THE HIGHLANDS OF CENTRAL INDIA

DEATH OF THE MAN-EATER

[*Frontispiece.*

THE HIGHLANDS
OF
CENTRAL INDIA

Notes on their Forests and Wild Tribes
Natural History and Sports

BY
CAPTAIN J. FORSYTH
BENGAL STAFF CORPS

NEW EDITION

WITH MAP AND ILLUSTRATIONS

GYAN

Published by

GYAN

Gyan Publishing House
5, Ansari Road
Darayaganj, New Delhi-110002
Phone: 011-47034999, 9811692060
E-mail: books@gyanbooks.com

Distribution Network
gyanbooks.com
India, USA, Canada, UK, Australia, France

ISBN : 978-81-212-4521-0 (HB)
First Published, 1871

2nd Impression 2020

Printed at: Gyan Press, Delhi.

The Highlands of Central India
Author: Captain J. Forsyth

CONTENTS

CHAPTER I

INTRODUCTORY

PAGE

CHAPTER II

THE NARBADÁ VALLEY

CHAPTER III

THE MÁHÁDEO HILLS

CHAPTER IV

THE ABORIGINAL TRIBES

CHAPTER V

THE LAY OF SAINT LINGO

CHAPTER VI

THE TEAK REGION

CHAPTER VII

THE TIGER

CHAPTER VIII

THE HIGHER NARÁBADÁ

LIST OF ILLUSTRATIONS

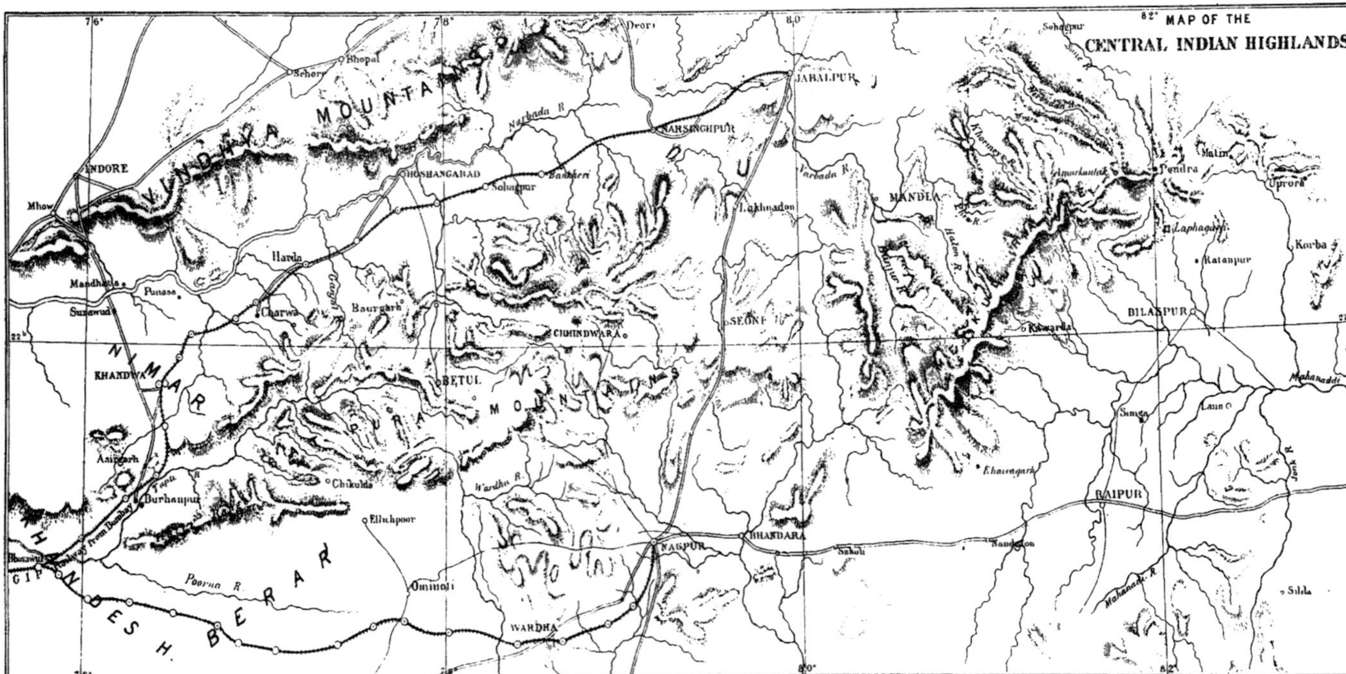

Vincent Brooks Day & Son Lith.

To face page 1]

THE HIGHLANDS OF CENTRAL INDIA

CHAPTER I

INTRODUCTORY

PEOPLE commonly talk of the "hills" and the "plains" of India, meaning by the former the great Himalayan range, and by the latter all the rest of the country. The mightiest mountains of the earth are called nothing more than "hills"; and popular geography has no name for the numerous excrescences of mother earth which intersect the so-called region of "plains." A range called the Nilgherries, in the south of the peninsula, approaching 9000 feet in altitude, is known to a few beyond the limits of India as a resort of invalids, and a nursery for cinchonas; but of lesser ranges than this, which would still be called mountains in any other country, the mass of "ordinary readers" has no cognisance.

Much of this has really been owing to the unexplored and undescribed condition of such regions; but something also to the overwhelming prominence of the great northern range, which rivets the attention of teachers of geography and their pupils, and also, from the exigencies of the art of chartography, renders it almost impossible to delineate on ordinary maps of India the features of inferior ranges.

Yet in the very centre of India there exists a considerable region to which the term Highlands, which I have adopted for a title, is strictly applicable; and in which are numerous peaks and ranges, for which the term "mountain" would, in any other country, be used. Several of the great rivers of India have their first sources in this elevated region, and pour their waters into the sea on either side of the peninsula—to the north the Són commingling with the Ganges, to the east the Mahánadí, flowing independently to the Bay of Bengal, to the south some of the principal feeders of the Godávarí, and to the west the Narbadá and the Táptí, taking parallel courses to the Arabian Gulf. If the reader will seek the head-waters of these rivers on the map, he will find the region I am about to describe. To be more precise, it lies on the 22nd parallel of north latitude, and between the 76th and 82nd of east longitude. It forms the central and culminating section of a ridge of elevated country which stretches across the peninsula, from near Calcutta to near Bombay, and separates Northern India, or Hindostan proper, from the Deccan, or country of the south. The traveller by the Great Indian Peninsular Railway from Bombay to Calcutta, after some 275 miles of his journey, will come to a point where the line branches into two. The northern branch leads him on up the Narbadá valley, and so, by Alahabád and the Gangetic valley, to the City of Palaces. If he takes the southern branch instead, he will be landed at Nágpúr, a city in the very heart of India, and its present terminal station. Between these two branches lies a triangle of country in which is situated the western half of the highlands I speak of. From its western extremity, in the fork of these lines, the mountainous region extends eastwards for a distance of about 450 miles, with an average width of about 80 miles.

The general level of what may be called the plains of Central India has here, by gradual, and to the traveller scarcely perceptible steps, reached an altitude of about 1000 feet above the level of the sea; and he will rise but little higher than this at any point on the lines of railway. So soon, however, as he leaves the railway, and proceeds a few miles towards the interior of the triangle, he will begin to come on ranges of hills, at first generally low, but in places attaining at once a height of about 1000 feet from the plain; and beyond them peaks and plateaux will present themselves evidently of much superior elevation. Valleys will everywhere be found penetrating the hills, by following which he may rise gradually to these higher regions; and soon he will exchange the rich cultivation of the flat land through which the railway passes for unreclaimed waste and rugged forest-covered steeps.

He will now find himself in a region where all is chaos to the unguided traveller; where hill after hill of the same wild and undefined character are piled together; where the streams appear to run in all directions at once; and it will not be until he has traversed the whole region, or closely studied a map, that some method will begin to evolve itself, and the geography become plain. He will find that at a height of about 1000 feet above the plain, that is of about 2000 above the sea, the hills have a tendency to spread out in the form of plateaux; some comprising the top of only one hill and a small area; others like a group of many hills, which support, like buttresses, on their summits, large level or undulating plains. From these again he will find shooting up still higher, a good many other solitary flat-topped hills, reaching the height of nearly 3500 feet; some of which in like manner unite into plateaux at about the same elevation. Yet higher than these, but never assuming the character of a plateau, he will see here and there a peak rising to nearly 5000 feet above the sea.

As is usual, the inhabitants of the hills themselves have no general name for the whole chain; each individual hill or minor range being called by a local name derived from the nearest village, or the species of tree it bears, or a god, or a river, or some other accidental circumstance. The Hindús of the plains have several terms for its different sections, calling the most easterly the Mykal, the centre the Máhádeo, and the western the Sátpúra Hills. Geographers have applied the name Sátpúra to the entire range; and the name is perhaps as appropriate as any which could be selected.

The watershed of these mountains varies in direction in their several sections. In the extreme east the range terminates in a bluff promontory with a precipitous face to the south, throwing the whole of the drainage of a vast area towards the north. This is the cradle of the

Narbadá river, which soon leaves its parent hills, and flows through a wide valley of its own along the northern face of the range. In the centre the range culminates in the bold group of the Máhádeos, crowned by the Puchmurree peaks, throwing the drainage almost equally to the north and south, the former into the Narbadá, and the latter into the Godávarí. The western section (the Sátpúras proper) is cleft in two by a deep valley, and drains inwards, forming the river Táptí, which, like the Narbadá, flows for but a short part of its course within the hills, before it leaves them altogether, and runs along their southern face to the sea. Such, however, is the tortuous formation of these mountains, that their streams frequently surprise one by turning short round in their courses, and making off towards the wrong river, as if they had suddenly changed their minds. The drainage of the great central Máhádeo block is a striking example of this. Two streams rise near its southern face, the Dénwá and the Sónbadrá. Both flow nearly south, away from the Narbadá, for a short way, when the former turns to the east, and the latter to the west. Presently, however, they find two vast cracks in the range, and turn sharp to the north, passing through them to the northern face, where they unite and fall into the Narbadá after all.

This extensive region emerged from the outer darkness that shrouds the early history of such immense tracts in India only within the last three centuries. Before then we have nothing to grope by in the thick darkness but the will-o'-the-wisp lights of tradition, and the scarcely more reliable indications of a few ruinous remains and vague inscriptions. The aborigines have never possessed a written language, and the Hindú races, who have within the last few centuries peopled the valleys that surround and interpenetrate the hills, have allowed their literature to remain the monopoly of a priestly caste, whose very existence was bound up in the necessity of falsifying all history. Their only writings which wear even the remotest semblance of history—the Máhábhárat and Rámáyan epics—speak of all India south of the Jamná as a vast wilderness inhabited by hostile demons and snakes. Religious hermits of the northern race are described as dwelling in leafy bowers in their midst, while heroes and demigods wandered about like knights-errant, protecting the devotees from their hostile acts, which seem more like the pranks of frisky monkeys than the actions of human beings. The snakes and demons have been conjectured, with some probability, to have been the black aborigines of the country, and the scenes of the epics to portray the gradual advance of the Aryan race and religion into their midst. The wandering Rájás are frequently described as allying themselves in marriage with the daughters of the potent demons, and so far the poems agree with what is otherwise shown to be probable. Nothing like a connected historical narrative is, however, to be extracted from the mass of Brahminical fiction; and whatever value such materials may yield to the investigation of the history of the Aryan or conquering races, they are worth nothing as bearing on that of the wild men of the wilderness, who are throughout regarded as being as much beyond the pale of humanity as their country was beyond the Aryan pale—the land of clearings and the black antelope.

We have a few architectural remains and inscriptions that tell of Aryan chiefs holding power in parts of the Narbadá valley and the central plateaux, between the fifth and the fourteenth centuries. But who and what they were, and what was really their position, there is nothing to show. Remains of religious edifices surrounded by fortifications point to the probability of their having been the heads of isolated bands of the warlike caste, protecting settlements of missionary priests, and perhaps, by superior courage and arms, holding in nominal subjection the aboriginal tribes around them. Traditions exist of a pastoral race, to whom is attributed every ancient building that cannot be otherwise accounted for. It is highly probable that the cow was unknown to the aborigines before it was brought by their Aryan invaders. Tradition would probably fix on so striking a feature as the possession of herds by those early colonists; and thus it does not seem necessary to suppose the existence of any peculiar pastoral people, distinct from other Aryan settlers in these central regions.

But what these early immigrants may really have been is unimportant. For, when first the light of true history breaks upon the country, at the period of its contact with the invading Mahomedan in the fourteenth century, all of them had ceased to have any separate existence. Most probably they had been absorbed in the great mass of the aboriginal tribes who surrounded them; and we find the country then called by the name of Góndwáná, from the tribe of Gónds who chiefly inhabited it. The petty tribal chieftainships into which, there is reason to believe, it had formerly been divided, had then been united into three considerable principalities, under the sway of chiefs whom all the evidence we have proves to have been of mixed aboriginal and Hindú (Rájpút) descent. Architectural remains, and the recorded condition of the country at the time mentioned, show that these little kingdoms had acquired a considerable degree of stability and development; and it has often been wondered how a tribe of such rude savages as the Gónds could have reached a stage of civilisation at that early period so greatly above anything they have since shown themselves capable of. The explanation seems to lie in the circumstance mentioned. The real establishers of these courts, and introducers of the arts, were not Gónds but Hindús.

It is the custom in all families which trace their lineage to the fountain-head of Hindú aristocracy among the Rájpút clans of Rájasthán to retain, like the Celtic chieftains of our own country, family bards, whose duty it is to record in a genealogical volume, and recite on great occasions, the descent and family history of their patrons. The bardic office is hereditary, and where the lineage of the family is really ancient, the bard is generally also a descendant of the bards of the original clan. Often he is the chief bard of the clan itself, and resides with its hereditary head at the family seat in Rájasthán, visiting at intervals the cadet branches of the house to record their domestic events. In Góndwáná, numerous chiefs claim either a pure descent from Rájpút houses, or, more frequently, admit their remote origin to have sprung from a union between some Rájpút adventurer of noble blood and one of the daughters of the aborigines. Few of them are admitted to be pure Rájpúts by the blue-blooded chiefs of Rájasthán; but all have their bards and genealogies. These, like such documents in all countries, often go back to fabulous times, and are overlaid with modern fiction; but the legendary portion of the bardic chronicle can generally be separated with little difficulty from a solid residue of probable fact.

The general conclusion to be drawn from the evidence of these writings, supported as they are by tradition and later history, is that during the fourteenth and fifteenth centuries, and it may be even earlier, a great immigration of the Rájpút clans took place into the country of the aborigines. The Mahomedan invaders of Upper India were then pressing hard on the country between the Ganges and the Narbadá rivers occupied by the Rájpúts; and it was doubtless the recoil from them that forced these colonies of Rájpúts southwards into the wilds of Central India. Here it would seem that they generally formed matrimonial alliances with the indigenous tribes. The superior qualities of the Aryan race would soon assert themselves among such inert races as these aborigines; and there is little doubt that before the arrival of the Mahomedans, not only the heads of what have been termed the Gónd kingdoms, but also many of the subordinate chiefs, were far more Hindú than aboriginal in blood. The unfailing evidence of physical appearance supports these indications of tradition. Most of the chiefs possess the tall, well-proportioned figure and light complexion of the Hindú, but allied with more or less of the thickness of lip and animal type of countenance of the pure aborigine. The mass of the tribes, on the other hand, are marked by the black skin, short squat figure, and features of the negretto race of humanity. Between them are found certain sections of the tribes, who would seem to have been also imbued with something of the foreign blood, though in a less degree than the chiefs. Like the latter they affect much Hindú manners and customs; and it is probable that they, too, are the result of some connection in long past times between immigrant Aryans and the indigenous tribes.

The Hindú proclivities of the chiefs appear to have early led them to encourage the settlement in their domains of colonies of the industrious agricultural races who had already reclaimed the soil of Northern and Western India. But no very extensive arrival of these races would seem to have occurred previous to the establishment, early in the seventeenth century, of a strong Mahomedan government, under the great Akber, in the surrounding countries. The impetus given to the development and civilisation of the dark regions of India by the wise rule of that greatest of eastern administrators can never be over-rated. Before the absorption into his empire of the minor Hindú and Mahomedan states, their history is one of continuous lawlessness and strife; and the further we investigate, the more certainly we perceive that political order, the supremacy of law, sound principles of taxation, a wise land system, and almost every art of civilised government, owe their birth to this enlightened ruler. His treatment of these unsettled wilds and their people was marked with the same political wisdom. While, in the surrounding countries, which had already been in a measure reclaimed by Hindú races, he everywhere broke up the feudal system, under which strong government and permanent improvement were impossible, he asked no more from the chiefs of these waste regions than nominal submission to his empire, and the preservation of the peace of the realm. Those on his borders he converted into a frontier police, and the rest he left to administer their country in their own fashion. Acknowledgment of his supremacy he insisted on, however, and, in case of refusal, sent his generals and armies, who very soon convinced the barbarous chiefs of their powerlessness in his hands. The influence of his power and splendour rapidly extended itself over even this remote region. The chiefs became courtiers, accepted with pride imperial favours and titles, and, in some cases, were even converted to the fashionable faith of Islam.

A vast development of the resources of these central regions followed the coming of Akber. A great highway between Upper India and the Deccan was established through a gap in the Sátpúra mountains. A vast city arose in the Táptí valley, which became the seat of government of the southern province of the empire. Armies marching to and fro, and the retinues of a great court, brought with them a demand, before unheard of, for the necessaries and the luxuries of life. The open country, under the rule of Akber, was rapidly reclaimed by Hindú immigrants, arriving simultaneously from the north and from the west. Nor were they long in extending into the fat lands of the great valleys in the territories of the Gónd princes. The reclamation of the heavy lands of the Narbadá valley, and the country now known as the Berárs, had probably been entirely beyond the resources of the aboriginal races. The immigrants brought with them the necessary energy and the necessary resources; and from this time a process commenced which resulted in the wholesale deprivation of the indigenous races of their birthright in the richest portions of their country, and the establishment therein of the arts of agriculture and commerce.

The Gónds retired to the higher plateaux and slopes of the central hills, where their hunting instincts, and rude system of raising the coarse grains on which they subsist, could still find scope; the more extensive plateaux were also soon invaded by the aggressive race, and their level black soils covered with crops of wheat and cotton. These elevated plains are surrounded by belts of rugged, unculturable country, which remained in the possession of the aborigines; and thus, ere long, the tribes were not only surrounded but interpenetrated by large bodies of Hindús.

The Brahman priest accompanied the warlike Rájpút and the industrious Hindú peasant to their new country; and brought with him the worship of the Hindú gods and the institution of caste. No separation from the holy mysteries of his faith was demanded from the immigrant. Not only was he persuaded that he was still under the protection of the old gods; but the gods themselves, and all their belongings, were bodily borne into exile along with their votaries. New scriptures were revealed, in which the religious myths of the race were transplanted wholesale, and fitted to local names and places. The Narbadá became more holy as a river than the Ganges. The mountain of Kailas, the fabled heaven of Sívá beyond the snows of the Himalaya, jutted to heaven in the peaks of the Máhádeo range. Krishná and Rámá passed their miraculous boyhood, and achieved their legendary feats, in these central forests, instead of in the groves of Mathúrá and the wilderness of Bindrában. Some remarks will be offered in another place on the social and religious influence of this contact with Hindúism of the aboriginal races who retired before the invaders. A few remained in the country occupied by the Hindús, chiefly in the position of agricultural serfs, of watchers of the villages against the inroads of their wilder brethren or of wild beasts, of hewers of wood, prevented only by the rules of caste from being also their drawers of water. A social status was assigned them below that of all but the outcasts of the other race; and they were compelled to segregate themselves in humble hovels, beyond the limits of the comfortable houses and homesteads of the superior castes.

The semi-aboriginal principalities of Mandlá Deogarh and Khérlá, which included the whole of this highland region, were thus permitted, by the policy of successive Mahomedan rulers, to maintain a little irksome feudatory position until the Maráthá power began to supplant that of the Moghuls in the latter part of the eighteenth century. Then the irrepressible hordes of the Deccan, having swallowed up the more settled dominions of the Moslem, began to overrun also the country of the Gónds. Before the close of the century, the three kingdoms had been entirely broken up, and are heard of no more in history. They seem to have at no time been more than a feudal agglomeration of numerous petty chiefships; and on the ruin of their heads they resolved themselves again into the same elements. The conquest of the Maráthás assumed little of a practical character in the interior of the hills, the mountaineers continuing to wage against them a desultory warfare from their fastnesses. The present century broke with the commencement of that "time of trouble," when the leaders of the Maráthá confederacy began to quarrel over their spoil, and entered on a deadly struggle for territory and power. The financial straits of the Maráthá chiefs now led to wholesale disregard for all rights of property inconsistent with their demand of a rack-rent from every acre of the soil commanded by their troops. The hill-chiefs were now reft of the last of their possessions in the plains; corrupt and overbearing farmers of the land-tax seizing on the last of their accessible resources. Then they took to the hills with their tribes, and turned their hands against the spoiler, till the name of Gónd and Bheel became synonymous with that of hill-robber. Whole tracts came to be distinguished by the title of the "country of robbers." There is not a district in all that long frontier between hill and plain where tales are not still related of the sudden downswoop of bands of hill-men on the garnered harvest of the plains, of bloodshed, torture, and blazing villages, and of the sharp and savage retaliation of Maráthá mercenaries. A little tributary of the Táptí river that comes down from the hills of Gávilgarh is still called the "stream of blood," from the massacre in its valley of a whole tribe of Nahals, man, woman, and child, by a body of Arabs in the service of Sindiá; and many similar tales have been related to me when travelling in the hills. Then, if not before, every pass in the hills was crowned by a fortified post of the mountain men, and every inhabited village of the plains by a wall of earthwork and a central keep. Then, too, arose the organised bands of mounted plunderers who have been called Pindárís—Ishmaelites of these central regions, who, like the vulture, sallied forth from their fastnesses in some secluded wild to gorge on the prey struck down by a nobler hand. Thenceforth, for nearly twenty years, the hill-tribes, Pindárí plunderers, and lawless Maráthá soldiery, with their daggers at each other's throats, were unanimous only in robbing the husbandmen of the plains, who ploughed their fields by night with swords and matchlocks tied to the shafts of their ploughs, or purchased peace by heavy payments of blackmail. Vast areas of the country that had been reclaimed by their industry were again abandoned to the jungle and the wild beast; and only round the walls of fortified villages, within which the people and their herds could retreat in time of need, was any tillage maintained at all.

In the year 1818 this unheard-of anarchy was terminated by our final success against the Maráthás, and the extermination of the Pindárí bands. But we entered on the possession of our new territories to find them almost desolated by a quarter of a century of the utter absence of government, with the hill population frenzied by the excitement of a life of plunder, and branded with the character of "savage and intractable foresters." The Ságar and Narbadá territories, as the northern half of the country was then called, were acquired by us in full sovereignty after this war. The southern portion remained nominally the territory of the feudatory Rájá of Nágpúr, but had long been under British administration when, in 1854, it too was annexed on failure of heirs. The Gávilgarh hills, in the extreme south-west, formed part of the Nizam's territory of Berár; but that also has for many years been under British management.

With the establishment of a strong government the hill-men soon proved how greatly they were maligned when described as "savage and intractable." Since they first came under our rule there has not been an outbreak among them of the least importance; and, on the contrary, they have long since gained the character of being a remarkably submissive and law-abiding people. The chiefs were early secured in their feudatory position, with the full proprietorship of such territories, both in the hills and in the plains, as they could establish a title to; and for many years they were left almost to themselves in the management of their internal affairs. Our early administrators were too fully occupied with the work of restoring prosperity in the open country to have much time to spare for the Gónd and his wildernesses; and thus we find that the interior of their country remained an almost unexplored mystery up to a very recent period.

Two and a half centuries ago the great Akber knew nothing of the Góńds but as a "people who tame lions so as to make them do anything they please, and about whom many wonderful stories are told";[1] and within the last twenty years even they have been described as going naked, or clothed in leaves, living in trees, and practising cannibalism. "So lately as 1853, when the great trigonometrical survey of India had been at work for half a century, and the more detailed surveys for some thirty years, Sir Erskine Perry, addressing the Bombay branch of the Royal Asiatic Society, wrote: 'At present the Góndwáná highlands and jungles comprise such a large tract of unexplored country that they form quite an oasis in our maps. Captain Blunt's interesting journey in 1795, from Benares to Rájámandrí, gives us almost all the information we possess of many parts of the interior.'"[2] Till within a few years, "unexplored" was written across vast tracts in our best maps; and, though lying at our very doors, unexplored in reality they were. With few exceptions, the civil officers of those days never dreamt of penetrating the hilly portions of their charges; and the writer is acquainted with one district containing some 3000 square miles of forest country, and inhabited by between 30,000 and 40,000 aborigines, in which one officer held charge for eleven years without once having put foot within this enormous territory. All accounts of such tracts were filtered through Hindú or Mahomedan subordinates, whose horror of a jungle, and its unknown terrors of bad air and water, wild beasts, and general discomfort, is such as to ensure their painting the country and its people in the blackest of colours.

But a new era dawned on these dark regions, when the conscience of the British rulers of India was awakened to the wants of their great charge, after a rebellion which

[1] Gladwin's *Ayeen Akberee*, vol. ii. p. 59.

[2] "Introduction to the Central Provinces Gazetteer," by Charles Grant, Esq., C.S.

nearly ousted them from their seat. Along with many more important provinces, this secluded region felt the benefit of the impulse then given to the administration of the empire. That great civiliser of nations—the iron road—was to be driven through the heart of its valleys; and Manchester had prophetically fixed an eye on its black soil plains as a future field for cotton. Something stronger than the divided and limited agency of the several local officers who had been sitting still over its affairs was wanted for the guidance of a country and a people who possessed all the elements of a rapid progress. Accordingly, in 1861, were constituted what have since been known as the Central Provinces, under the chief commissionership of the late Sir Richard Temple, of the Bengal Civil Service.

Then were seen strange sights in that unknown land; when distant valleys and mountain gorges, that had heard no other sound than the woodman's axe, echoed to the horse-hoofs of the tireless Chief, and his small knot of often weary followers; when the solitary Gónd or Bygá, clearing his patch of millet on the remote hill-side, was astonished by the apparition, on some commanding hill-top, of that veritable "Government" (Sirkar) in the flesh, which to him and his for several generations had been an abstraction, represented, if by chance he ever visited the district head-quarters, by a "Saheb" in his shirt-sleeves, sitting in a dingy office smoking a cheroot!

A Chief who thus, by dint of hard riding, insisted on seeing the requirements of the country for himself, was not long in perceiving that the highland centre of the province, with its extensive forests and mineral wealth, its limitless tracts of unreclaimed waste, and scanty, half-wild population, and its great capabilities for the storage of precious water, was worthy of a principal share of attention. It had already been whispered by a few that its forests, calculated on by the projectors of the railway lines, then being constructed through the province, for their supply of timber, were likely to prove a broken reed, having been already exhausted by a long course of mismanagement; and one of the first steps taken was the organisation of a Forest Department, for the detailed examination and conservation of the timber-bearing tracts. An officer[1] who had already interested himself in the question, and had travelled extensively in these regions, and who was admirably fitted for the task by physical qualities, and the possession of that faculty of observation which is not to be attained by the labours of the study, was selected as superintendent of the new department. During the five succeeding years several officers, *quorum unus fui*, were unremittingly employed in the exploration of the 36,000 square miles which may be taken to be the area of the central hills, besides doing much to examine an almost equally extensive tract of low-lying forest in the south of the province. In later years the regular civil officers of the district, those employed in the land revenue settlement, surveyors, missionaries, and many others, have traversed many parts of these mountains; and a great mass of information respecting their physical character and inhabitants has been accumulated, which, although of very unequal value, is yet a mine of useful ore from which much good metal may be extracted. Much of this has already been printed in the form of official Reports; and the cream of it has been abstracted into a Gazetteer of the Central Provinces, the Introduction to which, from the pen of Mr. Grant, late Secretary to the Chief Commissioner, is a *résumé* of the history of the province, admirable for its conciseness and research. Good maps of all but the remotest tracts have also now been made available; and statistical information of all sorts is annually prepared with much care and made public by the Government.

My design, then, in thus venturing before the public, is not that of attempting to rival these most complete official documents in accuracy or extent of information, but rather to present, in a more popular and accessible form, the lighter and more picturesque aspects of a country in which an increasingly large section of our countrymen take an interest. Though most of what I shall have to say is founded on, or corroborated by my

[1] Captain G. F. Pearson, of the Madras Army, now Conservator in the N.W. Provinces.

own observation during many years of acquaintance with the region described, I shall not refuse to avail myself of well-authenticated material collected by others.

The highland region is comprehended within eleven of the nineteen districts into which the province has been subdivided for administrative purposes. A portion of most of these districts lies also in the adjacent plains, either to the north or south of the hills, a judicious arrangement, which combines in one jurisdiction the hill and the plain people who have dealings together. The total area of these districts is, in round numbers, 44,000 square miles, of which about 11,000 are under cultivation, and the remainder waste. Where such extensive mountains are included, it will not be surprising to find that of this large unreclaimed area, about 20,000 square miles are estimated to be wholly incapable of tillage, the remaining 13,000 being probably more or less fit for improvement. These figures are obtained by the returns of the department employed in what is called the "settlement of the land revenue."[1]

Few readers will require to be told that in India the great mass of the land has always paid a tax to the Government (which is really of the nature of a rent-charge which had never been alienated by the original proprietor of all land—the State); and in these provinces most of the hill-chiefs even were found, on the country coming into our hands, to be liable to the land tax, which in their case, however, was usually a very light one. During the times of anarchy which preceded our rule, the proper amount of this tax had become very uncertain, the assessment, in fact, having very much resolved itself into a struggle between the rulers and the ruled, "that they should take who have the power, and they should keep who can." It was also by no means clear in many cases from whom the tax should be demanded, rights of property in land having fallen greatly into abeyance during a period when to claim the proprietorship was to invite spoliation and oppression. Our strong and equable rule so greatly

[1] The writer served for three years as settlement officer of one of these districts, and can vouch for the general accuracy of the statistics.

encouraged the arts of peace, that a population soon began to press upon the immediately available land; and this circumstance, together with the moderation and certainty of our land taxation, soon bestowed on property in land a value which it had never before possessed. Rival claimants then began to bring forward conflicting, and often long-dormant, claims to possession; and the courts established for the ordinary business of the country were soon swamped by the number and complexity of these cases. It was found, too, on inquiry, that there had never really existed any clearly recognised right of property, in our sense of the term, which would give the agricultural classes a real interest in the improvement of their lands, while many classes of persons had been allowed to exercise very undefined powers over the whole of this immense area of unreclaimed land. The culturable wastes were becoming much in demand by enterprising settlers, a demand which the opening of the country by the railway promised to largely increase. Such operations were clogged by these uncertain claims, and thus the progress of the country was in danger. The forest question also became urgent, timber being required in large quantities by the railways, while a fear arose of the impending exhaustion of the whole forests of the country. Nothing could be effected in this direction either, until the question of title in these wastes should be determined. The Government then determined to appoint special officers for the settlement of all these matters in every district of the province; and after ten years of hard work, they have now been set at rest. Few persons can conceive the amount of personal labour, in the field and in the office, involved in the settlement of one of these districts. Every village and hamlet has to be visited and every acre of land appraised and assessed; the title of every claimant to any interest in the land has to be investigated from the beginning of time; and finally a minute and accurate record of the whole process has to be drawn up, to form the substantive law for the disposal of future cases in the civil and revenue courts of the district. The grand result, as affecting rights and interests in the land, was, that where any title which could be converted into a right of property was established, the freehold, bearing liability to the fixed Government rent-charge, was bestowed on the claimants; while all land to which no such private title could be established was declared to be the unhampered property of the State. Most of the hill-chiefs were admitted to the full ownership of the whole of their enormous wastes, though certain restrictions as to the destruction of the forests have here (as in all civilised countries) been imposed on these proprietors.

Few parts of India present so great a range of interesting natural objects for investigation as this. Situated in the very centre of the peninsula, the ethnical, zoological, botanical, and even geological features of north and south, and of east and west, here meet and contrast themselves. As has been noticed above, two distinct streams of the so-called Indian Aryans, approaching from Northern and Western India, here meet and intermingle, differing considerably in appearance, in character, and in speech. Where the land has been suitable for their agricultural processes, the original dwellers of the land have been driven out to the central hills; and there we find them in several tribes, which yield to the investigator points of connection with several branches of the human race.

The total population of the tracts I have included in this sketch is about four and one-third millions, of whom about three and one-third millions are Aryans, and one million only belong to aboriginal races. The great majority of these are the Gónds, who have given their name to the country, and who are distributed in greater or less density over the whole of the hilly portion of the tract. The infallible test of language shows that the Gónds belong to the same family of mankind as the Tamil-speaking Dravidians of Southern India.[1] In the extreme north-east of the tract are found the tribe known in the Bengal hill-tracts as Kóls, a race closely allied to the Sántáls and

[1] A supposed connection between the Gónds and the Bráhúis, a Mahomedan tribe on the Sindh frontier, based on the correspondence of a few words in their languages, does not appear to bear the test of a closer examination.

other tribes of the north-east; and in the very centre of these highlands, on the high plateaux of Puchmurree and Gávilgarh, surrounded and isolated by the Góṇds, are found another race, called Kúrs or Korkús, whose language and general type are almost identical with these Kóls and Sántáls, though they themselves are utterly unaware of the connection. All these Kolarian tribes differ radically in language from the Dravidian Góṇds; and some connection has been traced between them and the aboriginal races of countries lying to the east of India. Further to the east again, in the Mykal range, and like the Korkus imbedded among the Góṇds, is found a small body of Bygás, who have not yet been traced either to the Kolarian or the Dravidian stock. They present, from many circumstances to be afterwards noticed, the most curious ethnical problem of all. Less raised above the condition of the mere hunting savage than any, and clinging to the most secluded solitudes, they have yet entirely lost all trace of their own language, and speak instead a rude dialect of the tongue of the Aryan immigrants. They present some points of affinity to the Bheels of Western India, of whom also, in the extreme west, some 20,000 are reckoned in this cauldron of peoples. The number of the aborigines is completed by about 25,000 souls, forming the fag-ends of tribes who have lost all semblance of distinct cohesion, without language or territory of their own.

Which of these entirely distinct families are the autochthones of the land, or which of them first settled here, may possibly never be known. None of them have any reliable tradition of their arrival; and no evidence bearing on the subject, beyond what has been already mentioned, has been discovered. It is not within the scope of my present purpose to attempt any elaborate investigation into the ethnical history or peculiarities of these tribes. The evidence yet recorded is too scanty to yield valuable results; and such has been the admixture of their customs, religion, and language with those of the Hindús, that it is improbable now that much of their original distinctive peculiarity remains to be discovered. Yet there is much that is curious and interesting in their present condition, gradually being absorbed as they are in the vast mixture of races composing modern Hindúism; and a grave problem remains unsolved in the question of our duty towards these races as a Government. What I have to say on these points will find a place further on.

The region is also remarkable as forming the meeting-ground of some forms of vegetable and animal life, which seem to be characteristic of North-eastern and South-western India. The principal forest-tree of upper India is the Sál (*Shorea robusta*), a tree whose habit it is to occupy, where it grows at all, the whole area, almost to the exclusion of others. It thus forms vast forests in the lower Himalaya, and covers also the greater portion of the hilly region to the south of the Gangetic valley. From the latter tract it stretches along the table-land of the subdivision of Bengal called Chota Nágpúr, and thence extends into the Central Provinces in two great branches separated by the open cleared plain of Chattísgarh. The southern branch reaches as far as the Godávarí river, and the northern embraces the eastern half of the highlands I have described, both branches ceasing almost exactly at the eightieth parallel of east longitude. To the west of this the characteristic and most valuable forest-tree is the Teak (*Tectona grandis*), which is not found at all in Northern India, or Bengal, and but scantily in the Central Provinces to the east of 80° longitude. The Teak tree is, however, not so exclusive in its habit of growth as the Sál, appearing rather in the form of scattered clumps among other forms than as the sole occupant of large areas.

Some explanation of this peculiar disposition of these two timber trees may perhaps be found in their habits of growth and relation to various soils. The Sál is a tree possessed of a remarkable power of propagating itself, shedding an enormous number of seeds, at a season (the commencement of the rains) when the usual jungle fires have ceased, and which sprout almost immediately on their reaching the ground. On the other hand, the Teak seeds after the rainy season, and the seeds themselves are covered by a hard shell, which must be decomposed by long exposure to moisture and heat before they will germinate. This necessitates their exposure throughout one hot season, when the whole of the grass covering the ground below is burnt in the annual conflagrations. Thus a large percentage of the seeds of the Teak never germinate at all. It is clear, then, that if these two species were growing together, on soil equally suitable for both, the Sál must possess an immense advantage in the "struggle for life" over the Teak. And if to this natural advantage be added an adventitious one, in the fact that the Teak is much more generally useful to man—particularly to man in a primitive state—as is really the case, there seems to be a sufficient reason why the Teak should disappear before its rival in tracts where the latter has obtained a footing and is equally suitable to the soil and climate. Now an examination of the tracts on which these trees are found in Central India shows that, while the Teak does not appear to shun any particular geological formation, it thrives best on the trap soils which predominate in the south and west of the province. But the Sál, on the other hand, clearly shuns the trap formation altogether. Not only is it unknown within the great trappean area to the west of the eightieth degree of longitude, but even to the east of that line, in its own peculiar region, it does not grow where isolated areas of the trap rocks are found. Further, I believe that in no part of India where this tree grows is there any of the trap formation. With the exception only of this volcanic rock, the Sál appears to thrive on any other formation, being equally abundant within its own area, where primitive rocks, or sandstones, or lateritic beds predominate. Thus I believe that the Sál, where the soil is suitable—that is, where there are no trap rocks —has exterminated the Teak, of which it is a natural rival. In other parts of India, where the Teak does not meet with this rival, as in Malabar and Burma, it flourishes on the soils from which it is here excluded by the Sál. The general conclusion appears irresistible, but sharp contrasts perhaps best illustrate such peculiarities. Many such might be mentioned, but two in particular are very noticeable. Within the Sál region, in the hills immediately to the east of the town of Mandlá, there is a considerable area covered by Teak, to the total exclusion of the Sál. The whole of this region is composed of a trap overflow; and all around it, as soon as the gigantic and lateritic formations recommence, the Sál again entirely abolishes the Teak. Again, within the area of the trap and Teak, in the valley of the Dénwá river, 150 miles west of the furthest limit of the general Sál region, is found a solitary isolated patch of the latter, occupying but a few square miles. Here the Sál grows on a sandstone formation. It is surrounded on three sides by trap rocks, and there it entirely ceases, and is supplanted by the Teak as the principal timber tree. But how to account for this small and unimportant outlier of the great Sál belt? To maintain our theory, some link to connect them together should be found. I think that a hypothesis, much less extravagant than many which are introduced into such arguments, will do so. Towards the fourth side of the Sál patch in the Dénwá valley lies the great open plain of the Narbadá, into which the sandstone formation extends, and passes on along with primitive rocks, and with little interruption from the trap, right up to the main body of the Sál forest at the head of the Narbadá valley. The Sál, it is true, ceases in the open Narbadá valley, but so does all forest, the country having been completely cleared and cultivated for many generations. It is not then a very violent assumption to suppose that the Sál forest at one time extended down the Narbadá valley as far as the Dénwá, and that, when the country was cleared, this little patch alone was left securely nestled under the cliffs of the Máhádeo range, in the secluded valley of the Dénwá, into which there was no road until within the last few years.

These are strange facts. But it would be still more strange if a corresponding distribution of animal life could also be demonstrated. Something of the kind is really almost possible. Equally with the Sál tree, several prominent members of the Central Indian fauna belong peculiarly to the north-eastern parts of India. These are the wild buffalo (*Bubalus Arni*), the twelve-tined "swamp" deer (*Rucervus Duvaucellii*), and the red jungle-fowl (*Gallus ferrugineus*). All these are plentiful within the area of the great Sál belt, but do not occur to the west of it, *excepting in the Sál patch of the Dénwá valley*, where the two latter, though not the buffalo, again recur. In the Dénwá valley there is but a solitary herd of the swamp deer, I believe; the red jungle-fowl are not so numerous as the rival species, *G. Sonneratii*, which replaces it in the west and south of India; and it is not surprising that the wild buffalo should have disappeared when his range had been reduced, by the clearance of the intermediate forest, to the narrow limits of this small valley. So large and prominent an animal requires a much larger range than deer and birds; and there is no part of the surrounding country suitable for his habits until we reach the Sál tracts again, though very probably the extensive black soil plains of the Narbadá valley were so before they were cleared. In corroboration of the probability of his formerly having extended further down the valley than at present, skulls and horns have been found in the upper gravels of the Narbadá in no way differing, except in superior size, from those of the existing species. Their greater size is not surprising, as they are not larger than the horns still occasionally met with in Assam, where also the average size is now rapidly diminishing under the attacks of sportsmen.

Two other large representatives of the eastern and western faunas, the wild elephant and the Asiatic lion, also appear to have formerly extended far into this region. In modern times, however, the advance of cultivation and the persecutions of the hunter have driven them both almost out of the country I am describing. The former, in the time of Akber (as is ascertained from Abúl Fuzl's chronicles), ranged as far west as Asirgarh, but is now confined to the extreme east of the province. Sir Thomas Roe, ambassador from James I. to the Court of the Great Mogul, in the seventeenth century, speaks of the lion as being then common in the Narbadá valley. It is now seldom heard of further east than Rajputána; although a solitary specimen sometimes appears in their old haunts further east. A lion was killed in the Ságar district in 1851, and another a few years ago only a few miles from the Jubbulpúr and Alahabád railway. The hog-deer (*Axis porcinus*) I have never met with in the west of the province, nor is it very numerous even in the east, though very common in the Sál tracts of Northern India. The black partridge (*Francolinus vulgaris*) of Northern India does not extend into these provinces at all, its place being taken by the painted partridge (*F. pictus*), a very closely allied species. The great imperial pigeon of Southern India does not, I think, cross the Narbadá to the north, though not uncommon in the higher forests to the south of that river. Scientific research among the minor forms of animal and vegetable life (for which I have had neither the time nor the knowledge) may possibly elicit many confirmations of the law of distribution I have thus roughly stated from observations that have presented themselves to me as a forester and a sportsman.

I need here only indicate another matter in connection with this subject. It has already been stated that a tribe called Korkús, closely connected with what is called the Kolarian stock, which is represented by the Kóls and Sántáls of Bengal, is found embedded among the Gónds of these central hills. Now the commencement of the range of this tribe precisely agrees with the isolated patch of the Sál forest in the Dénwá valley; and their nearest relatives of the same stock are the Kóls of the country to the north of Mandlá, where the Sál forest again commences. Thus we have an outlier of the human tribes of Eastern India existing along with an outlier of its vegetable and animal forms, and the country between the whole three and their nearest congeners occupied by other forms. It is a most singular coincidence; and such must be my excuse for devoting so much of my space to what must be to many an uninteresting discussion.

I have said that at the time the Central Provinces were constituted, little was accurately known regarding the forest resources of their vast waste regions. It had, indeed, been suspected that the projectors of the railways had over-calculated the possible supply; but it was little guessed that the exhaustion had gone so far as really proved to be the case. In another place will be found an account of the system of cultivation of the hill-tribes, who had for centuries devastated the forests, by the cutting and burning of their best timber to form ashes to manure their wretched fields of half-wild grain. This was itself almost sufficient to have proved the ruin of the forests, but other causes had not been absent. The most valuable timbers for the railway and other useful purposes are the Teak and the Sál; indeed, no others have been found to be really lasting when subjected to the great and sudden variations of an Indian climate. The Teak tree is perhaps the most generally useful in the whole world. In combined strength, lightness, elasticity, and endurance there is none to compare with it. At the present day its uses cover a wider range than those of any other timber, from the handle of an axe in its native forests to the backing of an ironclad in the navy of England. But it is unfortunate also that it is the easiest of all timbers to fell, and makes better firewood and charcoal than any other. It is little wonder, then, that on it almost exclusively, where found, had fallen the weight of the people's requirements, ever since the country was first populated by civilised tribes. I have already said that it is a most difficult tree to reproduce, the seeds being exposed to the extremities of danger before they have the opportunity to germinate. The seedlings also, with their great dried leaves like so many sheets of tinder, are more exposed to injury by fire than those of any other tree. Thus the Teak had everywhere been mercilessly cut down, and had to struggle with the most adverse circumstances to maintain a footing at all. Over great tracts, where it probably once grew, it has been utterly exterminated, giving place to a "shoddy aristocracy" of such worthless species as the *Boswellia*, which no one would dream of cutting, and on which nature has bestowed all the indestructible vitality of a weed. The Teak has but one rare and valuable property, by means of which it has alone continued to survive at all in many places. However much it may be cut and hacked, if the root only be left, it will continue to throw up a second growth of shoots, which grow in the course of a few years to the size of large poles. This is the sort of timber which was chiefly in demand for the small native houses before the introduction of our great public works; and thus, perhaps, may be explained the apathy with which the native Governments witnessed the destruction of the forests of large timber. A further reference to this matter will be found further on.

The Sál tree, again, as I have explained, possesses a much stronger vitality as a species than the Teak; though from its liability to heartshake, dry-rot, and boring by insects, as well as its want of all power (like most resinous trees) of throwing out coppice wood, the individual trees are much more perishable than the Teak. It is also not so generally useful, particularly for minor purposes, being hard to fell, of coarse grain, and making very inferior charcoal. It, however, yields a gum-resin valuable in commerce, and this has led to a very great destruction of the Sál forests. Again, the Sál tracts were very inaccessible from the populous regions, the nearest point where any great supply could be had for the railway being about a hundred miles, by a bad land route. This distance has up to the present time proved an insurmountable obstacle to the general utilisation of the Sál timber on the railway works. The supply of this timber is almost inexhaustible; and a stronger commentary on the commercial value of easy communications could not be found than this, that the railways have found it cheaper to import pine sleepers from Norway, and ironwood from Australia, than to carry the Sál timber growing within a hundred miles of their line.[1] There is something wrong where this is the case; and that something is the want of a good road into the Sál regions from the railway at Jubbulpúr, which road should have been made, for many other reasons besides this, long ago.

So much for the Sál forests. As regards the Teak, the supply available for railway uses had already been much reduced from the causes mentioned. A good deal

[1] I would not be understood to say that no Sál timber has been used; but its cost as compared with the imported material has been greater.

was, however, still left in the remoter forests, where communications were not so easy; and the forests, if properly taken in hand, might have yielded a steady supply of large timber for many years. But unfortunately the grave mistake was now made of announcing that *after a certain time* the forests would be brought under Government management and strictly conserved. This was the death-blow to the remainder of the Teak throughout the northern parts of the tract. The railway contractors, and numerous speculators, foreseeing the value that timber was likely to acquire, owing to railway operations and the closing of the forests, then went into the jungles with bags of rupees in their hands, and spread them broadcast among the wild tribes, with instructions to slay and spare not—to fell every Teak tree larger than a sapling that they could find, and mark them with their peculiar mark. It was only too faithfully done; and scarcely anything that was accessible, escaped the axe. Now came delay in the railway works, failure of the contractors, and want of money. The cut timber was abandoned wholesale where it lay. Teak wood is full of oil, and burns readily after lying for a short time. The jungle fires occurred as usual in the long dry grass where the logs were lying, and the great majority of them were burnt! The exact amount of the destruction can never be known. For years afterwards, when exploring in the forests, we continued to come on the charred remains of multitudes of these slaughtered innocents, most of them being quite immature and unfit for felling at any time. All that were worth anything were saved by the Forest Department in after years, and the value even of these amounted to many lacs of rupees. They were not a hundredth part of those that were cut, which should probably be reckoned by millions rather than thousands. The injury done to the forests and to the country by this most mistaken measure may never be recovered; certainly it cannot be recovered in less than two generations of the people's life. Such was one of the most material results of the utter ignorance of the administrative officers of that period regarding everything connected with the wilder portions of their charge. The mischief had been completed, and most of the timber speculators had bolted from their creditors, leaving their logs smoking in the forests, before the formation of the Central Provinces, and ere the Forest Department had entered on their labour of exploring and arranging for the protection of what was still worth looking after. Succeeding chapters will give some account of such of these explorations as the writer was engaged in, and of the penalties and pleasures that accompanied the early investigations in these Central Indian forests.

CHAPTER II

THE NARBADÁ VALLEY

Acting on instructions I proceeded to the Puchmurree (Pachmarhí) hills—the lofty block I have described as crowning the Sátpúra range to the south of the Narbadá river. There the centre of our operations in that extensive forest region was to be fixed; a permanent forest lodge was to be built in the heart of the country of the Gónds and Korkús, whose interests we were to endeavour to unite with our own in the preservation of the remnants of the fine forests that clothed the slopes of their hills. The country to be explored was little known; but it was sufficiently ascertained that plenty of rough work was before us in overcoming the obstacles presented by the rugged nature of the land and its inhabitants.

The organisation of such a camp as is admissible in such a wild country, occupies no great time. Since the return of my regiment to quarters a year or so before, I had been almost constantly out on detachment duty, or on shooting excursions; and had added little to the modest properties I found myself possessed of at the close of some three years of camping out in the sub-Himalayan Terae, and subsequent hunting up of skulking rebels over the stony wastes of Bandelkand. There are two ways of travelling in such tracts. The one is to take a full equipment of the large tents and their luxurious furnishings, which render marching about in India, under ordinary circumstances, so little attended by hardship, or even by inconvenience; a corresponding train of servants and baggage-animals; and a small army of horse and foot as a protection. Such a camp will perhaps number from fifty to eighty men, and half that number of animals of sorts. An array like this may be allowable or even proper for the civil officer, who has the dignity of his office to maintain, while traversing slowly a populous and well-supplied district of the plains. But the hardship of such an infliction on scattered tribes of poor and resourceless aborigines is sometimes forcibly brought home to the invaders, by finding the country, as they advance, utterly deserted in their track. When I come to describe the extreme poverty in resource of these outlying tracts, this circumstance will perhaps be more easy to realise.

In my shooting excursions I had always marched with only a single small tent, about eight feet square, of the sort called a *Pál*, which is composed of two or three thicknesses of common double-thread country cloth, sewn together, and thrown over a ridge-pole on two uprights, all of the hollow (female) bamboo, which combines strength with lightness in the highest possible degree. It has no doors nor windows, but one of the gable ends (so to speak) is slit up the middle and fitted with stout laces in case of storms. In ordinary weather this end is kept open to the breeze except at night, and such a tent really affords ample protection and accommodation to the traveller who has no heavy indoor business to do, unless perhaps in the extreme hot weather when no trees are available to pitch it under. It affords room enough for a light folding bedstead of bamboo, a cane stool, a small folding table, a brass basin and stand, and your portmanteau and guns, which is all the furnishing that the mere sportsman or explorer should require. All this, with a good supply of such eatables and drinkables as are not to be had in the wilderness, will go on a good camel; and such had been the extent of my personal requirements during many a rough expedition and hunting trip before the present march. On this occasion I added another tent twelve feet square, for the servants and a few newly-entertained native foresters who were to assist in my explorations; and we were also furnished with a somewhat larger double-roofed tent by the Government, which was to be pitched on the hill as a depôt while the contemplated masonry lodge was being erected. To carry these additional impedimenta I had four or five of the rough little unshod and unkempt country ponies, called *tattoos*—hardy little villains, whom no amount of work can tire out of immediate readiness for a daily battle royal with teeth and heels the moment they are cast loose from their loads to graze.

My own tent travelled as usual upon a camel. I don't think I would have ventured to take any other camel but "Junglee" into the country I was going to visit. Though the camel is far more at home in rough and difficult country than his ungainly-looking formation would lead one to suppose, there are many passes in the Máhádeo hills where these animals cannot carry their loads, and some where they could not proceed at all. But "Junglee" was a camel among camels. Of the low, stout, shaggy breed used by the Cabul merchants, who annually during the cold season hawk the dried fruits of their country over the plains of India, I had found and caught him running wild and ownerless among the hills along the Cane river in Bandelkand. When out shooting I was astonished to see him start out of a thicket, and flee like a deer over rocks and ravines; and a rare chase we had—sepoys, camel-men, and camp followers—before we got him into a corner, and bound his sprawling legs and threatening jaws with tent ropes, and led him away between a couple of tame loadsters, to have his nose rebored and be starved into a peaceful return to the uses of his race. He had probably been abandoned by some party of hard-pressed rebels, long enough before I saw him to have become perfectly at home in the jungles, and to have got into first-rate condition. A better beast to scramble over breakneck ground with a heavy load I never saw. Poor Junglee! he afterwards ended his days under the paw of a tiger in the Bétúl forests during one of his periodical relapses into the life of freedom he had tasted in the wilds of Bandelkand.

On the 11th of January, I bade adieu to the pretty little station of Jubbulpúr (Jabalpùr), and to my comrades of the gallant 25th Punjabees. I was really sorry to see the last of the jovial manly company of Sikhs who composed the regiment, one of the first of the force that rose on the ruins of the Bengal army in 1857. But soldiering in India, in time of peace, is truly one of the dreariest of occupations; and I confess I was far from doleful at the prospect of quitting the bondage of parade routine for the free life of the forest; and to think that—

> No barbarous drums shall be my wakening rude;
> The jungle cock shall crow my sweet reveillé.

For the first five marches (eighty-two miles), my route lay down the open and well-cultivated valley of the Narbadá. In the first march I went off the highway to pay a last visit to a remarkable scene of beauty, a few miles to the south of the road. What visitor to Jubbulpúr can ever forget the Marble Rocks! In any country a mighty river pent up into a third of its width, and for a space of two miles or more boiling along deep and sullen between two sheer walls of pure white marble, a hundred feet in height, must form a scene of rare loveliness. But in a bustling, dusty, Oriental land, the charm of coolness and quiet belonging to these pure cold rocks, and deep and blue and yet pellucid waters, is almost entrancing. The eye never wearies of the infinite variety of effect produced by the broken and reflected sunlight, now glancing from a pinnacle of snow-white marble reared against the deep blue of the sky as from a point of silver; touching here and there with bright lights the prominences of the middle heights; and again losing itself in the soft bluish grays of their recesses. Still lower down, the bases of the cliffs are almost lost in a hazy shadow, so that it is hard to tell at what point the rocks have melted into the water, from whose depths the same lights in reverse order are reflected as clear as above, but broken into a thousand quivering fragments in the swirl of the pool.

Here and there the white saccharine limestone is seamed by veins of dark green or black volcanic rock; a contrast which only enhances, like a setting of jet, the purity of the surrounding marble. The visitor to these Marble Rocks is poled up through the gorge in a flat-bottomed punt as far as the "fall of smoke," where the Narbadá makes her first plunge into the mighty rift; and there is no difficulty in dreaming away the best part of a day in the contemplation of this marvellous [1] scene of beauty.

The only drawback to the peaceful enjoyment of the

GORGE IN THE NARBADÁ. THE MARBLE ROCKS. (*From a Photograph.*)

scene is the presence of numerous colonies of bees, whose combs are to be seen attached to most of the jutting ledges of the rocks on the left bank. In cold weather

[1] A fiend in human shape has perpetrated a pun, in the visitors' book kept at the little rest-house above the cliff, which will here be sufficiently obvious.

D

these insects seem to be inoffensive; but from about March to July, anything disturbing or irritating them is almost certain to bring them down in swarms on the offender. Their attack is of a most determined character; and, not long before my visit, had proved fatal to an engineer employed in sounding the river for a projected crossing of the railway. It is believed that, on this occasion, the bees were roused by some of his companions above shooting at the blue rock pigeons that build in the cliffs, on which they attacked furiously this gentleman and a friend who were together in a boat below. After a while both gentlemen sought protection by taking to the water. The one by taking long dives under water, managed to elude the angry insects and hide in one of the few accessible clefts of the rock; but the other, although a practised swimmer, was never lost sight of by the exasperated creatures, and in the end was drowned and carried down the stream. He lies buried above the cliff, under a marble slab cut out from the rock beneath which he met his death.

The species of bee that frequents these rocks is, I believe, the common *Bonhrá* (*Apis dorsata*), which attaches its large pendent combs indiscriminately to such rocks and to the boughs of forest trees. There are two other species of bees common in Central India, both much smaller than the Bonhrá, and neither of them inclined to act on the offensive. The Bonhrá is of very common occurrence in many forest tracts; and I have myself several times been attacked by them. If attacked, the only resource is to rush into the nearest thick bush, break off a leafy branch, and lay about with it wherever there is an opening. On one occasion, when marching in the Mandlá district, my baggage animals and servants were attacked, and scattered in every direction. Many of the men and animals were so severely stung as to be laid up for several days; and one of the baggage ponies, who could not get rid of his load, was killed on the spot. Our kit was flung about all over the jungle, and was not all collected for several days. On another occasion a valuable elephant was attacked, and driven away into the jungle;

and was so panic-stricken that she could not be recovered for days. I have heard of a large force of troops in the Mutiny days being routed, horse and foot, by a swarm of these terrible insects, in the neighbourhood of Lucknow. The honey and wax of this and the other species of bee are regular articles of export from our forests. The people who engage in the business of taking them seem to possess not a little of the art of the bee-master; but they usually resort to more forcible measures, and rob the combs after suffocating the tenants at night with the smoke of torches. Their richest harvests are got from cliffs like this on the Narbadá; and some of their slender ladders of bamboo slips may usually be seen at the Marble Rocks, hanging from the edge of the cliffs over the abyss of water. The honey is inferior in quality to that of the domesticated bee of Europe; and is sometimes even of a poisonous quality, owing to the bees having resorted to some noxious flower. It is easy to procure a comb by slicing it off the face of the rock with a rifle ball; and I once had the gratification of thus operating on the colonies at the Marble Rocks, from a safe position on the opposite bank, sending several large comb-fulls to a watery grave in the depths below.

The presence of these inhospitable bees renders it a matter for congratulation that the finest impression of the Marble Rocks is to be got "by the pale moonlight." The bees are then quite harmless; and, if the scenery has then lost something in brilliancy of contrast in its lights and shades, it has gained perhaps more in the mysteriousness and solemnity that well befit a spot seemingly created by Deity for an everlasting temple to Himself. I am sorry to say that, in the old Jubbulpúr days, we not unfrequently used to desecrate the sanctuary by unholy moonlight picnics, in which plenty of champagne, brass bands, and songs that were sometimes very much the reverse of hymns, bore the most prominent part. It was very jolly, though, like most things that are wrong.

A spot so naturally remarkable as the Marble Rocks could not escape sanctification at the hands of the

Brahmans. Nothing more completely refutes the accusation of want of taste for natural beauty, so often made against the Hindús, than their almost invariable selection of the most picturesque sites for their religious buildings. Many of the commonest legends of Hindú mythology have, as usual, been transplanted by the local priests to this neighbourhood. The monkey legions of Hanúmán here leapt across the chasm on their way to Ceylon; and the celestial elephant of Indra left a mighty footprint in the white rock which is still exhibited to the devout pilgrim. Several picturesque temples dedicated to Sívá crown the cliff on the right bank; and by the river's edge is a favourite *ghát* for the launching of the bodies of devout Hindús into the waters of Mother Narbadá. A pleasure party to the rocks is apt to be not a little marred by a collision with one of these unsavoury objects in mid-stream. In India many a fair scene has its foul belongings and fell inhabitants; and these lovely waters are polluted by ghoul-like turtles, monstrous fishes, and repulsive crocodiles, that batten on the ghastly provender thus provided for them by the pious Hindú.

I believe the common *Magar* of the rivers and tanks of the Central Provinces is identical with that of upper India (*Crocodilus biporcatus*). The other species of Indian crocodile (*Gavialis Gangeticus*), the long-nosed *Gavìál*, is found in these provinces only in the Máhánadí river, which falls into the Bay of Bengal. The long still reaches of the Narbadá all contain a goodly complement of broad-snouted magars; but, so far as I have observed, they do not attain in our rocky-bottomed rivers nearly to the dimensions I have seen in the slimy tributaries of the Ganges and Jamná. Eight or nine feet in length I take to be here about the limit of the magar's growth. Nor have I ever heard an authentic case of an adult human being having been killed by a crocodile in our rivers. Small animals are frequently carried off, and children sometimes disappear from the gháts in a suspicious manner. A dog employed in retrieving wild fowl is almost certain to be sooner or later made a meal of by the saurian. The fall of a duck in his neighbourhood generally brings the reptile near the spot; and many a shot bird thus disappears, as if by magic, before the eyes of the gunner. But he will prefer your plump retriever, should he see him nearing the duck as he comes up. A dear old spaniel of mine named "Quail," possessed of an uncontrollable "craze after the deuks," had so many narrow escapes of this sort that I never taught any of the four generations of his descendants I have possessed to retrieve from water.

Although our crocodiles are thus little noxious to life, and may even advance some claims to merit as scavengers, it is not in human nature to refrain from destroying so hideous a reptile when a chance occurs. There is a spot in the gorge of the Marble Rocks where such a chance is seldom wanting. A flat and slightly hollowed rock-shelf at the water's edge invites to noontide repose these unlovely monsters of the deep. Cold weather and a warm sun seem to be the most favourable conditions. The place is on the left bank, some quarter of a mile above the rest-house; and is marked by the droppings of the brutes, and of the aquatic birds that invariably watch over their slumbers. If now, as midday approaches, you will take your rifle and cross over below the house, and get you round to where a cleft in the rocks commands the spot, and if the place has not recently been much disturbed, you will shortly perceive (if he is not there before you) the seeing and smelling apparatus of one or more of the reptiles floating slowly in from mid-stream, like two bungs out of a cask. Nothing but experience will enable you to distinguish them at this distance from the pieces of drift wood always floating down the stream, so marvellously does nature protect even the most loathsome of her productions. The crocodile approaches the projected scene of his siesta with immense caution. Long and keenly he reconnoitres it from a distance; and if he has any suspicions he will sink and rise again and again during his approach. If not he will descend after the first good look, and then swim right in under water; and the next thing you will see of him will be his rugged head lying on the ledge of rock below you, and a pair of fishy eyes slowly revolving in a last survey of the neighbourhood. This done, he will heave his huge bulk and serrated tail sideways out of the water, and lie extended along the edge, ready to "whammle" in again on the slightest alarm. You will aim at him in the centre of the neck, just where it joins the head; and if you then shoot plumb-centre, but not otherwise, he will never stir. A different shot might eventually perhaps be fatal; but this alone will prevent his reaching the water and escaping, to float up in a day or two a sickening mass of corruption. Nothing possesses such a frightful, "ancient fish-like smell" as a crocodile that has been dead for even a few hours. You can seldom get near enough to one of these creatures in a boat to kill him with certainty; and the only certain plans are to watch for them at noon as I have described, or to bait with a noisy puppy dog in the evening, at which time they appear to be most on the feed.

Few things are more enjoyable than marching along during the cold season in a rich open country like the Narbadá valley with a well-appointed camp, and plenty of leisure to linger over the numerous objects of interest or amusement presented by such a tract. Very little of this sort of thing fell in the way of the forest officers of those days, however. Our work lay in the depths of distant forests, or at most in the half-reclaimed frontier belt lying between the hills and the plains, where timber transactions generally took place, and the chief depôts for forest produce had been established. When by chance our direct route from forest to forest led across such an open region, our movements were as rapid as man and beast could make them; and at the earliest possible moment we hurried again from the face of civilisation, like ghosts at cock-crow, to bury ourselves again in the depths of the wilderness. In after years, when employed in revenue work in a populous district, I saw the reverse of the picture. Marching by fair roads and easy stages with a duplicate set of canvas houses (for such our large Indian tents really are), one of which goes on over-night and is pitched ready for your arrival in the morning, in the deep shade of some mango grove, near a populous village which supplies all your wants; starting after the morning cup of hot coffee to ride slowly along through green fields and grassy plains; and looking on the forest-covered hills on the blue horizon only as an agreeable vanishing point in the landscape, or as unpleasantly complicating the questions of liquor excise and police administration! It is amazing what a difference the point of view makes. The man who has dwelt for years among the forests, and their simple wild inhabitants, will regard nearly every question that arises in a wholly different light from him whose experience has lain only among the corn fields of the plains, and their tame and settled tillers. And each of them will probably arrive at a conclusion as little comprehending the whole bearings of the question as the other.

The climate of Central India in the cold season, that is, from November to March, is almost perfect for the life of combined outdoor exercise and indoor occupation which forms the healthiest sort of existence in India. The midday sun, if a little hot for hard work in the open air, is just sufficient to make the temperature under canvas delightful, while the mornings and evenings are cool and bracing, and the nights cold enough to make several blankets a necessity. In January, ice will generally be found on water that has been exposed all night. Nothing can, in my opinion, exceed the exhilarating effect of a march at such a season, with pleasant companions, through a country teeming with interest in its scenery, its people, and its natural productions, such as is this region of the Narbadá valley.

The valley was not long ago—not long, that is, in the history of countries—a hunting ground of the Góṇds and other wild tribes who are now chiefly confined to the hills which surround it. At most, it could have been but scantily patched by their rude tillage before the arrival of the Hindú races, who have cleared its forests, driven the wild elephant that roamed through them to the far east, and covered its black soil with an unbroken stretch of wheat cultivation that strikes every visitor with admiration.

In less than three centuries this has been done; and yet it is the custom to say that India is an unprogressive country, that she has been standing still since the beginning of history! Everything shows that this country is still in its very youth. The people, strong-limbed and healthy, rejoicing in the rude abundance that falls to the lot of energetic races tilling an almost virgin soil. Tilling it roughly, it is true, getting from it nothing approaching to the quantity of produce extracted by the denser populations of long-reclaimed tracts from much inferior soils; but still, tilling it in the way which is the most profitable to a scanty population with a poor accumulation of wealth and stock. The example of all new countries with much available land, even when, as in America, all the resources of capital and machinery are available, shows that a comparatively rough culture of a large area is more remunerative than the higher tillage of a smaller area; and this alone is the cause of the rude state of agriculture still observed in this and many other parts of India. At present, plenty for all is the rule, poverty the very rare exception. Well-built houses, well-stocked cattle yards, and a general air of comfort and happiness, cannot fail to arrest the attention in Hindú villages. It is true that the people of the soil, those of the Gónds who have preferred to stay and serve a Hindú master to a retreat to the hills, are poorly clad and housed, living like outcasts beyond the limits of the Hindú quarter; but they, too, are at least sufficiently fed; and nothing but their own innate apathy and vice prevents them from receiving a greater share of the surrounding plenty.

As the influence on the aborigines in the past, and at the present time, of their contact with these invading Hindú races will afterwards form matter of consideration, it is important to understand of what material these Hindú races themselves are really composed. They have generally been comprehended in the category of "Aryan," as distinguished from the "Tauranian" peoples who are believed to have preceded the fair-complexioned Aryan invaders from Upper Asia in the occupation of Hindostan, and among whom are included the remnants of wild tribes still found in the hills. But it needs but little observation of these Hindú races to perceive that they themselves have long been subjected to some influence which has greatly modified the original high Aryan type—a type which includes the noblest races of mankind; the Caucasian of Europe, the Persian of high Asia, and the Sanscrit-speaking "fair-skinned" people who entered India from the north uncalculated ages ago. That influence cannot have been one of climate only, which would have affected all their descendants equally; whereas we see existing the greatest range of diversity, from the light-coloured, noble-featured Brahman of the extreme north-west to the black and negro-like chamar or pariah of the east and south. Everything shows that the cause has been a mingling of the immigrant race with the inferior Tauranian tribes whom they found occupying the soil before them. To judge from physical appearance, few but the highest castes of Northern India can have any claim to purity of Aryan blood; and the admixture of indigenous blood, as indicated by colour and feature, appears to be greater and greater the further we proceed from the seat of the original Aryan settlements in the north-west. It can scarcely be doubted, then, that the modern Hindús are a composite race, resulting from the absorption of a wave of Aryanism in a great ocean of peoples of a far inferior type—the type, in fact, represented by such of them as have still remained undiluted in their inaccessible hills. The force of the wave diminished as it proceeded; and the gradations in the extent of its influence are now so subtle, that it is hard to say where the line should be drawn to denote a preponderance of the one element over the other. The difficulty is further increased by the circumstance that the Aryan language, customs, and beliefs appear to have been carried far beyond any perceptible influence of the Aryan blood, so that whole races, who show little or nothing of the latter, have become thoroughly imbued with the former.

Not, however, without notable modifications have the Aryan language, religion, and customs thus permeated the masses of the inferior races. In language, while the tongue of the most northern high-caste races has changed from the classical Sanscrit scarcely more than was inevitable from the wear and tear of use through such long ages, that spoken by the masses of lower physical type has suffered so radical an alteration that a large proportion of its vocables, in some parts as much as half, are not traceable to Sanscrit at all; while in Southern India, where the aboriginal type has been little modified, purely aboriginal languages, unconnected with Sanscrit, are still spoken. Still greater has been the effect on the Aryan religion of contact with these lower races. The gods of the primitive Aryans have almost disappeared from practical recognition. The backbone of the original system survives its priesthood and ceremonial, just as the backbone of the language survives in the grammatical forms of the invaders. But, as the vocables of the tongue have frequently been adopted from the aborigines, so probably have the popular gods of the pantheon been largely drawn from aboriginal sources. No religious system possesses such facility for proselytising as a polytheism; and history shows that when two such systems meet, there is nothing to stand in the way of their coalescing but the rivalry of their priests. Here there probably was no such rivalry. To judge from those which remain, the aboriginal tribes had no regular priesthood, and no systematic mythology. They had only inchoate gods, without a history, and numerous as the natural objects whose forces they represented. And when the tribes accepted the Hindú priest and his ceremonial, the priest found no difficulty in admitting to his accommodating pantheon a sufficient number of these to satisfy the conscience of the aboriginal Pantheist. The leading deities in the existing Hindú pantheon, Sívá and Vishnú, were wholly unknown to the early Aryans; and even they themselves are at the present day scarcely worshipped at all, in their radical forms, by the great body of the people, but only in the form of mythological consorts and sons, and incarnations in many forms, most of which are probably adaptations of the gods and heroes of the races thus absorbed within the accommodating pale of Hindúism. Nor is this all. Even such secondary forms of the regular gods of the Brahmans receive but little of the real devotion of the people, which is paid rather to tribal and village deities, unheard of in recognised mythology, and to the Lares and Penates of the householder. And these, the Brahman priest, who is paid for his services, has no scruple in recognising as orthodox. Superficial inquirers have quoted Hindúism as a faith which cannot admit of a proselyte; but nothing could be more completely the reverse of the truth. Anything in the way of new gods may be brought by new worshippers within the pale of orthodoxy, provided only that they agree to accept the dominion of the Brahman priest, together with the caste rules and ceremonial by means of which he exercises his power.

It was, then, with a race thus already modified, and with a social and religious system which had thus already engulfed the great mass of the indigenous nations of India, and which was still ready to absorb in a similar manner any number more of them, that the aborigines of Central India came in contact. What has been the result will be discussed in a future portion of this work.

In a new country like this, few objects of antiquarian interest attract the attention of the traveller. Allusion has already been made to the traces of isolated settlements of Aryans in the country, who had all been swept away again, or had been absorbed in the indigenous element surrounding them, before the true history of the country opens; and a few shapeless ruins still remain to mark the sites of some of these settlements "in the unremembered ages." Generally, however, even the religious edifices, which in the East seem to outlast all others, will be found to be of very modern date, and of little pretension to interest. They will frequently be met with standing on the embankment of some water-tank, covered with the lotus in full bloom, and shaded by great trees of mango, tamarind, and fig. Very often the camp will be pitched alongside of them, for the sake of the fine shade; and the wild fowl and snipe that frequent the tanks will probably form an attraction, to the sportsman at least, superior to the allurements of such poor antiquities.

Snipe and wild fowl begin to arrive in these central regions of India, voyaging from the frozen wilds of Central Asia, early in October; and, before the end of November, every piece of water and swampy hollow affords its contingent to the gun. The common teal,[1] and the whistling teal,[2] are the most numerous, as well as the first to make their appearance. The lovely blue-winged teal [3] is scarcely less common; and of larger ducks, the red-headed pochard,[4] the wigeon,[5] the pintail,[6] and the gadwall,[7] are found throughout the winter on nearly every tank of tolerable size. On the main rivers, and on the larger reservoirs, such as those of Bhandára and Lachorá, in Nimar, which, though owing their existence to the hand of man (the giants of past days, who knew the requirements of India better than their successors), yet approach the dignity of lakes, many other species of wild fowl will be found, including that king of ducks, the mallard,[8] the common gray goose,[9] and the black-backed goose.[10] The latter species is extremely common; the others, which are much superior for the table, are comparatively infrequent. Numerous wading birds, storks, herons, and cranes, haunt every pool and marsh. Few of these offer much temptation to the sportsman, except the Demoiselle crane,[11] generally known as the Coolen, which is much sought after, and is therefore difficult to approach. Few extensive wheat or *gram* fields in the Narbadá valley will be found at this season without a flock of these delicious birds stalking across it, in the morning and evening, grazing on the young shoots.

If encamped in the neighbourhood of a river or swamp, the traveller will probably be aroused at daybreak by the quavering and sonorous call of the giant Sárus crane,[12] a

[1] *Querquedula crecca.*
[2] *Dendrocygna awsuree.*
[3] *Q. circia.*
[4] *Anthia ferina.*
[5] *Mareca penelope.*
[6] *Dafila acuta.*
[7] *Chandlelasmus streperus.*
[8] *Anas boschas.*
[9] *Anser cinereus.*
[10] *A. melanonotus.*
[11] *Anthropoides virgo.*
[12] *Grus antigone.*

bird revered by the Hindús as a type of conjugal affection. They are nearly always seen in pairs, and, should one of them be shot by the ruthless gunner, the companion bird will return again and again to the spot, to hover and lament over its slain friend in a manner that generally prevails on the hardest hearted to grant immunity to the race for ever after. A contrast to this happy union of lovers is found by the Hindú in the Braminy ducks,[1] which also associate in pairs, but, by a cruel fate, are compelled to pass their nights on the opposite banks of a stream, wailing forth their unavailing love in the melancholy "chukwa, chukwi," which few travellers by the rivers of India have failed to hear in the dusk of the evening. Their unfitness for the table, probably more than the Hindú adage against their slaughter, protects them from the gun.

Of other winged game, the gray quail—best of Indian game birds, in my opinion—will be found in good numbers in most grain fields. I have never seen them here in such swarms as in some parts of upper India, where eighty or a hundred brace may be bagged in a day; but the sport is none the worse for that. Twenty brace is a first-rate bag in Central India, and generally the sportsman has to be contented with much less. The common gray partridge, which closely resembles in appearance the English bird, abounds in many places. It hugs the vicinity of villages, and feeds foully. I have seen a covey of them run out of the carcase of a dead camel, and speed across the plain like so many hares. These nasty habits, and its skulking nature, much belie its appearance as a bird of game. Far different is the gallant painted partridge,[2] which here takes the place of the black partridge[3] of upper India. I have seen the latter in Bandélkand; but I am positive that it nowhere occurs in the Central Provinces. The appearance of the two species is so alike, and their habits are so identical, that assertions to the contrary have no doubt arisen from mistake. No game bird could afford more perfect shooting than the painted partridge. Of handsome plumage,

[1] *Casarca rubila.* [2] *Francolinus pictus.* [3] *F. vulgaris.*

and excellent on the table, his habits in the field admirably adapt him for the purposes of the gun. He frequents the outskirts of cultivation, in spots where bushes and grass-cover fringe the edge of a stream, for he seems to be very impatient of thirst. The proximity of some sort of jungle seems to be as necessary as the neighbourhood of crops. Morning and evening small coveys or pairs of them will be found out feeding in the stubble of the cut autumn crops, that latest reaped being the most likely find. On being disturbed they seldom run farther than to the edge of the nearest cover, from which, on being flushed, they rise like rockets, with a great *whirr*, straight up for twenty or thirty yards, and then sail away over the top of the cover to a distance of a few hundred yards; this time plumping into the middle of the cover, from which it is not so easy to raise them again. This beautiful bird is most common in the extreme west of the Central Provinces, and in good spots a bag of ten to fifteen brace to each gun may be made in Nimár and the Táptí valley.

The most common way of shooting quail and partridges is by beating them out with a line of men; but it is a poor sport compared to shooting them over dogs. I have used both pointers and spaniels in this sport. The former secure the best of shooting in the early morning and late in the evening, while the birds are out of cover and the scent good, and four hours' shooting may thus be had in the day. But a team of lusty spaniels is, I think, on the whole preferable, as they are useful also for many sorts of cover shooting where pointers could not be worked. They also keep their health better, and degenerate less in breeding than any other imported dog, which is probably due to their descent from a race originated in a warm climate. They make the best of all companions, and are not so liable to "come to grief" in many ways as larger dogs. Fresh imported blood is, however, required, at least once in every two generations, to keep all English sporting dogs up to their best in India. The spaniels should either be large Clumbers, or of the heavy Sussex breed, as a small dog like a cocker cannot penetrate the jungle cover. The noble Clumber, otherwise faultless, has the fault for this particular purpose of giving no tongue on game; I commenced the breed, which I maintained for twelve years in India, with a strain of pure Clumber in the never-to-be-forgotten "Quail"—a dog that for looks and quality surpassed anything of the breed I can now discover in England. All his descendants were more or less crossed with Sussex or cocker blood; but none of them ever gave tongue till the fourth generation, when symptoms of it began to appear. On the whole, then, I think I would prefer the heavy Sussex breed.

On one occasion the whole of my spaniels were very nearly being "wiped out" by one of a class of accidents that must be looked for in India. I was shooting quail in a grain field near Jubbulpúr, with "Quail," "Snipe," "Nell," and "Jess," when, on a sudden, they all began to jump violently about, snapping at what seemed to me to be a large rat. But coming nearer I made out that it was a huge cobra, erect on his coil, and striking right and left at the dogs. I lost no time in pelting them off with clods of earth, and then cut the brute's head off with a charge of shot; when I found that the snake had been in the act of swallowing a rat, of which the hind-legs and tail were protruding from his jaws, so that his repeated lunges at the dogs had fortunately been harmless. All these spaniels were famous ratters, and had no doubt been attracted by the cobra's mouthful, for they generally had, like all dogs of any experience in India, a wholesome dread of the snake tribe. I never lost any of these dogs by an accident, though exposed to all the dangers of panthers, hyenas, wolves, snakes, and crocodiles; and all of them lived to a good age, in excellent health. As with men, English dogs keep healthy enough if properly treated in accordance with the climate.

Of larger game, the principal animal met with in the settled parts is the black antelope,[1] which has probably followed the clearings made by the immigrant races. The aversion of this animal to thick uncleared jungle has made it, in the Hindú sacred literature, a type of the Aryan pale, of the land fitted for the occupation of

[1] *Antelope cervicapra.*

the fair-skinned races; and the appropriate seat of the devotee is still upon its black and white skin. It is too well known to require any minute description. Suffice it to say, that not even in Africa—the land of antelopes —is there any species which surpasses the "black buck" in loveliness or grace. In Central India, although this antelope attains the full size of body, the horns of the buck (the female is hornless and of a fawn colour) rarely exceed a length of 22 inches. I have shot one with horns 24½ inches, and seen a pair that measured 26 inches. The longest horns are probably attained in Gújerát, and about Bhurtpúr in Northern India. In all the corn districts of Central India it is found in considerable herds, and does much damage to the young crops. I have seen herds in the Ságar country, immediately after the Mutiny of 1857, when they were little molested, which must have numbered a thousand or more individuals. A tolerable shot could at that time kill almost any number he chose. In most cultivated districts, tracts of the poorer land are kept under grass for cattle-grazing, etc., and these preserves are generally the favourite midday resorts and the breeding-grounds of the antelopes. Thence in the evening they troop out in squadrons on to the cultivated lands in the vicinity; and all the night long continue grazing on the tender wheat shoots, returning in the gray of the morning to their safe retreat. Many will, however, remain in the fields the whole day, sleeping and grazing at intervals, unless driven off by the cultivators. In such places the voices of the watchers in the fields will be heard in the still night shouting continuously at the antelopes; but they seldom succeed in effecting more than to move them about from field to field, doing more damage probably than if they were left alone, for a buck killed in the morning will always be found filled nearly to bursting with the green food. Although many of them are shot by the village shikárís at night, and more snared and netted by the professional hunters called Párdís (who use a trained bullock in stalking round the herds to screen their movements), the resources of the natives are altogether insufficient, in a country favourable to them, to keep down the numbers of these prolific and wary creatures; and it is a perfect godsend to them when the European sportsman hits on their neighbourhood as a hunting-ground.

There are many ways of circumventing them. Living quite in the open they rely principally on the sense of sight for protection, although at times warned also by their power of smell. One way is to drive up to them in one of the bullock-carts commonly used in agriculture. The native shikárí often gets near them by creeping up behind a screen of leaves which he works before him. Where they have not been much harassed the European sportsman, in sad-coloured garments, can usually stalk in on them when passing between the grass plains and the crops. In the very early morning, if a station be taken up in their usual route, they are nearly sure to come within shot, the grunting of the bucks warning the sportsman of their approach some time before they emerge from the darkness. One of the most successful and interesting plans is to ride a steady shooting horse nearly up to the herd. When within say four hundred yards, slip off and walk on the off side of the horse in such a direction as will lead past the herd within shot, if possible on the down-wind side. If they have been so shot at in this way as to be shy of the horse, take a groom and pass them further off; and when a convenient bush or hillock intervenes drop behind, and let the man lead the horse on, passing well clear of the herd. They will probably be so intent on watching them out of the way, that you will generally be able to creep in on them without much difficulty. Shots at antelope in populous districts are seldom got much under 150 yards nowadays, which is, however, near enough for modern rifles to make sure work. One great advantage of employing a horse in stalking is that it will often enable you to follow and spear a wounded buck which might otherwise escape. If you have a brace of good greyhounds in the distance ready to slip, the chances will be still better. A wounded buck often gives a beautiful run with greyhounds, which have never been known to catch an untouched and perfect antelope on fair hard ground, though under conditions unduly favourable to the dogs they have sometimes done so. A shooting horse, like several which I have possessed, who is quite steady under fire, does not need to be tied, and will come to call, is a perfect treasure for many sorts of sport in India. As in all good qualities, the Arab is the most likely to develop such a character; but most horses are capable of being taught something of the business. Should neither horse nor hounds be at hand, a wounded buck should not be followed up too quickly. If left to himself he will probably lie down in the first cover he comes to; and by watching the line he takes you may often follow up and secure him.

In upper India they are frequently shot by approaching them on a riding camel. The more bells and gay trappings he has on him the better, as the antelope on this plan fall victims to their curiosity and amazement. I brought down to Central India with me a trained camel, with which I had thus bewildered many an antelope into rifle distance; but after getting some dangerous tumbles, owing to the yawning cracks that form in the black soil in these provinces after the rains, I had to abandon the camel as a shooting vehicle. As a sport antelope-shooting palls upon the taste. There is too much of it, and it lacks variety. So I should think also would be the case with much of the African sport we read of. To the beginner in Indian sport, however, there is no pursuit more fascinating. The game being nearly always within sight, the excitement is maintained throughout the day's sport. Simple as it seems, it takes a good man and a good rifle to make much of a bag when the antelope have been much disturbed. The old hand is apt to smile at the enthusiasm of the "griff" when he dilates on the glories of antelope-stalking; but the time was when he too passed through the stage at which the acquisition of a particular long spiral pair of horns was more to him than the wealth of all the Indies, and when nothing impressed him so profoundly with the vanity of all human affairs as the miss of "a few inches" under or over, which so frequently terminated the weary stalk. Perhaps

I may be allowed to quote a description of the pursuit of a master buck, written many years ago, when I myself was in the throes of the "buck fever."

"I had frequently seen in my rambles over the antelope plains a more than ordinarily magnificent coal-black buck. I had watched him for hours through my 'Dollond,' but my most laborious attempts to reach him by stalking had as yet proved futile. His horns were perfection, of great size, well set on, twisted and knotted like the gnarled branch of an old oak tree. As the sun glanced on his sable coat, it shone like that of a racehorse fit to run for the Two Thousand Guinea Stakes—in fact, he was the *beau ideal* of a perfect black buck. Of course, the more difficult the task appeared, the more determined was I that these superb horns should be mine, and that in future I would disregard every buck except the one. He was constantly attended by two does, to whom he confidently entrusted the duty of watching over his personal safety—and faithful sentinels they were. They seemed to relieve each other with the precision of sentries, and clever indeed would be the stalker who could approach within many hundred paces ere the warning hiss of the watchful doe aroused the grand signior from his siesta. It was then grand to see the majestic air of the buck, as, after stretching his graceful limbs, he slowly paced towards the object of his suspicion, still too far distant to cause him any alarm. Now he stops, and, tossing his nostrils in the air, snuffs the breeze that might convey to his delicate sense the human taint. Now he lazily crops a blade or two of grass, or scientifically whisks a fly from his glossy haunch with the tip of his horn; anon he saunters up to one of his partners, and seems to take counsel regarding the state of affairs. Again, as some movement of the distant figure catches his eye, his sudden wheel and prolonged gaze show that, despite his careless mien, not for a moment has he lost sight of his well-known foe. But soon the does begin to take real alarm; and after fidgeting round their lord, as if to apprise him of the full extent of the danger, trot off together towards some other haunt. Now they halt a moment, and look round appealingly to the buck, and again with feigned consternation start off at a gallop, every now and then taking imaginary ten-barred gates in their stride. At last the buck, after remaining behind a decent time to maintain his character for superior courage, follows them at a pace that mocks the efforts of every animal on the face of the earth but one—the hunting leopard.

"Such was the invariable result of my best efforts for upwards of a week. I would not risk a long shot, as it might drive him for ever from that part of the country. His favourite haunt was a wide grassy plain, intersected here and there by dry watercourses, up which I had many a weary crawl, *ventre à terre*. I soon found out his usual feeding and drinking places; and observed that to reach the latter he almost daily crossed a deepish dry nullah about the same place. This struck me as affording the means of circumventing him, so I took up my position in the nullah; but as luck would have it, *my* buck took his water in some other direction for the next two days. Many other herds of antelope constantly passed within easy shot of where I was ensconced; but not until I was almost giving up hope on the third day, and was taking a last sweep of the plain with my binocular, did the well-known form of the master buck greet my vision, as he slowly wound his way with his two inseparable companions towards the pool to which he had watched so many of his species passing and repassing in safety.

"The wind was favourable, and the buck came steadily on till he arrived within a long rifle shot of where I was posted. Here he suddenly threw up his head, and, after standing at gaze for a few moments, turned sharp to the left and started off at a canter for a pass in the nullah, about a quarter of a mile from where I was. I knew he could neither have seen nor smelt me, and was at a loss to account for his sudden panic till, on turning round in disgust, there was the cause behind me, in the shape of a small parcel of does, which had evidently been returning from the water, but, having discovered my unprotected rear, were now pulled up in a body, and staring at me with an air which had telegraphed the state of affairs to the old buck in an unmistakable manner. I felt very much inclined to sacrifice one of the inquisitive does to my just wrath, but preferred the chance of a running shot at the buck; so I started at a crouching run (somewhat trying to the small of the back) up the bed of the nullah, in the hopes that the buck might have pulled up ere he crossed, and would still afford me a shot. Nor was I mistaken, for, on turning a bend of the tortuous nullah, there he stood, broadside on, in all his magnificence, not eighty yards from my rifle; but, alas! who could shoot after a run, almost on all-fours, of some 500 yards or so? When I attempted to bring the fine sight to bear on his shoulder, my hand trembled like an aspen leaf, and the sight described figures of eight all over his body. There was no help for it, however; he was moving away, and I might never have such another chance. So, almost in despair, I fired. I was not surprised to see the ball raise the dust a hundred yards or so on his further side, and with a tremendous bound of, I fear to say how many yards, straight in the air, away went the buck like an arrow from the bow. In for a penny, in for a pound! Once fired at, I might as well have the other shot; so stepping from my cramped position, I held my breath as I tried to cover his fleeting figure with the second barrel. He had gained at least 150 yards ere I touched the trigger, but the ball sped true, and over rolled the buck in a cloud of dust. Short was my triumph, however, for ere I had well taken the rifle from my shoulder he had regained his feet, and was off with hardly diminished speed. It is very rarely that an antelope thus suddenly rolled over does not succeed in regaining his legs. Their vital power is immense, and nothing but a brain shot or broken spine will tumble them over for good on the spot. When shot in the heart they generally run some fifty yards and then fall dead, and I much prefer to see an antelope go off thus, with the peculiar gait well known to experienced shots as the forerunner of a speedy dissolution, than to see even the prettiest somersault follow the striking of the ball.

"In the present instance I watched the antelope almost to the verge of the horizon. Now and then he slackened his pace for a few seconds, and looked round at his wounded flanks, and then, as if remembering that he had not yet put sufficient distance between him and the fatal spot, he would again start forward with renewed energy. The two does, as is generally the case when the buck is wounded, had gone off in a different direction; and were now standing on the plain, a few hundred paces from where I stood, gazing wistfully from me to their wounded lord. Such are the scenes that touch the heart of even the hardest deer-stalker, and for a moment I almost wished my right hand had been cut off ere I pulled trigger on this the loveliest of God's creatures.

"When he dwindled before the naked eye till he seemed as a black speck on the far horizon, I still continued to watch him through my glass, in the hope that he might lie down when he thought himself concealed, in which case I might steal in and end his troubles by another shot. Suddenly I saw him swerve from his course, and start off in another direction at full speed. Almost at the same instant a puff of smoke issued from a small bush on the plain—the buck staggered and fell, and, many seconds afterwards, the faint report of a gun-shot reached my ears."

The person who came to my aid in so timely a fashion was a native sportsman, whom I then saw for the first time. He was more like the professional hunter of the American backwoods than any other native of India I have ever met. His short trousers and hunting-shirt of Mhowa green displayed sinewy limbs and throat of a clear red brown, little darker than the colour of a sun-burnt European. An upright carriage and light springy step marked him out as a roamer of the forests from youth upwards; and the English double-barrelled gun, and workmanlike appointments of yellow sámbar leather, looked like the genuine sportsman I soon found him to be. Many a glorious day did I afterwards pass with him in the pursuit of nobler game than black bucks.

The *Chikárá*, or Indian gazelle,[1] is another antelope very common in Central India. It is called often the "ravine deer" by sportsmen; and, as regards the first part of the name, is so far well denoted. Its favourite haunts are the banks of the shallow ravines that often intersect the plain country in the neighbourhood of rivers, and seam the slopes of the higher eminences rising out of the great central table-land. These are generally thinly clothed with low thorny bushes, on the young shoots and pods of which it browses like the domestic goat. Of course it is wrong to call it a "deer," which term properly belongs only to the solid-horned *Cervidæ*. Considerably smaller than the black antelope, the gazelle also differs much from it in habits. It prefers low jungle to the open plain; and trusts more to its watchfulness and activity than to speed, which, however, it also possesses in a high degree. It is very rare to catch a gazelle, or still more a herd of them, off their guard; and it is surprising how, on the least alarm, the little creatures manage to disappear as if by magic. They have probably just hopped into the bottom of a ravine, sped along it like lightning for about a hundred yards, and are regarding you, intent and motionless, from behind the straggling bushes on the next rising ground. Should you follow them up, they will probably repeat the same manœuvre, but this time putting three or four ravines between you and them instead of one. They also resort to the cultivation to feed, though not so regularly as the black antelope; and their numbers are not sufficient to do any notable damage. In the morning they may often be found picking their way back to the network of ravines, where they stay during the day. Should you disturb them at this time, they will most likely seek their cover at top speed; and what that amounts to will amaze you if you let slip a greyhound at them. Chikárá have not yet learned the range of the modern "Express" rifle; and consequently they still often let one get almost within

[1] *Gazella Bennettii.*

the killing distance of the old weapon, and are easily knocked over with the "Express." The depth of their slender bodies is so small that a bullet must be planted in a space little wider than a hand's-breadth to make sure of stopping them. Shots are generally got at a distance of from 100 to 150 yards; and the difficulty of such fine shooting at uncertain distances, together with their peculiar "dodginess" in keeping out of sight, makes the stalking of them a more difficult, and I think more interesting, sport than the pursuit of the larger antelope. Their art has little variety in it, however; and there is something to the experienced eye in the features of the ground which will almost infallibly tell whereabouts one is likely to have stopped after his first disappearance. Unless they have been seen to go clean away, they should always be followed up on the chance of being found again.

The last of the antelopes met with in the open country is the Nílgáe,[1] the male of which, called a "blue bull," will stand about 13½ hands high at the shoulder. The female is a good deal smaller, and of a fawn colour. Their habitat is on the lower hills that border and intersect the plains, and also on the plains themselves wherever grass and bushes afford sufficient cover. The old sites of deserted villages and cultivation, unfortunately so common, which are usually covered with long grass and a low bushy growth of Palás and Jujube trees,[2] are seldom without a herd of nílgáe. They are never found very far from cultivation, which they visit regularly every night. When little fired at, the blue bull is very easily approached and shot. It is very poor eating, and affords no trophy worth taking away, so that it is not much sought after by the sportsman. The beginner, however, who is steadying his nerves, or the inventor who wants a substantial target for a new projectile, will find them very accessible and convenient. The blue bull is an awkward, lumbering, stupid brute; and it is highly ludicrous to observe the air of self-satisfaction with which a blockhead of a bull, who has allowed you to walk up

[1] *Portax pictus*. [2] *Butea frondosa, Zizyphus jujuba*.

within fifty yards of him, will blunder off to the other side of a nálá, then turn round and stand still within easy range of your rifle, and look as if he thought himself a very clever fellow indeed for so thoroughly outwitting you. He is a favourite quarry with the unenterprising Mahomedan gentleman. The antelope his style of dress and powers of locomotion do not allow him to approach; the rugged ground and thorny underwood prohibit his succeeding with the forest deer; the tiger he likes not the look of, and the pig he may not touch; so he gets him into a bullock-cart, and is driven within a few paces of an unsuspecting blue bull, whose carcase, when shot and duly cut in the throat after the rules of his faith, makes for him the beef which his soul loveth. Awkward and inactive as he looks, however, the blue bull, when fairly pushed to his speed, will give a good horse as much as he can do to overhaul him. It is in vain to attempt it in or near the jungle; but if you can succeed in getting at him when he has a mile or two to go across the open plain, a real good run may be had with the spear. I have never heard of a blue bull attempting to charge when brought to bay, in which respect, therefore, the sport of riding them is inferior to pig-sticking.

Such are the principal animals which form the objects of the sportsman's pursuit in the open country. As, however, in a state of nature, there never are herbivorous creatures without their attendant carnivora to form a check and counterbalance to them, so we find various natural enemies attendant on the herds of antelope and nílgáe, whose acquaintance the sportsman will occasionally make. The nílgáe is a favourite prey of the tiger and the panther. But it is in the low hills where he retires during the day, rather than in the plains where he feeds at night, that he meets these relentless foes; and the chief carnivorous creatures of the open country are the hunting leopard,[1] the wolf,[2] and the jackal.[3]

I have several times come across and shot the hunting leopard when after antelope; but they cannot be called common in this part of India. They live mostly in the

[1] *F. jubata.* [2] *C. pallipes.* [3] *C. aureus.*

low, isolated rocky eminences called *Torias*, that rise here and there like islets in the middle of the plains, and on the central plateau, and which are frequently surrounded by grassy plains where they hunt their prey. They are of a retiring and inoffensive disposition, never coming near dwellings, or attacking domesticated animals, like the leopard and panther; and I never heard of their showing any sport when pursued. Their manner of catching the antelope, by a union of cat-like stealth of approach and unparalleled velocity of attack, has often been described. A few are kept tame by the wealthier natives, but more, I think, for show than real use in hunting.

The common jackal, always ready for food of any description, seldom fails to make a meal of any wounded animal, and I have seen a small gang of them pursue a wounded antelope I had just fired at. The fawns of the antelope and gazelle frequently become their victims.

The wolf is extremely common in the northern parts of the province; frequenting the same sort of ground as the antelope and chikárá. I have very seldom met with them in forest tracts; and I think that in India they are clearly a plain-loving species. They unite in parties of five or six to hunt; the latter being the largest number I have ever seen together. More generally they are found singly or in couples. I have several times observed them in the act of hunting the antelope; their method being to steal in on all sides of a detached party of does and fawns, and trust to a united rush to capture one or more of them before they attain their speed. Fast as the wolf is (as you will learn if you try to ride him down), I do not believe he is capable of running down an antelope in a fair hunt, though doubtless old or injured animals are thus killed by him. When game is not to be had, the wolf seldom fails to get a meal in the neighbourhood of villages, in the shape of a dog or a goat. They are deadly foes to the former; and will stand outside a village or the traveller's camp at night, and howl until some inexperienced cur sallies forth to reply, when the lot of that cur will probably be to return no more. Unfortunately, the wolf of Central India does not always confine himself to such substitutes for legitimate game; and the loss of human life from these hideous brutes has recently been ascertained to be so great that a heavy reward is now offered for their destruction. Though not generally venturing beyond children of ten or twelve years old, yet, when confirmed in the habit of man-eating, they do not hesitate to attack, at an advantage, full-grown women and even adult men. A good many instances occurred, during the construction of the railway through the low jungles north of Jubbulpúr, of labourers on the works being so attacked, and sometimes killed and eaten. The attack was commonly made by a pair of wolves, one of which seized the victim by the neck from behind, preventing outcry, while the other, coming swiftly up, tore out the entrails in front. These confirmed man-eaters are described as having been exceedingly wary, and fully able to discriminate between a helpless victim and an armed man.

My own experience of wolves does not record an instance of their attacking an adult human being; but I have known many places where children were regularly carried off by them. Superstition frequently prevents the natives from protecting themselves or retaliating on the brutes. I was once marching through a small village on the borders of the Damoh district, and accidentally heard that for months past a pair of wolves had carried off a child every few days, from the centre of the village and in broad daylight. No attempt whatever had been made to kill them, though their haunts were perfectly well known, and lay not a quarter of a mile from the village. A shapeless stone representing the goddess Deví, under a neighbouring tree, had instead been daubed with vermilion, and liberally propitiated with cocoa-nuts and rice! Their plan of attack was uniform and simple. The village stood on the slope of a hill, at the foot of which ran the bed of a stream thickly fringed with grass and bushes. The main street of the village, where children were always at play, ran down the slope of the hill; and while one of the wolves, which was smaller than the other, would ensconce itself among some low bushes between the village and the bottom of the hill, the other would go round to the top, and, watching an opportunity, race down through the street, picking up a child by the way, and making off with it to the thick cover in the nálá. At first the people used to pursue, and sometimes made the marauder drop his prey; but, as they said, finding that in that case the companion wolf usually succeeded in carrying off another of the children in the confusion, while the first was usually so injured as to be beyond recovery, they ended, like phlegmatic Hindús as they were, by just letting them take as many of their offspring as they wanted! An infant a few years old had thus been carried off the morning of my arrival. It is scarcely credible that I could not at first obtain sufficient beaters to drive the cover where these two atrocious brutes were gorging on their unholy meal. At last a few of the outcaste helots who act as village drudges in those parts were induced to take sticks and accompany my horsekeeper with a hog-spear, and my Sikh orderly with his sword, through the belt of grass, while I posted myself behind a tree with a double rifle at the other end. In about five minutes the pair walked leisurely out into an open space within twenty paces of me. They were evidently mother and son; the latter about three-quarters grown, with a reddish-yellow well-furred coat, and plump appearance; the mother a lean and grizzled hag, with hideous pendent dugs, and slaver dropping from her disgusting jaws. I gave her the benefit of the first barrel, and dropped her with a shot through both her shoulders. The whelp started off, but the second barrel arrested him also with a bullet in the neck; and I watched with satisfaction the struggles of the mother till my man came up with the hog-spear, which I defiled by finishing her. In the cover they had come through, my men said that their lairs in the grass were numerous, and filled with fragments of bones; so that there was little doubt that the brutes thus so happily disposed of, had long been perfectly at home in the neighbourhood of these miserable superstitious villagers.

Dogs that are in the way of hunting jackals will readily pursue a wolf, so long as he runs away. But the wolf generally tries the effect of his bared teeth on his pursuers before running very far, and only the most resolute hounds can be brought to face them. I have several times had my dogs chased back close up to my horse by a wolf they had encountered when out coursing foxes and jackals; and only once saw the dogs get the better of one without assistance from the gun. On that occasion I had out a couple of young greyhounds, crossed between the deer-hound and the Rampore breed; and along with them was a very large and powerful English bull-mastiff, rejoicing in the name of "Tinker," whose exceedingly plebeian looks in no way belied his name. He was an old hand at fighting before ever he left the purlieus of his native Manchester; and in India had been victor in many a bloody tussle with jackal, jungle cat, and pariah dog. His massive head and well-armed jaws combined in a high degree the qualities of a battering-ram and heavy artillery; and his courage was in full proportion to his means of offence. On the present occasion the three dogs espied the enemy sitting coolly on his haunches on the top of a rising ground, and the young dogs, taking him no doubt for a jackal, went at him full speed, Tinker as usual lumbering along in the rear. Soon, however, the hounds returned in a panic, with their tails well down, and closely pursued by the wolf, a large dark-gray fellow, snapping and snarling at their heels. The greyhounds fled past Tinker, who steadily advanced, dropping into the crouching sort of run he always adopted in his attack. No doubt Master Wolf thought he too would turn from his gleaming rows of teeth and erected hair, as all his canine assailants had done before. But he never was more mistaken, for the game old dog, as soon as a pace or two only remained betwixt him and the enemy, suddenly sprang to his full height, and, with a bound, buried his bullet head in his advancing chest. I saw the two roll over and over together, and then the gallant Tinker rose on the top of the wolf, his vice-like jaws firmly fastened on his throat. At this point of a combat he usually overpowered his antagonist utterly, by using his immense weight and power of limb to force him prostrate on the earth, the while riving at the throat with a force that often scooped a hollow in the earth under the scene of action. His efforts were now directed to effect this favourite manœuvre; but the wolf was too strong for him, and repeatedly foiled the attempt. But the young hounds, who were not at all without pluck, soon returned to his assistance, and seizing the wolf by different hind-legs, made such a spread-eagle of him, that Tinker had no difficulty in holding him down while I dismounted and battered in his skull with the hammer-head of my hunting-whip. None of the three dogs had been bitten, Tinker having got his jaws in chancery from the very first. I am sure that the three, or even Tinker alone, would have killed him in time without my assistance; for Tinker never let go a grip he had once secured, and though not so large, was not much inferior to him in strength.

The catalogue of amusements offered to the sportsman in the open plain would be incomplete without a mention of the "mighty boar." He is to be found almost everywhere—in the low jungle on the edge of cultivation, and sometimes in the sugar-cane and other tall crops; and with a liberal expenditure of self and horse may be ridden and speared in a good many places. Generally, however, the country is highly unfavourable to riding, the black soil of the plains being split up into yawning cracks many feet in depth, or covered with rolling trap boulders, both sorts of country being equally productive of dangerous croppers. The neighbourhood of Nágpúr affords the best ground; and there there is a regular "tent club," which gives a good account of numerous hogs in the course of the year. The sport has been so voluminously described that I believe nothing remains to be said about it. The hogs that reside in the open plains are not much inferior in size to those of other parts of India; but those met with in the hills are generally much smaller, and far more active. A brown-coloured variety has sometimes been noticed among them. The common village pig of the country shows every sign of having been derived from the wild race originally.

My march down the Narbadá valley led along the tortuous and rugged cart track, through the deep black loam of the surrounding fields, which, before the construction of the railway, was the only means of communication through these fertile districts. Broken carts strewed the roadside, and clumps of thorny acacias overgrew the path. These were justly called the "cotton thief" by the people, their branches being laden with bunches of the fibre dear to Manchester, torn by their thorns from the unpressed bales, as they lumbered along on antediluvian buffalo carts towards the distant coast.

Large gangs of aboriginal Gónds from the nearer hill tracts were labouring on the railway works. The really wild tribes of the interior of the hills were not yet attracted by the labour market in the plains, preferring a dinner of jungle herbs and their squalid freedom to plenty earned by steady toil under the eye of the foreign taskmaster. But the semi-Hindú tribes of the borderland, who are now the most numerous of the race, and whom long contact with the people of the plains has imbued with wants and tendencies strange to their wilder brethren, have reaped a rich harvest from this sudden demand for labour arising at their doors. How far it has been to them an unmixed advantage will be discussed further on. As labourers, their innate distaste to steady toil, born of long years of a semi-nomadic existence, renders them inferior to the regular Maráthá navvy of the Deccan, who is also their superior in muscular power, and can double the wages of any Gónd at this sort of work.

On the 25th of January I quitted the main road down the valley, near the little civil station of Narsingpúr, and struck off nearly at right angles to the south, marching direct for the hills that bounded the horizon in that direction. About half-way through the march of fifteen miles, the level deep black soil of the valley began to give place to a red gravelly tract of undulating conformation; and numerous fine *Mhowa* trees, forming groups that at a little distance much resembled oaks, and half-cleared fields, gave indications of the approach of the border belt of half-reclaimed land which intervenes between the open plain and the forest-covered hills. The Mhowa (*Bassia latifolia*) is one of the most useful wild trees in this part of India. It is not cut down like other forest trees in clearing the land for tillage, its value being at first greater than that of the area rendered unproductive by its shade and roots. As the country gets more thickly peopled, however, the case is reversed, and it generally disappears in long-settled tracts. As a singular instance of the influence sometimes exerted by social customs on the physical character of a country, I may mention an exception to this rule in the case of the district of Nimár, which, even in its fully cultivated parts, is still thickly dotted with Mhowa trees. The reason of this I believe to be that, during the "times of trouble" referred to in my first chapter, the majority of the small proprietors of the land were ousted from possession of their fields; but the custom having been established that possession of the fruit-trees growing on it did not necessarily pass with the land, they mostly retained the proprietorship of these trees. Thus it has happened that the land is often owned by one party and the trees by another. The rent is paid only by the landholder; and thus, though it would pay him to clear off the trees, it would not pay the tree-man; and so they have remained, doubtless to the very great advantage, and certainly to the beauty, of the district.

The value of the Mhowa consists in the fleshy corolla of its flower, and in its seeds. The flower is highly deciduous, ripening and falling in the months of March and April. It possesses considerable substance, and a sweet but sickly taste and smell. It is a favourite article of food with all the wild tribes, and the lower classes of Hindús; but its main use is in the distillation of ardent spirits, most of what is consumed being made from Mhowa. The spirit, when well made and mellowed by age, is by no means of despicable quality, resembling in some degree Irish whisky. The luscious flowers are no less a favourite food of the brute creation than of man. Every vegetable-eating animal and bird incessantly endeavours to fill itself with Mhowa during its flowering season. Sámbar, nílgáe, and bears appear to lose their natural apprehensions of danger in some degree during the Mhowa season; and the most favourable chances of shooting them are then obtained. The trees have to be watched night and day if the crop is to be saved; and the wilder races, who fear neither wild beast nor evil spirit, are generally engaged to do this for a wage of one-half the produce. The yield of flowers from a single tree is about 130 lbs., worth five shillings in the market; and the nuts, which form in bunches after the dropping of the flowers, yield a thick oil, much resembling tallow in appearance and properties. It is used for burning, for the manufacture of soap, and in adulterating the clarified butter so largely consumed by all natives. A demand for it has lately sprung up in the Bombay market; and a good deal has been exported since the opening of the railway. The supply must be immense; and probably this new demand will be the means of greatly increasing the value of the trees.

I encamped at the end of this march at a place called Mohpání, the scene of the works of the "Nerbudda Coal and Iron Company." Most of the miners employed at that time were Góṇds, whose courage in diving into the bowels of the earth was found to be superior to that of other races. The universal pantheism of the Gónd stands him in good stead on such occasions. From his cradle he has looked on every rock, stream, and cavern as tenanted by its peculiar spirit, whom it is only needful to propitiate in a simple fashion to make all safe. So he just touches with vermilion the rock he is about to blow into a thousand fragments with a keg of powder, lays before it a handful of rice and a nutshell full of Mhowa spirit, and lo! the god of the coal-mine is sufficiently satisfied to permit his simple worshipper to hew away as he pleases at his residence. If utility is, as some have thought, a good quality in religions, surely we have it in perfection in a pliable belief like this.

Near Mohpání is one of the best snipe *jheels* in the province. I went out to it in the afternoon with one of the gentlemen connected with the works, who surely never could have seen a snipe before. We took opposite sides of the long swamp, which swarmed with the long-bills; and when we met at the end I had got twenty-seven and a half couples, while my friend had collected a miscellaneous bag of snippets, plover, paddy-birds, and *minas*, and not *one* snipe among them.

My next march lay under the northern face of the main range of the Sátpúras, which here form a bluff headland rising some 500 feet above the plain, crowned by an old fortress called Chaoragarh. This is one of the many extensive fortifications constructed by the chiefs of the country to the south of the Narbadá, at the time when the resistless tide of Mahomedan conquest, after engulfing the Hindú kingdoms of upper India and the Deccan, was rolling against the principalities of these central regions. The works of these forts generally enclose a considerable space on the summit of a naturally inaccessible hill, having been designed for the retreat of large bodies of the inhabitants, and of armies, in times of successful invasion. The flat-topped and scarp-sided hills of the trap formation are the most suitable for such strongholds, and there are consequently more of them in the trap country than elsewhere. Such additional works as are necessary are composed of massive blocks of rock, roughly squared and laid without masonry. Inside tanks have generally been excavated in the rock to hold a plentiful supply of water, natural hollows being always taken advantage of to avoid labour as much as possible. Before the days of artillery such places must have possessed great strength; but we rarely hear of their being vigorously defended by their possessors, and they were generally surrendered after a short investment. Doubtless the chief cause was usually want of provisions, masses of people being suddenly huddled into the place, and being unable to carry with them the scanty provender afforded by a poor country in the face of danger. In 1564 the great Akber sent his lieutenant to reduce the Gónd chieftain of Mandlá. The Gónd troops, led by the heroic Dúrgáwatí, the Rájpút widow of the last chief, made a noble resistance to the invader near Jubbulpúr; but, the battle at last going against them, their leader stabbed herself rather than suffer the disgrace of defeat; and this fort of Chaoragarh immediately afterwards fell into the hands of the Moslem, together with property and treasure valued in the chronicles at an altogether fabulous amount. The summits of these old forts usually contain a little water in the old tanks; and being generally covered with thick jungle are favourite resorts of the tiger and other animals in the hot weather.

From my camp at Chaolpání a single peak of the Puchmurree hills was visible. It had not a very imposing appearance, however, as I find it recorded as "like half an egg sticking out of an immense egg-cup!" A couple of bears came close up to the camp at night and commenced to fight, making a fearful noise, it seemed to me, as I awoke, inside the tent ropes. The horses were tearing at their pickets, and all the camp in a hubbub. I started out with a gun, but the people said they had just passed through the camp, rolling over each other and growling; and it was so pitch dark that I could not see any distance before me, and had to come back. The next march was fourteen miles to Jhilpá, the last village before the ascent of the hills begins. The view of Puchmurree was lost during this march from our being too close under the intervening range of hills. On the way I shot a young sámbar stag; and after arriving in camp a messenger from the village I had left in the morning came in breathless to say that a tiger had killed a bullock in the morning within half a mile of my camp. At that time of year, when the jungle is very green and thick, and tigers always on the move, it was not worth while to go back, even if I had had the time.

This day's march was through a much more jungly country than I had yet met. It could not be called a forest; for the trees were all of the secondary growth, which marks land repeatedly cleared and abandoned again; and the cultivation, such as it was, was still carried on with the regular bullock-plough, after the manner of the plains. In many places there was a thick growth of teak poles from old stumps of trees; and many of the fields had been hewn out of these coppices, the poles being burnt on the ground as manure, in the manner to be hereafter described. The clear and pretty stream of the Dénwá, which comes down from Puchmurree, was crossed several times by the track we followed, and contained on its sandy banks many footprints of tigers. There was evidently a good deal of forest game about. The valley is one of those tracts on the border between open plain and dense jungle, where much of the nocturnal life of the forest creatures is passed. In such a tract the traveller will often be astonished at the quantity of signs of animals he will see in the morning all about his night's camp, while not a wild creature of any sort will he find in the neighbourhood if he goes to look for them after the sun is up. The fact is that deer, bears, pigs, etc., travel such long distances at night to their feeding grounds, and depart again to the remoter hills so early in the morning, that unless a very early start be made, nothing but the tracks they have left behind will ever be seen. The tigers and panthers, again, which prey on them, although not usually retreating so far, yet seek the most secluded thickets and ravines of the neighbourhood at an equally early hour, and in the cold weather are so much on the alert, and can so easily hide in the thick vegetation, that the chances with them, except by sitting up over a bait at night, are equally poor. The native shikárí, watching by night, kills a great deal of game at this season. But it is very slow and cold, as well as rather poaching work, and few Europeans are cat-like enough to succeed in it. Now, as most Europeans who attempt shooting at all in India (and who does not at first?) only go out during the cold season, and never go deeper into the forest than this semi-cleared belt, the reason of much of the want of success complained of is not far to seek. To ensure success the animals must be followed up into the deeper jungles.

CHAPTER III

THE MÁHÁDEO HILLS

In the eyes of the Hindú inhabitants of the neighbouring plains, the whole of the range of hills which culminated in the Puchmurree plateau is sacred to their deity Sívá, called Máhádeo, or the Great God; and the hills themselves are called by his name, the Máhádeos. A conception of awe and mystery had always been associated with their lofty peaks, embosomed among which lies one of the most sacred shrines of the god, to which at least one pilgrimage was a necessity in the life of every devout Hindú. But excepting at the appointed season for this pilgrimage, no dweller of the plains would venture at the time of which I am writing, to set his foot on the holy soil of Máhádeo's hills; and, as we approached its neighbourhood, gloomy looks began to gather on the faces of my followers, whose fears had been acted on by the conversation of the people they had met. The road to the top was represented as impassable from natural difficulties; and guarded by wild beasts, goblins, and fell disease.

I halted a day at Jhilpá, the last village on the plains, to make arrangements for the ascent, and procure guides; and on the 22nd packed my small tent and a few necessaries on a pony, and with two attendants started up the hill on foot. For the first ten miles or so the pathway led up an easy and regular ascent over shelving rocks and scanty soil, whereon grew a thin forest of the commoner sorts of trees, Sálei (*Boswellia thurifera*), Dhäorá (*Conocarpus latifolia*), and Sáj (*Pentaptera glabra*), being the most numerous species; the grass and vegetation on these slopes had begun already to assume the yellow tinge of the dry season. Such a prospect as this, which is typical of vast tracts in the jungles of Central India, is sadly disappointing to him who looks for the luxuriant tropical forest of low-lying equatorial regions. Forests like those of Southern Africa and the littoral countries of Asia, with their close array of giant trunks, dense

CAMP AT PUCHMURREE. BUDDHIST CAVES IN THE BACKGROUND.

canopy of vegetation, impenetrable underwood, gorgeous flowers, and mighty tangled creepers—

> From branch to branch close wreaths of bondage throwing,

are unknown in these central regions of India; and their character is rarely approached save in some occasional low moist valley, where the axe of the woodcutter has not penetrated, and the stagnation of some stream has united with the heat of a close valley in giving to the vegetation a more truly tropical character. Indeed, but for the preponderance of yellows where rich reds and browns should be, and the rare appearance of a palm or other eastern form, most of these low forest tracts might be taken after December for a late autumn scene in a temperate climate. Nothing is more striking than the absence of brilliant flowers, which, contrary to popular idea, are far more characteristic of temperate than of tropical regions. The Palás (*Butea superba*) is almost the only tree in our forests which possesses really bright colouring.

When an elevation of about 2000 feet (above the sea) had been attained, the character of the scenery began to change. Vertical scarps of the red sandstone which forms the higher plateau began to rise into view at every turn of the path, which now plunged into narrow and gloomy glens, following the boulder-strewn bed of a small stream. The dried and yellow grasses and naked tree stems of the lower slope gave place to a green vegetation thickly covering the soil, and in places almost meeting overhead. The moist banks of the stream were covered with ferns and mosses, and the clear sparkle of the little brooks appeared singularly refreshing after our long walk up-hill in the heat of a sultry and lowering day. The baggage-pony found considerable difficulty in scrambling over the boulders that now began to block the road; and we relieved him by putting about half of his load on the two guides. After scrambling thus along the sides and bottoms of ravines for some miles, steadily rising at the same time, we suddenly emerged through a narrow pass, and from under the spreading aisle of a large banyan tree (from which this pass gets its name of the Bur-ghat), on to an open glade, covered with short green grass, and studded with magnificent trees, which I found was the commencement of the plateau of Puchmurree.

Heavy masses of cloud had now gathered overhead, and large drops of rain began to fall, betokening, as it proved, the coming of one of the short but severe storms to which these hills are liable at this season. The village of Puchmurree was still some miles distant, and we hurried along over the now almost level plateau to get shelter as soon as possible, as we had already walked about seventeen miles, and the sun was almost set. The road now lay over a hard and gently undulating sandy soil, crossed by many small streams running swiftly in their rocky beds. Immense trees of the dark green Harrá (*Terminalia Chebula*), the arboreous Jáman (*Eugenia Jambolana*), and the common Mango dotted the plain in fine clumps; and altogether the aspect of the plateau was much more that of a fine English park than of any scene I had before come across in India. By and by, through the vistas of the trees, three great isolated peaks began to appear, glowing red and fiery in the setting sun against the purple background of a cloud-bank. The centre one of the three, right ahead of us, was the peak of Máhádeo, deep in the bowels of which lies the shrine of the god himself; to the left, like the bastion of some giant's hold, rose the square and abrupt form of Cháurádeo; while to the right, and further off than the others, frowned the sheer scarp of Dhúpgarh, the highest point of these Central Indian highlands.

We had little leisure to enjoy this splendid view, however, for a blinding rain, accompanied by thunder and lightning, now came on; and some distance still intervened from the village when we were compelled to seek shelter in a grove of trees. Fortunately there was among them a large hollow banyan tree, within which we all found shelter, including "Quail" and "Snipe," who I forgot to say were of the party, and had revelled in spur fowl all the way up.

I sent on the two guides to the village to procure us some firewood and water; for I determined to encamp here, rather than go further, and probably fare worse, among the unknown disagreeables of a Korkú village. A swampy hollow lay betwixt us and the village, and after we heard the guides go splashing through this and disappear in the darkness it was full two hours before we heard them floundering back again with three or four Korkús carrying bundles of sticks, grass, pots of water, and the various natural productions which have always to be procured from the village where camp is pitched.

Meanwhile we sat in our tree and smoked, and very cold and disagreeable it was, though tolerably dry. With the help of the Korkús the little tent was soon pitched, and I transferred myself and dogs to its shelter, while a fire was lit in the hollow of the banyan, and the natives were soon crouching over it as jolly as sand-boys; while my servant plucked and grilled over its embers one of the spur fowl I had shot as a "spatch-cock." About midnight the rain ceased, and the sky cleared. It was an excessively cold night; and when I got up shivering in the morning I found my men had stayed up the greater part of the night by the fire for the sake of the warmth.

The morning broke fine and bright, however, and I started off for a ramble over the plateau. In passing through the swamp below the tent, the dogs put up, and I shot several couples of snipe, and among them a fine specimen of the solitary or wood snipe.[1] This fine snipe is of rare occurrence in Central India, and in fact I have only met with it on one other occasion, in the Mandlá district. I suspect this is the bird that has stood for the woodcock in the stories told of the latter's occurrence in the Central Provinces; for though I have hunted every likely spot in the hills for the latter bird, I never found a single one of them.

There were two small settlements of Korkús on the plateau: one at Puchmurree itself, and another about a mile to the north of it. The former was the larger of the two, consisting of about thirty houses, and, besides the Thákúr, a few families of traders from the plains lived in it. The functions exercised by these Hindú dealers in the rural economy of the aborigines will form the subject of some remarks further on.

A brother of the Thákúr of Puchmurree accompanied me in my ramble, a fine, athletic, intelligent young fellow of eighteen or twenty, and an ardent sportsman, who was afterwards my guide over the whole of this wonderful mass of mountains. We were out nearly all day, the succession of fine views from the different heights and

[1] *Gallinago nemoricola.*

bluffs luring me on and on, till what was meant for a stroll ended in a pretty hard day's work.

I found that the plateau had something of a cup-like shape, draining in every direction from the edges into the centre, where two considerable brooks receive its waters and carry them over the edge in fine cascades. The general elevation of this central valley is about 3400 feet, the ridge surrounding it being a few hundred feet higher, and here and there shooting into abrupt peaks, of which the three I had seen the evening before attain a height of 4500 feet. The area of the plateau is altogether about twelve square miles, some six of which, in the centre, resemble the portion I had before passed through, and consist of fine culturable, though light, soils. Everywhere the massive groups of trees and park-like scenery strike the eye; and the greenery of the glades, and various wild flowers unseen at lower elevations, maintain the illusion that the scene is a bit out of our own temperate zone rather than of the tropics. Though the ascent on the side I had come up was generally gradual, I found that in all other directions the drop from the plateau was sudden and precipitous. There are three other pathways by which a man can easily, and an unladen animal with difficulty, ascend and descend. Subsequently we took lightly laden elephants (which, when there is *room* for them, are the most sure-footed of all creatures) up and down both of the passes leading to the south; but the eastern pass (Kánjí Ghát) has never, I believe, been traversed by any baggage animal. The view from the edge of the plateau, in almost any direction, is singularly fine; and a still more extensive sweep is commanded from the top of the higher peaks.

To the south, as far as the eye can see, lie range upon range of forest-covered hills, tumbled in wild confusion. To the east a long line of rampart-like cliffs marks the southern face of the Máhádeo range, the deep red of their sandstone formation contrasting finely with the intense green of the bamboo vegetation, out of which they rise. Here and there they shoot into peaks of bare red rock, many of which have a peculiar and almost fantastic appearance, owing to the irregular weathering of their material—beds of coarse sandstone horizontally streaked by darker bands of hard vitrified ferruginous earth. Looking across this wall of rock, to the north-east, a long perspective of forest-covered hills is seen, the nearer ones seeming to be part of the Puchmurree plateau, though really separated from it by an enormous rift in the rock, the further ranges sinking gradually in elevation, till, faint and blue in the far distance, gleams the level plain of the Narbadá valley. Standing on the eastern edge of the plateau, again, the observer hangs over a sheer descent of 2000 feet of rock, leading beyond, in long green slopes, down to a flat and forest-covered valley. Its width may be six or seven miles, and beyond it is seen another range of hills rising in a long yellow grass-covered slope, dotted with the black boulders, and ending in the scarped tops that mark the trap formation. That is the plateau of Motúr (Mohtoor), with which the general continuation of the Sátpúra range again commences, after the break in it occasioned by the Máhádeo group. On this side, the forest that clothes the valley and the nearer slopes presents a very dark green and yet brilliant colouring, which will be noted as differing from the vegetation in any other direction. This is the Sál forest, which I have mentioned before (p. 22), as forming so singular an outlier far to the west of the line which otherwise limits the range of that tree in Central India. It fills this valley of the Dénwá, almost to the exclusion of other vegetation, and, creeping up the ravines, has occupied also the south-eastern portion of the plateau itself.

A remarkable feature in the configuration of the plateau is the vast and unexpected ravines or rather clefts in the solid rock, which seam the edges of the scarp, some of them reaching in sheer descent almost to the level of the plains. You come on them during a ramble in almost any direction, opening suddenly at your feet in the middle of some grassy glade. The most remarkable is the Ándeh-Kóh, which begins about a mile to the east of the village, and runs right down into the Dénwá valley. Looking over its edge, the vision loses itself in the vast profundity.

A few dark indigo-coloured specks at the bottom represent wild mango trees of sixty or eighty feet in height. A faint sound of running water rises on the sough of the wind from the abyss. The only sign of life is an occasional flight of blue pigeons swinging out from the face of either cliff, and circling round on suspended pinion, again to disappear under the crags. If a gun is fired, the echoes roll round the hollow in continually increasing confusion, till the accumulated volume seems to bellow forth at the mouth of the ravine into the plain below. If tradition be believed, no mortal foot has ever trodden the dark interior of the Ándeh-Kóh. I myself never found an entrance to it, though, with the aid of ropes, I got once at the easiest place within a few hundred feet of the bottom. I may say, however, for the benefit of adventurous explorers, that a way in may probably be found by going round behind the Máhádeo peak, and following down the bed of the stream which issues from the cave of the shrine I am about to describe, and which, I think, eventually falls into the Kóh under the scarp of Cháurádeo.

Legend has made the Ándeh-Kóh the retreat of a monstrous serpent, which formerly inhabited a lake on the plateau, and vexed the worshippers of Máhádeo till the god dried up the serpent's lake, and imprisoned the snake himself in this rift, formed by a stroke of his trident in the solid rock. It needs no very ingenious interpreter of legend to see in this wild story an allusion to the former settlements of Búddhists (referred to as snakes in Brahminical writings) on the Puchmurree hill, and their extinction on the revival of Brahmanism in the sixth or seventh century. Certain it is that there once was a considerable lake in the centre of the plateau, formed by a dam thrown across a narrow gorge, and that on its banks are still found numbers of the large flat bricks used in ancient buildings, while in the overhanging rocks are cut five caves (whence the name of Puchmurree), of the character usually attributed to the Búddhists. Beneath the lower end of the lake lies a considerable stretch of almost level land, on which are still traceable the signs of ancient tillage, in the form of embankments and watercourses. Looking from the portico of the rock-cut caves, it is not difficult for the imagination to travel back to the time when the lower margin of the lake was surrounded by the dwellings of a small, perhaps an exiled and persecuted, colony of Búddhists, practising for their subsistence the art, strange in these wilds, of civilised cultivation of the earth, and to hear again the sound of the evening bell in their little monastery floating away up the placid surface of the winding lake.

Another very striking ravine, called Jambo-Dwìp, lies on the opposite side of the plateau from the Ándeh-Kóh. About a thousand feet of steep descent, down a track worn by the feet of pilgrims, leads to the entrance of a gorge, whose aspect is singularly adapted to impress the imagination of the pilgrim to these sacred hills. A dense canopy of the wild mango tree, overlaid and interlaced by the tree-like limbs of the giant creeper,[1] almost shuts out the sun; strange shapes of tree ferns and thickets of dank and rotting vegetation cumber the path; a chalybeate stream, covered by a film of metallic scum, reddens the ooze through which it slowly percolates; a gloom like twilight shrouds the bottom of the valley, from out of which rises on either hand a towering crag of deep red colour, from the summit of which stretch the ghostly arms of the white and naked *Sterculia urens*, a tree that looks as if the megatherium might have climbed its uncouth and ghastly branches at the birth of the world. Further on, the gorge narrows to a mere cleft between the high cliffs, wholly destitute of vegetation, and strewn with great boulders. Climbing over these, and wading through the waters of a shallow stream, the pilgrim at length reaches a cavern in the rock, the sides and bottom of which have been, by some peculiar water action, worn into the semblance of gigantic matted locks of hair; while deep below the floor of the cavern, in the bowels of the rock, is heard the labouring of imprisoned waters shaking the cave. It is small wonder that such a natural marvel as this should be a chosen dwelling-place for the god to whom all these mountains are sacred, and that it forms

[1] *Bauhinia scandens.*

one of the most holy and indispensable points in the circuit which the devout pilgrim must perform.

The place has also a slight historical interest. During the last of our struggles with the Maráthás, Áppá Sáheb Bhonslá, Rájá of Nágpúr, on his way to an exile justly earned by repeated acts of treachery, escaped and fled to the fastnesses of the Máhádeo hills; and it was in this secluded ravine, if tradition speaks the truth, that he was concealed by the fidelity of his aboriginal subjects till he finally made his escape, while detachments of British troops were hunting for him in every other nook and recess in the mountains.

Beyond the Jambo-Dwìp, or "great ravine" as we called it, and between it and the valley of the Sonbhadrá, lies another group of wild hills, a little lower than the Puchmurree block in elevation, and with few level plateaux of any extent. One or two poor hamlets of Korkús occupy its most sheltered nooks; but the soil is everywhere extremely thin, and there is a great absence of water in this section of the Máhádeo range, so that it is almost uninhabited. The Sonbhadrá valley itself can only be entered where it leaves the southern face of the hills, by a difficult pathway along the edges of the rapid stream; but the scene is well deserving of the scramble of eight or ten miles on foot by which it is reached. It is utterly untenanted even by animals, save a few melancholy bears, and its steep precipices, and long slopes of gray and naked rock, interspersed with scanty moor-like vegetation, are singularly suggestive of a comparison with the well-known valley of Glencoe.

These deep and gloomy dells that seam the Puchmurree block are the home of a splendid squirrel (*Sciurus maximus*), measuring two and a half to three feet in length, and of a rich, deep claret colour, with a blue metallic lustre on the upper parts of the body, the lower parts being rufous yellow. They dwell in the upper branches of the wild mango trees, making nests of the leaves, generally in the very top. They live chiefly on the mango fruit, lavishly squandering the supply while the fresh mangoes are attainable, and afterwards cracking the discarded stones for their kernels. They seem to be of a retired and melancholy nature, appropriate to the sunless ravines they reside in; and they are not very numerous either here or at Amarkantak, which is the only other part of the hills where I have met the species. They are easily captured in the nests when young, but make most foolish and uninteresting pets, having a singularly vacant expression of countenance, and nothing of the light-hearted vivacity of the other members of the squirrel family. If an exquisite fur for a lady's muff or a sporran is an object, some pretty shooting may be had in knocking them off the tops of the high trees with a small rifle. Numerous vultures and birds of the rapacious order build on the ledges of the cliffs. Among them is the grand imperial eagle (*A. imperialis*), whose wings measure eight feet from tip to tip, and whose soaring flight and harsh scream form a grand feature in the scenery of this range of mountains.

On my return to the tent I had an interview with the Thákúr, or chief, of Puchmurree. This potentate is the proprietor of a considerable tract of hill and forest in the Máhádeo range, and the valleys at its base. He is the representative of one of the families already referred to as having been established in the early days of Aryan colonisation, by an intermixture of the blood of the adventurous Rájpút with that of the aboriginal (in this case Korkú) occupants of the soil. In personal appearance and habits the family exactly correspond to their descent. Taller and fairer by far than the undiluted Korkús about them, they still possess the thick lips and prominent jaw of the aborigines. With all the love of tinsel and sounding form of the vain Rájpút, they unite much of the apathy and unthrift of the savage. In religion they are (like all converts) ultra Hindú, worshipping Sívá, looking on the slaughter of a cow with horror (though they will kill the nearly related bison of their hills), wearing the holy thread of the twice-born castes, and keeping a family Brahman to do their household worship for them. The Puchmurree Thákúr was a well-grown young man of about twenty-five, but awkward in manner and incapable of any sort of conversation. I subsequently found that he was, like most of these petty chiefs, a confirmed opium-eater. By his side, however, stood the Brahman "Dewan," or minister of state (!), whose glibness of tongue was fully sufficient for both. Behind them came four or five tatterdemalion retainers, in quilted garments of many hues, girded as to their loins with broad embroidered belts of sámbar leather, in which were stuck, or suspended, swords, daggers, and the cumbrous appointments of a matchlock-man, the matchlock itself being borne, with smoking match, over the shoulder of each. These were mostly of the same breed as the Thákúr, being his poor relations in fact. This description would serve sufficiently well for the great majority of these petty semi-aboriginal chiefs, who are so numerous in the hills of Central India. Though the breed between the Rájpút and the aborigine produces the best of all shikárís and foresters, in a somewhat higher sphere they are chiefly remarkable for debauchery, and a vain and silly pride which leads them into expenditure beyond their means, and ruinous debt. They all call themselves "Rájás," and keep up minute standing armies of these ragamuffin retainers, as well as one or two Brahman bloodsuckers to manage their holy and clerkly affairs. As they are always seeking for brides for their sons in families with higher claims to Rájpút descent than their own, they have to pay enormous sums for marriage expenses, and this is probably the chief cause of their generally hopeless poverty.

I found I was likely to have a good deal of trouble in getting the wild hill people to help in building our lodge. The Thákúr made all sorts of excuses for withholding from us his influence with his "subjects." There was great scarcity among them, owing to a failure of their precarious crops; they had nearly all left the hills to seek service in the plains; they were engaged in preparing the land for their crops; they hated work they had not been accustomed to; they would be afraid to help in making a house on Máhádeo's hill—and so on. Truth was, I saw the chief himself and his advisers hated our intrusion. With some truth they feared we were come to break up their much-beloved seclusion, and untrammelled barbarism; their rich harvest from the taxation of pilgrims to Máhádeo's shrine they thought was in danger; and they would have none of us. They promised, however, to send me a gang of men to start wood and grass cutting next morning. Of course they did not come; and the Thákúr I found had gone off to a village he had below the hill, and quite out of reach of my camp; and he did not return to Puchmurree, except when I sent for him, all the time I was there. Luckily I had a friend in council in the shape of the younger brother, who had shown me the lions of the place. Not being a chief he had little to live on, and was, in fact, scarcely to be distinguished in position or worldly wealth from the common Korkús about. He promised to use his influence to get them to come and work for me, and went off on a visit to the neighbouring hamlets, partly with this object, and partly to look for traces of any bison or other larger game there might be on the hills, as I contemplated a grand hunting party at which I hoped to overcome the shyness of the jungle population.

They were really in great distress owing to the failure of the previous harvest, on which great part of their subsistence for the year depends. The system of cultivation of all the wild tribes of these provinces is much the same, and is, in fact, almost identical with the method followed by all the unreclaimed aboriginal races throughout India. Though large tracts of splendid level land lie untilled on the Puchmurree plateau, and in the valleys below, the Korkú has no cattle or ploughs with which to break it up. He has nothing in the way of implements but his axe. This is enough, however, for his wants. He selects a hillside where there is a little soil, and a plentiful growth of grass, timber, and bamboos. He prefers a place where young straight teak poles grow thick and strong, as they are easiest to cut, and produce most ashes when burnt. He cuts every stick that stands on the selected plot, except the largest trunks, which he lops of their branches and girdles so that they may shortly die. This he does early in the dry season (January to March), and leaves the timber thickly piled on the ground to dry in the torrid sun of the hot season. By the end of May it will be just like tinder, and he then sets fire to it and burns it as nearly as he can to ashes. With all his labour, however (and he works hard at this spasmodic sort of toil), he will not be able to work all the logs into position to get burnt; and at the end of a week he will rest from his labour, and contemplate with satisfaction the three or four acres of valuable teak forest he has reduced to a heap of ashes, strewn with the charred remains of the larger limbs and trunks. He now rakes his ashes evenly over the field and waits for rain, which in due season generally comes. He then takes a few handfuls of the coarse grain he subsists on and flings them into the ashes, broadcast if the ground be tolerably level; if steep, then in a line at the top, so as to be washed down by the rain. The principal grains are Kódon (*Paspalum*), Kútkí (*Panicum*), and coarse rice. But nearly all the ordinary crops raised in the plains during the autumn season are also grown more or less in these *dhya* clearings, as they are called, though usually from greatly degenerate seed, the produce of which is often scarcely recognisable as the same species. A few pumpkins and creeping beans are usually grown about the houses in addition to the dhya crop. Such is the fertilising power of the ashes that the crop is generally a very productive one, though the individual grains are far smaller than the same species as cultivated in the plains. A fence against wild animals is made round the clearing by cutting trees so as to fall over and interlace with each other, the whole being strongly bound with split bamboos and thorny bushes. The second year the dead trees and half-burnt branches are again ignited, and fresh wood is cut and brought from the adjoining jungle, and the same process is repeated. The third year the clearing is usually abandoned for a fresh one. Sometimes the owner of a dhya will watch at night on a platform in the middle of the field and endeavour to save it from wild animals, but oftener he does not think it worth the labour, and lets it take its chance till ripe, while he earns his livelihood in some other way.

The dhya clearings are of course favourite resorts for all the animals of the neighbourhood. The smaller species of these—peafowl, partridges, hares, etc.—are often trapped in ingenious "deadfall" traps set in runs left open on purpose; and the larger are frequently shot by the sportsmen of the community. None of the Gónds of the Central Hills now use the bow and arrow; but few villages are without their professional hunter, who is generally a capital shot with his long heavy matchlock, and as patient as a cat in watching for game. He usually takes it in turn to sit up at night in all the dhya clearings of the village, getting as remuneration all that he kills, and a basket of grain at harvest time besides. The skins of sámbar are of considerable value in the market for making the well-known soft yellow leather—the best of all materials for sporting leggings and other accoutrements.

The abandoned dhya clearings are speedily covered again with jungle. The second growth is, however, very different from the virgin forest destroyed by the first clearing; being composed of a variety of low and very densely growing bamboo, and of certain thorny bushes, which together form in a year or two a cover almost impenetrable to man or beast. I have often been obliged to turn back from such a jungle after vainly endeavouring to force through it a powerful elephant accustomed to work his way through difficult cover. In such a thicket no timber tree can ever force its way into daylight; and a second growth of timber on such land can never be expected if left to nature. The scrub itself does not furnish fuel enough for a sufficient coating of ashes to please the dhya cutter; and so the latter never again returns to an old clearing while untouched forest land is to be had. Now, if it be considered that, for untold ages, the aboriginal inhabitants have been thus devastating the forests, the cause of the problem that has puzzled railway engineers —namely, why, in a country with so vast an expanse of forest-covered land, they should yet have to send to England, or Australia, or Norway for their sleepers—will not be far to seek. Stand on any hill-top on the Puchmurree or other high range, and look over the valleys below you—the dhya clearings can be easily distinguished from tree jungle—and you will see that for one acre left of the latter, thousands have been levelled by the axe of the Gónd and Korkú. In fact I can say, from an experience reaching over every teak tract in these hills, that, excepting a few preserved by private proprietors, no teak forest ever escaped this treatment, unless so situated in ravines or on precipitous hill-sides as to make it unprofitable to make dhya clearings on its site.

The system of cultivation thus adopted by the wild tribes, which seems to be a natural consequence of their want of agricultural stock, necessitates a more or less nomadic habit of life. The larger villages, where the chief of a sept, and the Hindú traders who effect their small exchanges, reside, is usually the only stable settlement in a whole tract; the rest of the people spreading themselves about in small hamlets of five or six families, at such intervals as will give each a sufficient range of jungle for several years of dhya cutting. Their huts are of the most temporary character, and made from materials found on the spot—a few upright posts, interlaced with split bamboos, plastered with mud, and thatched with the broad leaves of the teak, and an upper layer of grass. It costs them but the work of a day or two to shift such a settlement as this in accordance with the changes of their dhya sites.

The system of cultivation, if it can be so termed, I have thus described is of course of the most precarious character. The holding off of rain for a few weeks after the seed is sown, or when the ear is forming, will ruin the whole, and then the owner may be compelled to subsist entirely on what always largely supplements his diet—the wild fruits and products of the forest. Nature has been very bountiful in these forests in her supply of food for their wild human denizens. Many species of tree and bush ripen a wholesome and palatable fruit in their season; and the earth supplements the supply by many nourishing roots. The Mhowa flower before referred to (p. 64), the plum of the ebony tree (*Diospyros melanoxylon*), and the fruit of the wild mango, are the staples in these hills. The berries of the Chironjí (*Buchanania latifolia*), and the Bér (*Zizyphus jujuba*), the seeds of the Sál (*Shorea robusta*), the bean of the giant Bauhinia creeper, and many other products of trees, are also eaten in different parts of the hills. A species of wild arrowroot (*Cúrcuma*), and a sort of wild yam, are also dug out of the earth and consumed.

The rare occurrence of the general seeding of the bamboo forests, is a godsend to the aboriginal tribes. A certain number of bamboos seed every year, but a general seeding is said to occur only once in about thirty years. Then every single bamboo over a vast tract of country will drop its leaves, and form at the end a large panicle of flowers, to be followed by the formation and shedding of myriads of seeds which are hardly to be distinguished from grains of rice. This done, the parent bamboo itself immediately dies, while a fresh and vigorous crop at once begins to spring from the seed. For some years the scarcity of so useful an article as the bamboo may be severely felt, though it is not often that all the sources of supply are at once cut off; but in the meantime an abundant supply of wholesome grain is afforded, not only to the wild tribes but to multitudes of the poorer inhabitants of the open country, and the cities around, who crowd to the spot to obtain their share of the heaven-sent provender. There is a proverb that this occurrence portends a failure of the common food staples of the country; but like many such it has not been verified by experience. It would probably be in vain to guess the cause of this sudden renewal at long intervals of the whole crop of bamboo.

This diet of herbs is varied and improved by the flesh of wild animals, procured by extensive drives in which the whole population of a tract will unite; and many small fish are also captured in the mountain streams, chiefly by poisoning the pools with various vegetable substances, of which I am acquainted only with the leaves and fruit of the species of *strychnos* that grow wild in these hills.

Those of the wild men who live in the neighbourhood of the plains, and have got accustomed to contact with their inhabitants, add considerably to their means of subsistence by trooping out in large numbers, after they have cut their own dhyas, to the reaping of the wheat harvest of the plains in the month of March, much after the fashion of the gangs of Irishmen who cross the Channel about harvest time. But the genuine hill-man of the far interior cannot yet bring himself to this, and is often put to severe straits by the failure of his scanty crop.

Such was now the case with the Gónds and Korkús in and about the Puchmurree hills; and I soon saw that to make anything of them I must appeal to their bellies. I accordingly sent down to the nearest large market in the plains, and purchased a mighty store of wheat and millet —about twenty-five bullock loads, I think—and had it sent up by the agency of some of the Banjárá [1] carriers, who are in the habit of penetrating the remotest tracts of these hills with loads of salt, and taking back forest produce in return.

In the meantime I got up the remainder of my camp, pitched the large tent, and erected a hut of wattle and daub as a storehouse for the grain and tools, and made myself comfortable. At the same time I arranged for a few artificers, carpenters, and masons, being sent up from the plains; but it was long before any of them could be induced to venture into the dreaded region. Though the geological surveyor of the Narbadá valley had given no hope of limestone being found in these hills, I discovered

[1] These Banjárás are a curious race of nomads who are found everywhere in Central India, acting as carriers with herds of pack bullocks. Their name means "Forest Wanderer," and they appear to be perfectly distinct both from Hindús and from the known aboriginal tribes. It has been conjectured with some probability that they are gipsies. They are a fine, stalwart, light-coloured people, ready for any adventure, and of dauntless courage. With the aid of their splendid dogs they do not scruple to attack and spear the wild boar, the bear, and even the tiger; and they are at all times ardent and indefatigable sportsmen. Each *tanda*, as their camps are called, is commanded by a chief called the *naik*, whom all obey, and who, in council with the elders, disposes of intertribal offenders, even to the extent of capital punishment, it is believed. The old men and many of the women and children remain encamped at some favourite grazing spot during the expeditions, where all return to pass the rainy season and recruit their cattle. Though eminent in the art and practice of highway robbery, the Banjárás are scrupulously faithful in the execution of trusts, and are constantly employed in the interchange of commodities between the open country and the forest tracts.

an excellent supply of it in one of the deep glens a little below the scarp of the plateau. After searching long and wearily for it in vain, and receiving on all hands assurances that such a thing had never been heard of, I was directed to the place by a Korkú whom I incidentally saw in the unwonted occupation of chewing *paun*, in the composition of which lime has a place. I found a huge block of pure white crystalline limestone jammed in the bottom of this ravine; and it is curious to conjecture by what fortunate geological process this immense boulder of an article without which building would be impossible at Puchmurree, could have been brought and so conveniently deposited at an elevation of at least 2000 feet above the nearest formation of the kind. Though I believe I have at one time or other been in almost every other ravine in these hills, I never found another piece of limestone but one—a smaller boulder of the same sort, similarly situated, but at a rather lower elevation.

The young Thákúr came back in a day or two, with about half-a-dozen Korkús from the neighbouring hills, and news of a herd of bison in the Bángangá valley, behind and below the high peak of Dhúpgarh; so I determined to have our grand hunt in that place. Invitations were sent to all the Gónd and Korkú chiefs in the neighbourhood, with their followers, and every available man in the hills was sent for to beat. A store of grain enough to feed them all was sent down to the little hamlet at the bottom of the Roríghát pass, where the beat was expected to end; and one of the Puchmurree grog-shops was taken bodily down to the same place to supply the drinkables.

In after days I spent many a long day in the chase of the bison on these splendid hills; and have also made the acquaintance of the mountain bull in many other parts of the province. Some account of his habits may, therefore, not be out of place here, particularly as they are frequently a good deal misrepresented. And first as to his name. The latest scientific name for him is *Gavœus Gaurus*, but what he is to be called in English is not so easily settled. Sportsmen have unanimously agreed to call him the "Indian Bison," which naturalists object to, as he does not properly belong to the same group of bovines as the bisons of Europe and America. They would have us call him the *Gaur*, which appears to be his vernacular name in the Nepalese forests. I would, however, put in a plea for the retention, by sportsmen at least, of the name "Indian Bison." In the first place it fully accomplishes the object of all names in distinctly denoting the animal meant. Ever since he became known to Europeans he has been so called, and no other animal has ever shared the name. Then his structural distinction from the true bisontine group appears to consist chiefly, if not solely, in his having thirteen instead of fourteen or fifteen pairs of ribs, and somewhat flattened instead of cylindrical horns (Jerdon). Lastly, there is no vernacular name universally applicable to him, "Gaur" being unknown in Central India; while his occasional Central Indian name of *Bhínsa* (with *Bun* or "wild" prefixed to it) is almost identical in sound with "bison," and is no doubt derived from the same root. If you ask for "bison" in these forests where he is known (and speak a little through your nose at the same time), you will certainly be shown *Gavæus Gaurus* and no other animal.

The respective ranges of this animal and the wild buffalo (*Bubalus*) have sometimes been defined by sportsmen in the saying that the bison is not found north, nor the buffalo south, of the Narbadá river. Like most apophthegms, however, this contains little more than a flavour of the truth. Not only does the bison inhabit many parts of the Vindhyá Mountains, directly to the north of the Narbadá, but he also stretches round the source of that river and penetrates into the hills of Chotá-Nágpúr and Midnapúr, and crosses over to the Nepalese Terae, and the hilly regions in the east of Bengal. The wild buffalo also covers the whole of the eastern part of the Central Provinces far to the south of the latitude of the Narbadá, and also the plateau of Mandlá and the Godávarí forests, directly to the south of that river. In fact, the bison appears to inhabit every part of India where he can find suitable conditions. These appear to be, firstly, the close proximity of hills, for though he is

[To face page 88.

BISON ON THE PACHMARHÍ HILLS—VIEW LOOKING WEST

sometimes found on level ground, he is essentially a lover of hills, and always retreats to them when disturbed; extensive ranges of forest little disturbed by man or tame cattle, for, unlike the buffalo, he cannot tolerate the proximity of man and his works; a plentiful supply of water and green herbage; and lastly, so far as I have observed, the presence of the bamboo, on which he constantly browses. In the Central Provinces of India all these conditions are unfortunately still present over enormous tracts of country. Thousands of square miles in the Central range, much of which will one day be reclaimed to the uses of the plough, are now the very perfection of a preserve for the bison.

Perhaps he is nowhere more completely at home than in the Máhádeo hills. There, as a general rule, he will be found to frequent at any season the highest elevation at which he can then find food and water. During the cold season succeeding the monsoon, they remain much about the higher plateaux, at an elevation of 2000 to 3000 feet, where they graze all night on the bamboos that clothe their sides, and on the short, succulent grasses fringing the springs and streams usually found in the intervening hollows. They generally pass the day on the tops of the plateaux, lying down in secure positions under the shade of small trees, where they chew the cud and sleep. Their object in lying under trees seems more the concealment thus afforded to their large and dark-coloured bodies than shelter from the sun, as the shade is seldom dense, and a secure windy position is always secured irrespective of the sun. I have observed that single animals always lie looking down wind, leaving the up wind direction to be guarded by their keen sense of smell; and, in my experience, it is far easier to baffle their sense of vision in a direct approach, than to stalk them down wind, however carefully the approach may be covered. It is extraordinary how difficult it often is to distinguish so strongly coloured an object as a bull bison when thus lying down in the flickering shadow of a tree.

The colour of the cows is a light chestnut brown in the cold weather, becoming darker as the season advances.

The young bulls are a deeper tint of the same colour, becoming, however, much darker as they advance in age, the mature bull being almost black on the back and sides, and showing a rich chestnut shade only on the lower parts of the body and inside of the thighs. The colour of both bulls and cows varies a good deal in different localities. The lightest coloured are those of the open grass jungles in the west, the darkest those of the deep bamboo forests of Puchmurree and the east. The white stockings, which are so characteristic a marking of this species, also change with advancing age, assuming a much dingier colour in the old bulls. A singular change also occurs in the growth of the horns, which will be well illustrated by the accompanying plate of a photographed series belonging to bulls of different ages shot in the same locality (Nimár). No. 1 belonged to a young chestnut-coloured bull of about five years old. Its shape, it will be seen, approximates to that of the cows (No. 5), being, like them, slender and much recurved at the points. No. 2 pertained to a very dark, but not black, bull, evidently a year or two older than the first, but not quite mature. The horns have considerably increased in girth at the base, and have assumed a more outward sweep, with less incurvature at the points. No. 3 are still thicker and more horizontal, with some signs of wear at the tips, and were taken from a full-grown, jet-black bull, the lord of a herd. No. 4 adorned a very old and solitary bull, and are, it will be seen, extremely rugged and massive, with scarcely any curve, and are considerably worn and blunted at the points. They measure thirty-seven and a half inches across the sweep, and seventeen round the thickest part. No. 3 are the longest round the curve of the horn, each measuring twenty-five and a half inches, the extreme girth being only fifteen and a half inches. The largest of these bulls measured exactly seventeen and a quarter hands (five feet nine inches) at the shoulder, measuring fairly the right line between two pegs held in the line of the foreleg. I once measured a bull in the Puchmurree hills which was two inches taller than this, and I am convinced that this is about the extreme height attained by them in this

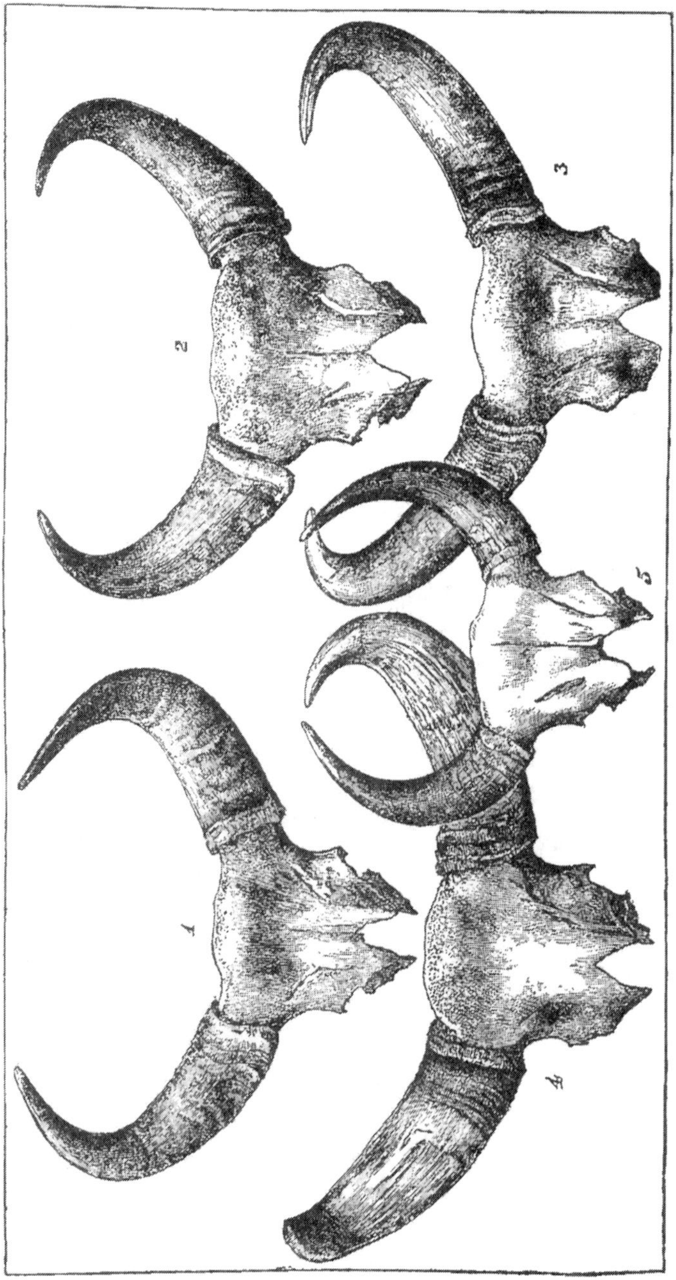

GROWTH OF HORNS OF "GAVÆUS GAURUS."

part of India. I strongly suspect that the much greater heights often given have been taken from unfair measurements. A common way is to take an oblique line from the fore-foot to the top of the dorsal ridge, and follow the curvatures of the body besides. In this way twenty-two hands may doubtless be made out, but we might as well measure the distance from nose to tail for the height as this.

At this season of the year (the winter months), the bison are rutting, and they will be found collected in herds numbering ten or twelve cows, with one bull in the prime of life, and a few immature males, the remaining old bulls being expelled to wander in pairs, or as solitary bachelors, in sullen and disappointed mood. Very old bulls with worn horns are almost always found alone, never, apparently, rejoining the herd after being once beaten by a younger rival. These solitary gentlemen wander about a great deal; while the herd, if undisturbed, will constantly be found in the same neighbourhood. Each herd appears to possess a tract of country tabooed to other herds; and in this are always included more than one stronghold, where the density of the cover renders pursuit of them hopeless. When frequently disturbed in and about one of these, they make off at once to one of the others.

As the hot season advances, and the springs in the higher ranges dry up, the bison come lower down the hills; and may even, if compelled by want of water, come out into the forest on the plains, drinking from the large rivers like other animals at that season. But they are always ready to retreat to their mountain fastnesses when much disturbed; and as soon as the fall of the rains has renewed the supply of water, and freshened the grass in the higher hills, they retire again to their favourite plateaux. At this season the cows begin to calve, and separate a good deal, remaining for two or three months secluded in some spot where grazing and water are plentiful. The bulls and young cows are then often found together in herds of six to ten, the oldest bulls, however, always remaining alone. During the lulls in the monsoon, a species of gadfly appears in the jungles, which is exceedingly troublesome to all animals. At such times the bison seek the high, open tops of the mountains; and I have then seen a solitary bull standing for hours like a statue on the top of the highest peak in the Puchmurree range.

Though at first sight a clumsy-looking animal, which is chiefly due to his immensely massive dorsal ridge, the bison is one of the best rock climbers among animals. His short legs, and small, game-like hoofs, the enormous power of the muscles of the shoulder, with their high dorsal attachment, and the preponderance of weight in the fore part of the body, all eminently qualify him for the ascent of steep and rocky hills. For rapid descent, however, they are not so well adapted; and I have known cases of their breaking a leg when pushed to take rapidly a steep declivity; a bull with one fore-leg broken is at once brought to a standstill.

Terrible tales are told of the relentless ferocity of the bison by the class of writers who aim rather at sensational description than at sober truth. I have myself always found them to be extremely timid, and have never been charged by a bison, though frequently in a position where any animal at all ferocious would certainly have done so. In all my experience, I have only heard of one or two cases of charging which I consider fully authentic, and in these the animal had previously been attacked and wounded. Captain Pearson was once treed by a wounded bull in the Puchmurree hills, which charged and upset his gun-bearer; and an officer was killed by one some years ago near Asírgarh. Often the blind rush of an animal bent on escape is put down by excited sportsmen as a deliberate charge. Much, too, of the romance attached to the animal must be attributed to his formidable appearance; for the sullen air of a mighty bull just roused is very impressive; and much to the wild tales of the people in whose neighbourhood they live, who always dilate on their general ferocity, but can seldom point to an instance of its effects, and who are, moreover, frequently from religious prejudice, desirous of withholding the sportsman from their pursuit. Still there is sufficient evidence on record of the occasional fierce retaliation of the bull bison when wounded and closely followed up, in some resulting even in the death of the sportsman, to invest their pursuit with the flavour of danger so attractive to many persons, and to render caution in attacking them highly advisable. The ground on which they are usually met is fortunately favourable for escape if the sportsman be attacked, trees and large rocks being seldom far distant.

Although a closely allied bovine, the Gayal of trans-Bráhmápútrá India, has for ages been domesticated and used to till the land, all attempts to do so with the subject of my remarks, or even to raise them to maturity in a state of captivity, have failed. After a certain point the wild and retiring nature of the forest race asserts itself, and the young bison pines and dies. It has always struck me as curious why the most difficult of all animals to reclaim from a wild state are precisely those whose congeners have been already domesticated. The so-called wild horses, and the wild asses, are almost untamable; so also with the wild sheep and goat, the wild dog and the jungle-fowl. A young tiger or hyena is infinitely easier to bring up and tame than any of these.

This unconquerable antipathy of the Indian bison to the propinquity of man is slowly but surely contracting its range, and probably diminishing its numbers. Gradually cultivation is extending into the valleys that everywhere penetrate these hills; and the grazing of cattle, which extends far ahead of the regularly settled tracts, is pushing the wild bull before it into the remotest depths of the hills. I have, in a comparatively brief acquaintance with these hills, myself known considerable areas where bison used to be plentiful almost entirely cleared of these animals. Other wild beasts retire more slowly before the incursions of man, partly subsisting as they do on the products of his labour. The tiger who finds himself suddenly in the middle of herds of cattle merely changes his diet to meet the situation, and preys on cattle instead of wild pigs and deer. Even deer seldom live entirely in the deep forest, but hang on the outskirts of cultivation, and, mainly subsisting on it, need not materially decrease in numbers so long as there remain uncleared tracts to furnish a retreat when pressed. But the bison admits of no compromise. I have never heard of his visiting fields even when he lives within reach; he never interbreeds with tame cattle; and the axe of the clearer and the low of domestic cattle are a sign to him, as to the traditional backwoodsman, to move "further west."

On the day appointed for our grand hunt I started early, with the young Thákúr and a few of the Korkús, by a way that led right over the top of Dhúpgarh. After walking along the open plateau for about three miles we commenced the ascent of the hill, which is close on 1000 feet above the plateau. The zigzag track was hardly distinguishable among the grass and bamboos that clothe the hill; and every here and there a road had to be cleared with the axe, no one having passed that way since the preceding rainy season, when all vestiges of paths in these hills become obliterated. We were amply rewarded, however, for the climb by the magnificent prospect that awaited us when we gained the summit—the finest by far in all this range of hills. The further slope of Dhúpgarh was not nearly so precipitous as that we had come up, but fell, by steps as it were, to the bottom of a deep and extensive glen, which was the one we were about to beat. Beyond this again rose the mural cliff that buttresses the whole of this block to the south; and far past this, to the left, stretched out below us the wilderness of forest-clad hills, that reaches with scarcely a break to the Táptí river—a distance, as the crow flies, of sixty or seventy miles. All this immense waste is the chosen home of the bison; and beyond it, on either side of the Táptí, on the elevated Chikaldá range, and in the wild hills of Kálíbhít, lies another tract of equally wide extent, where, too, the mountain bull roams, as yet scarcely troubled with the presence of man or cattle. This is the region of the Teak tree *par excellence* in this central range of mountains, to which I will have the pleasure of conducting the reader in a future chapter.

Tracks of bison and sámbar were numerous on the top

of the hill, which is covered with bamboo clumps and with a low thicket of the bastard date.[1] I have frequently, on other occasions, found both bison and sámbar on the very top of Dhúpgarh in the early morning. The descent of the farther side of the hill, over long slopes of crumbled sandstone, and the curious vitrified pipes of ironstone that exfoliate from the decomposed surface of these hills, was fully more tiresome than the ascent. Many a time after this did I tread the same path to reach this valley, where bison were nearly always to be found, and many an effort did I make to discover a shorter and less precipitous road. But all in vain; for the sheer ravines that everywhere else hem in the flanks of the Dhúpgarh mountain render a passage round it a matter of infinitely greater time and toil than the way over the top. At the bottom of the valley, below a shady grove of wild mango trees, where the stream that drains the large valley has formed a considerable pool in a rocky basin, I found assembled three or four of the Ráj-Gónd chiefs whose possessions lie in the hills to the south of Puchmurree. They differed not at all from him of Puchmurree, unless that they were somewhat more intelligent and polished in manner. Each had brought his small retinue of matchlock men, and a large gang of common Gónds and Korkús to beat; so that altogether we mustered some twenty guns, and between two and three hundred beaters. The people were well acquainted with all the beats and passes, having always several great hunts of this sort during the year; and everything had been arranged before I came. The bulk of the beaters had gone on hours before to surround the valley, and, as we were a little later than was expected, it was likely that they would already have commenced to beat.

We lost no time, therefore, in taking up our posts, which stretched in a long line right across the lower end of the valley. First, however, I had to furnish powder to load the whole of the matchlocks of my native friends; and had I not guessed that such would be the case, as usual, I would certainly not have had sufficient in my flask.

[1] *Phœnix sylvestris.*

Six fingers deep is the rule for these weapons, and it is of no avail to point out the superior strength of our powder. They will have six fingers of Hall's No. 2, whatever the consequence. As they put generally two bullets, a leaden and an iron one, on the top of this charge, and wad with a handful of dry leaves, the result often is the bursting of the barrel, and always considerable contusion of the user's shoulder.

This was to be a silent beat; that is, the people were to advance without noise, beyond the rapping of their axes against the trees, as there was another dense cover lower down which usually held bison, and sometimes a tiger, and which was to be beaten also in the afternoon. I had sat an hour at least behind the screen of leaves that had been put up for me when the first sign of the beat appeared, and for another half-hour nothing was heard but the occasional knock of an axe-handle on a tree. Presently a shot rang from the extreme flank of the line of guns, then another, and a clatter of hoofs inside showed that a herd of something had been repulsed in an attempt to escape. As the beat advanced more shots were heard on either side, and the galloping about of the imprisoned animals, now and then met by a shout from behind when they attempted to break back, became productive of considerable excitement on my part. At last a rush of animals advanced down the side of the stream where I was posted, and eight or ten sámbar clattered past within half a stone's throw. I had just fired both barrels of my rifle at a couple of the stags, dropping one of them in his tracks, and had advanced a few paces towards it, when I heard a shot on my immediate right, and a fine bull bison, with two cows and a small calf, trotted past almost in the same line as the sámbar had taken. Those were not the days of breech-loaders, and though I had another rifle it was a little behind, leaning against the tree, and before I could get hold of it nothing but the sterns of the "beeves" (as a friend used to call them were to be seen. When I got it I favoured the bull with both barrels *à posteriori*, but there was no result. The young Thákúr, who occupied the post on my right, had been more successful; and when the beaters came up immediately afterwards I found a fine four-year-old bull lying dead, with two of his bullets through the centre of his neck. All the guns now came dropping in, and gathered in a group round the slain bison. One had seen a bear, another a couple of sámbar, and so on. All had fired, and of course hit hard, but the net result was the Thákúr's beeve, my sámbar, and two little "jungle sheep," as they are called, the proper name being the four-horned antelope.[1]

I had never seen a bison before, and though this was only a young chestnut-coloured bull with small horns, I was much struck with the bulk and expression of power belonging to the animal. Such was the width of the chest that when lying on the side, the upper fore-leg projected stiff and straight out from the body, without any tendency towards the ground. The head in particular has a fine high-bred and withal solemn appearance, which is still more noticeable in old bulls. From the eye of a newly slain bison, turned up to the sunlight, comes such a wonderful beam of emerald light as I have seen in the eye of no other animal; and the skin emits a faint, sweet odour as of herbs.

We tracked the wounded sámbar and bison a little way down the valley, the former showing signs of being hard hit, and a little blood was found also on the track of the bull. We left a few of the best trackers to follow up their trail with the next beat, and went round to take up our places about a mile further down, and close to my camp at Roríghát. The same process was repeated here, and this time with much shouting and hammering of drums, as a tiger was usually somewhere in this part of the valley, and his tracks had been seen in the morning. I did not get a shot on this occasion. One of the Gónd Thákúrs shot another sámbar; and my wounded stag was found and killed with their axes by the Gónds. The wounded bull was in the beat, and broke near one of the Thákúr's retainers, who was too astonished to fire. The rest of the bison, or another herd, broke through the side of the beat, and plunged down a very steep and rocky descent,

[1] *Titraceros quadricornis.*

which the people said they had never attempted but once before, when one of them had broken a leg. Certainly I should not have thought that any animal so large as a bison could go down that place and live.

Nothing had been seen of the tiger, and had I known him as well as I afterwards did, I would not have been surprised. I knew that tiger intimately for many months after this, and yet I never once saw him. He was a very large animal indeed, but entirely a *jungle* tiger, that is, preying solely on wild animals, and keeping during the day to the most inaccessible ravines and thickets. He frequented the bison ground round Dhúpgarh, and hung on the traces of the herds, apparently with an eye to the young beeves. I never came across evidence of his killing any of them, though I once saw a place on the plateau where the whole night long he had evidently baited an unfortunate cow with a calf. Within a space of some twenty yards in diameter the grass had been closely trampled down and paddled into the moist ground by their feet, the footprints of the calf being in the centre, while the tiger's mighty paw went round outside, and the poor cow had evidently circled round and round between the monster and her little one. I am glad to say that I tracked the tiger off in one direction, and the courageous mother and her calf safe in another. The tiger cannot, I believe, kill even a cow bison, unless taken at a disadvantage; and with a bull he could have no chance whatever. I seldom went out without meeting the tracks of this tiger; and often followed him through his whole night's wanderings, which were laid out as on a map in the clean sand of the stream beds; but I always lost him in the end, though I believe he often let me pass within a few yards of him. He came at rare intervals, like the bison, on to the plateau; but his regular beat was round the bottom of Dhúpgarh, a thousand feet lower down. Once, long ago, a tiger took up his post on the plateau, and became a man-eater, almost stopping the pilgrimage to Máhádeo, till he was shot by the uncle of the Thákúr.

I followed the wounded bison bull for about a mile from where he was last seen; but he was moving fast, and the blood had ceased to drop. He would never stop, the people said, till he got to a stronghold of the bison of these hills, about five miles off, a hill called the Búrí-Má (Old Mother); and so I reluctantly gave up the pursuit. When I returned all the beaters were assembled; and a more wild and uncouth set it never before had been my lot to see. Entirely naked, with the exception of a very dingy and often terribly scanty strip of cloth round the middle, there was no difficulty in detecting the points that mark the aborigine. They were all of low stature, the Korkús perhaps averaging an inch or two higher than the Gónds, who seldom exceed five feet two inches; the colour generally a very dark brown, almost black in many individuals, though never reaching the sooty blackness of the negro. Among the Gónds a lighter-brown tint was not uncommon. In features both races are almost identical, the face being flat, forehead low, nose flat on the bridge, with open protuberant nostrils; lips heavy and large, but the jaw usually well formed and not prominent like that of the negro; the hair on the face generally very scanty, but made up for by a bushy shock of straight black hair. In form they are generally well made, muscular about the shoulders and thighs, with lean, sinewy forearm and lower leg. The expression of face is rather stolid, though good-humoured. Some of the younger men might almost be called handsome after their pattern; but the elders have generally a coarse, weather-beaten aspect, which is not attractive. All the men present carried the little axe, without which they never stir into the forest, and many had spears besides. During the beat they had killed a good many peafowl and hares, and one little deer, by throwing their axes at them, in which they are very expert.

The Korkús, I found, were prevented by prejudice acquired from the Hindús from eating the flesh of the slain bison; so the Gónds from Almód, and a number of a tribe called Bharyas, who had come from the Motúr hills, had him all to themselves, while the Korkús set to work on the sámbar with their sharp little axes, which are all that is wanted for skinning and cutting up the carcase of the largest animal. My servant secured the tongues and marrow-bones, and a steak out of the under-cut of the bison—all delicacies of the first water for the table of the forest sportsman; and the remainder of the flesh was given up to the hungry multitude. As night fell, they lit fires where the bison had fallen, and near the village where they had brought the deer; and for hours after continued carrying about gobbets of the raw meat, which they hung up on the surrounding trees, broiling and swallowing the titbits during leisure moments. This was only the preliminary to the great feast, however—the dozen of oysters to whet the appetite for turtle and venison. Soon the trees were fully decorated with bloody festoons, and the savages set to work in earnest to gorge themselves with the half-cooked meat. The entrails were evidently the great delicacies, and were eaten in long lengths, as Italians do macaroni. The gorging seemed to be endless, and I sat outside my little tent for hours looking on in wonder at the bloody orgie. The bonfires they had lighted threw a ruddy glow over the open glade, and on the crimson junks of flesh hanging on the trees, bringing the dusky forms of the revellers into every variety of picturesque relief, and forming a wild and Rembrandt-like picture which I shall not soon forget. Till a late hour many new arrivals continued to add to their numbers, winding down the steep path that leads over the Rorígbát, with lighted torches and loud shouts to show the way and scare wild beasts. All were welcome to a raw steak and a pull at the pot of Mhowa spirit that stood beside every group. Ere long they began to sing, and then to dance to a shrill music piped from half-a-dozen bamboo flutes. The scene was getting uproarious as I turned in; and my slumber was broken through the greater part of the night by the noise and the glare of the great fires through the thin canvas of my tent.

Next morning I was roused by the crow of the red jungle-fowl, which swarm in the bamboo cover of this little valley, and by the unremitting "hammer, hammer" of the little "coppersmith" barbet,[1] of which there

[1] *Xantholæma indica.*

seemed to be more in this valley of Rorígbát than in all the rest of the country. I found the revellers lying like logs just where they had been sitting; and it was no small labour to rouse and get them together. A couple of days' supply of flour was served out to each, as remuneration for their labour in the drive; and plenty more was promised if they would come and help to build the lodge at Puchmurree. I also gratified the chiefs by presenting them with sundry canisters of powder and all my spare bullets; and we parted, I believe, mutually pleased with each other, and with promises of plenty more hunting-meets of the same sort. I had had enough of that sort of sport, however; and, excepting once with the Thákúr of Almód, never again drove the hills for game. It is poor sport in my opinion, and is seldom very successful even in making a bag.

Two days after this, parties of my aboriginal friends began to drop in at the bungalow work; and, as a few masons and brickmakers had also arrived from the plains, our prospects looked cheerful. The wild people brought their women and children along with them, and in half a day erected huts of boughs sufficient for their accommodation. They were all told off in parties to cut and bring in Sál poles for rafters, and bamboos and grass for thatching, to break and carry up lime from the ravine, to puddle earth for brick-making, etc. The wood-cutting part of the work they were well accustomed to; but those to whose lot fell the lime and earth business were much disgusted, and were with difficulty kept to their work. All payments were made in kind, the convoy of Banjárá bullocks being now unremittingly employed in carrying grain from the plains. The work rapidly progressed, and was but slightly interrupted by the absconding after a while of all our masons and brickmakers, who had very unwillingly come up from the plains. Their places were at once taken by the Gónds who had been employed under them, and whom I had selected to learn these branches of the work, with a view to such a contingency. An old foreman carpenter, who stuck by us and superintended the work, had fortunately some knowledge of bricklaying, and with his help we soon began to get the Góndș to turn out very respectable work indeed. Nobody knew how to turn an arch, however; and I had to evolve the idea of one out of my own consciousness, and build the first over the fireplace myself. The Gónds were immensely amused at the idea of the *Koitor*, or "men," as they call themselves, dabbling in bricks and mortar, and laughed and joked over it from morning till night. Regular industry, however, was not to be got from these unreclaimed savages; and there were seldom half of those on the muster-roll actually present. Every now and then, too, they would walk off in a body, and have a big drink somewhere for a couple of days, returning and setting to work the next morning without appearing to think a word of explanation necessary. The height of absurdity was reached when I imported a plough and a pair of bullocks from below, and sent a Korkú to work with them to plough up a piece of land for a garden. He really made a sad bunglė of it at first, having no conception of the business; and I had to set one of my peons, who had followed the plough before he donned the badge of office, to help him. In a little while, however, several of the Korkús because quite *au fait* at ploughing; and an acre or so of fine soil in the old bed of the tank was soon fenced in, deeply ploughed, and prepared for gardening operations at the commencement of the rainy season.

For the next few weeks, my spare time was pleasantly passed in exploring the neighbourhood of the hills and their productions. I visited the Sál forest in the Delákárí valley to the east of Puchmurree. It was one of the few forests in this part of the country which had till then escaped destruction at the hands of the timber-speculator or the dyha-cutting aborigine, being inaccessible to the former from want of roads, and unsuited from its level character and the size of the trees to the operations of the latter. It, however, affords an example of one of the great difficulties of growing large timber in the dry upland regions of Central India. Though the trees bore every appearance of being fully mature, their size was by no means first-rate, the largest averaging no more than six or eight feet in girth, while most of them, when subsequently cut down, were found to be almost useless from heart-shake and dry-rot. It belonged to the Thákúr of Puchmurree and another chief; and I soon after concluded a lease of it for Government with them, and laid out a road connecting it with the open country. The view looking upwards to the Puchmurree heights from the Dénwá valley, or across from the opposite Motúr hills, is exceedingly fine, the rich reds of the sandstone scarp mellowing into an indescribable variety of delicate shades of purple and violet in the evening sun, while broad belts of shadow thrown across the green slopes at the foot, and gathering in the recesses of the ravines, seem to project the glowing summits of the rocks to an unnatural height in the soft orange-tinted sky.

Here I ascertained the existence of the Bárá-Singhá, or twelve-tined deer (*Rucervus Duvaucellii*), an animal which, like the Sál forest in which it lives, had been supposed not to extend to the west of the Sál belt in the Mandlá district. I was not so fortunate as to shoot a stag myself in this place; but I shot two does, and saw a frontlet of the male in the possession of a native shikárí, with the unmistakable antlers attached. Since then, too, I have heard of a fine stag being shot there by a railway engineer. I believe they are not very numerous here; indeed, the Sál forest, to which I believe their range is confined, covers an area of only a few square miles.

I also found that the red jungle-fowl of North-Eastern India (*G. ferrugineus*) inhabits this Sál forest and the hills around it, although, so far as I am aware, it is not found anywhere else in these hills further west than the great Sál belt of Mandlá. The other species of jungle-fowl, which properly belongs to Western and Southern India (*G. Sonneratii*), is also to be met with on the Puchmurree hills; and I have shot both species in the same day in the ravine where the Máhádeo Cave is situated. The red fowl could hardly be distinguished from many a specimen of the domesticated race either in appearance or voice, while the gray fowl does not crow like a cock, and is, I think, a much handsomer bird than the red. His peculiar hackles, each feather tipped as with a drop of yellow sealing-wax, are much valued for fly-dressing. Jungle-fowl shooting with spaniels in these hills is capital fun. The cover they frequent is very thick, and they take a good hustling before they fly up and perch on the trees. When you approach they generally fly off, and are very clever at putting a thick cover between themselves and the gun, making the shooting by no means so easy as it looks, so that a couple of brace are a good bag for a morning's sport. I never saw reason to suppose that the two species interbred, nor that either of them crosses with the domestic fowl of these hills.

I have already remarked on the singularity of thus finding a patch of the forest peculiar to Eastern India, together with its most characteristic mammals and birds, isolated among the vegetation and fauna of the west, at a distance of about one hundred and thirty miles from the nearest point of the main forest to which they belong.

Two species of spur-fowl are pretty common on the hills. The one is the common little red bird,[1] which, but for its size, might easily be mistaken for the red jungle-fowl, being very like a small bantam cock. The other species is, I think, the same as the painted spur-fowl,[2] an exceedingly handsome bird, with a long double spur on each leg. The latter species is generally found on the edges of the ravines, down which it drops, when flushed, like a stone, and can seldom be found again. The red bird I found chiefly on the little broken hills that surround the plateau, and in the same places as the jungle-fowl; and very pretty sport it gives with spaniels.

The common chikárá gazelle of the plains inhabits the undulating part of the plateau; and the little four-horned antelope, already referred to, is not uncommon in the thicker parts. The black antelope is quite unknown, though on the similar plateau of Toran Mál, in the western Sátpúras, it is said to be common. Hares are very numerous. The Korkús have a curious way of killing them at night. I discovered it by observing a strange will-o'-

[1] *Galloperdix spadiceus.* [2] *G. lunulosus*, Jerdon.

the-wisp-like light flitting about the edges of the little eminences across the valley below my tent, accompanied by a faint jingle as of bells. It is very simple. One man carries a pole across his shoulders, from the fore end of which is slung an earthen pan full of blazing fagots of the torch-wood tree,[1] arranged so as to throw the light ahead. The pan is made out of one of their ordinary earthen water-vessels, by knocking out the side. It is balanced at the other end by a basket of spare fagots. Another man carries a long iron rod, with a number of sliding rings, that jingle as he walks. Three or four lusty fellows follow, carrying bamboos fifteen or twenty feet in length; and the party proceed to move about the edge of the thickets, where unsuspecting hares come out to feed after nightfall. As soon as one appears in the streak of bright light thrown across the ground by the fire-pan, the whole party rush towards her, jingling frantically at the bells, and keeping her terror-stricken form in the circle of light. Poor puss seldom attempts to escape, but sits stupefied by the glare and noise, till a bamboo brought down on her back ends her existence. A party generally gets five or six hares in this way in a few hours. They sometimes come across small deer, and kill them in the same way; and I have heard stories of panthers and even tigers being met with, and turning the tables on the fire-hunters in an unexpected fashion. I once took a gun out with one of these parties; but found that it spoiled the whole affair, all the hares in the neighbourhood retreating to the cover at the first shot.

I have already said that tigers rarely come on to the plateau. Bears are equally scarce; in fact, I don't think I ever saw the track of one above the passes, and very few below. The opposite range of Motúr, however, as well as the Máhádeo hills further west, are full of them. The panther, on the other hand, is pretty common in Puchmurree. The first night my camp came up, one of a small flock of sheep I had brought, in case of provisions running short, was killed by a panther close to my tent. He dropped from an overhanging branch into an enclosure

[1] *Cochlospermum gossypium.*

of prickly bushes that had been put up round the sheep; and his attempts to drag it through the fence created such a disturbance among the people that he left it and leaped out in the confusion. The next night he seized one of my Clumber spaniels at the door of my tent; but a big greyhound named "Jack" flew to the rescue, and little "Nell" escaped with a few scratches and a great fright. The same panther became afterwards very troublesome on the hill when the workmen at the bungalow had left, attacking my dogs, sheep, and goats nearly every night, and coming boldly through the very rooms of the house. He was a toothless old brute, however, to which circumstance the dogs owed several escapes out of his very jaws; and though so daring at night in attacking our animals he would never face the men. Several times my horsekeepers and dog-boys sent him skulking off sideways, like a crab, from the vigour of their applications of long bamboos across his back. I never could kill him, though I tried every conceivable plan. One night I might have shot him as he passed along below the raised plinth of the house in the moonlight; but of course I had seized the only unloaded gun in the rack in the hurry, and the locks snapped harmlessly within a foot of his back. He was shot by a shikárí after I had left the hill.

Coursing foxes was another great amusement. A colony of the pretty little fox of the plains[1] inhabited a small open glade a little to the west of my camp. They had a great many burrows almost in the centre of the plain, all of which appeared to run into each other. I never failed to unearth one or more foxes here by the aid of "Pincher," a minute black-and-tan English terrier, with the spirit of a lion, who could get into any of the holes, and would die rather than not get out his fox. Often he showed signs of severe subterranean combats; and once I thought he was done for, when the greyhounds ran a fox into the very hole he had gone in at. We had to get picks and spades and dig down to him, and we found him lying with one fox before him pinned up in the end of a blind hole, which he had already half killed,

[1] *Vulpes Bengalensis.*

and another blocking the way out behind him. Poor gallant little Pincher! He died of a sunstroke some three months later, from being dragged through a long eighteen-mile march in the hot sun by a brutal dog-boy, without getting a single drop of water. I had two brace of capital greyhounds at that time; one couple crossed between the English and Rámpúr breeds, and the other bred from a Scotch deerhound out of a Bunjárá bitch. The Indian fox is not above half the size of English Reynard, but he has an astonishing turn of speed, and doubles with wonderful agility. These dogs had, however, the speed of them, and the run was generally much in a circle; so that though the ground was well suited for riding, I generally went on foot, along with some of the workpeople who greatly enjoyed the sport, and some of whom (Bharyás) ate the foxes afterwards. It was capital training for bison-shooting, which severely tries the wind, and in which I also spent a day or two now and then.

Stalking the bison in these hills is very severe work indeed. At times they may be found pretty near at hand, but more generally the Dhúpgarh hill, or the great ravine, has to be crossed first, and either implies a good many miles of stiff work before the sport really begins. The bison, though they seem to move slowly, are often really going very fast; and, as scarcely a yard of the country they live in is anything like level, what is apparently nothing to them is really a very hard pull for their pursuer. The bottoms of the valleys are also very hot even at this time of year; and at all times exercise under an Indian sun is much more fatiguing than in a cold climate. A wounded bison never stops going while he can, short of nightfall, and must be pursued while a ray of hope remains. Thus hill after hill, and ravine after ravine, are put between one and home in the excitement of the chase, till suddenly you pull up and realise what an immense distance you have come, and that you cannot possibly get back before the middle of the night. If you have anything to eat, the best course under such circumstances is to sleep where you are. I often used to bivouac thus when out after bison; and seldom found it much of a hardship. A good fire can always be lit in a few minutes,

To face page 108.

RAJ-GOND FROM NURSINGPORE

dry wood being never far off in an Indian jungle. An elevated place, at the same time sheltered from the wind, should be chosen for the purpose, as the valleys are more malarious at night. A shelter of boughs should always be knocked up, which your wild men will do handsomely in five minutes. I learned more of the simple nature of the forest people during the few hours' chat by the fire on these occasions than I believe I would have done otherwise in as many years. I think they got attached to me a good deal; and, though they are not very demonstrative at any time, I was often touched by some simple act of thoughtfulness one would hardly have expected from their untutored natures.

About the hardest day I had was after a couple of bulls I had seen grazing on the very top of Dhúpgarh, looming against the sky-line like two young elephants in the red sunlight. It was evening when I found them, and, as the spot was inaccessible by stalking, I sent round a couple of Korkús to move them, while I posted myself on the road they would be most likely to take down the hill. They went, however, by a pass a few hundred yards further on; and though I ran over the intervening bare and slippery rocks as hard as I could to get a shot, I was only in time to see them floundering down the hill-side like two great rocks, and they never pulled up till far down in the blue haze that hung over the bottom of the valley they looked scarcely bigger than a couple of crows. As they had not been alarmed by shooting, and would probably be found in the valley next day, I went home and prepared for a long hunt. We took the road round by the great ravine, instead of going over Dhúpgarh, because it was rather shorter when the bottom of the valley had to be made for, and also because we expected to find another herd on the way. We were disappointed, however, in this, seeing nothing till we got to the valley except a bear with her cub, the former of which I shot. Arriving in the valley, we spread about in all directions to look for bison-tracks. The young Thákúr of Puchmurree, the best hunter and tracker in the hills, was unfortunately laid up with a sprain he had got the preceding day; but we picked up two capital bison-trackers out of a lot of Korkús from a village across the great ravine, whom we found cutting a dhya on one of the hill-sides as we passed. I had found the footprints of the Dhúpgarh tiger in the bed of the stream, and was following them up with one of the Korkús, when I was recalled by a whistle to a place where the tracks of the two bulls had been discovered. They were making for a high plateau covered with thick bamboo jungle at the top of the valley, and we at once started on the trail. It was clear everywhere, and the men ran it at a sharp walk nearly to the top of the hill. Here, however, a sheet of rock intervened, and above it was a mass of large boulders intermixed with heavy clumps of bamboo. We were a long time puzzling the track through here, as the bulls had stopped and fed about on the young bamboo shoots. At last, however, one of the men we had picked up took a long cast over the top of the hill, and returned with the news that the bulls had separated, one going off to the south, apparently in the direction of a well-known haunt in the Borí teak forest, while his companion had gone off up the hill in the opposite direction. We decided to follow the latter, as it led more nearly in the direction of home. The wilderness of bamboo-covered hills and deep intervening rocky-bottomed or swampy dells, over and through which we carried that trail till the sun was getting low, is beyond description. Every now and then we thought we were just upon him, freshly-cropped bamboos and droppings showing that he was not far in front. But he had never stopped for long. This restlessness I afterwards found to be the habit of bison which have recently been disturbed. He was evidently making off steadily for some distant retreat. We started several herds of sámbar and solitary stags, and once a bear bustled out of a nálá we were crossing, and bundled off down the hill-side; but we were bent on nobler game and durst not fire at them. By evening we had got right to the further side of the great ravine beyond Jambo-Dwìp, and the peak of Dhúpgarh glowed pink and distant in the rays of the declining sun. We were descending a long slope among thin trees and high yellow grass, and I was a little ahead of the rest, when I suddenly saw the head and horns of a bison looking at me over a low thicket, and was putting up my rifle to fire when, with a loud snort, the owner wheeled round, and plunging noisily down the hill disappeared. This snort, which sounds like a strong expulsion of air through the nostrils, is very commonly uttered by bison when suddenly disturbed, and is the only sound I ever heard from them, except a low menacing moan, which I have heard a bull utter when suspicious of approaching danger, and the quivering bellow which they sometimes emit in common with most other animals when *in articulo*. I ran to the edge of what proved to be a deepish ravine full of bamboos, and was just in time to see a small herd of six or seven cows and calves disappearing over a low shoulder on the opposite side. But behind them slowly stalked one bull—a majestic fellow nearly jet-black, and towering like a young elephant in the rapidly closing gloom of the evening. As he reached the top of the rise he paused and turned broadside on, his solemn-looking visage facing in our direction. He was about ninety yards from where I sat, with the heavy 8-bore rifle I had wearily dragged after him all day rested on my knee; and, forbidding though he looked, I sighted him just behind the elbow and fired, fully expecting him to subside on the receipt of two ounces of lead driven by six drachms of powder. But there was no result whatever, save a dull thud as the bullet plunged into his side; and he slowly walked on over the brow as if nothing had happened. My other barrel caught him in the flank, and then I seized the spare rifle that was thrust into my hand, and sped across the intervening ravine. I was toiling up the other side, very hot and much out of breath, when a heavy crash beyond fell upon my delighted ear. I had been in agony lest I had missed the mighty target after all; but it was not so. There he lay as he had fallen, and rolled over down the hill until stopped by a clump of bamboos. A mighty mass of beef, truly, secured at last. But we were six or seven miles from Puchmurree, and there was no more than half an hour of daylight left. The road I knew was frightful, with hundreds of ravines besides the great one to cross, and it was not to be thought of at night. After due consideration we determined to go and sleep at a recently cut dhya that was known by the people, about a mile from where we were; so, leaving the fallen bull to the shadows of night, we went and made ourselves sufficiently comfortable for the night, under a canopy of the newly cut branches, on couches spread deeply with the springy shoots of the bamboo. We had walked at least twenty miles in the course of the day, and that over fearful ground. I was very tired, but happy, and never slept sounder in my life. On the whole I think stalking the mountain bull among the splendid scenery of these elevated regions, possesses more of the elements of true sport than almost any other pursuit in this part of India.

HEAD OF BULL BISON.

CHAPTER IV

THE ABORIGINAL TRIBES

SOMETHING has already been said regarding the intermixture of Hindú blood, manners, and religion, that has taken place among the aboriginal races of Central India. Were this an isolated event in the ethnical history of the country it would possess a comparatively feeble interest. Its high importance lies in its furnishing us with a living example of a process which has, as already suggested, played an important part in the development of the races which compose the mass of modern Hindúism. It is the uppermost and most accessible stratum of a geological series of untold antiquity; and, as the geologist interprets ancient formations by the analogy of the processes he sees still going on around him, so it may be that some light may be thrown on the construction of modern Hindúism by the process of transformation which is here going on before our eyes.

It is difficult to say how far the actual admixture of blood has taken place. There is small room for doubt that the so-called Gónd Rájás of pre-Mahomedan times were nearly, or quite, pure Hindú Rájpúts, exercising a feudal authority over numerous petty chiefs of mixed descent. The former have been nearly swept away, their only remaining representative being the pensioned Gónd Rájá of Nágpúr; the latter remain in their descendants, and, almost to a man, show the clearest signs of possessing a mixture of the Hindú and aboriginal blood. The Hindú element in such cases has not been the debased article current among the masses of the labouring population, but the purer strain derived from the aristocratic families of Rajputána. It is as it were the *first cross* in the mixed breed, and thus, as might be expected, shows the characteristics of both sides clearly developed. In other cases, among the lower races of aborigines, crosses also appear to have taken place; but in such cases it appears to have been the already debased Hindú of the lower orders that has furnished the foreign element, and the result has been a breed which little approaches the high Aryan character, and is, in fact, only a slight advance on the purely aboriginal type. Among the chiefs the cross appears to have taken place with all the different tribes of indigenes. Towards the east the mixed breed call themselves Gónd-Rájpúts, or shortly Ráj-Gónds, and are the direct result of the alliance between the Rájpút adventurer and the Gónd. In the Korkú country the same thing seems to have occurred between the Rájpúts and the Korkús. In this case, however, the tribe being an influential one, the descendants are only known as Korkús. But they differ in many respects from pure Korkús, being tall and fair-complexioned, ultra-Hindú in their observances, and marrying only among their several families, or into purer houses—never among the undiluted aborigines. In the extreme west a distinct race called Bhilálás has originated from the cross between the Rájpút and the Bheel. The Bheels were for a much longer period in close contact with Hindús than any other tribe, and that during a period of Indian history when the restrictions of caste were almost entirely in abeyance. Búddhism, and its offspring Jainism, were the ruling faiths in that part of the country up to the eleventh or twelfth century; and thus it is probable that a much greater admixture of the races occurred there than in countries where the Brahminical forms prevailed. The Bhilálás are now very numerous, occupying large tracts as almost the sole population, but still there is a marked distinction between these and the land-holding chiefs of the same descent. The distinction is, in fact, identical with that between the Ráj-Gónd and Korkú chiefs and the numerous commoner classes of the same tribes who are nominally pure aborigines, but are really half Hindú.

As is the case with the divers people now included among modern Hindús, it would be wholly impossible now to gauge the extent to which the infusion of the Aryan element has taken place among these aboriginal races. The facility for amalgamation between them—the chemical affinity, so to speak, between the races—seems to be so great, that in a very few generations the points denoting the predominance of one or the other become obliterated. And yet the traveller among them will come on stratum after stratum showing in the clearest manner the intermediate stages between the two races. And, as a rule, variation of physical type will be found to be accompanied in almost equal ratio by divergence from aboriginal manners and religious ideas in the direction of Hindúism. It is probable that the further commixture of blood, excepting through the occasional immorality of the races, has in recent times ceased as regards the masses, though the chiefs are still unremitting in their endeavours to purify their families by alliance with more blue-blooded Rájpút houses than their own. Blue blood being a marketable commodity here as in other countries, the chiefs have to pay highly for such privileges; and nothing has so much tended to pauperise these families as these constant bribes for the ennoblement of their race, and the equally heavy cost of conciliating the priestly arbitrators of their quality.

For it is through this chink that the influence of Brahmanism has mainly succeeded in penetrating to the very core of these indigenous tribes. The test of purity of caste among races of uncertain descent is much more the extent of their observance of the Hindú code of purity and ceremonial than actual proof of lineage. The Brahmans form a sort of Heralds' College, to be inscribed on the rolls of which for a few generations entitles an aspirant to ally himself with families who have already attained a higher status than himself. Strict reverence for the Brahmans, and adherence to ceremonial purity, are necessary to secure this; and thus it is that all these semi-Hindú chiefs spend the greater part of their time and means in striving to attain the utmost rigour of attention to Hindú religious and social rule. To this end they have abandoned the gods of their fathers for the deities of the Brahmans. They have retained Brahmans as their councillors and to conduct the worship of the gods. They eat nothing unsanctioned by the Brahminical law; and some even employ Brahmans to cook their food, sprinkling the fagots employed for the purpose with holy water. Thus they have gradually separated themselves from the mass of their aboriginal subjects, and formed a separate caste of their own, either inter-marrying among families similarly situated, or if possible seeking brides, as I have said, in houses superior to themselves. Some of them have thus succeeded in almost eradicating the aboriginal taint; and by continued reversion to the purer stocks have attained to an equality of physical type with the higher races. Their social status has come to be acknowledged as that of the Rájpút rather than the aborigine; and many have assumed the sacred thread, the wearing of which denotes membership of one of the twice-born castes. Most of them, however, whether from motives of policy or of superstition, still concede something to their semi-aboriginal descent; worshipping perhaps in secret the tribal deities, and, in cases, placing at certain festivals the flesh of cows, abhorred of Hindúism, to their lips, wrapped in a thin covering of cloth. Many of them also require to be installed on their succession to the chiefship by a ceremony which includes the touching of their foreheads with a drop of blood drawn from the body of a pure aborigine of the tribe they belong to.

Such an example on the part of their influential chiefs was certain to be followed by large sections of their subjects; and in particular by such of them as were themselves in some degree of mixed descent. Accordingly we find the tribes much subdivided into clans, or castes, distinguished from each other by a more or less close adoption of Hindú customs and religious forms. A theory has arisen that the Gónds are divided into twelve and a half formal castes according to the number of the gods they worship, after the pattern of the Hindús; but, as in the case of the latter such a division is purely nominal, the actual number of Hindú castes being almost infinite, so also among the Gónds this distinction accords with nothing to be seen in practice; and their subdivisions differ in almost every district, being founded partly perhaps on tribal descent, but chiefly on imported distinctions arising from the extent of their approximation to Hindúism. Some of these castes have already succeeded, like their chiefs, in attaining to the status of Rájpúts; and the process is still going on before our eyes in places where the sacred thread is openly sold to aspirants by the chiefs and their obsequious Brahmans.

As might be expected, the Gónds have gone further in the adoption of these Hindú sentiments than the other tribes. They are far more numerous; they occupy large tracts of low country intermixed with the Hindús; their semi-Hindú chiefs possessed the ruling power of the country for many generations; and possibly they belong to a branch of the human race more susceptible of modification than the others. Their Tamulian congeners in Southern India, while losing little of their aboriginal physical type, have conformed *en masse* to the customs and religion of Hindúism; while the Kolarian stock, wherever found, has obstinately resisted intermixture with the Hindú.

In the next chapter I propose to give a sample of the legends current among the Gónds, which indicate their own consciousness of the importance of the change that has been wrought among them by their acceptance of Hindú ideas; and in the meantime will proceed to some description of the aboriginal beliefs and institutions, which still lie, in the most advanced of their sections, but a little way below the surface, and which, among the undiluted denizens of the wilder regions, are yet found in their primitive purity.

It is not an easy matter for the inquirer among such tribes really to ascertain the peculiarities of their language, religion, or ideas. Like all savages there is a child-like vagueness about their conceptions which it is very difficult to get the better of, and to this is added a suspiciousness which frequently leads them to deliberately withhold information the object of which they are unable to comprehend. In the case of these particular tribes, moreover, the admixture of Hindúism has proceeded so far that one has to be constantly on his guard against admitting as belonging to them what is in fact of foreign origin. An intimate acquaintance with Hindú beliefs and peculiarities is therefore the first essential quality of him who attempts to ascertain the distinctive features of these races; and from the want of this great mistakes have constantly been made in describing them. The poverty of their languages is another great obstacle to the inquirer. In the aboriginal tongues there seem to be no expressions for abstract ideas, the few such which they possess being derived from the Hindí. In fact, the aboriginal roots are really almost confined to the expression of the barest necessities of savage existence. The names even of most of their personal deities, the nomenclature of religious ceremony, of moral qualities, and of nearly all the arts of life they possess, are all Hindí. The form, and particularly the termination, of these imported words is, however, frequently a good deal modified, the pronunciation being as a rule broadened; and thus an imperfect acquaintance with the dialects of Hindí frequently leads to the acceptance of such phrases as purely aboriginal. The greatest difficulty, however, is their vagueness of conception, and their want of abstract ideas. Thus, for instance, in all the recorded vocabularies it will be found that the term for "sky" is nothing but the Hindí name for "clouds," or "sun," or "moon," or some specific object in the sky, not for the sky generally, for which they do not seem to possess a name. It is only in the remotest wilds that either Gónds or Korkús are now found who do not know sufficient Hindí to carry on a simple conversation, although they generally employ their own tongue in talking among themselves. The tribes bordering on the plains, who visit some bazaar town once a week for purposes of exchange, and who are constantly in contact with the people of the plains, have in many cases lost all knowledge of their own language, and speak the Hindí of the plains. There is nothing that is worth preserving in these rudimentary indigenous tongues; and their inevitable absorption in the more copious *lingua franca* of the plains is not at all to be regretted.

In religion the Gónd tribes have passed through all the earlier stages of belief, and are now entering on that of idolatry pure and simple—the last in which religion is still altogether dissevered from ideas of morality. As has been generally observed, however, the objects of worship of each new stage of development here form additions to those formerly reverenced, rather than supplant them.

The foundation of their creed appears to be a vague pantheism, in which all nature is looked upon as pervaded by spiritual powers, the most prominent and powerful of which are personified and propitiated by simple offerings. Every prominent mountain top is the residence of the Spirit of the Hill, who must be satisfied by an offering before a dhya can be cut on its slopes. The forest is people by woodland sprites, for whom a grove of typical trees is commonly left standing as a refuge in clearing away the jungle. When the field is sown, the god of rice-fields (Khodo Pen) has to be satisfied, and again when the crop is reaped. The malignant powers receive regular propitiation. The Tiger God has a hut built for him in the wilderness that he may not come near their dwellings. The goddess of small-pox and of cholera receives offerings chiefly when her ravages are threatened. Among such elementary powers must be reckoned the ghosts of the deceased, which have to be laid by certain ceremonies. These consist in conjuring the ghost into something tangible, in one case into the body of a fish caught in the nearest water, in another, into a fowl chosen by omen. The object, whatever it is, is then brought to the house of the deceased, and propitiated for a certain time, after which it is formally consigned to rest by burial, or in one case by pouring it (in solution) over the representation of the village god. The spirits of persons killed by wild animals are believed to be especially malignant, and are "laid" with much care and ceremony. To this practice has been superadded by some the rite of periodical propitiation of deceased ancestors by sacrifice, implying their continued existence in another world, an entirely different thing it may be observed from the rite already described, which implies only a restless and spiteful existence in *this* world of a ghost which may be made an end of by a ceremony. I believe the superior belief to be entirely derived from the Hindús, with whom it is a prime article of faith.

None of these powers of nature are represented by idols, nor have they any particular forms or ceremonies of worship. They are merely localised by some vague symbol; the mountain god by a daub of vermilion on some prominent rock; the tree god by a pile of stones thrown round the stem of a tree—and so on. At these the simple savage pays his devotion, almost furtively, as he passes in the gray of the morning to his day's labour, by a simple prostration, or perhaps by the offering of a handful of rice or an onion! More elaborate acts of worship are engaged in by the community at certain seasons, and then these primitive powers may be joined with the more personal deities derived from their neighbours in the general act of worship.

In the next stage the tribes have added certain Fetishes to the list of powers. The principal of these is an iron spear-head called Phársá Pén, and he is supported by the Bell god, the Chain god, a god composed of some copper money hung up in a pot, shapeless stones, and many other objects, the power attributed to which is purely arbitrary, and unconnected with any natural agency. To this stage appears to belong the medicine man and dealer in witchcraft, who still possesses considerable power among the tribes. These medicine men can scarcely be called priests, and are not an hereditary caste. Their business is to exorcise evil spirits, to interpret the wishes of the fetish, to compel rain, and so on. Some of them seem to have acquired the power of throwing themselves into a sort of trance in which they are visited by the deity; but in this respect they are far behind the sorcerers of the Bygá race further to the east, who will be subsequently alluded to.

In a still more advanced stage, the Góuds have resorted to hero worship; but it is curious that all the deified heroes they reverence are of purely Hindú derivation. The chief are Bhímá, one of the five Pándú brethren, who is represented by his mythical club either in stone or wood; Hardyál, a Rájpút hero of much later date; Dulha Deo, the apotheosis of a bridegroom, and many others.

Lastly come the recognised divinities of the Hindú pantheon. Amongst a race whose blessings are few and hardships many it is not surprising that the malevolent members of the Hindú pantheon should have found more acceptance than the benevolent deities. Vishnú is scarcely recognised by them, except in his one terrible development of Narsingha or the Man-Tiger; while Sívá the Destroyer, with his formidable consort Kálí, and son Bhairavá, are the favourite objects of reverence among the more advanced of the tribes. These are represented by rude idols, Sívá himself in his usual Phallic form; and a Brahman in many cases officiates at their shrines. Here for the first time we find mythology—the science of priests—at work. In their earlier stages the tribes had no priests, no hierarchy of gods, and consequently no mythology. Now legends are invented to connect the tribes, and their earlier gods, with the great web of Hindú fiction, and bring them within the dominion of caste and priestdom. In the succeeding chapter will be found a version of one of these fragments. Their art is of the rudest character, often outraging the requirements of Hindú orthodoxy—suited, in fact, to the mental calibre of a people scarcely yet emerging from mere fetishism.

Many have conjectured that the worship of Sívá and his mythic companions, which forms so incongruous an intrusion into the milder faith of the Aryan Hindús, has been, in fact, derived from the aboriginal races of India. As regards Sívá himself in his Phallic form there seems to be little foundation for such an hypothesis. The emblem has nowhere, I believe, been found as an object of adoration among the indigenous races where Brahminism has not penetrated, whereas it was a very ancient form of worship among the peoples of Western Asia, and was even prevalent in heathen Rome more than sixteen hundred years ago. It was, as in India, so in the countries of Western Asia, connected with human sacrifices. It is true that this form of the Hindú religion is chiefly prevalent in the wilder parts of the country, where the aboriginal element prevails, many of its chiefest shrines being in fact situated in secluded wildernesses, and guarded by aboriginal, or semi-aboriginal, custodians. It may be, then, that the personified forms of this deity were adaptations from the cultus of some of the aboriginal races that have been absorbed in Hindúism; but I think we must go further back in the history of this movement to find the originals of Kálí and Bhairavá than to anything we know of the indigenes as they now exist. May it not have been in the earliest days of Brahminical revival, when competitors for the adherence of the people in the great struggle with Búddhism had to be sought for among the popular deities—when Vishnú was transformed into the popular demigods Rama and Krishna, into the Tortoise, and the Fish, and the Man-Tiger, to suit the tastes of a variety of half-Hindúised races—that then Sívá was also imported from the West, and allied with the sterner objects of worship of the wilder races, to draw them into the great net of the priests, as the incarnations of Vishnú in their popular heroes and totems were employed to draw the more civilised classes of the people? Were these deities really indigenous amongst the Gónds we should certainly see their worship a matter of more widespread and heartfelt devotion than it is. It is in truth still almost confined to the chiefs and their half-Hindú dependents, and to a few of the most advanced, and probably half-blooded, sections of the tribes. In the great periodical acts of public propitiation of the gods they are either not admitted, or if so, frequently have to sit under one of the fetishes or nature-gods of the primitive faith.

The chief of these ceremonies occur at the marked periods of their agricultural season—when the crops are sown or reaped, and at the flowering of the valuable Mhowa tree—also when severe pestilence threatens the community. On such occasions a row of small stones, taken from the nearest hill-side, are set up in a row and daubed with vermilion, to represent the presence of all the gods that are to be included in the propitiation. Sometimes small pieces of iron hung up in a pot are used instead. A bigger stone or bit of iron represents the "Bará Pén," or Great God of the occasion, who is usually the one supposed to want most attention at the time. Cocks and goats, and libations of Mhowa spirit, are then offered with much ceremony, dancing, and music; and the affair, like most of their great occasions, usually winds up by the whole of them getting abominably drunk. Such is still the real religion of these peoples, notwithstanding the lacquer of Hindúism many of them have received; and such I may add is not very different from that of the vast mass of the so-called Hindús of the plains, who look on Vishnú and Sívá as little nearer to them than do these savages, and pay their real devotion to the village gods, to the gods of the threshing-floor, and to their lares and penates—all unrecognised by the orthodox priest. In both cases their religious belief is wholly unconnected with any idea of morality. A moral deity, demanding morality from his creatures, is a religious conception far beyond the present capacity either of the aborigine or the ordinary Hindú.

The idea of a Great Spirit, above and beyond all personal gods, and whom they call Bhagwán, is, however, accepted by all Hindús, and has been borrowed from them by the Gónds. He is the great First Cause of all things, but himself endowed with neither form nor moral qualities. He is unrepresented, and receives no adoration. A Hindú will accurately describe all the gods of his pantheon; but of Bhagwán he has no idea, except that he is the great Creator. He is, in fact, that "Unknown God" whom humanity has never yet learned to approach save through the medium of some human or anthromorphous substitute.

I have not yet touched on the religion of the Korkús. It is, I think, purer than that of the Gónds. The powers of nature are equally adored, such as the Tiger God, the Bison God, the Hill God, the Deities of Small-pox and Cholera. But these are all secondary to the Sun and the Moon, which, among this branch of the Kolarian stock as among the Kóls in the far East, are the principal objects of adoration. I have seen nothing resembling Fetishism among them; and if, as some consider, that is the earliest form in which the religion of savages develops itself, the Korkús would seem in this respect to have advanced a stage beyond the Gónds. The sun and the figure of a horse (a Scythian emblem of the sun) are carved on wooden posts, and receive sacrifices. They also sacrifice to the manes of their dead, but only for a certain period, to "lay" them. Belief in sorcery and witchcraft is not so prevalent among them as with the Gónds and Bygás. Their semi-Hindú chiefs have accepted Sívá and his companions; but the common Korkús seem to care little about them, excepting in the immediate neighbourhood of his great shrine in the Máhádeo hills. A few glorified heroes receive attention, but not to nearly so great an extent as among the Gónds.

In disposing of the dead, the aboriginal tribes all appear to have formerly practised burial; but those who have been much Hindúised resort by preference to cremation. The process being an expensive one, however, it is not lavished on all alike, women and children being still mostly buried, while adult males are burnt. Also during the rainy season, when burning is inconvenient, burial is often adopted for all alike. Most of the tribes erect some sort of a memorial to the dead; the Gónds generally in the shape of little mounds, covered by slabs of stone; while the Korkús carve elaborate pillars of teak-wood, with emblems of the sun and the crescent moon, and of the deceased party mounted on a horse, which they erect under a tree appropriated to the purpose near each of their villages. A very populous cemetery of this sort may be seen close to the village of Puchmurree.

I have already described the personal appearance of the men of the Gónd and Korkú tribes. Their women, I think, differ among themselves more than do the men of these races. Those of the Gónds are generally somewhat lighter in colour and less fleshy than the Korkús. But the Gónd women of different parts of the country vary greatly in appearance, many of them in the opener parts near the plains being great robust creatures—finer animals by far than the men; and here Hindú blood may be fairly suspected. In the interior, again, bevies of Gónd women may be seen who are liker monkeys than human beings. The features of all are generally strongly marked and coarse. The young girls occasionally possess such comeliness as attaches to general plumpness and a good-humoured expression of face; but when their short youth is over, all pass at once into a hideous age. Their hard lives, sharing as they do all the labours of the men except that of hunting, suffice to account for this. They dress decently enough, in a short petticoat, often dyed blue, tucked in between the legs so as to leave them naked to the thigh, and a mantle of white cotton covering the upper part of the body, with a fold thrown over the head. The most eastern section of the Korkús (hence called *Pothrias*) add a bodice, as do some of the Hindúised Gónds. The Gónd women have the legs as far as they are suffered to be seen tattooed in a variety of fantastic patterns, done in indigo or gunpowder blue. The Pardháns are the great artists in this line, and the figures they design are almost the only ornamental art attempted by these tribes. It is done when the girl becomes marriage-

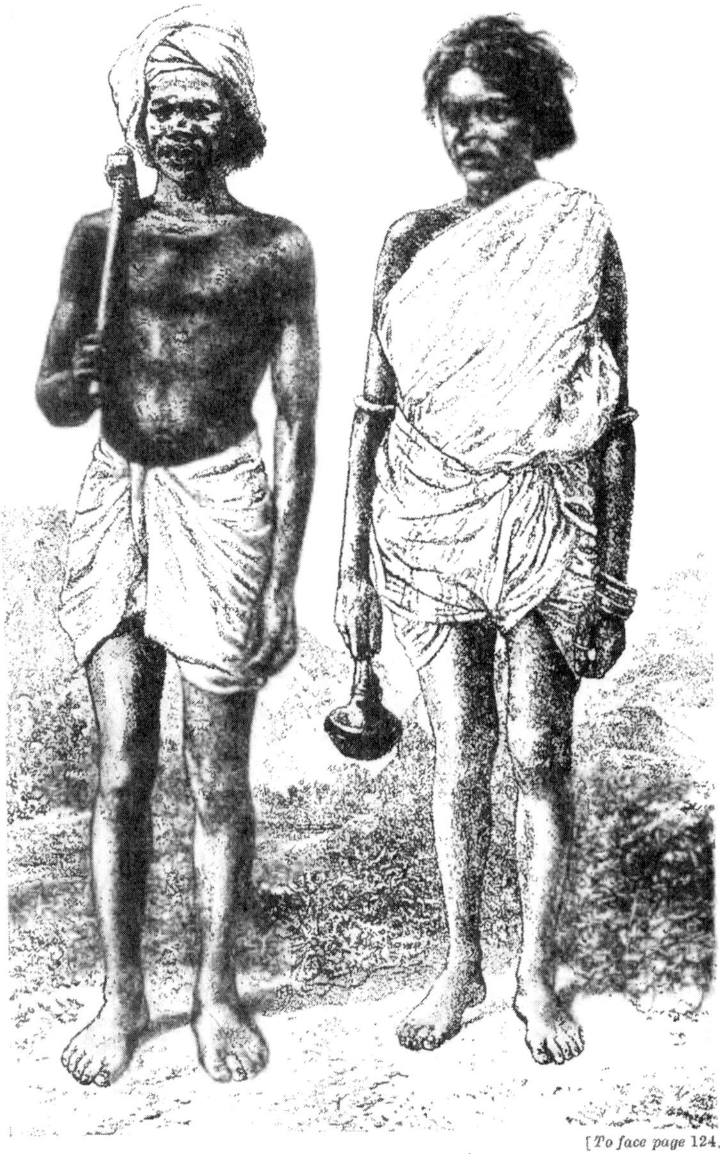

[*To face page* 124.

MALE AND FEMALE GÓND

able; and the traveller will sometimes hear dreadful screeches issuing from their villages, which will be attributed to some young Góndin being operated upon with the tattooing-needle. Like all barbarians, both races deck themselves with an inordinate amount of what they consider ornaments. Quantity rather than quality is aimed at; and both arms and legs are usually loaded with tiers of heavy rings—in silver among the more wealthy, but, rather than not at all, then in brass, iron, or coloured glass. Ear and nose rings and bulky necklaces of coins or beads are also common; and their ambrosial locks are intertwined on State occasions with the hair of goats and other animals.

In marriage customs they differ from the Hindús chiefly in the contract and performance both taking place when the parties are of full age. Polygamy is not forbidden; but, women being costly chattels, it is rarely practised. The father of the bride is always paid a consideration for the loss of her services, as is usually the case among poor races where the females bear a large share in the burden of life. The Biblical usage of the bridegroom, when too poor to pay this consideration in cash, serving in the house of his future father-in-law for a certain time, is universal among the tribes. The youth is then called a *lamjan;* and it frequently happens that he gets tired of waiting, and induces his fair one to make a moonlight flitting of it. The morality of both sexes before marriage is open to comment; and some of the tribes adopt the precaution of shutting up all the marriageable young men at night in a bothy by themselves. Infidelity in the married state is, however, said to be very rare; and when it does occur is one of the few occasions when the stolid aborigine is roused to the extremity of passion, frequently revenging himself on the guilty pair by cutting off his wife's nose, and knocking out the brains of her paramour with his axe.

The marriage ceremony is very elaborate and childish, and is generally borrowed in great part from the Hindús. The bride is in some tribes selected from among first cousins by preference. More usually, however, connection is sought among another tribe. Usually an understanding is come to privately before the formal "asking" takes place, so that a "refusal" is scarcely known. The Pardhán is the ambassador, and arranges the articles of the "marriage settlement." In contradistinction to the Hindú practice, it is at the bridegroom's house that the ceremony takes place, so that the whole of the expense may fall upon him. Hindúised tribes, however, practise the reverse. The actual ceremonies consist, first, of an omen to discover the propitious day, on which commences a series of repeated carryings to and fro, anointings and sprinklings with various substances, eating together, trying the garments together, dancing together round a pole, being half drowned together by a douche of water, and the interchange of rings—all of which may be supposed to symbolise the union of the parties. The bridegroom sometimes places his foot on the bride's back to indicate her subjection; and a feigned forcible abduction of the bride is often a part of the ceremony—the usual relic of olden times of the strong hand. Sacrifice to the gods, and unlimited gorging and spirit-drinking, are usually the wind-up of the affair. Widows are not precluded from re-marriage; and among the Gónds it is even the duty of a younger brother to take to wife the widow of an elder. The converse is not, however, permitted. A widow's re-marriage is accompanied by little ceremony.

There is little in any of these customs, it will be seen, to distinguish these tribes from other races of savages; and it would be unprofitable to devote further space to a record of their details. They may nearly all be found repeated among large masses of the so-called Hindú population of the plains; and, in fact, so far as religious and other customs are concerned, I believe that, were the Gónds not associated with hills and forests into which the Hindús have not penetrated very far, they would long since have come to be looked on merely as another caste in the vast social fabric of Hindúism. The Korkús are more peculiar, and, I think, a far superior race in most respects; and the Bygás or Bhúmias of the eastern hills are still more worthy of observation by the ethnologist. Something will be said of them in future chapters.

It is more important, as regards the Gónds and Korkús of the central and western hills, to inquire into their present economical position and their probable future. Their methods of subsistence in the interior of the hills have already been described; and their life has been shown to be one of great hardship and toil. Although so far inured to malaria as to be able to exist, and in some measure continue the race, in the heart of jungles which are at some seasons deadly to other constitutions, the effect of the climate and a poor diet is seen in impoverishment of the constitution, constant attacks of fever and bowel diseases, and often chronic enlargement of the spleen. Imported diseases like cholera and small-pox also commit dreadful ravages among them. The life of labour which both sexes undergo, and their low physical vigour, result in very small families, of whom moreover a large percentage never attain maturity. There has been no accurate enumeration of the hill tribes at intervals, from which to judge whether they are increasing or the reverse. I suspect the latter as regards those in the interior, though the better fed and less exposed tribes in and near the plains may probably be increasing.

Until lately, habits of unrestrained drunkenness have aggravated the natural obstacles to their improvement. The labour of their peculiar system of cultivation, though severe, is of a fitful character, a few weeks of great toil being succeeded by an interval of idleness, broken only by aimless wanderings in the jungle or hunting expeditions. Periods of rude plenty, when the rains have been propitious to the crops, the hunt successful, and the crop of Mhowa abundant, have been succeeded by times of scarcity or even of want. Such a thing as providing for a rainy day has never been thought of. The necessity for constantly shifting the sites of their clearings and habitations has created a want of local attachment, and a disposition to anything rather than steadiness of occupation. Occasional periods of hardship are sure to be followed, in such a character, by outbursts of excess; and thus the life of the Gónd has usually consisted of intervals of severe toil succeeded by periods of unrestrained dissipation, in which anything he may have earned has been squandered on drink. It is this unfortunate want of steadiness that has led to most of the misfortunes of the race, to the loss of heritage in the land, and in a great many cases practically even of their personal liberty. Inferior races give way before superior whenever they meet; and whether, as here and in America, the instrument selected be "fire-water," or as in New Zealand, it be our own favourite recipe of powder and lead, the result is the same.

The case of the Gónd has hitherto little differed, whether he has preferred to cling to his rugged hills and struggle with nature, or has remained on the edge of civilisation and toiled for the superior races. Everywhere the aboriginal is the pioneer of the more settled races in their advance against the wilderness. His capacity for toil that would break the heart of a Hindú, his endurance of malaria, and his fearlessness of the jungle, eminently qualify him for this function; and his thriftlessness and hatred of being long settled in a locality as certainly ensure the fruits of his labour reverting as a permanency to the settled races of the plains. The process is everywhere much the same. The frontier villages in the possession of Hindú landholders, or of the Gónd Thákúrs, or chiefs, usually comprehend large areas of culturable but uncleared land, and there are always numbers of the aborigines floating about such frontiers, earning a precarious livelihood by wood-cutting and occasional jobs, or working as farm-servants, who can be induced to break it up. They have, of course, no capital, and seldom any security to offer; and the risk of loss must therefore be borne by the landholder. He either lends money himself for the purchase of a plough and pair of bullocks, and the other small farm-stock required to commence with, or becomes security for such a loan borrowed from the banker who is found in every circle of villages, with money always ready to be lent on any such speculation. The interest charged on such a money loan is never less than twenty-four per cent. per annum. Seed grain has also to be borrowed; and this, as well as sufficient food to last the cultivator till his crop is ready, is generally borrowed in kind, the arrangement being that double the quantity borrowed shall be repaid at harvest time. As grain is cheaper at harvest than at seed time, this does not *quite* represent a hundred per cent. interest! Such rates of interest seem high, but the risk of such speculations is very great, the principal being not seldom lost altogether. The short-sighted policy long followed by our Legislature, which rendered the recovery of such debts a matter of the greatest difficulty and uncertainty, greatly aided in maintaining these rates of interest. This policy is not even yet extinct, there being, in the Central Provinces at least, a rule which prohibits procedure against the farm-stock of a debtor, although it may all have been purchased with the borrowed money to recover which execution is sought.

It is obvious that transactions of this nature are really of the nature of a partnership between the labourer and the capitalist, the former furnishing nothing but his personal labour and supervision. Sometimes the partnership takes a more explicit form, when the man of money furnishes the oxen against the manual labour of the cultivator. All the other expenses, including the wages of the cultivator's family, if he has any, are deducted from the gross produce of the farm, with interest to the capitalist if he has advanced any part of such expenditure, and the balance is then divided equally between the owner of the oxen and the cultivator. In either case the result usually is that all the profit, beyond the bare wages his labour would fetch in the market, is absorbed by the man that supplies the money and takes the risk. But the cultivator is far better off also than if he had been working for hire, for then he would not have laboured half so steadily as his interest in the result of the crop induces him to do.

Until recently, the habits of debauchery I have mentioned, together with the low value of agricultural produce, usually prohibited the advance of the aboriginal cultivator from this stage. The harvest reaped, any grain that might fall to his share was at once taken to the spirit-dealer (who usually combined grain-dealing with his more pernicious trade), and converted into Mhowa spirit—gangs of Gónds at this season being constantly to be seen rolling about in a perpetual state of drunkenness, or sitting, blear-eyed, at the door of the bothy, until the last of their earnings had been dissipated. This effected, they had no resource but to work during the rest of the season, until sowing-time should again arrive, at occasional jobs of wood-cutting or road-making, or anything that might turn up, always getting drunk whenever opportunity served.

Great numbers of them, when once they had resorted to the grog-shop, never again became their own masters, remaining practically the bond slaves of the spirit-dealer ever after. And this introduces one of the most pernicious evils with which we had to contend in the early days of forest conservation. A very great amount of timber, bamboos, grass, and other forest produce is annually required by the people of the plains for house-building and repairing, fencing their fields, and other agricultural purposes. The timber-bearing tracts in the neighbourhood of the cultivated plains having long since been cleared, all this has to be brought down from the interior of the hills; and such work can only be done by the bold and hardy aborigines. Almost the whole of this trade had got into the hands of the Kúlars, or spirit-dealers, by means of the power they had obtained over the tribes by their devotion to strong potations. Badly off as the poor Gónd was in the hands of the agricultural money-lender, he was at least paid in wholesome grain or hard coin; but here the universal practice was to pay him *in liquor*, all except the pittance necessary to keep body and soul together in the way of food and raiment. Often the Kulárs united the *three* trades, making the Gónd cultivate an autumn crop of grain for his own subsistence and the trader's profit at a season when forest operations were impossible, exchanging his surplus grain for liquor immediately after, until he had him deep in his books again, and then sending him out to the forests to cut wood to repay him, and to purchase back some of his own grain for subsistence. He was clean done and cheated at every turn, having to labour like a horse, and getting out of it nothing but a scanty subsistence, and as much vile liquor as he could swallow without interfering too much with his working power. This trade had become enormously profitable. The numbers of the caste of Kulárs, who alone can legitimately deal in spirits, were limited; and they soon were rolling in wealth. A dissolute flaunting set by nature, they did no good with the money they thus earned, spending it chiefly in gambling and debauchery, and in loading themselves and their women with massive golden ornaments. The evils of the system were incalculable. In his wild state the Gónd or Korkú has been recognised to be truthful and honest, occasionally breaking out into passion which might lead to violent crime, but free from tendency to mean or habitual criminality. Now he became a thief and a scoundrel. His craving for drink made him a ready tool in the hands of every designing knave; and to the dangerous temper of the drunken savage he soon began to add the viciousness of a debased and desperate character. To the forests the injury was scarcely less. Having no implements but their little axes, and their employers being wholly indifferent to economical processes, these woodcutters procured their material in the most wasteful way possible. To procure a post for a cattle-pen a straight young teak sapling of ten or fifteen years' growth would be felled, and a piece six feet long taken from its middle, all the rest being left to perish. To procure a plank for a door a mature tree would be cut down, and hewn away to the requisite thickness with the axe. Timber was then doubtless cheap because nothing but the labour of these downtrodden races was expended in procuring it, and as many of them as they desired could be procured by the spirit-dealers for a wage which to the latter was almost nothing. In those days, the excise arrangements being very lax, the duty levied on spirits was very low; and enough liquor could be brewed to make a Gónd drunk for about a penny of our money. No forests could stand such a drain as this; and this wasteful system of working them was one of the main causes of their impending exhaustion.

It is fortunate that, under an improved administration, means were found at once to put a stop to this wholesale waste, and to greatly ameliorate the condition of the aboriginal labourer. The first step in this direction was the introduction of a new excise law, under which the formerly unrestricted power of establishing spirit-stills and grog-shops among the aborigines was withdrawn. Liquor was allowed to be distilled only at certain central places, and on payment of a fixed and considerable still-head duty. A certain number of retail shops only were allowed, sufficient in number and position to supply all the proper requirements of the people, and capable of being regulated by the police, without forcing temptation in the way of the less provident classes. The licenses for this restricted number of shops were let by public auction. Now came a just retribution on the whole race of Kulárs. There were far more of them engaged in the liquor-trade than were required to man these shops; all were wealthy and reckless, and also jealous of each other; and so a strong competition for the licenses set in among them. Fabulous sums were bid at the auctions in many cases; and everywhere the price of liquor was so forced up by this and the heavy still-head duty that the poorer classes could no longer afford to drink it in excessive quantity. Sales thus diminished, while the expenses of a shop were largely increased; and the result was the almost universal ruin of the Kulárs, and the complete breaking up of their system of traffic. The gold ornaments they had flaunted to the world gradually disappeared, and many of them ended in utter bankruptcy. It may, perhaps, be regretted that a less sudden and seemingly oppressive method of curing the canker that was eating into the frontier society did not suggest itself; but it is difficult to pity so vicious and unscrupulous a tribe as these Kulárs. Though the consumption of liquor has fallen off immensely, the state revenue has not suffered, the avowed object of getting "the maximum of revenue with the minimum of consumption" being fully attained.

The complement to this overhauling of the excise law was the introduction of our system of forest conservation. So large a subject, regarding which so little knowledge existed, could not be expected to be dealt with in an entirely satisfactory manner all at once. Some mistakes were made, the chief of such being to attempt too much on a sudden, and with insufficient means. The management of all our immense tracts of waste was thrown upon one or two officers, who had not yet even explored the country, and had nothing besides to guide them, and who were expected to administer a code of rules in detail, throughout this area, which was afterwards found to be much too strict, and to bear very hardly on the people. It could not be done; and things came, ere long, to a dead lock, till solved by the rules themselves passing into a dead letter. Presently the proper remedy was applied, by reserving the most promising forests to be directly managed by the special Forest Department, while the greater portion was left to be looked after by the ordinary civil officers. Improved experience has still further improved the system; but the main features of it were struck out as early as 1864. Restrictions on the method of felling timber were imposed, and a fixed timber-duty levied. These measures, if in some cases not unopen to exception, at least had the effect of inducing a more economical system of working the forests. The aborigines still furnish the labour in the forests, and, being paid in coin at the regular market value of their work, are enabled to profit by whatever they can earn. For some time the breaking up of the Kulár system left a want of private agency in the timber trade; and the Forest Department itself had to step in and arrange for the supply of the country. At the time this was beneficial in many respects, enabling us to utilise most of the fully ripe standing trees, and the logs lying in the forest, by enhancing the price until it became remunerative to take these out. Now, however, this has ceased to be necessary, and there are sufficient legitimate dealers in the trade to supply all wants.

It was some time before we ventured to interfere with the devastation caused by the wild tribes in their system of tillage by axe and fire which has been described. Having acquired the reputation of "savage and intractable foresters," it was with considerable hesitation that the first steps were adopted. The most promising forests were encircled by boundary lines, marked by terror-inspiring masonry pillars, within which the formation of dhya clearings was prohibited. The people obeyed with scarcely a murmur; and presently the rules were extended to the great mass of the wastes, in so far that the cutting of valuable timber for clearings was forbidden, except under such arrangements as afforded a prospect of the reclamation of the land being permanent. To the wildest of the tribes certain areas were assigned, sufficient to afford room for a rotation of sites for their dhya-fields. It cannot be said that these comprehensive restrictions have been everywhere enforced to the letter, nor was it to be expected. But the general effect has been very marked: the "intractable foresters" have shown a ready acquiescence in arrangements, the object and necessity of which were carefully shown to them; and year by year the influence of law is more fully acknowledged and felt in the forest regions.

The habits of the aborigines are now greatly changed for the better. Excessive and constant drunkenness is almost unknown, though drinking to a greater extent than is good for them on occasions has not entirely ceased. The whole of their earnings is not now dissipated in drink; and the accumulation of the little capital needed to start cultivation on a more regular system is now possible to them all. An immense assistance in this respect has been derived from the great enhancement in the value of all agricultural produce, consequent on the opening up of the country and the American War. Large areas in the west of India, which formerly yielded cereals, have been devoted to the production of cotton, and a great extension of cultivation to supply the consequent scarcity of food-grains has taken place, and is still progressing, wherever the country is fitted by proper communications to yield an exportable supply. The great undertakings in railways, and other public works, which have marked the last decade, have also much increased the demand for labour; and even the natural produce of these central wilds has acquired a commercial value which it never before possessed. Before I left India, the agents of Bombay mercantile houses were probing the recesses of my district (Nimár) in search of various articles of natural production which had suddenly become valuable for export, such as the oil-yielding seeds of the Mhowa (*Bassia latifolia*), and the pure gum of the Dháora (*Conocarpus latifolius*). Altogether a new era has dawned for these "children of the forest." The relation between labour and capital, long unfavourable to the former, has been reversed, and hard rupees are finding their way into the hills of Góndwáná, to the material improvement of the circumstances of its denizens, instead of the poisonous liquor which was fast hurrying them to destruction. Their contact with the Hindú races was long to them nothing but a curse; but there is now a general agreement of opinion that of late they have been fast improving, both in well-being and in character. Where they still continue to work as farm-servants they receive better wages, and save something out of them; and, either from such savings or from their large earnings on the railway works, many have found the means to settle down as small farmers on their own account. Even as borrowers their credit is much improved. A great deal of capital is now seeking the profitable investment offered by agriculture; and loans are given on easier terms even to these still somewhat unreliable settlers. "The high price obtainable for oil-seeds of late years has perhaps done more towards this than anything else. It takes a mere handful of seed to sow an acre of *tillee* (sesamum); it flourishes with the rudest tillage on half-cleared land, for which no rent is usually paid for the first three years; and it is cut and sold by the beginning of November. I know two 'unencumbered' Korkús who in 1867 cleared thirty acres of light land, and sowed it with tillee. They borrowed 80 rupees (£8) to buy bullocks and implements, and two *manees* (1920 lb.) of *jowaree* (millet) to eat. The interest on the money-debt was 20 rupees, and as usual, double the quantity of grain had to be paid back at harvest. They had no other expenses, no rent being charged, and they themselves doing all the labour. The produce was 75 *maunds* (6150 lb.) of oil-seed, which sold for 215 rupees (£21 10*s*.), from which they repaid the 80 rupees' worth of grain and 100 rupees in cash, leaving them gainers of 35 rupees (£3 10*s*.), after paying off the whole of their debt. Thus they got a stocked farm, free from debt, in a single season, by their own manual labour alone, which would afterwards yield them at least £10 apiece per annum, or much more than they could live on in comfort. The money-lender at the same time cleared 40 per cent. on his money in eight months."[1] Such a farm as this may appear rather a miserable little affair to the English reader; but such are the units of which the vast extent of Indian tillage is made up; and to obtain possession of such a holding, with its slender stock, is an object of ambition to millions of labourers for a bare subsistence.

[1] Extract from a Report, by the writer, on the Settlement of the Nimár district.

There can be small room for doubt that the permeation of these aboriginal tribes with Hindú ideas, manners, and religion, is steadily progressing; and it may be hoped that this influence is now working rather for the better than for the worse. The flighty, debauched, half-tamed Gónd was a being much deteriorated from his original state of rude simplicity; but the steady and sober, if illiterate and superstitious, Hindú cultivator of the soil is a type towards which we should by no means regret to see the aboriginal races advancing. It is true that in thus joining the great mass of Hindúism they will exchange their rude forms of religious belief for a submission to the powerful priestly influence which still prohibits the advance of the people of India beyond a certain point, and for a superstition which is morally no better than their own. The missionary may lose his chance in the meantime of getting them to accept some of his fetishes[1] in the place of their own. But probably they will then be no further, if so far, from the acceptance of a pure religion of morality than they are at present; and when the distant day dawns for the dusky peoples of India, when the light of education shall dissipate their hideous superstitions, and lead them to inquire after a pure belief, they will be there, elevated and improved by contact and assimilation with a race superior to themselves.

Such seems to be the probable future of those sections of the aborigines who lie on the confines of Hindúism in the plains. But so long as the vast wildernesses of these Central Highlands remain uncleared, which physical causes will in great measure render a permanent necessity, so long must human inhabitants of a type fitted to occupy them continue to exist. For, such civilisation as we call it is impossible, and undesirable if it were possible. All that can be done for them is to eliminate by thoughtful administration causes which lead to their depression or demoralisation, and to avoid any treatment irksome to their wild and timid nature which is not necessitated by the general requirements of the country.

To return to my doings at Puchmurree. Towards the end

[1] Of course I mean what would prove fetishes to them in their present intellectual stage—not that they are so to the missionary!

[To face page 137.

SHRINE OF SÍVÁ IN THE MÁHÁDEO HILLS

of February numbers of Hindú pilgrims from the plains to the great shrine of Sívá in the Máhádeo hills began to pass my camp. They usually encamp at the foot of the hill below the shrine; and, besides the road over the plateau, come by a way which leads through the Dénwá valley below the Puchmurree scarp. Several other roads lead in from the south, all of which are rugged and difficult, and are traversed in fear and trembling by the pilgrims. About this time I crossed over from Puchmurree to visit the opposite plateau of Motúr, which was also at that time under examination as a possible site for a sanitarium in these provinces. The Dénwá valley lay between, necessitating a descent and ascent of about 2500 feet each way. On my return from Motúr on the 26th of February I found the little plain in the Dénwá valley below the shrine, through which my road lay, swarming with the pilgrims, some forty thousand of whom had collected in this lonely valley in a few days, and were now crowding up into the ravine where the cave is situated—a ravine through which a week or two before I had tracked a herd of bison!

Most of these annual gatherings of pilgrims are, to the majority of the Hindús who attend them, very much what race-meetings and cattle-shows are to the more practical Englishman—an episode in their hard-worked and rather colourless existence, in which a nominal object of little interest in itself is made the excuse for an "outing," the amusements of which chiefly consist in bothies for the sale of all sorts of miscellaneous articles, universal gossiping for the elders, and peep-shows and whirligigs for the younger members. It is surprising how the familiar features of a fair at home come out, in an oriental costume, at these so-called religious gatherings. The cow with five legs and the performing billy-goat adequately represent the woolly horse and the dancing bear of our childhood. The acrobats are there to the life, tying themselves into identical knots we loved so well. The begging gipsy appears in the fantastic Jogee. Ginger-pop and oranges are even faintly typified in Mhowa grog and sticky sweetmeats. Aunt Sally alone is nowhere: there is nothing at all resembling the uproarious mirth of that ancient lady.

Doubtless at all these gatherings there are a certain number of genuine pilgrims, whose end in coming is the performance of sacred rites at these holy shrines at such holy seasons; for the fairs are all held at times when the worship of the local deity is held to be particularly efficacious. But generally their number is no greater a proportion of the whole than is that of the "members of the ring" in a Derby crowd. Such gatherings usually occur near the large centres of population, where solemn temples crown some sacred eminence by the holy Narbadá. But the gathering at the Máhádeo shrine was of another character from these holiday outings. It draws its multitudes into a remote and desolate valley surrounded by the "eternal hills," where the Great God has his chiefest dwelling-place in these central regions. No gorgeous temples or impressive ritual attract the sight-seer. The pathways leading to the place are mere tracks, scarcely discernible in the rank jungle, and here and there scaling precipitous rocks, where the feet of countless pilgrims have worn steps in the stone. Young and old have to track out these paths on foot; and all the terrors of pestilence, wild beasts, and the demons and spirits of the waste surround the approach in their excited imaginations. Arrived at the foot of the holy hill, the pilgrim finds neither jollity nor anything more than the barest requirements of existence awaiting him. His food is dry parched grain, his couch on the naked earth, during his sojourn in the presence of Máhádevá. Should he be among the first to arrive, the tiger may chance to dispute with him the right to quench his thirst at the watering-place in the Dénwá river.[1] Those who come to a place like this for pleasure must be few indeed.

On my way back to Puchmurree, as I passed through the assembled multitudes, many of them were starting, after a dip of purification in the holy stream, to scale the heights that contain the shrine. My way also lay up the pilgrims' pass; and as I went I passed through numerous groups of them slowly toiling up the steep

[1] As I went to Motúr on this occasion I saw the track of a tiger where the pilgrims drink. They had not then arrived, of course.

ascent of nearly two thousand feet. Both men and women formed the throng, the former stripped to the waist and girded with a clean white cloth, the horizontal marks of red and yellow which distinguished them as worshippers of Síví being newly imprinted on their arms and foreheads. The women retained their usual costume; but the careful veiling of face and figure, attended to on common occasions by high caste ladies, was a good deal relaxed in the excitement of the occasion (and besides, were they not on their way to be absolved of all sin?); and not inconsiderable revelations of the charms of many of the good dames, of light brown skins and jet black eyes, were permitted by the wayward behaviour of their flowing robes as they turned to stare in astonishment at the *saheb* and his strangely attired attendants pegging away past them up the hill with double-barrelled rifles on their shoulders. All were talking and laughing gaily—now and then shouting out "Jae, Jae, Máhádeo!" (*Victory to the Great God*). The cry raised by each as he took the first step on the hill was taken up by all the forward groups, till it died away in a confused hum among the crowd who had already reached the shrine, far up in the bowels of the hill. Gloom and terror are the last sentiments in the religious feeling of the Hindú, even when approaching the shrine of the deity who has been called the Destroyer in their trinity of gods. It is considered sufficiently meritorious to perform such a pilgrimage as this at all, without further adding to its misery by wailing and gnashing of teeth. They believe it will do them good, because the priests say so; but they do not think it necessary to weep over it, and "boil their peas" when they can. But at the best it is a hard clamber for those unused to toil. The old and decrepit, the fat trader, and the delicate high-bred woman, have to halt and rest often and again as they labour up the hill. The path was a zig-zag; and at every turn some convenient stone or rocky ledge had been worn smooth by these restings of generations of pilgrims.

For a long way before the shrine was reached the path was lined on either side by rows of religious mendicants and devotees, spreading before them open cloths to receive alms, clothed in ashes picked out by the white horizontal paint marks of the followers of Sívá, with girdle of twisted rope and long felted locks, hollow-eyed and hideous, jingling a huge pair of iron tongs with movable rings on them, and shouting out the praises of Máhádeo. The clang of a large fine-toned bell and the hum of a multitude of voices reached our ears, as, surmounting the last shoulder of the hill, we entered the narrow valley of the shrine. A long dim aisle, betwixt high red sandstone cliffs, and canopied by tall mango trees, led up to the cave. The roots of the great mangoes, of wild plantains, and of the sacred *Chumpun*,[1] were fixed in cracks in the pavement of the rock, worn smooth by the feet of the pilgrims, and moist and slippery with the waters of the stream that issues from the cave.

The cave itself opens through a lofty natural arch in a vertical sandstone cliff; and for about three hundred feet runs straight into the bowels of the hill. It is without doubt natural; and a considerable stream of clear cold water issues from a cleft at its further end. Here is set up the little conical stone (lingam) which represents the god, and attracts all these pilgrims once a year. No temple made with hands, no graven image, nothing of the usual pomp and ceremony of Brahminical worship, adorns this forest shrine. Outside on a platform a Brahman sits chanting passages in praise of the god, out of the local Sívite gospel (the *Réwa Khanda*); and a little way off an old woman tolls the great bell at intervals. But within there is no officiating priest, no one but a retainer of the aboriginal chief whose right it has been from time immemorial to act as custodian of the shrine, and to receive the offerings of the pilgrims. No pilgrim ever brings more up the hill with him than he means to offer; for he may take back nothing—his last rupee, and even the ornaments of the women, must be left on the shrine of the god. Before passing into the cave the pilgrim leaves with the Brahmans outside (along with a sufficient *douceur*) his pair of small earthen vessels for the receipt of holy water.

[1] *Michelia Champaca.*

These they fill from the stream, seal up, and return to the pilgrim, who then proceeds to make the tour of the holy places on the Máhádeo hills. This takes him the whole of the remainder of the day. At each place a cocoa-nut is offered; and little piles of stones, like children's card-houses, are erected at some point of their peregrinations to signify a desire for a mansion in Kailás—the heaven of Sívá. Many of the places which should in theory be visited are very inaccessible, such as the top of the Cháoradeo peak, and very few of the pilgrims make the whole round.

I sat for some hours in the ravine sketching the entrance to the cave and the picturesque throng about it. A few sulky looks from the professional religionists, and a drawing closer of their garments by the ladies, when they saw my occupation, were all the notice I met with. The bright colouring which gives such a charm to congregations of Hindús was heightened by the general holiday attire of the worshippers on this occasion; and, in the mellowed light from above, which percolated rather than shone through the canopy of foliage, would have formed a subject worthy of a much better artist than myself. It was hard to believe that all this gay gathering had come in a day, and would go in another, leaving the valley again to the bison and the jungle-fowl. Unlike most shrines where such pilgrimages occur, no one remains to look after the god when the pilgrims are gone. The bell is unslung and taken away, being evidently looked upon as the only thing of value in the place. When I first visited the cave I found that the Great God had been better attended to by the wild beasts of the forest than by his human worshippers—a panther or hyena having evidently been in the daily habit of leaving the only offering he could make before his shrine!

It is a common idea amongst Europeans that the worship at these Sívite shrines includes rites or mysteries of an obscene character. I believe this to be wholly groundless. No such thing could take place, here at any rate, except in public among a dense crowd; and neither here nor at any other of the many shrines that I have visited have I either seen or heard of such a practice. It is undoubted that the small sects who worship of Sáktí, or female power of Sívá, do indulge in such obscenity. Their unholy rites are not, however, practised at the public shrines, but in the dark seclusion of their secret meeting-places; and their existence I believe is wholly unknown to the great majority even of the ordinary followers of Sívá.

There is one object which will attract attention near this shrine of Sívá, and which will receive a remarkable explanation. Projecting from the edge of a sheer and lofty cliff above the sacred brook is hung a small white flag. Innocent-looking enough it is; but it marks a spot where, "in the days that are forgotten," human victims hurled themselves over the rock as sacrifices to the bloody Kálí and Kál-Bhairavá, the consort and son of Sívá the Destroyer. The British Government, which cannot be accused of timidity in forbidding so-called religious customs which are contrary to humanity, has long since put a stop to these bloody rites. For centuries, however, they were a regular part of the show at these annual pilgrimages, both here and at other principal shrines of Sívá. They are connected with the worship of the terrible mythical developments of the god above mentioned—forms which have, with some probability, been conjectured to be aboriginal deities imported into the Brahminical pantheon.

Far to the west of Puchmurree, in the district of Nimár, is a rocky island in the Narbadá river called Mándháttá, on which is situated the shrine of Sívá called Omkár—one of the oldest and most famous in all India. Like that at Puchmurree, it is situated among rugged hills and jungles; but it has evidently at one time been the seat of a great centre of Sívite worship. Ancient fortifications surmount its scarps; and the area of nearly two square miles enclosed is piled up with the ruins of a thousand gorgeous temples. The most ancient of the temples at which worship is still paid are held by aboriginal Bheels as their custodians, and the more recent by a Bhilálá family, who admit their remote derivation from the former. A legend is here current, and based on writings of some antiquity, that Kálí and Kál-Bhairavá were here worshipped by the Bheels, long before the worship of Omkár (Sívá) was introduced along with the Rájpút adventurer and his attendant priest, who were the ancestors of the present Bhilálá custodian and of the hereditary high priest of Sívá's shrine. The Rájpút is said, by alliance with the Bheels, to have obtained the headship of the tribe; and the holy man who accompanied him, to have stayed by his austerities the ravages of their savage deities, locking Kálí up in a cavern of the hill (and if you do not believe it you may still see the cavern closed up), and vowing to Bhairavá an annual sacrifice of human beings. Listen now to the inducements which the local Sívite gospel[1] holds forth to devotees to cast themselves from the rock. "At Omkár-Mándháttá is Kál Bhairavá. Regarding it, Parbatí (wife of Sívá) said unto twenty-five crores of the daughters of the Gandharvás (angels): 'Your nuptials will be with persons who shall have cast themselves over that rock.' Whoever thus devotes himself to Kál Bhairavá will receive forgiveness, even though he had killed a Brahman. Let the devotee make a figure of the sun on a cloth; and take two flags, a club, and a *chawar*[2] in his hands, and proceed joyously with music to the rock. Whoever shall bodily cast himself down and die, will be married to a Gandharvá. But if he fall faint-heartedly his lot will be in hell. Whosoever turns back again in terror, each step that he takes shall be equivalent to the guilt of killing a Brahman; but he who boldly casts himself over, each step that he takes is equal in merit to the performance of a sacrifice. *Let no Brahman cast himself from the rock.* A devotee who has broken his vows, a parricide, or one who has committed incest, shall by thus sacrificing himself become sinless."

In 1822, a European officer of our Government witnessed the death of almost the last victim to Kál Bhairavá at this shrine. The island then belonged to a native State

[1] The Narmadá Khandá, which professes to be a part of the Skandá Puráná. A more detailed account of the Holy Island and its Shrines, by the author, will be found in the "Central Provinces Gazetteer," second edition.

[2] A yak's tail used for fanning, etc.

(Sindiá), and our Government had not then begun to interfere with such bloody rites. The political officer who wrote the account of it was therefore unable to prevent it by force. I came on the description a few years ago in MS., hidden away among many other forgotten papers in the Government record room of the Nimár district. The concluding portion may be interesting, as perhaps the only account on record, by an eye-witness, of such an occurrence. After narrating how he vainly urged every argument on the youth to dissuade him from his design, the writer proceeds to relate how he accompanied him nearly up to the fatal rock. "I took care," he says, "to be present at an early hour at the representation of Bhyroo (Bhairavá), a rough block of basalt smeared with red paint, before which he must necessarily present and prostrate himself, ere he mounted to the lofty pinnacle whence to spring on the idol. Ere long he arrived, preceded by rude music. He approached the amorphous idol with a light foot, while a wild pleasure marked his countenance. As soon as this subsided, and repeatedly during the painful scene, I addressed myself to him, in the most urgent possible manner, to recede from his rash resolve, pledging myself to ensure him protection and competence for his life. I had taken the precaution to have a boat close at hand, which in five minutes would have transported us beyond the sight of the multitude. In vain I urged him. He now more resolutely replied that it was beyond human power to remove the sacrifice of the powerful Bhyroo; evincing the most indomitable determination, and displaying so great an infatuation as even to request me to save him from the fell dagger of the priestess,[1] should he safely alight upon the idol. So deep-rooted a delusion could only be surmounted by force; and to exercise that I was unauthorised. While confronted with the idol, his delu-

[1] The priestess here referred to was probably the Bheel custodian of the shrine. There is nothing to prevent the hereditary custodian from having been a female at that time; but *priestesses*, properly speaking, have never existed in India. Her receipt of his collections from the people also indicates this conclusion.

sion gained strength; and the barbarous throng cheered with voice and hand, when by his motions he indicated a total and continued disregard of my persuasions to desist. He made his offering of cocoa-nuts, first breaking one; and he emptied into a gourd presented by the priestess his previous collection of pice and cowries. She now tendered to him some ardent spirit in the nut shell, first making her son drink some from his hand, to obviate all suspicion of its being drugged. A little was poured in libation on the idol. She hinted to him to deliver to her the silver rings he wore. In doing so he gave a proof of singular collectedness. One of the first he took off he concealed in his mouth till he had presented to her all the rest, when, searching among the surrounding countenances, he pointed to a man to whom he ordered this ring to be given. It was a person who had accompanied him from Oojein. An eagerness was now evinced by several to submit bracelets and even betel-nuts to his sacred touch. He composedly placed such in his mouth and returned them. The priestess at last presented him with a *pann* leaf,[1] and he left the spot with a firm step, amidst the plaudits of the crowd. During the latter half of his ascent he was much concealed from view by shrubs. At length he appeared to the aching sight, and stood in a bold and erect posture upon the fatal eminence. Some short time he passed in agitated motions on the stone ledge, tossing now and then his arms aloft as if employed in invocation. At length he ceased; and, in slow motions with both his hands, made farewell salutations to the assembled multitude. This done, he whirled down the cocoa-nut, mirror, knife, and lime, which he had continued to hold; and stepping back was lost to view for a moment—a pause that caused the head to swim, the heart to sink, and the flesh to creep. The next second he burst upon our agonised sight in a most manful leap,[2] descending feet foremost with terrific rapidity, till, in mid career, a projecting rock reversed his position, and caused a headlong fall. Instant

[1] The usual signal for the termination of a formal interview.

[2] The place is called the "Bír-Kalí" rock, which I believe means literally the "manful leap."

death followed this descent of ninety feet, and terminated the existence of this youth, whose strength of faith and fortitude would have adorned the noblest cause, and must command admiration when feelings of horror have subsided. Thus closed the truly appalling scene."[1]

With the exception of the murder of a poor old woman who shrank from the fatal leap when brought to the brink, but was mercilessly pushed over by the excited religionists, this was the last of these sacrifices that was permitted, the country coming in 1824 under our administration.

But the powers of evil were not yet to be baulked of their victims. The British Government could prevent deluded and drugged devotees from casting themselves over the Bír-Káli rock; but it could not deprive Kálí and Kál-Bhairavá of their fell executioner—the cholera demon. Year by year the pestilence invaded the encampments of the pilgrims. Sanitary science would say that it arose from the germs of disease brought from the festering gullies of the great cities, and pushed into activity by the exposure, bad food, defiled neighbourhood, and poisoned water, of the pilgrim camps. But the Hindú saw nothing in it but the wrath of the offended Divinity claiming his sacrifice. Year after year the gatherings were broken up in wild disorder. The valley of the cave, the steep hill-side, and that green glade in the Sál forest, were left to bury their dead, while the multitude fled affrighted over the land, carrying far and wide with them the seeds of death. Everywhere their tracks were marked by unburied corpses; and the remotest villages of the Narbadá valley and the country of the south felt the anger of the destroying fiend. A pilgrim fleeing from the fatal gathering could find no rest for the sole of his foot. The villages on his road closed their gates against him as if he were a mad dog; and many who escaped the disease perished in the jungle from starvation and wild beasts. At last, after a terrible outbreak of cholera in 1865, the Government prohibited the usual gathering at

[1] Extract from a letter of 29th of November, 1822, from Captain Douglas, Political Assistant in Nimár, to the Resident at Indore.

the Máhádeo Cave. The people made no complaint. They do not seriously care about these things when left alone by the priests; and here the priests were satisfied by the continuance to the hereditary custodians, on whom they were dependent, of their average income from the pilgrimage, in the form of a pension. It is very different when their gains are affected. Two years ago a cholera epidemic threatened in Nimár, and the pilgrimage to Omkár Mándháttá was closed by order. The priests and guardians of the shrine were up in arms at once, basing their objections entirely on the money loss they would suffer. Since the closing of the Máhádeo pilgrimage the deities of destruction have been baulked of their prey. The valley of the Dénwá, although now opened up by a good timber road made to penetrate the Sál forest, no longer witnesses the annual pilgrim congress. The Cave of the Shrine is silent and deserted.

The interruption to the business of the country caused by these cholera outbreaks used to be terrible. Whole villages were sometimes swept away. I once marched nearly twenty miles to a small Gónd village on one of the pilgrim tracks, in the district of Bétúl. I had been eluding the tracks of cholera the whole of the hot season, and had escaped without a single case of the disease in my camp. My people were almost exhausted with such a long march in the height of the hot season; and I joined them at the village, likewise much knocked up by a long exploration in the hills. I found my tent-pitcher and one or two others who had arrived struggling to pitch the large tent, without the usual assistance rendered by the villagers at the camping place. They placidly told me that the village was no longer the home of the living, every one in the houses being dead of cholera! The only living object in the place was a white kid, wandering about with a garland round its neck. It was the scape-goat which these simple people, after the manner of the Israelites of old, send out into the wilderness on such occasions to carry with it the spirit of the plague. Tired out as we were, it was death to stay in this place; so we re-loaded the things and marched eight miles further, straight into the jungle; and at nightfall pitched our camp by the banks of the wide Táwá river, far from human habitation. No one was seized by the disease; and during all my marching, humanly speaking I believe owing to proper sanitary precautions, I never had a single case in my camp.

CHAPTER V

THE LAY OF SAINT LINGO

THE Pardháns, or bards, of the Gónd tribes are in possession of many rudely rhythmical pieces, which it is their function to recite on festive occasions to their assembled constituents, to the accompaniment of the two-stringed lyre. The best and most complete of these, extending to nearly a thousand bars or lines, was laboriously taken down in writing from the lips of one of these Pardháns by the late Rev. Stephen Hislop, of the Free Church of Scotland mission at Nágpúr. But the lamented death of that indefatigable investigator into the history and manners of the Central Indian peoples prevented his furnishing it in a complete form. In a collection of his papers afterwards published under the editorship of Sir R. Temple, this legend appeared at length, with a translation of each word as it stood, only so far modified as to conform to the first requirements of English grammar. In this guise, although well suited to the purposes of the student, the piece is almost unintelligible to ordinary readers; and, if it be considered that the Gónds have never had any written language, and that these pieces have only been preserved by tradition from one of these *troubadours* to another, it will not be surprising that a good deal of recension is requisite before it can be made suitable to the general reader. Whether or not the piece has any original foundation in purely Gónd tradition may be matter of doubt; but it is certain that it has become greatly overlaid with the spirit and phraseology of Hindúism. It professes to recount the creation of the original Gónds at the hands of Hindú (Sívaic) deities; what may be called their subsequent fall through the eating of meats forbidden by Hindú law; their exile and imprisonment by the offended Hindú deity; the appearance by miraculous birth and life among them of a Hindú saint named Lingo,[1] whom they ungratefully put to death, but who rises again, and, after much penance and suffering, delivers them from bondage, introduces Hindú observances, the arts of agriculture, and the worship of tribal gods, and eventually disappears and goes to the gods. The programme thus bears a singular resemblance in many respects to the legend of Hiawatha, the prophet of the Red Indians; and to some an even more startling parallelism may suggest itself.

My own opinion is that its origin is comparatively recent, subsequent to the propagation among the Góṇds of Hindú ideas and rules. It seems to possess little value as bearing on their origin, assigning to them a northern descent, which is contradicted by the strong southern affinities of their language, and which is obviously only introduced as part of the Hindú machinery which pervades the piece. As a composition it has little merit, though here and there exhibiting something of beauty, and more often a good deal of quiet humour. The style of the original is very discursive, constantly losing sight of the narrative, often apparently leading to nothing, and full of repetition—defects which are probably the natural result of its usage as a ballad, handed down by mere word of mouth. It gives the idea of having been composed by the gradual accretion round a very slender thread of original story of successive episodes, manufactured by the semi-Hindú Pardháns for recitation before the almost entirely Hindú chiefs of the Góṇds. Yet even as such it possesses some interest, as exhibiting, in a somewhat dramatic form, the recent Hindúisation of many of the Góṇd tribes; and I have, accordingly, endeavoured to throw it into a shape that will not greatly fatigue my readers. I have excised from it most of the Hindú mythology with which it was overlaid, and which was often anything but orthodox; and I have thought it

[1] This name is probably typical of the Lingaet sect, who are known to have actively propagated the worship of the Phallic Sívá in the Deccan.

best to omit nearly the whole of the latter part, which consists of tiresome details of marriage and other ceremonial, which do not even possess the value of being an accurate account of the practice of the present day.

Thus the present version is greatly reduced in bulk, and is rather a paraphrase than a translation, though in many parts it will be found to adhere almost literally to the original, and little will be detected which has not some foundation therein. I should, perhaps, apologise for the adoption of the Hiawathian metre and style, and in a few cases even of the words of the American poet, in a piece which may appear almost like a burlesque of his Red Indian legend. It is probable that the originals of the two legends may not have differed greatly in character; and the close and curious parallelism between them could only be brought out by the adoption of the method introduced by the author of *Hiawatha*, and now familiar to the public. But the "noble savage" of North America is a very different character from the poor squalid Gónd of Central India; and not even the genius of a Longfellow or a Fenimore Cooper could throw a halo of sentiment over the latter and his surroundings. I have therefore thought it best to give full play to the grotesque element in the tale, for which, it must be confessed, the Hiawathian style is provokingly well adapted. I should add that the serious student of Gónd institutions had better, perhaps, prefer the original to the version now offered.

I.—THE CREATION AND TRIBULATIONS OF THE GÓNDS.

In the Glens of Seven Mountains,[1]
Of the Twelve Hills in the Valleys,
Is the mountain Lingáwangad,
Is the flowering tree Pahindí;
In that desert far out-spreading
Twelve *coss* round arose no dwelling:
"Caw" saying, there no crow was;
"Chee" saying, there no bird was;
"Raghum" saying, there no tiger was.
And the Gods were greatly troubled.
In their heavenly courts and councils
Sat no Gods of Gónds among them.

[1] The *Sátpúra* mountains are probably here referred to.

Gods of other nations sat there,
Eighteen threshing-floors [1] of Brahmins,
Sixteen scores [1] of Telingánás;
But no Gods of Góndś appeared there
From the Glens of Seven Mountains,
From the Twelve Hills in the Valleys.
Then the Strong God Kárto Subal,[2]
The first-born of Máhádevá,
Of the Great God Máhádevá,
Pondered deeply in his bosom
O'er a circumstance so curious;
Pondered much, and then he fasted,
Devotee-like prayed and fasted
For the coming of the Gónd Gods
From the Glens of Seven Valleys
To the councils of the Godhead.
Pondered thus till on his left hand
Rose a most Portentous Tumour,
Tumour boil-like, red, and growing
Bigger daily, daily bigger,
Till it burst, and from its centre
Came the Koitor,[3] came they trooping,
Sixteen threshing-floors they numbered.
Came and spread them o'er the country,
On the hills, and in the valleys,
In the arches of the forest,
Everywhere they filled the country;
Killing, eating, every creature;
Nothing knowing of distinction;
Eating clean and eating unclean;
Eating raw and eating rotten;
Eating squirrels, eating jackals,
Eating antelope and sámbar,
Eating quails and eating pigeons,
Eating crows and kites and vultures,
Eating Dokuma the Adjutant,
Eating lizards, frogs, and beetles,
Eating cows and eating calves,
Eating male and female buffaloes,
Eating rats, and mice, and bandicoots;
So the Gónds made no distinction.
For half a year they bathed not,
And their faces nicely washed not
When they fell upon the dunghills—
Thus at first were born the Koitor
From the hand of Kárto Subal.
Soon a stench began to issue
From the forests and the mountains—
Stench of Gónds that lived so foully.
Rose the stench to Máhádevá,
To his mountain Dewalgirí.[4]
Wrathful then became the Great God,
Called his messenger Naráyan,
Said he, "Bring these Gónds before me—
Outcast wretches! How their stink has
Spread o'er all my Dewalgirí."
Then the messenger Naráyan
Called the Koitor all together,
Called them up to Dewalgirí
To the Great God Máhádevá,
Ranged them all in rows before him

[1] Such expressions are used throughout the legend to denote indefinite numbers.

[2] Kártik Swámi, the son of Sívá (Máhádevá), is thus termed in the legend.

[3] Koitor is the national name for all the Gónds of different tribes. It signifies properly "men."

[4] Dewalgirí is one of the highest peaks of the Himalaya range; and is here used as identical with Kailás, the mythic heaven of Sívá.

In the courtyard of the Great God.
Then the Great God washed his body,
Washed a little of the dirt off;
Fashioned it into the likeness
Of the King of Squirrels—Wárché;
Breathed the breath of life into it;
Down before the Koitor threw it.
Straight the Squirrel then his tail made,
Seeking passage to escape them,
Jerking in and out among them;
And the Gónds began to chase it,
Crying, "Catch it!" crying, "Kill it!"
"Let us catch and skin and eat it."
Some took sticks and some took stones,
Some took clods, and off they scurried
After Wárché, King of Squirrels,
Hip-cloths streaming out behind them.
But the Squirrel—Artful Dodger—
Jerking in and out among them
Popped into a hole convenient
In the mountain Dewalgirí.
And the Gónds all ran in after—
All but four that stayed behind them.
Then a stone took Máhádevá,
A great stone of sixteen cubits,
Shut them up within the cavern
In the mountain Dewalgirí;
Shut them up, and placed the demon—
Monster horrid, fierce Basmásur—
Placed him guardian o'er the entrance.
And the four that were remaining
Swiftly fled from Dewalgirí,
Fled across the hills and valleys,
Fled to hide them from the Great God,
From the wrath of Máhádevá.
Long they wandered thus in terror,
But no hiding-place discovered;
Till a tree at last ascending,
On a hill a straight-stemmed date tree,
Thence looked forth and saw a refuge—
Saw the Red Hills, Lahúgadá,
The Iron Valley, Kachikopá.
There they sped them through the forest,
And they hid them from the Great God.

Now the goddess-queen Párbuttee—
Consort she of Máhádevá—
On the mountain top was sleeping,
On the top of Dewalgirí.
Waked she shortly from her slumber,
Waked to find a something wanting
In the air of Dewalgirí.
Then she grieved, and thought within her,
"Where can all my Gónds have gone to?
Many days our hill is silent,
Once that echoed to their shouting;
Many days no smell ascendeth,
Pleasant smell of Gónds ascending;
My sweet-smelling Gónds, where are they?
And my Máhádevá, also,
Him I see not; much I fear me
He has done my Gónds a mischief."
And she grieved, and took no dinner,
Prayed and fasted like a hermit,
Devotee-like penance doing
For her lost sweet-smelling Koitor.
Six months thus she prayed and fasted,
Till the King of Gods, Bhagwantál,[1]

[1] This is intended for Bhagwán, the unworshipped Creator of the Hindús (*vide* p. 123). His introduction here as a mythical personage is not consonant with the usual practice in Hindú writings.

Swinging in a swing and snoozing,
By her penance greatly moved was—
Moved to rise and look about him;
Sent the messenger Naráyan,
Sent him forth to Dewalgirí,
Sent to see what she was up to,
Why so sadly she was grieving.
Soon she told her little grievance,
How her pleasant-smelling GóndS had
Disappeared from Dewalgirí.
Then Bhagwantál sent and told her
He would try if he could find them;
And betook him to his swinging,
And bethought him how to do it.

II.—THE COMING OF LINGO.

On the mountain Lingáwangad,
Grew the flowering-tree Pahindí.
Flowers budding, still unopened,
Yellow flowers of the Pahindí,
Saw the King of Gods Bhagwantál;
Saw and thought him of the Koitor,
Wandering sadly in the mountains,
Pining deep in Dewalgirí;
Saw, and came as comes a raincloud,
Spreading fanlike, came in thunder.
Lightning flashed, the sky was darkened,
Thus the God came to the Flower.
Darkness spread around her cover,
Gently oped the flower her blossom,
Softly fell the quickening shower—
Thus conceived the flower Pahindí.
In the fourth watch of the night time
Fell a heap of yellow saffron;
Fell beneath the tree Pahindí.
Morning dawned, the clouds were opened;
Thundering still the clouds were opened.
Burst the yellow flower Pahindí,
Cracking burst it in the sunlight.
Sprang to life from it my Lingo,
Sprang into the heap of saffron;
Sat and wept among the saffron,
Till his tears the God Paternal
Dried with sprinkling of the saffron;
Sent the Gúlar tree beside him,
Honey dropping from its branches,
Dropped it in the mouth of Lingo.
Sweetness drinking then he cried not.
Blew around him noontide zephyrs;
Grew my Lingo in their breathing.
In a God-sent swing reposing
Gently slept he till the evening.
Purest water may be stainèd;
Stainless all and pure was Lingo.
Diamond sparkled on his navel;
On his forehead beamed the Tíká,
Mark divine of fragrant sandal,
Mark of godhead in my Lingo.
Playing grew he in the saffron,
Swinging slept he in his cradle,
Honey sucking, nothing eating
Of the wild fruits in the forest.
Nine years old became my Lingo,
When his soul began to wonder
Whether all alone his lot was
In that forest shade primeval.
There no wild deer cropped the herbage,
Manlike form there none appearèd;
Somewhere they must be, thought Lingo;
I will seek them, I may find them.
Then he rose and wandered onwards,
Wandered on by brook and meadow,

Through the forest shade primeval,
Till before him rose a mountain,
Mountain pointed like a needle.
Thither climbing, on the summit
Lingo saw the tree Mandítá,
Saw beneath it Kirsádítá,
Sweetly-flowering Kirsádítá.
There its perfume sweet inhaling
Lingered Lingo for a little.
Then he climbed the tree Mandítá,
Climbed and looked forth o'er the forest,
To the valley Kachikopá,
To the Red Hills, Lahúgadá.
Saw a little smoke ascending,
Saw and very greatly marvelled
At this circumstance portentous.
Wandered on, and soon discovered
In that forest shade primeval,
Manlike forms four discovered—
Saw the four Gónds that remainèd
Hiding fearful of the Great God.
Forest quarry having stricken,
Steaks of venison were roasting,
Pieces raw at times devouring.
Seeing Lingo up they started;
Seeing them our Lingo halted;
Long time gazed they at each other.
But the brothers inwards pondered,
Brothers four we are, bethought them,
Let us take him for a fifth one,
Let us take him to our wigwams.
Then they brought him to their wigwams,
To their wigwams in the forest,
And set meat before their brother.
But he asked them whence the meat was,
And they answered, "Of a wild boar."
Then he asked them for its liver;
And they sought long for the liver,
But no liver could discover.
Then they told him, "Lo, a strange thing!
Without liver is this creature
We have slain in the forest."
Lingo laughed at this conception
Of a creature without liver,
Asked to see it in the forest—
Living creature without liver.
Then the brothers much considered
Where on earth they might discover
In the forest or the mountains
Living creature without liver.
One suggested, "He is little,
We are big, and practised roamers
Of the forest shades primeval.
Let us take him to the mountains
Rough and stony, to the thickets
Close and thorny; he will fagged be,
Thirst for water, get so hungry,
Glad he will be to sit down, and
Give up looking for a creature,
Living creature, without liver."
Then they took their bows and arrows—
Bows of bamboo from the mountains,
Shafts of bulrush from the marshes;
And they went by deepest thickets
Of that forest shade primeval.
Kurs the Antelope—they saw it,
Killed it, found it had a liver.
Mawk the sámbar—found and slew it,
Found it also had a liver.
Malól the Hare—they saw and killed it,
In it too they found a liver—
All the creatures had a liver.
Tired and weary were the Brothers;
Lingo only was not wearied.
Thirsty very were the Brothers;
Clambered up upon a hill-top
Seeking water, but they found none.
Clambered down again, and wandered
Through a close and thorny jungle,
Where a man could scarcely enter.
There they found a spring of water,

Cool and sparkling in the shadow.
And they plucked the leaves of Pulás,
Making cups, and drank the waters,
And refreshed were from their labours.
Then said Lingo, "Wherefore stay ye?
We have not yet seen the creature,
Living creature without liver.
Without liver creature is not."

And he said, "Here in the forest
Let us clear a field and plant it.
Down the trees here—let us fell them;
And the ground here—let us dig it;
Seed of rice here—let us sow it.
I will sleep here for a little
While ye clear away the forest."
Then slept Lingo, slept and dreamed he,
Dreamed he of twelve threshing-places,
Threshing-floors that full of Gónds were.
And his soul was greatly troubled;
And he rose and looked about him.
Found the Brothers sadly hewing,
Hewing sadly at a big tree;
And their hands had blisters on them,
Blisters large as fruit of Aolá.
And their hatchets—down they threw them;
And went off and down they squatted.

Then our Lingo up an axe took,
Took and hewed he at the big tree,
Hewed and levelled all the forest,
Felled the trees and grubbed their roots out—
In an hour the field was finished.
And the Gónds said, "Mighty Lingo!
Lo our hands were sore and blistered,
Hewing sadly at one big tree,
Which we left still undemolished.
In an hour has Lingo done it!
He has levelled all the forest;
Black the land appears below it;
Thick the rice is sown upon it;
High a hedge is raised around it;
Single left an entrance to it;
Strong a gate is placed before it."
Then they rose and turned them homewards,
Homewards went they to their wigwams.

Soon the rainy season cometh,
Black a little cloud appeareth,
Strong the winds from heaven are loosened.
All the sky is clouded over;
Now the rain begins to patter.
In a while the streams run knee-deep,
All the hollows flooded brimfull.
Thus three days and nights it rainèd,
Then it stopped as it begun had.
And the rice began to shoot up;
Green became the field of Lingo.
High as fingers four it sprouted,
Sprouted thus high in a day's time.
In a month 'twas somewhat higher,
With a man's knee it was level.

In that forest shade primeval
Sixteen scores of Deer were dwelling;
Chief among them Uncle Mámán;
Nephew Bhásyal—heir apparent.
Rich the odour reached their noses
Of that rice-field in the clearing.
First the Uncle sniffed the odour,
And the Nephew sniffed it after.
Then the Nephew fetched a gambol,
Upwards leaped he, joints all cracking,
And his ears with pleasure cocking.
To his Uncle near he trotted,
And he said, "My ancient Uncle,
See this lovely field of green stuff.
May we have it for our dinner?"

But the Uncle, ancient Mámán,
Warning, chiding, spake in this wise—
"Ere you leap 'twere wise to look well.
In the valleys of the forests
Many fields there are of green stuff;
Touch ye not the field of Lingo—
Go and graze on some one else's.
Sixteen scores of Rohees are ye;
But of all your noble sixteen
Neither buck nor doe will left be
If ye touch the field of Lingo."
Then spake Bhásyal the Nephew,
Spake disdainfully in this wise—
"Old are you and somewhat feeble,
We are young and rather frisky;
Seven-foot-six about the mark is
We can clear a running high jump—
Stay behind, Old Ninkampúpo!
They might catch you if you tried it."
Then his ears pricked twitchy-witchy,
And his tail cocked jerky-perky,
And went forward to the rice-field.
And the Uncle, deeply thinking,
Greatly grieving, left behind was.
But he slowly followed after.
At the fence the Nephew halted,
And prospected for an entrance;
But an entrance nowhere found he,
For the sixteen scores of Rohees.
And the sixteen scores to mutter
'Mong themselves began in this wise—
"Left behind is ancient Mámán,
He the very wise among us.
Now this Bhásyal, youthful Nephew,
He must show us how to do it.
Uncle Mámán spake of Lingo,
Said that very sapient uncle,
Look behind and look before you,
Ere ye touch the field of Lingo."
Answered them the valiant Nephew—
"Keep not company with ancients,
Full of years and slack of sinews,
Follow me"—and then he bounded
O'er the hedge into the rice-field.
After him the Rohees leapt all—
Leapt the sixteen scores of Rohees;
Leapt they straight into the rice-field,
And the rice began to graze on.
Soon the Uncle coming after
By the hedge stood and looked over;
And his mouth began to water
Like a dripping spring in summer.
But no entrance seemed to offer,
And his joints were stiff and feeble;
So he stayed outside, reproachful,
While those sixteen scores of Rohees
Eat up all the field of Lingo.
Eat it up, and back they leapt all,
Stood beside that ancient Mámán,
Who in words of solemn wisdom
Warning, chiding, spake in this wise—
"Hear, ye sixteen scores of Rohees!
O my children, my poor children!
Very nicely ye have done it—
Eaten up the field of Lingo.
Father Lingo, he the powerful,
When he comes to see his rice-field,
What on earth will he think of it?"
Then the very youthful Bhásyal,
To the sixteen scores of Rohees
Counsel offered, spake in this wise—
"Listen, brethren! let us speed now
To our forest shades primeval.
On the stones our feet well placing,
On the leaves our footsteps keeping,
On the grass our way selecting,
On the soil no footmarks leaving,

Let us cunningly our way take
To our forest shades primeval."
As he said so did the Rohees,
Lightly stepping left no traces,
Marks of footsteps none appearèd;
Reached their forest shades primeval.
Some to sit down, some to sleep went,
Some to stand up in the cool shade,
'Gan these sixteen scores of Rohees.
'Midst the perfume sweet of flowers,
Swinging in a swing, was Lingo;
Swinging slept he, and he dreamèd,
Dreamt of sixteen scores of Rohees,
Of a devastated rice-field.
And his soul was greatly troubled;
And he rose and looked about him.
Lookėd, and went to reconnoitre
By the way of Kachikopá;
Went he through the Iron Valley,
To the Red Hills, Lahúgadá,
Went the very valiant Lingo;
Saw the devastated rice-field;
Thence returning, to the Brothers,
Brothers sleeping in their wigwams,
Spake our Lingo — "Listen, Brothers,
Listen to my doleful story,
How these sixteen scores of Rohees
All our rice-field have demolished."
Then the Brothers, greatly troubled
By this doleful tale of Lingo,
Wailed a wail of disappointment,
Spake the words of bitter anguish—
"To the gods our yearly firstfruits,
Firstfruits that we yearly offer,
Now of what shall we give firstfruits,
Since our rice-field is demolished?"
Answered Lingo—"Lo a firstfruit
To the Gods of Rohees' livers,
Of the sixteen scores of Rohees
Liver firstfruits shall we offer.
On the perfume of the flowers
I, a devotee, can prosper;
Ye are Gónds with hungry stomachs,
Wherewithal shall they be fillèd,
Now these sixteen scores of Rohees
All our rice-field have demolished?"
Then the Brothers took their weapons—
Bows of bamboo from the mountains,
Shafts of bulrush from the marshes;
And in wrath they sought the rice-field,
Where the soil was black and naked,
Saw they nothing but the stubble
Of the rice that waved so greenly.
Then a flame of mighty anger,
From the heels of Lingo rising,
To his matted head ascended.
Reddened were his eyes like firebrands,
Bit his fingers till the blood came;
Said he—"Search ye for the footprints
Of these sixteen scores of Rohees."
Then the Brothers bent them downwards,
Searching closely for their traces,
Traces nowhere that appearèd
Of the sixteen scores of Rohees.
Searched they long and found a footmark,
Single footmarks scarce appearing,
Thence the jungle trodden down was
To the forest shades primeval.
Fast they followed on the traces,
But the sixteen scores they saw not.
Soon a Peepul tree appearèd
Towering high above the forest;
Clambered Lingo to its summit,
Looked he from it o'er the forest,

Spied the sixteen scores of Rohees,
Rohees in the shade reclining,
Rohees sleeping, Rohees frisking
In the forest shade primeval.
Then said Lingo to the Brothers—
"Take your bows and take your arrows;
Quickly get ye round about them,
To the four sides of the Rohees.
Slay and spare not, smite the rascals!
Hence my bolts I will deliver."
Then the Brothers stalked around them,
To the four sides of the Rohees;
Thence their bulrush shafts delivered;
Shot our Lingo from the Peepul.
Smitten were the herd of Rohees,
Only Mámán, Uncle Mámán,
And one little female Rohee,
Of those sixteen scores remainèd.
Then our Lingo aimed an arrow
At that Uncle, ancient Mámán;
But the arrow from his hand fell.
Thought he, surely here's an omen
That this very ancient Mámán
Of our rice has nothing taken.
Then to run began the Rohee,
Female Rohee that remainèd;
And to run began the Uncle.
Brothers all behind them followed,
Shouting "Catch them" to each other.
But they vanished and were seen not.
And the Brothers, much disgusted,
Back returnèd to their Lingo.
Then said Lingo, "Search ye, Brethren,
For a firebox in your waistbelts."
Flints and steel they forthwith brought out,
Struck a spark among the tinder,
But the tinder would not burn.
Thus the whole night long they tried it,
Tried in vain until the morning,
When they flung away the tinder.
And to Lingo said, "O Brother,
You're a prophet, can you tell us
Why we cannot light this tinder?"
Answered Lingo, "Three *coss* onward
Lives the Giant Rikad Gowree,
He the very dreadful Monster,
He the terrible Devourer.
In his field a fire is smoking;
Thither go and fetch a firebrand."
Then the Brothers went a little,
Went a very little, onwards;
Thence returned, and said to Lingo—
"Nowhere saw we Rikad Gowree,
Nowhere have we found this Giant."
Then said Lingo, "Lo my arrow,
By its pathway see ye follow."
Then he fitted to his bowstring
Shaft of bulrush straight and slender;
Shot it through the forest thickets,
Shot it cleaving through the branches,
Shot it shearing all the grass down;
Cut a pathway straight and easy;
Fell it right into the fireplace
Of the Giant Rikad Gowree;
Fell, and glanced it from the fire-place,
Glanced, and sped into the door-way
Of the wigwam of the Giant;
Fell before the seven daughters,
Seven very nice young women,
Daughters fair of Rikad Gowree.
Then those seven nice young women
Took the arrow and concealed it.
For they oft had asked the old man,
Asked him when they would be married;
And he always answered gruffly,
"When I choose that you be married

Good and well, if not you won't be."
And they thought this was an omen.
Now the Brothers, greatly fearing
Lest they all should eaten up be,
Counsel taking, sent the youngest,
Sent Ahkeseral the youngest,
To prospect the Giant's quarters.
By that pathway straight and easy
Went this very young Ahkeseral;
Saw the Giant's smoke ascending;
Coming nearer saw the Giant.
Saw him, like a shapeless tree trunk,
Sleeping by the fire and snoring—
By the fire of mighty tree stems,
Stems of Mohwá, stems of Ánjan,
Stems of Sájná, stems of Téktá;
Blazing red, its glow reflected
From that form huge and shapeless
Of the Giant Rikad Gowree,
Of that very dreadful Rákshis,
Of that terrible Devourer.
Then his knees began to quake all,
O'er his body came cold shudders,
Leapt his liver to his throat all,
Leapt the liver of Ahkeseral.
But he crept up to the fireplace,
Crept and snatched a blazing firebrand,
Blazing brand of Támádítá.
Groaned the Giant, fled Ahkeseral,
Dropped the firebrand, and a spark flew,
Flew and lighted on the Giant,
On his shapeless hip it lighted.
Raised a blister like a saucer;
Started up the Giant swearing;
Also feeling very hungry,
Feeling very much like eating.
Saw that very young Ahkeseral,
Plump and luscious as a cucumber,
Saw him running and ran after,
Ran and shouted loud behind him.
But in vain he followed after.
For the very young Ahkeseral,
Speeding swiftly through the forest,
Shortly vanished and was seen not.
And the Giant, much disgusted,
Then returnèd to his fireside.
And Ahkeseral, returning,
Told his greatly trembling brothers
Of that very dreadful Giant.
But the very valiant Lingo
Said, "Repose ye here a little,
I will go and see this monster
That so much has discomposed you."
At the crossing of a river,
In that straight and easy pathway,
Lingo saw the stick Wadúdá
Floating down upon the current.
Saw he too a bottle-gourd tree,
Saw it growing by the river;
Pulled a bottle-gourd from off it,
Fished Wadúdá from the river,
Stuck the one into the other,
Plucked two hairs wherewith to string it,
Made a bow and keys eleven,
Played a tune or two, and found he
Had a passable guitar.
Pleased was Lingo, and proceeded
To the field of Rikad Gowree;
Rikad Gowree lying snoring
By the fireside, mouth wide gaping,
Tushes horrible displaying,
Lying loglike with his eyes shut.
Close by grew the tree called Peepul,
Peepul tall with spreading branches.
Quickly Lingo clambered up it,
Climbed aloft into its branches;
Sat and heard the morning cock crow,
Thought this Giant soon would waken.
Then he took his banjo Jántur,
Struck a note that sounded sweetly,

Played a hundred tunes upon it.
Like a song its music sounded;
At its sound the trees were silent;
Stood the mighty hills enraptured.
Entered then that strain of music
In the ears of Rikad Gowree,
Quickly woke him from his slumber;
Rubbed his eyes and looked about him;
Looked in thickets, looked in hollows,
Looked in tree-tops; nothing finding,
Wondered where on earth it came from,
Came that strain of heavenly music,
Like the warbling of the Mainá.
Back returning to his fireside,
Sat down, stood up, sat down, stood up;
Listened, wondered at the music;
Jumped and danced he to the music,
Sung and danced he to the music;
Rolled and tumbled by the fire-side
To the warbling of the music.
Soon at daybreak his old woman
Heard that strain of heavenly music;
Came she wondering to the fire-side,
Saw her old man wildly dancing—
Hands outstretching, feet uplifting,
Head back reeling, dancing, tumbling,
To that strain of heavenly music.
Saw and wondered, saw and called out—
"Ancient husband, foolish old man!"
Looked he at her, nothing said he,
Danced and tumbled to the music.
Said she, listening to that music,
"I must dance too." Then she opened
Loose the border of her garment,
Danced and tumbled to the music.
Then said Lingo, "Lo my Jántur!
To thy strain of heavenly music
Dance this old man and his woman;
All my Koitor thus I teach will,
Thus in rows to sing and dance all,
At the feasting of the Gónd Gods,
At the feast of the Dewálí,
At the feast of Búdhal Péná,
At the feast of Jungo Reytál,
At the feast of Phársá Péná—
Salutation to the Gods all
From this various tuneful Jántur!"
Then he ceased the wondrous music;
Hailed the old man from the tree-top,
Saying—"Uncle, Rikad Gowree,
See your nephew on this tree-top!"
Then the Giant, looking upwards,
Saw our Lingo on the tree-top;
Called him down, shook hands, and said that
He was very glad to see him.
Asked him in and made him sit down;
Rang and called for pipes and coffee;
Apologised for having thought of
Making breakfast of Ahkeseral;
Thanked our Lingo very kindly
For his offer of the livers
Of those sixteen scores of Rohees;
In return proposed to give him
All those seven nice young women,
With their eyes bound, will they nill they,
To be wedded to the Brothers.
And those seven nice young women
When they heard about the young men,
Of those young men faint and fasting

Waiting fireless by the Rohees,
Forthwith packed they up their wardrobes,
On their heads they took their beds up,
Back to Lingo gave his arrow—
Arrow of the truthful omen—
Saying good-bye to their parent,
Followed Lingo to the forest,
To that forest-shade primeval.
Reached those young men by the Rohees,
Made a fire, and had some luncheon
Of the livers of the Rohees.

Then the brothers 'gan to squabble
O'er those seven nice young women.
Holy Lingo, virtuous very,
Quite refusing to be wedded,
Somewhat easier made the problem;
And he soon arranged it this wise—
That the eldest of the brethren
Each should take two nice young women,
While the very young Ahkeseral
Should be fitted with the odd one.

Then returning from the forest,
By the valley Kachikopá,
To the Red Hills, Lahúgadá,
Holy Lingo joined the Brothers
To those seven nice young women,
To the daughters of the Giant.
Water brought and poured it o'er them,
Bowers of branches raised around them,
Garlands gay he threw about them,
Mark of Turmeric applied he—
And declared them duly wedded.

Then the Brothers mighty pleased were
With their good and virtuous Lingo;
Said they'd go forth to the forest,
Go and smite the bounding red-deer,
Bring its liver to their Lingo,
Gather wild flowers for their Lingo,
While those Sisters seven should swing him,
Swing him gently as he slumbered.
Then their bows and arrows took they,
Took and started to the forest.
And the sisters swinging Lingo
Thus began to say among them—
"See this Lingo! who so solemn
As this brother of our husbands?
Neither laughs he, neither speaks he,
Neither looks he even at us.
He must laugh, and speak, and gambol,
Must this very solemn Lingo;
Let us pinch and pull and hug him."
And they pulled him by the arms,
Pulled his feet and pinched his arms;
But the more they pulled and pinched him
All the sounder slept our Lingo.
Till the sisters, vexed to find him
Nothing caring for their toying,
Took to hugging rather closely,
Hugged that very virtuous Lingo,
Till they woke him from his sleeping.
Wrathful then was holy Lingo,
At those wanton Giant's daughters
Rose the flame of indignation
From his boots up to his top-knot;
Looked about him for a weapon,
For a weapon to chastise them;
Saw a pestle hard and heavy,
Pestle made for husking rice with;
Bounded from his swing and seized it,
With it thrashed those Giant's daughters;
Thrashed them till they bellowed loudly,

Fled and roared like Bulls of Bashan,
Fled and hid them in their wigwams.
Soon the Brothers back returning,
Bringing game and bringing wild flowers,
Found their Lingo quietly sleeping;
Sisters none his swing were rocking.
Much astonished, they betook them
To the wigwams of the Sisters.
But had scarce begun to scold them
Ere they found the tables turnèd—
" Pretty fellows are you truly!
Thus to leave your wives behind you
And go hunting in the forest,
While your very holy Lingo
Tries his arts upon our virtue.
We have quite made up our minds now
Not to stay another minute,
But to take our beds and wardrobes,
And return to where we came from—
To our poor deceived Papa!"
Then the Brothers said among them—
" O that sinful, wicked Lingo!
How the villain has deceived us!
When we offered him the fairest,
No, he wanted none, he told us;
Called them sisters, called them mothers;
Now to play so mean a trick on
Us when hunting in the forest!
Let us get him to the jungle,
Kill him there, and pull his eyes out.
Hares and antelopes we've hunted,
Now we'll hunt our little Lingo.
Bread or water let us touch not
Till we've played a game of marbles
With the eyes of faithless Lingo."
Then they went and wakened Lingo,
Saying, " Rise, our youngest brother."
And he rose, and wondering asked them
Why so late they had returnèd,
Bringing nothing from the forest.
And they answered, " Lo, a Creature,
Mighty strong, appeared before us;
And we fought him with our arrows,
But this mighty Creature fell not,
Neither fled he; come then with us."
Then rose Lingo, and before them
Stalked he on into the forest,
To the forest-shade primeval.
Looked for traces of the Creature
In the grass, among the bushes;
But this mighty Creature saw not.
Then they sat them down and rested
By the Tree called Sárekátá.
And the Brothers went for water,
Went and pondered how to kill him;
And returning softly, hidden
By the stem of Sárekátá,
From their bows four arrows sped they,
Bulrush shafts, at holy Lingo.
Split his skull was, pierced his neck was,
Cleft the liver was of Lingo.
Down he dropped, and out his life passed,
By the Tree called Sárekátá.
Then a knife they took and gouged him,
Out the eyes they bored of Lingo;
In a hole they put the body;
Strewed it over with some branches;
Pulled some leaves and made a goblet
For the bored-out eyes of Lingo;
Tied it up into a waistcloth,

Hied them homeward to their wigwams;
Called their wives, and lit some torches,
Blazing torches made of flax-stalks;
Played their horrid game of marbles
With the bored-out eyes of Lingo.
So the Brothers four of Lingo
And those seven nice young women
Chucked his eyes about like marbles
For an hour's time by the torch light.

III.—THE RESURRECTION OF LINGO, AND DELIVERY OF THE GÓNDS.

In the Court of great Bhagwantál
Sat the Deities assembled;
Sat they in the Upper World,
Wondering where, in earthly regions,
Lay the body of their Lingo:
Wondered much, but nothing knew they
In what region it had fallen.
Then Bhagwantál took a basin,
Washed a little of his body,
Washed a little of the dirt off:
Took and made of it an image;
Breathed the breath of life into it;
Made Kagésur, Lord of Ravens.
Amrit[1] sprinkled he upon it.
From his hand released it, saying—
"Search the forests, search the mountains,
Search the valleys, search the rivers,
For the body of my Lingo."
Then Kagésur, Lord of Ravens,
He the very black and cunning,
Swiftly sped him on his errand;
Searched he first the Upper Regions,
Thence descended to the Lower;
Searched their hills and glens and forests,
Till he reached the Iron Valley,
In the Red Hills, Lahúgadá.
Peered among the forest thickets,
Saw the twigs that covered Lingo,
Looked below them, found our Lingo,
Looking horrid, with his eyes out,
Split his skull, and pierced his liver.
Hied him back to great Bhagwantál,
Told the doleful tale of Lingo.
Then the God said, "Ha! I see it,
By his birth-place has he fallen,
By the flowering tree Pahindí."
Then he sent for Kárto Subal,
Gave a flask of heavenly Amrit
(Bade him well to shake the bottle),
For external application
To the skull and neck and liver
Of the gouged and butchered Lingo;
And despatched him with Kagésur
To the valley Kachikopá,
To the Red Hills, Lahúgadá.
Flew the Raven straight before him;
Reached the place; then Kárto Subal
Took the flask of heavenly Amrit,
Poured it o'er his wounds and bruises,
Stitching up the chiefest openings
In his head and his abdomen.
Soon his eyes began to open,[2]
And he saw the Lord of Ravens;
Thought he'd slept a little soundly;

[1] The water of immortality.
[2] It is not related how these organs were restored to him.

Asked them, "Had they seen his
Brothers?"
And was very much astounded
When they told him how they
found him
Gouged and butchered by his
Brothers.
Then he thought perhaps 'twere
better
Now to leave this lot of Brothers,
And their seven nice young
women;
And go seek those other Sixteen,
Sixteen threshing-floors of Koitor.
So the Strong God and the
Raven
Hied them back and told Bhag-
wantál
Of their surgery successful.
And our Lingo *Redivivus*
Wandered sadly through the forest,
Wandered on across the mountains
Till the darkening of the evening,
Wandered on until the night fell.
Screamed the panther in the
forest,
Growled the bear upon the moun-
tain,
And our Lingo then bethought him
Of their cannibal propensities.
Saw at hand the tree Nirúdá,
Clambered up into its branches.
Darkness fell upon the forest,
Bears their heads wagged, yelled
the jackal—
Kolyál the King of Jackals.
Sounded loud their dreadful voices
In that forest-shade primeval.
Then the Jungle-Cock Gugótee,
Mull the Peacock, Kurs the Wild
Deer,
Terror-stricken screeched and
shuddered
In that forest-shade primeval.
But the Moon arose at midnight,
Poured her flood of silver radiance,
Lighted all the forest arches,
Through their gloomy branches
slanting;
Fell on Lingo, pondering deeply
On his Sixteen Scores of Koitor.
Then thought Lingo, I will ask
her
For my Sixteen Scores of Koitor.
"Tell me, O Moon!" said Lingo,
"Tell, O Brightener of the dark-
ness,
Where my Sixteen Scores are
hidden."
But the Moon sailed onwards,
upwards,
And her cold and glancing moon-
beams
Said, "Your Gónds, I have not
seen them."
And the Stars came forth and
twinkled—
Twinkling eyes above the forest.
Lingo said, "O Stars that twinkle!
Eyes that look into the darkness,
Tell me where my Sixteen Scores
are."
But the cold Stars, twinkling ever,
Said, "Your Gónds, we have not
seen them."
Broke the morning, the sky red-
dened,
Faded out the star of morning,
Rose the Sun above the forest,
Brilliant Sun the Lord of Morning,
And our Lingo quick descended,
Quickly ran he to the eastward,
Fell before the Lord of Morning,
Gave the great Sun salutation—
"Tell, O Sun!" he said, "dis-
cover
Where my Sixteen Scores of Gónds
are."
But the Lord of Day reply made—
"Hear, O Lingo, I a Pilgrim
Wander onwards through four
watches
Serving God, I have seen nothing
Of your Sixteen Scores of Koitor."
Then our Lingo wandered on-
wards
Through the arches of the forest;
Wandered on until before him

Saw the grotto of a hermit,
Old and sage, the Black Kumait,
He the very wise and knowing,
He the greatest of Magicians,
Born in days that are forgotten,
In the unremembered ages.
Salutation gave, and asked him—
"Tell, O Hermit! Great Kumait!
Where my Sixteen Scores of Gónds are."

Then replied the Black Magician,
Spake disdainfully in this wise—
"Lingo hear, your Gónds are asses,
Eating cats, and mice, and bandicoots,
Eating pigs, and cows, and buffaloes;
Filthy wretches! wherefore ask me?
If you wish it I will tell you.
Our great Máhádevá caught them,
And has shut them up securely
In a cave within the bowels
Of his mountain Dewalgirí,
With a stone of sixteen cubits,
And his bulldog fierce Basmásur.
Serve them right too, I consider,
Filthy, casteless, stinking wretches!"
And the Hermit to his grotto
Back returned, and deeply pondered
On the days that are forgotten,
On the unremembered ages.

But our Lingo wandered onwards,
Fasting, praying, doing penance;
Laid him on a bed of prickles,
Thorns long and sharp and piercing;
Fasting lay he devotee-like,
Hand not lifting, foot not lifting,
Eye not opening, nothing seeing.
Twelve months long thus lay and fasted,
Till his flesh was dry and withered,
And the bones began to show through.

Then the Great God Máhádevá
Felt his seat begin to tremble,
Felt his golden stool all shaking
From the penance of our Lingo.
Felt, and wondered who on earth
This devotee was that was fasting
Till his golden stool was shaking.
Stepped he down from Dewalgirí,
Came and saw that bed of prickles
Where our Lingo lay unmoving.
Asked him what his little game was,
Why his golden stool was shaking?
Answered Lingo, "Mighty Ruler!
Nothing less will stop that shaking
Than my Sixteen Scores of Koitor
Rendered up all safe and hurtless
From your cave in Dewalgirí."
Then the Great God, much disgusted,
Offered all he had to Lingo,
Offered kingdom, name, and riches,
Offered anything he wished for,
"Only leave your stinking Koitor
Well shut up in Dewalgirí."
But our Lingo all refusing
Would have nothing but his Koitor;
Gave a turn to run the thorns a
Little deeper in his midriff.
Winced the Great God, "Very well then,
Take your Gónds—but first a favour.
By the shore of the Black Water
Lives a bird they call Black Bindo;
Much I wish to see his young ones,
Little Bindos from the sea-shore;
For an offering bring these Bindos,
Then your Gónds take from my mountain."

Then our Lingo rose and wandered,
Wandered onwards through the forest,
Till he reached the sounding sea-shore,

Reached the brink of the Black Water,
Found the Bindo birds were absent
From their nest upon the seashore,
Absent hunting in the forest,
Hunting elephants prodigious,
Which they killed and took their brains out,
Cracked their skulls, and brought their brains to
Feed their callow little Bindos,
Wailing sadly by the sea-shore.
Seven times a fearful serpent,
Bhawarnág the horrid serpent,
Serpent born in ocean's caverns,
Coming forth from the Black Water,
Had devoured the little Bindos—
Broods of callow little Bindos
Wailing sadly by the sea-shore,
In the absence of their parents.
Eighth this brood was. Stood our Lingo,
Stood he pondering beside them—
"If I take these little wretches
In the absence of their parents
They will call me thief and robber.
No! I'll wait till they come back here."
Then he laid him down and slumbered
By the little wailing Bindos.
As he slept the dreadful serpent,
Rising, came from the Black Water,
Came to eat the callow Bindos,
In the absence of their parents.
Came he trunk-like from the waters,
Came with fearful jaws distended,
Huge and horrid. Like a basket
For the winnowing of corn
Rose a hood of vast dimensions
O'er his fierce and dreadful visage.
Shrieked the Bindos young and callow,
Gave a cry of lamentation;
Rose our Lingo; saw the Monster;
Drew an arrow from his quiver,
Shot it swift into his stomach,
Sharp and cutting in the stomach,
Then another and another;
Cleft him into seven pieces;
Wriggled all the seven pieces,
Wriggled backwards to the water.
But our Lingo, swift advancing,
Seized the head-piece in his arms,
Knocked the brains out on a boulder,
Laid it down beside the Bindos,
Callow wailing little Bindos.
On it laid him, like a pillow,
And began again to slumber.
Soon returned the parent Bindos
From their hunting in the forest;
Bringing brains and eyes of camels,
And of elephants prodigious,
For their little callow Bindos
Wailing sadly by the sea-shore.
But the Bindos young and callow
Brains of camels would not swallow;
Said—"A pretty set of parents
You are truly! thus to leave us
Sadly wailing by the sea-shore
To be eaten by the serpent—
Bhawarnág the dreadful serpent—
Came he up from the Black Water,
Came to eat us little Bindos,
When this very valiant Lingo
Shot an arrow in his stomach,
Cut him into seven pieces—
Give to Lingo brains of camels,
Eyes of elephants prodigious."
Then the fond paternal Bindo
Saw the head-piece of the serpent
Under Lingo's head a pillow.
And he said, "O valiant Lingo,
Ask whatever you may wish for."
Then he asked the little Bindos
For an offering to the Great God.
And the fond paternal Bindo,
Much disgusted, first refusing,
Soon consented; said he'd go too
With the fond maternal Bindo—
Take them all upon his shoulders,

And fly straight to Dewalgirí.
Then he spread his mighty pinions,
Took his Bindos up on one side
And our Lingo on the other.
Thus they soared away together
From the shores of the Black Water.
And the fond maternal Bindo,
O'er them hovering, spread an awning
With her broad and mighty pinions
O'er her offspring and our Lingo.
By the forests and the mountains
Six months' journey was it thither
To the mountain Dewalgirí.
Half the day was scarcely over
Ere this convoy from the sea-shore
Lighted safe on Dewalgirí;
Touched the knocker on the gate-way
Of the Great God Máhádevá.
And the messenger Naráyan
Answering, went and told his master—
"Lo, this very valiant Lingo!
Here he is with all the Bindos,
The Black Bindos from the sea-shore."
Then the Great God, much disgusted,
Driven quite into a corner,
Took our Lingo to the cavern,
Sent Basmásur to his kennel,
Held his nose, and moved away the
Mighty stone of sixteen cubits;
Called those Sixteen Scores of Gónds out,
Made them over to their Lingo.
And they said, "O Father Lingo!
What a bad time we've had of it,
Not a thing to fill our bellies
In this horrid gloomy dungeon."
But our Lingo gave them dinner,
Gave them rice and flour of millet,
And they went off to the river,
Had a drink, and cooked and eat it.

IV.—SETTLEMENT OF THE GÓNDS, AND PASSING OF LINGO.

Then they rose and followed Lingo,
Followed onwards to the forest,
From the mountain Dewalgirí;
Followed on till night descended,
And before them saw a river,
Dark and swollen with the torrent
Bursting down from Dewalgirí,
From the snows of Dewalgirí.
On that river nothing saw they,
Boat nor raft, to waft them over.
Nothing saw they in the torrent
But the Alligator Púsé,
And the River-Turtle Dámé,
Playing, rolling, in the water.
Then our Lingo called them to him,
Called them brother, called them mother;
Bound with oaths to bear them over.
And the Alligator Púsé,
Looming long upon the water,
Bore the Gónds into the torrent,
Through the black and roaring water:
And the River-Turtle Dámé
With our Lingo followed after.
Soon the faithless Alligator,
In the deep and roaring water,
Slipping from below his cargo,
Left them floundering in the water.
Then our Lingo stretched his hand out,

Fished them out upon the Turtle;
Faithful Dámé bore them onward
O'er that black and roaring torrent,
Bore them on across the river.
And the Sixteen vowed to cherish
Name of Dámé with them ever,
Who had borne them safe and hurtless
O'er that dark and foaming river.

Then they travelled through the forest,
Over mountain, over valley,
To the Glens of Seven Mountains,
To the Twelve Hills in the Valleys.
There remained with Holy Lingo.
He the very wise and prudent,
Taught to clear the forest thickets,
Taught to rear the stately millet,
Taught to yoke the sturdy oxen,
Taught to build the roomy wagon.
Raised a city, raised Nárbúmí;
City fenced in from the forest.
Made a market in Nárbúmí.
Rich and prosperous grew Nárbúmí—
So they flourished and remainèd.

Then our Lingo called them round him,
Ranged them all in rows beside him,
Spake in this wise—"Hear, O Brethren!
Nothing know ye of your fathers,
Of your mothers, of your brothers,
Whom to laugh with, whom to marry;
Meet it is not ye should be so
Like the creatures of the forest."

Then he chose them from each other,
Chose and named their tribes distinctive;
Chose the first and said, "Manwajjá."
Thus began the tribe Manwajjá.
By the hand took Dáhakwálí,
Bard he called him "Dáhakwálí."
Koilabútal named another,
And another Koikobútal—
Koikobútal wild and tameless.
Thus he named them as he chose them,
Till the Sixteen Scores were numbered,
Till the Tribes had all been chosen.
Next among them chose the eldest,
Chose an old man hoary headed,
Chose and called his name "Pardháná,"
Priest and Messenger he called him.
Called and sent him on a message
To the Red Hills Lahúgadá,
The Iron Valley, Kachikopá;
To those Brothers four he sent him,
Sent to ask them for their daughters
To be wedded to his Koitor—
Thus the Tribes our Lingo mated.
Thus they grew and multipliėd.
Then he chose them into houses,
Into families of seven,
Of six, of four, he chose them.

And he said, "O Koitor listen!
Nowhere Gods of Gónds are worshipped;
Let us make us Gods and worship."
Then made Ghagará the Bell-God.
Made and gave he to Manwajjá.
Brought the Wild Bull's Tail and named it
Cháwardeo; brought the War God—
God of Iron, Phársá Péná;
Manko Reytál, Jango Reytál—
Thus their tribal Gods he fashioned.
Taught them how to raise their altars;
Taught to offer sacrifices—
Hoary goats, white cocks a year old,
Virgin cows, and juice of mhowa;
Taught to praise with voice and psalter,
Twang of Jántur, sound of drumming—

Drum of Beejásál resounding—
Dancing, singing, by the altars.
Thus he taught them, Holy Lingo;
And his last words then he uttered—
"Keep your promise to the Turtle,
To the River-Turtle Dámé;
To the Gods I now am going."
Then he melted from their vision;
And they strained their eyes to see him.
But he vanished, and was seen not.

GÓNDS OF THE SAHPÚRA RANGE. (*From a Photograph.*)

CHAPTER VI

THE TEAK REGION

ON the 28th of March, having seen our forest lodge in a fair way to completion, I left the Puchmurree plâteau, and entered on the first of many long journeys of exploration among the forests of the Seoní, Chindwárá, and Bétúl districts. I have already described these as being situated on the great central table-land of this mountain range, from the centre of which juts up the still higher formation called the Máhádeo (or Puchmurree) group. The general elevation of the table-land is about 2000 feet above the sea; but this general level is broken by numerous minor projections, besides the great one of the Máhádeo range, which generally exhibit the peculiar flat-topped outline of hills of the trap formation.[1] The overflow of basalt has indeed been nearly universal over all this vast region, the great Máhádeo sandstone block, and a few isolated peaks of granite, known at once by their sharp and splintered peaks, being the only notable breaks in the great volcanic ocean. To judge from the great extent of table-land lying at about the elevation of 2000 feet, this would appear to have been the original level of the trap overflow, the higher peaks of that formation, which reach in a few places to 3000 feet, being more probably the result of subsequent upheaval. The plateau has, however, been generally denuded by the larger streams to a depth of about 1000 feet, where they still run over

[1] Many of these isolated hills, being flat-topped and surrounded by precipitous scarps, and frequently furnished with depressions in which rain-water collects, are natural fortresses of an almost impregnable strength; and, with the addition of some rude masonry works, were generally occupied for this purpose by the hill Chiefs in former times.

volcanic beds at the level of the great southern plain of the Deccan. The extent of level plateau is thus much diminished, on the one hand by the ramifications of the drainage system, and on the other by the higher ranges, and the long sloping valleys which connect them with the plateau.

I have called this volcanic region also the region of the teak tree in Central India. It is so *generally*, but, strictly speaking, the teak tree does not actually confine itself to the trap formation; nor, on the other hand, is the teak the only, or even the principal, timber tree of the trap country. No such close lines of distinction exist in nature, but the coincidence is, I think, sufficient to warrant the inference of some link of connection between them. More or less, teak is scattered all over this region, but the principal forests are found clinging to the skirts of the higher ranges rising from the general level of the plateau. The more extensive level portions of the country have long been cleared of jungle for purposes of cultivation, and for a long way around these settlements the forests have been hacked down into mere scrub for the common requirements in timber and fuel of the people. The outer slopes of the plateau, towards the lower plains, have also been long ago swept of all valuable teak; and, moreover, from their sterile nature, have probably at no time produced any large quantity of timber. Even in the higher and more secluded tracts, where forests of teak yet remain, the causes already referred to have now reduced the number of mature and well-grown trees to a very small proportion of the whole, so small that in few places are there more remaining than will suffice to reproduce the forests by their seed in a period of fifty to a hundred years. Everywhere the teak grows very much in patches intermixed with other species, the principal hardwoods of which in these forests are the Sáj (*Pentaptera*), the Bíjásál (*Pterocarpus*), the Dháorá (*Conocarpus*), and in a few localities the Anjan (*Hardwickia*). Many other species have been observed, of which a list will be found in an Appendix.

The mature teak tree of Central India attains a girth

of from ten to fifteen feet, with a bole of seventy or eighty feet to the head of branches. Perfect specimens are, however, rare, the majority of such trees as remain having suffered injury in the sapling stage from fire or axe, so as to permanently contort their form. The soft scaly bark, large flabby leaves, and generally straggling and "seedy" habit of growth of the teak, are certainly, I think, disappointing to those accustomed to the trim firm aspect of other hardwood forests, and particularly to such as have had the opportunity of comparing it with the striking appearance of the evergreen Sál forests of the more eastern regions. In the rainy season the teak tree is surmounted by a heavy head of large green leaves, supporting masses of yellowish white flowers; and when in considerable masses it then gives a peculiar and not unpleasant character to the scenery. The large umbrella-like leaves are admirably fitted for the great function of vegetation at that season, in breaking the direct impact of the rain torrent on the soil of the hill slopes, which would otherwise soon end in depriving the rocky skeletons of the hills of their covering of earth and vegetation. But this foliage is very deciduous, and by the month of March little of it remains on the tree. Then the yellow brittle fallen leaves in many places strew the ground so thickly as to make silent walking impossible. As a facetious friend once expressed it, in a very unnecessary whisper, when we were trying to creep up to a stag sámbar in such a cover—"It was like walking on tin boxes."

Forests containing any great number of tolerably large teak trees are, however, now extremely few; and, as I have said, the teak has been indiscriminately hacked down for every sort of purpose, for many generations, over nearly the whole area where it is found. Among its numerous other valuable qualities, however, it includes that of rapidly throwing up a head of tall slender poles from the stumps, if they are allowed to remain in the ground. In five years this coppice wood will attain a height of twenty-five or thirty feet, and a girth of one to two feet. Such poles are invaluable in a country where habitations are in great measure very small, and built of wood alone—far more valuable, in fact, than larger timber, which is only useful for the exceptional class of structures comprising the residences of wealthy persons, European houses, and public edifices. It was thus, perhaps, scarcely very surprising that when we suddenly demanded from the forests a large and permanent supply of large timber for our railway system, we found that they could not afford it, though it by no means follows that the forests were not in a useful state to meet the ordinary requirements of the country.

Our treatment of this question of the teak forests is a good example of the difficulties in Indian administration which arise from the absence of accurate information on the real requirements of the country, and the obstacles in the way of reconciling the conditions of a low and almost stationary stage of society with nineteenth-century "progress" and high-pressure civilisation. In the cry for great timbers for our railways we totally forgot, or neglected, the demand of the masses of the population for small timber for their houses and many other purposes. We shut up every acre of the teak-producing country we could, and referred them to inferior sorts of wood, all the best species besides teak having been *tabooed* along with it. The other species of timber, when used young, mostly decay in a year or two in an Indian climate; and so the people were put to a vast unnecessary expenditure of labour in renewals, while we strove, by pruning and preserving, to make large timber grow out of the scrubby coppice wood which had before supplied their wants; and, as it proved, strove entirely in vain. This pollarded teak will not grow straight and large, prune we never so wisely. It will grow well to a certain size, the size the natives require it, but after that it decays and twists into every variety of tortuous shape. What we should have done was to reserve the best forests for timber purposes proper, and apply to the rest—the vastly greater part of them—only such measures as would ensure the best and quickest production of coppice wood for the requirements of the people. It has been said that they should learn to do as European nations do, convert large trees to smaller scantlings by the saw, as it is an undoubted fact that forests yield a larger aggregate supply of timber when the trees are allowed to mature. The argument is one of a sort too readily applied to many Indian subjects. Theoretically it is true enough, and in the distant future it may be realised. But in the meantime the people have not the capital wherewith to do it, even if the large timber were growing ready for them, which it is not.

Of other trees than teak these forests produce a great variety, some producing highly ornamental woods for fancy purposes, others useful in the arts, and a good many, when fully matured and seasoned, capable of almost supplanting teak for ordinary building purposes. The useful sorts, however, on the whole, bear a very low proportion to the great mass for which no general use has as yet been found. Round the settlements the valuable sorts have mostly been exterminated; and such parts as are not actually under tillage are covered with a scrub composed of such thorny species as *Acacia Arabica*, *A. catechu*, *Zizyphus Jujuba*, and others. It is remarkable, I think, how the thorny species, which are the best armed to resist destruction, have thus won the race for life in such tracts.

Vast areas, again, do not produce, and do not seem to be capable of producing, any species but such as are, from the softness of their timber, almost useless to the carpenter. A typical example of such a tract is found in the upper valley of the Táptí river, a river which forms so good an example of the streams of this region as to be worthy of some description. Rising among the western spurs of the Máhádeo range, it flows for a short distance over the level plateau of the Bétúl district, in a shallow channel, which, in the hot season, forms a chain of silent pools fringed by great Kowá trees and by the thick green cover of Jáman and Karondá, in which tigers delight to dwell. The surrounding country in this part of its course is partially cleared and cultivated with rice and sugarcane. Presently, however, it commences its descent towards the level of the lower plains, plunging into a glen riven through the basalt, and assumes the character of a mountain torrent. Here and there it widens out into little bays of level valley land; but is henceforth, for a hundred miles or so, generally shut in between high banks rising from the edge of its channel. Through these the rapid drainage of the higher hills has cut innumerable narrow channels down to the level of its bed, which spread out above into an interminable series of rocky gullies, seeming in every direction a long succession of rolling basaltic waves. The surface of these tracts has been weathered in places into a penurious soil, bearing multitudes of round black boulders of trap, ranging in size from an egg to a small house, and salted over with small white agate splinters, both apparently eliminated from the mother rock in the process of decomposition. This surface is covered with a growth of coarse grass, varying according to the depth of the soil from a few inches to several feet in height, and is studded with small trees, of which ninety-nine in every hundred are the Sálei, or frankincense tree (*Boswellia thurifera*).

This tree has hitherto been regarded as a mere incumbrance to the ground. Its timber is soft and spongy, and is certainly valueless for building and such purposes. It has also been rejected as firewood, its specific gravity being so low that a great bulk of it has to be transported in comparison with teak and other hard woods to produce a given effect. Yet it produces excellent charcoal, and is perfectly adapted for most ordinary purposes of fuel; and, wherever the carriage of better sorts from remote parts has rendered their use more expensive, the Sálei has been actually used instead. This points to another mistake we have hitherto made in our Indian forestry. Undoubtedly this and other soft wood trees should have been forced into common use by the people as fuel long ago, instead of our giving way to their outcry for hard woods and bamboos, the use of which should be confined to certain special requirements. The *Boswellia* possesses other properties, which will probably at some future time render these great desolate tracts of high economical value. It yields a fragrant gum resin, which is burnt as incense in Hindú temples. It was long thought to be the Olibanum of the ancients, employed for a similar purpose; but Dr. Birdwood, in a pamphlet, attempted to show that this substance was procured from other species of the *Boswellia* in countries to the west of India. It is, however, singular that its Sanscrit name, *labáná*, should still so closely resemble that of antiquity; and it may perhaps be doubted if our knowledge of the ancient commerce of India suffices to exclude India from the list of countries which contributed the frankincense of the *Boswellia* to the fanes of heathen gods. It is highly probable that some much more general utility would be found in this gum resin, were the attention of persons capable of testing it drawn to the subject. It is also not unlikely that the soft woody fibre of the tree would prove to be adapted for the manufacture of coarse paper or cloth. Should any economic value be found to attach to any portion of the tree, the supply would be practically unlimited; and reproduction of the forests would be easy in the extreme, large stakes when stuck in the ground during the rainy season rapidly taking root and shooting into trees. This quality of the tree has recently been taken advantage of by the railway company for the construction of live fence-posts on which to stretch their fencing wires. The Sálei is of a highly social character, emulating in this respect the Sál (*Shorea*), but admitting in a greater degree than it the companionship of other species. The principal of these are the Sáj (*Pentaptera*); the Torchwood tree (*Cochlospermum*), with its bright yellow solitary flowers gleaming on the extremities of its naked branches; and the Ironwood tree (*Hardwickia binata*), which is perhaps the most graceful forest tree in these regions.

The aspect of these vast forests of the *Boswellia*, of which the country about the Táptí is a specimen, and which cover, I should say, fully one-half of the whole of this trap region, is very remarkable. During the height of the monsoon (July to October) the grass is green, and the trees have thrown out a thin foliage of small, bright green pinnated leaves. The river beds, too, are then filled by foaming torrents, and the fervour of the sun is moderated by a canopy of gray clouds. At this season one might almost mistake the valley for a scene in some northern primeval wilderness. But gradually, as the clouds clear off and the rain ceases, a change occurs. The rivers shrink in their beds, till a trickling stream in a wide bed of boulders represents the resistless mountain torrent of a month before, while the higher gullies are utterly dried up. The grass turns from green to yellow, and bristles with a terrible armature of prickles, like needles of steel with the barbs of a fish-hook, which catch in each other and mat together into masses. Woe betide the undefended pedestrian in grass like this. Unless defended by leather, before he has gone half a mile every stitch of his clothing will be run through and through, and pinned to his flesh by multitudes of these barbs, causing the most intolerable pain. The foliage of the Sálei withers and droops after a few weeks of sunning; and its naked yellow stems then fill the prospect like a vast army of skeletons. But this stage is not even the worst. It continues till the month of April introduces the torrid summer season, when the fierce sun laps up the last particle of moisture in these basaltic regions. Then the grass has become like tinder, and a thousand accidents may set it on fire. The traveller dropping a light from his pipe, the wind carrying a spark from an encampment of jungle-haunting Banjárás, the torch of the belated traveller, and, should it escape these accidents, then certainly the deliberate act of the graziers, who bring herds of cattle with the first fall of rain in June into these tracts to graze on the resulting new crop of grass, will start a jungle fire which nothing can stop till it burns itself out. Early in the hot season it is a fine sight to watch at night the long creeping red lines of the jungle fires on distant hill-sides. From the hill fortress of Asírgarh the eye ranges over the whole of the upper Táptí valley; and at this season the whole country appears at night ringed with these lines of fire, curving with the curvature of hills; here thin and scarcely visible where the grass is scanty on a bare hill-top; there flaring through tracts of long elephant grass, or wrapping some dried and sapless tree-stem in immense tongues of flame. By night a ruddy glow colours all the heavens above the spot;

while by day a thick pall of smoke hangs over the valley. Near the scene the air is stifling and thick with falling flakes of ash. Wild animals have fled the neighbourhood; and clouds of insects rise before the advancing flames, to be devoured by myriads of birds collected seemingly from every end of the country. Innumerable snakes and noxious vermin of all sorts perish in the fire, including many of the curious grass snakes of these regions, which a diligent search will frequently discover twined among the matted masses of the spear-grass. It is a harmless creature, living on insects, and changes its colour from green to yellow, along with the grass. When the fires are burnt out, the spectacle is a dismal one indeed. Hill-side after hill-side of blackness, relieved only here and there by a long streak of white ashes where a prostrate trunk has been consumed, and by the wilderness of Sálei skeletons, scorched at the base, and above more yellow and ghastly than ever.

Yet, even in the heart of those parts of the basaltic region to which this description most fittingly applies, there are few tracts where, at a little distance, some oasis will not be found. The larger ravines are often filled with clumps of bamboo which never entirely lose their verdure; and here and there a sheltered valley will be met, where there is either a pool of water, or moisture not far below the surface, with its fringe of verdure, and a few Mhowa or Mango trees, perhaps marking the site of some old village, deserted long ago beyond the memory of living man. In the central valley of the Táptí also will be found at intervals bays of rich, deep soil, with a moist substratum that is never entirely parched up, and carrying a greener grass which it is hard to burn, and often a covering of forest trees. Most of these tracts have been at one time reclaimed to the plough, and thickly populated. That was in the days when the Mahomedan Viceroy of the Deccan held court at the city of Burhánpúr, some fifty miles lower down the valley, and great armies marching between the Deccan and Hindostan had to be fed. The bays in the valley are still dotted over with the sites of the villages of those times, and with the ruined forts and tombs and mosques of their Mahomedan rulers. Near the ancient site of Sájní, the chief town of one of these tracts, may be seen a banyan tree of immense spread, whose trunk has embraced and lifted bodily up from off the ground the domed masonry tomb, about twelve feet in all dimensions, of some Moslem notable, and so enveloped it with its thousand folds that not one stone of it is to be seen outside, while, passing inside by a narrow opening, the arch of the dome and the wall will be seen to be almost perfect. A Moslem could scarcely desire a fitter entombment than to be suspended thus between heaven and earth, like the prophet of his faith.

It is now some years since the malaria of the encroaching jungle and famine in the country, caused by the failure of the rains of heaven and the still more terrible strife of men, desolated these settlements in the Táptí valley. The rank jungle then sprang on the deserted clearings, rendered fertile to weed as to cereal by the labour of man, and has now clothed them with a thicket of vegetation of such thickness, and guarded by a miasma so deadly, as to baffle all attempts at renewed occupation by the Hindú cultivators densely crowded in the adjoining open country. Here and there the Korkús, whose constitutions seem impervious to malaria, have settled down on some neighbouring rising ground, and built a neat little village of Swiss-like cottages of bamboo, and have cleared and tilled the opener parts of the valley, raising such crops of wheat on the unexhausted black soil as are the envy of the laborious tiller of the hard-used lands in the outer valley. But it is a terrible and unequal struggle between the aborigine, even so far reclaimed as these Korkús are, and the jungle with its immense and unremitting strength of vegetation, and tribes of noxious wild beasts. Every now and again the heart of the Korkú fails him, and he abandons the contest, flitting off to some hill-side where he may more easily contend with axe and fire against the less exuberant vegetation of the thin mountain soils. On the whole, however, the habits of the Korkús of the Táptí valley are a great advance on those of the tribes inhabiting the Máhádeo hills further east. Their cultivation is performed with the bullock plough instead of the axe, and is of a much more permanent character. Their villages and houses are much more substantial, and are seldom changed; and habits of providence and steady industry have been developed among them which are unknown to either Gónd or Korkú of other parts. Much of this may, no doubt, be due to their fortunate occupation of a country where cultivation by annual cutting down the forest is scarcely possible, owing to the scantiness of timber and of soil on the slopes of the hills, while the neighbourhood of so large a city as Burhánpúr must always have furnished them with a regular and remunerative market for their produce.

The grass-burning, universal in the jungles of these provinces, is undoubtedly beneficial in a great variety of ways. It allows, and assists by the manure of the ashes, a crop of green and tender grass-shoots to appear for the grazing of vast herds of cattle, which form great part of the wealth of the people in the neighbourhood of jungle tracts. It kills multitudes of snakes and noxious insects. It probably prevents much malaria that would arise from the vegetation if gradually allowed to decay. It destroys much of the harbour for wild beasts. And the ashes no doubt form a valuable ingredient in the deposits of soil carried down by the drainage of these hills to lower regions, and in the cultivable crust gradually forming in these uplands themselves. It has been held by some that these fires are very injurious to the growth of saplings of teak and other valuable trees. But it is an undoubted fact that teak seeds will germinate and produce seedlings where the grass has been fired better than where it has not; and it is not well established that much permanent injury is afterwards done to the seedlings.

The labour of exploring such forests as those I have described during the hot season, when alone they are sufficiently open and free from malaria, is immense—day after day toiling over those interminable basaltic ridges, where many marches have often to be made without meeting an inhabitant, without often a single green tree for shelter, and dependent for water on a few stagnant pools puddled up by the feet of wild animals. This was what often fell to the lot of the forest officers of those early days. I doubt if many of them would have gone on with the task but for the love of sport and adventure which probably led to their original selection of a jungle life; and there is not one of them whose health did not, after a few years, give way under the combined assaults of malaria and a fiery sun.

Vast tracts of the most sterile portion of this region are absolutely without water during some months of the hot season; and in many others there is no more than perhaps a single small pool, in some shaded hollow of the rocks, for many miles on end. The only animal which can inhabit such wastes as these is the nílgaí, which can and does pass many days without drinking; and scattered herds of them are accordingly found even in the driest parts. The bison wanders over the whole of the forest and hilly portion of the tract, wherever the absence of man and cattle, and abundance of bamboo cover and water, afford him the needful conditions. The deer tribe comprises the Sámbar (*Rusa aristotelis*) and the Axis or Spotted Deer (*Axis maculatus*) in large numbers, and, more rare, the Barking Deer (*Cervulus aureus*), besides the little four-horned antelope already mentioned. The Hog Deer (*Axis porcinus*) does not, I believe, occur so far to the south-west as the trap country. The spotted deer is never found except in the neighbourhood of the larger rivers. Abundance of water and green shade appear to be first conditions of its existence. A few barking deer are found scattered all over the tract, though never very far from water.

Sámbar are rarely found in the very dry interior, but sometimes travel to rest during the day to a long distance from the water hole or stream where they drink at night. On the level table-land they are not very numerous, preferring the slopes and summits of the hills. But no animal changes its location so much, according to the season of the year, abundance of food, etc., as the sámbar. Wherever the bison is found, the sámbar is certain to be as well; but his range is not so confined as the bison's, being much more tolerant of the propinquity of man and of grazing herds of domestic cattle. While the crops of the table-land and lower plains are green the herds of sámbar come out to feed on them at night, remaining during the day near the edge of the jungle, unless disturbed and driven into the depths of the forest by man. They also feed, however, on a great variety of jungle products; and move about in apparently the most capricious manner in search of them. The short green grass that clothes the banks of pools and springs, and the tender shoots of young trees and bushes, may be said to be at all times the foundation of their fare, and during the rainy season almost their only resource. Later on, in late autumn, the young wheat and grain crops of neighbouring clearances are made to pay heavy toll; and with the commencement of the hot season comes a great variety of wild fruits, all greatly relished by the deer. At one time (March and April) it is the luscious flower of the Mhowa tree, which they share with the Gónd and the bear and most other animals and birds. The Tendú, the Chironjí, the Áolá, the Bhér, and many other trees, also fruit plentifully in spring; and a little later the pods of numerous species of acacia, chiefly Babúl,[1] Reunjá,[2] Kheir,[3] and of the tamarinds which have overgrown many deserted village sites, and the fruit of several species of wild fig,[4] amply support the sámbar through the hot season. Wherever any of these are plentiful, there the marks of nightly visits by sámbar will be found in the morning. But by the earliest break of day the animals will have disappeared; and, having drunk well at some neighbouring water, will probably be well on their way to their resting-place for the day. For the next hour or two they are often to be found at a few miles' distance, apparently loitering about, but all the time slowly making their way in a certain direction, higher up the hills and towards denser cover, and keeping a heedful watch on possible pursuers. As they penetrate deeper into the waste country their watchfulness diminishes, but they generally take a long and

[1] *A. Arabica.*
[2] *A. Leucophlœa.*
[3] *A. catechu.*
[4] *F. indica, F. religiosa,* and *F. guleria.*

keen survey of all their surroundings before lying down for the day. At all times but the rutting season (October and November) the heavy old stags remain mostly solitary, a few young animals only remaining with the herd, which consists of ten to fifteen individuals. The old stags usually travel deeper into the forest and higher up the hills before lying down than the herd, which is often found within a mile or so of their feeding ground. In all cases a patch of longish grass is selected, and a regular form like that of a hare is made by each individual. Each form is usually in the shade of a small tree, the side or top of the hill, where grass is long but trees not very numerous or thick, being preferred to very dense thickets; and it is curious with what skill the spot is selected, so that the deepest shade shall fall on the form at about three o'clock in the afternoon, which is the hottest portion of the day. Hundreds of forms will sometimes be found in one locality, every one of them at precisely the same point of the compass from its sheltering tree. The large stags do not seem to care so much about shade, and generally lie on the side of some little depression on a hill top, sheltered only by long grass. Their forms can be readily distinguished from those of the others by their greatly superior size. These forms are generally made when the grass is green, and are occupied at intervals all the rest of the year. More than one herd and a few solitary stags will not usually be found in the same tract of country; but in the rutting season they collect together in much larger numbers on the tops of the high plateaux; and the hoarse roar of the stags may then be heard echoing far and wide in the silent night. When lying down for the day, sámbar, and particularly the solitary stags, will frequently allow one to approach and pass them quite close without getting up, trusting to concealment in the grass; and it is really almost impossible in many places for the sportsman on foot to see them unless he actually stumbles on their forms. The hard, yellow grass, while unburnt, leaves next to no trail of the passage of a single deer, and thus the search for sámbar on foot after the hour when they lie down is seldom very successful.

If information can be got from the people who frequent

the jungles for wood-cutting, etc., of whereabouts the sámbar are feeding and resting at that particular season, capital sport can be got with them in the daytime with the aid of a riding elephant. This enables you to see over the grass, and generally starts any sámbar that may be lying down within about a hundred yards. The elephant must be thoroughly trained to stop dead short on deer getting up, and should not be furnished with a howdah, the simple pad or *chárjámá* being preferable for this sort of shooting; and the smaller and more active the elephant is the better. You should start about eleven o'clock and hunt till sundown, proceeding as silently as possible through the longest patches of grass, with rifle on full cock, for you do not generally get much time to make ready once the deer get up. The presence of recently used forms (which will be known by the droppings) will indicate the probable proximity of deer; and it is better to beat thoroughly a limited area than hastily a large extent of country. Where the hills rise by steps, as is often the case in the trap country, the outer edge of each step is the most likely place, and the sámbar will almost always run up-hill. A standing shot may sometimes be had during a few seconds after the sámbar first rise, but more generally they dart off at full speed at once, and then comes into play the most difficult of all the arts of the rifleman—snap-shooting at running game off an elephant. The elephant is never *perfectly* still for more than a moment, and its short swing must be allowed for as well as the pace of the deer. The sámbar is, of course, from its great size and distinct colour, much more easy to hit than the spotted deer, or barking, or hog, deer; but still it is amazing what a preponderance of clear misses the best shots will make at even running sámbar off the elephant, until long and constant practice has given the peculiar knack which is so difficult to attain. It is, however, by far the most deadly as well as one of the most enjoyable ways of hunting the sámbar. The best stags will, however, seldom be obtained by this method, lying as they do on the tops of remote hills, where one might search for and not find them for a week.

Driving a large extent of country with a long line of beaters is the commonest method of hunting sámbar. It is frequently successful, and often secures a good stag; but for my own part I have very rarely resorted to it. It is difficult often to get a sufficient number of beaters without oppression, and accidents often occur to them from the enclosure of dangerous wild beasts. The whole country is disturbed; the shooting of a creature driven up to you, without the exercise either of skill or any other manly quality on your own part, is not sport; and lastly, to prove successful, a large number of sportsmen are required to guard the numerous passes; and it never has been my fortune (not that I have much regretted it) to be out with a large hunting party in India. A few times, however, I have helped to drive a jungle, generally for some other game than sámbar, and these have sometimes proved memorable occasions.

In the Jubbulpúr district, I was beating a wooded hill-side for sámbar as the shades of evening were drawing on, and the beaters had nearly reached the end of the drive when I suddenly saw them swarming up trees, and the shout reached me of "Two tigers are afoot!" I was then trying for the first time a rifle made on Jacob's principle for explosive shells, and congratulated myself on having so good an opportunity for testing it. Anxiously I waited behind my little green bush, the beaters creating a din enough to deafen a dozen tigers, till at last I saw a striped form glide across an open spot in front, and advancing in my direction. With finger on the trigger I was awaiting his appearance at the next break in the low jungle, when suddenly I heard the bushes crashing on my left, and a large tiger bounded into the jungle pathway on which I was standing, and cantered towards my position. Wheeling round, I delivered the right barrel of the Jacob in his left shoulder, on receiving which he rolled over like a rabbit. At the moment I fired my eye caught a glimpse of the other tiger close by, in the direction I had first seen him; so, seeing the first disposed of, I again fronted, and, with a steady aim, gave No. 2 the left barrel through the neck. As luck would have it, the spine was broken, and he dropped on the spot. All this occupied but a few seconds, being as quick a right and left as ever I fired. On turning my attention again to the first tiger, I was just in time to see him reach the thick jungle some twenty paces off, and, before I could seize another gun, he had disappeared. I had time to perceive, however, that his right hind leg was broken in the body; the shell must, therefore, as he was hit in the left shoulder, have traversed his body from stem to stern; and yet here were none of the immediate paralysing effects ascribed to these shells at close quarters. On walking up to the second "tiger," what was my disgust to find that it was not a tiger after all, but only a huge striped hyæna I had shot, having mistaken his disproportionately large head in the imperfect light for that of the jungle king! The shell had passed completely through his neck, but, if it exploded at all, must have done so after passing out. The other was a veritable tiger, however. We followed him a little way by his footprints and blood, but it was getting very dark, and prudence compelled us to leave him till the morning. We failed, however, to find him then, though we hunted about the whole day; and it was not till some days after that a cowherd found his rotting remains beside a pool of water, many miles away.

On another occasion I secured the largest sámbar horns I have ever seen, in a drive. It was in the Borí teak forest, a lovely little valley nestling under the northern scarp of the Máhádeo hills, and surrounded on three sides by its mural precipices. Being very inaccessible from the plains, more teak trees have here escaped the destroying timber contractor than almost anywhere else; and R., D., and myself were engaged in demarcating its boundaries as a reserved forest. Having toiled for some days putting up cairns of stones along the open southern border, where it is not enclosed by precipices, and completed the business, we decided to wind up with a drive in the forest itself for sámbar, and the chance of a few bison whose tracks we had seen during our work. The grass was so long and the forest so thick that driving was then almost the only possible way of getting game. We had had a number of

Gónds and Korkús out with us at the boundary work, and the prospect of abundance of meat readily induced them to beat for us. A long slope of broken ground between the foot of the scarp and the bottom of the glen was to be beaten crossways; D. took the post just below the scarp, R. remained near the bottom, and I had the middle place. I screened myself behind the thick double trunk of a teak tree, forking from the ground. The beat was a short one, and I had not waited long before a tremendous crashing on the hill-side above me, followed by a shot from D., announced the approach of some heavy animal. I thought it was a bull bison at least, and was surprised when a sámbar stag burst through the underwood just in front of me, and, with horns laid along his flanks, clattered down the steep hill-side. He was going full speed, and was much screened by the long grass and dry bamboos, which he scattered on every side in his passage, so that I had not much confidence in the broadside shot wherewith I greeted him proving successful. Something told me I had hit him, however—a sportsman who has shot much is seldom mistaken in his inward heart as to the truth of his aim—and although he crashed away apparently untouched I ran eagerly to the place where he had passed to look for blood. Before I arrived I heard the ring of a rifle in R.'s direction, and then a long holloa which told me that the stag was down. Though greatly disappointed at losing the magnificent head which I saw he carried, I went on to the trail, and there I found great gouts of the red and frothy blood that tells of a shot through the lungs. Some of the Gónds now came up, and I left them to run the trail down-hill, while I hastened down to where the stag had fallen. He lay on his side, close to R.'s post, which he had been passing full speed when he fired and toppled him over. The shot hole was, however, in his haunch, and that wound I knew would never stop a stag like this. So we turned him over and found my bullet hole on the other side, just a little too high for the heart. It was a true enough shot after all, and I was very glad when I measured by spans his splendid horns, though sorry for the disappointment of a brother sportsman.

Though not a very large stag, he was very old and rather mangy, and had a perfect head with the usual three points on each horn, and measuring from base to tip forty-one inches, round the base ten inches, and eight and a half at the thinnest part of the beam. I have never seen a larger head altogether than this in Central India. It is figured at the end of the present chapter. The horns of sámbar vary greatly in development, some being very massive but short, and others very long but slender. Really good heads every way like this one are the rare exception, and would not be seen once out of perhaps fifty animals shot. About thirty to thirty-five inches is the average length of the horns even of mature stags. Occasionally more than three tines are seen on one or both antlers; but this is an abnormal development, and such heads will generally be found of stunted growth and devoid of symmetry. Sometimes the inner and sometimes the outer tine of the terminal fork will be found the longer.

I have taken much pains to assure myself of a fact, of which I am now perfectly convinced, namely, that, neither in the case of the sámbar nor the spotted deer (both belonging to the Asiatic group of Rusinæ as distinguished from the Cervidæ or true stags), are the antlers regularly shed every year in these Central Indian forests, as is the case with the Cervidæ in cold climates.[1] No native shikárí, who is engaged all his life in the pursuit of these animals, will allow such to be the case; and all sportsmen out at that season must have seen stags with full-grown horns during the hot weather and rains, when they are supposed to have shed them. Hornless stags are seen at that season, but the great majority have perfect heads. I have also known certain stags for successive years always about the same locality, and which I have

[1] Probably on the higher hill ranges they shed them more regularly; on the Nílgherry hills I saw a number of stags in the month of July, and none of them had full-grown horns. I may add here that but one species of this deer is now recognised as inhabiting all India, including the *Gerow* of the Himalayas, and that I believe, after inspecting large collections of horns, etc., it nowhere attains greater development than in Central India.

repeatedly stalked at intervals during this time along with natives who constantly saw them, so that I could not be mistaken as to the individual; and all the time they never once dropped their horns.

One of these was a very peculiar animal, almost jet black in colour, and with large horns so white as to look almost like a cast pair bleached by the weather. He frequented, during several years I knew him, an open part of the Móná valley, a good deal resorted to by wood and grass cutters. He never could be found like other stags in the morning; but seemed to lie down before daylight in some strategical position whence he always managed to effect an escape without being seen till far out of shot. I had never even fired at him though I had seen him often, when very early one morning I was walking over the grassy plain where he was often seen, and some cart-men who were loading hay told me they had seen a stag lie down on the side of a hillock not far off. I made a long circuit to get to the other side of it, and then slowly, inch by inch and with beating heart, drew myself over the brow. Nothing was to be seen from there, and, with finger on the trigger of my little single "Henry," I crawled down the slope. Just then a stick crackled on my left, and looking round, I saw the stag running in a crouching, tiger-like fashion along the bottom of a watercourse I had not noticed, but which, doubtless, had been duly considered in the selection of his position. I had only time for a snap shot, which caught the top of his shoulder and heavily lamed him. He could go just a little faster than myself after this, and had frequently to stop. But he always got the start of me when I came up, and thus carried me some four or five miles towards the base of the hills, before a lucky shot at a very long range caught him in the centre of the neck and finished the business.

It is curious how often incidents like that one with the Borí sámbar occur. A beast shot in the lungs will run on, particularly down-hill, for several hundred yards before he drops, though then he will generally fall stone dead; and the collapse frequently occurs just when he receives another wound, though it may be a very slight one, or when anything occurs to interrupt his impetus. I remember when shooting in the Rohilkhund Terái, a hog deer ran the gauntlet of a whole line of elephants. I had fired at him first on the right with a little rifle carrying a very peculiar bullet, but we all thought we had to register a miss when he fell to the Joe Manton of old Col. S. on the extreme left of the line; and it was not till we were examining the goodly heap of slain brought in by the pad elephants on our return to camp that I thought of looking for my shot, and found that the death wound was from my rifle after all, as we cut out the little bullet from the top of its shoulder, while the Colonel's round ball had only just grazed its quarter. On another occasion I had fired at a large tiger sneaking through some thin jungle in the Bétúl district. The brute dashed ahead out of sight with loud roars, but presently came wheeling round in a circle, galloped along the bottom of a small ravine, and came up the bank of it right opposite me, as I thought with the determination of making a home charge. As his head appeared over the top I fired at it, at the distance of only some dozen paces, and he tumbled back again to the bottom, where he lay dead. My astonishment was not small to find that I had missed him clean the last time, and that he had died just in the nick of time from the first shot through his shoulders.

By far the finest sport afforded by the sámbar is when he is regularly stalked in his native wilderness, without either elephant or beaters. I will not waste a word on so vile a practice as that of shooting him at night, when he comes to the crops or drinking places. None but a native shikárí, or an European with equally poaching proclivities, would ever think of such a thing. To succeed in stalking, the camp must be pitched as near as possible to where they have been ascertained to resort at night to feed and drink. A party of the aborigines of the place must be entertained to act as scouts, people who thoroughly know the country and the haunts and habits of the deer, and who are not afraid to traverse any part of the jungles in the dark. These must be sent out in couples long before daylight to crown the most commanding hill-tops in the neighbourhood, with instructions to mark any sámbar they may see on the way from their feeding grounds to the midday resting place. When deer are observed one should remain to watch them, while the other hastens with the news to some well-marked central point, whither the sportsman himself must leisurely proceed, starting half an hour or so before daybreak, accompanied by one or two of the wild men. It is very likely he may fall in with a deer himself by the way, and get a stalk; but if not some of the scouts are almost certain to bring information in time to get at the deer before they have lain down. This method of scouting also succeeds well with bison in thin jungles where they are sometimes found; and I do not know any place where the sport of stalking the bison and sámbar in this fashion can be followed with better chance of success than in the jungles on either side of the upper Táptí valley. Indeed, the very best of this sport can be had within an easy morning's ride of the large city of Burhánpúr, in the Nimár district, situated on the Táptí, a few miles below the point where the narrow rugged valley opens out into a wide basin of fertile and highly cultivated black soil. Here the Táptí is joined by the Moná, a beautiful stream which flows clear and sparkling out of a branch of the Sátpúra range called the Hattí hills. It is one of the most singular parts of the great basaltic formation, and forms the extreme westerly termination of the highland region I am describing.

In the end of February we rode out from Burhánpúr to our camp, which was pitched at the last village in the open plain. Next morning a small tent was sent up to a little fort called Gharrí, that crowns the northern face of the Hattí range, and we ourselves took different lines through the hills on foot to the same place. The inhabitants of these hills are all Bheels, a good deal spoilt by "civilisation," being mostly lazy and thriftless, and confirmed opium eaters. They are the descendants of ancestors who were nominally converted to Mahomedanism in the days when a strong Moslem power was established at Burhánpúr, but now retain scarcely anything of their faith besides the name of the Prophet and the practice of its most elementary rites. In Mahomedan times the chiefs of these Bheels were subsidised and constituted wardens of the hill passes in this range, over which ran the main highways between the valley of the Táptí and Berár; and they still continue to receive from our Government this subsidy, which is nothing but a compensation for the blackmail levied by their turbulent ancestors from the adjoining plains. A few unconverted Bheels still remain in this country, who are chiefly the hereditary village watchmen of the Hindú villages bordering on the hills. They are usually a good deal Hindúised in manners, but retain much of the keen natural qualities that render the wilder members of the race such excellent hunters. Bheels of the wildest character are also found in the mountain region west of Asírgarh, depending for subsistence much on their bows and arrows, and still ready for any undertaking of lawlessness and peril. It is scarcely, however, within the province of this work to devote space to this tribe, which is but scantily represented in the highland region of which it treats.

The road to Gharrí lay up a fine, level, though narrow, valley in the Hattí hills, containing the sites of several old villages marked by ancient trees and Mahomedan tombs. As we overlooked, from the height of Gharrí, its long, level reach, and the narrow gorge formed by a transverse chain of little hills at its mouth, with the level, black-soil plain of the Táptí valley stretching away into the distant haze beyond, the thought suggested itself at the same time to both of us, how remarkably suited the spot was for an irrigation reservoir. Without—the land thirsting for water, being underlaid by a sandy subsoil so deep that no well can tap the stratum of moisture below it, and crowded with a dense population who pay for their dry and unfertile acres the rent that in many places is given for irrigated sugar-cane land. Within—a natural reservoir, fed by the drainage of forty square miles, and only wanting an embankment of a few hundred yards to hold back sufficient water to convert the whole of the plain without into an evergreen garden. Such sites as these, though not always so favoured by a combination of circumstances as this one, are met with at intervals along almost the whole of the frontier line between the highlands and the open plain. But, alas! the means at the command of so poor a country as India are unequal to the task of realising her own future; and the wealth of life-giving water that annually escapes through these unguarded outlets must still, for many a generation, it may be feared, be allowed to waste itself in destructive inundations and fruitless floods. We are only just beginning to realise that at the bottom of all India's wretched poverty and backwardness lies the exceeding unfertility of her land in the absence of artificial irrigation. What might be the changes in the physical conditions and economy of India were the annual rainfall saved which now escapes to the sea, it is impossible to foresee. An almost incredible increase in the productiveness of the low country, and the final banishment of the famine demon, would probably be combined with a great amelioration of the climate, and improvement of the forests of the higher regions.

Gharrí is situated on the edge of a table-land of considerable extent, but of very irregular outline; on the north winding round the head of long ravines which drain down into the valley below, and towards the south coming suddenly to a steep drop into the plains of Berár. The more open parts of this table-land have at some remote period been cultivated, the trap boulders having been cleared off and piled into rough walls enclosing large square fields. The land is in many places very deep and rich, and, the elevation being about 2000 feet, it would no doubt grow tea and coffee well. Now it is utterly waste, the lazy Bheels being satisfied with their subsidy from Government, while want of roads, and probably a bad climate, deter the cultivators of the neighbouring plains. There is plenty of water on the top, and one day it will doubtless be the seat of a considerable settlement.

At Gharrí, T. went out in the evening, and found two sámbar stags feeding on the pods of some acacias on the site of a deserted village. Being a capital stalker and a good shot, he got close in upon them, and bagged both with a right and left shot. Next day we crossed the plateau to a place called Bingárá, near which T. had a survey station to put up. The road for some distance lay over a tolerably level plain of black soil, covered by a thin scrub of teak poles and thorny bushes; but presently, leaving the plateau, passed on to a very narrow ridge which forms the backbone of these singular hills throughout their length. In some places an exceedingly steep slope of a thousand feet or so led down from this saddle-back to the plains on either side, leaving scarcely room for the path we were treading. It was a terrible business getting the baggage camels along these narrow places, studded as they were with trees, and encumbered with boulders of trap; and though we had a number of Bheels with axes to clear a passage for them they did not get in till nightfall. The views at the turns where the plains on both sides could be seen were remarkable, though scarcely to be called picturesque. At our feet steep hill-sides of crumbling basalt, covered with long yellow grass beaten almost flat by the western blasts that sweep the hills at this season, and studded over with large black boulders and the naked yellow stems of the Sálei tree. Above, short scarps of dark gray trap leading up to the flat tops of the range; and below, so near looking that you would expect a stone thrown over to light on it, and yet so far beneath that towns, and groves, and corn-fields were all melted in one indistinguishable blue haze, the long, level cotton-yielding plains of Berár.

At Bingárá the Mahomedan Nawábs of Berár had, some hundreds of years ago, constructed a pleasure house after their earnest fashion, which, despite the effects of a destructive climate, and the searching roots of the peepul and banyan figs, remains to this day, though probably never repaired, an example of the solidity of their style of construction. The massive domes, thick walls, and narrow openings combine in these buildings to form the coolest structures to be found in India. The building at Bingárá is erected on the banks of a small artificial lake, the waters of which, however, now escape a good deal through the rotten embankment, leaving behind a slime which by no means adds to the attractions of the place. The building itself was the habitation of bats and owls; and so we pitched our little tent a short way back from the lake under the shade of some immense banyan trees. Just as we arrived some dogs belonging to the Bheels, which had been ranging in the jungle, passed across the dry bed of the lake in full cry after a doe sámbar they had roused. Of course we flew to our rifles, but were just in time to miss her handsomely as she dashed into the thick jungle, followed for a little way by the dogs, who soon came limping back, however.

Next morning we took different directions to explore and hunt, each with a few Bheel attendants. My way lay along the backbone of the range beyond Bingárá. After walking some miles, examining carefully with glass and eye the declivities on either side, my Bheel henchman, a sharp lad called Chánd, or "the Moon," fixed a longer look than usual on the slope of a distant hill-side, and after a while motioned me up to him, and directed my binocular to the centre of a scrubby patch of teak forest. Presently I caught the glint of the sun on something moving, and made out a noble sámbar stag standing under the trees motionless, except that he slowly turned his antlered head from side to side, sweeping with keen vision the whole semicircle within his ken. He was not more than a mile off in a direct line; but to get to the spot it would be necessary to go several miles round the head of a long ravine. As he was almost certain to lie down where he was, we carefully marked the spot, and slipping back over the edge of the saddle started off at a brisk walk to circumvent him. The sun was well up now, and it is very hot in March even at that early hour; so that by the time we had got round into the ravine below, our temperature was considerably higher than when we started. Now commenced an excruciating advance on tiptoe, with bended backs, over a stratum of fallen teak leaves of the "tin-box" description, to step on a single one of which would be fatal to the stalk. As the only alternative foot-ground was on rounded trap boulders, given to rolling away from beneath the unwary foot, the heat developed by the exertion was greatly out of proportion to the progress made. At last, however, we sighted the red-topped tree under which we had marked our stag; and then "the Moon," stripping himself of next to his last fragment of raiment, swarmed up a teak pole to look out ahead. Nothing was seen, however, and so we stole on again, friend Chánd swarming up trees at intervals, and I balancing myself in fear and trembling on the rounded boulders. We were not to succeed, however; for the Bheel in coming off a tree accidentally stepped on a leaf, and the game was up. Though I dashed ahead at once, knowing that we could steal in no further, it was too late; and all I saw was a dark form running low, but at a great pace, through the teak scrub, too far off for a shot. I believe that this was about the only sámbar then on the hills; for though the forms where they had been lying were numerous, and both T. and I hunted the livelong day for them, not another hoof or horn did we see. The Bheels said they had all gone to "Dhowtea"—a place which we afterwards found was so difficult of access that very few of them had ever been there; and so they used it, much as we do "Jericho," to express an indefinite region where everything that can't be found elsewhere must certainly have gone.

Greatly to the surprise of the Bheels, we did shortly after this go to Dhowtea; and if its name was great before, it certainly became much more so after we had been there. Neither of us ever saw anything so extraordinary in our lives; and to the Bheels there was nothing short of magical devilry in what we found, or rather did not find. Dhowtea was a hollow on the top of the range surrounded by flat plateaux of small elevation, with a fine stream of water in the centre, and long grass all about. After a long struggle, through thick jungle and over desperate rocky ground, we reached it long after sundown, and encamped uncomfortably in the open plain for the night. The place was perfectly puddled up with the feet of sámbar, the footmarks ranging from a day to weeks old; and in the grass around were literally thousands of sámbar forms, while every second or third tree was peeled of its bark by the rubbing of the stags' horns against them. Next morning we started off, with an extra supply of ammunition, in different directions, our only fear being that we had not people enough to carry in all the enormous stags we expected to bag. For my part, I wandered round and round the plateaux, and over their tops, and through the hollow ground, and everywhere within six miles on my side of the hill; and though the sámbar signs were everywhere plentiful and recent, and there were droppings of bison also of some weeks old, not a dun hide of stag or hind did my eyes behold that morning. It was truly amazing, and I almost feared to return to camp lest all the beasts should have gone across to T.'s side, and I should find him smoking the pipe of satisfaction amid a hecatomb of slain. He had returned before myself, however; and mutual delight was no doubt displayed in our countenances when we found that each was in precisely the same plight as the other—not having seen hoof or horn between us! Half believing with the Bheels that the place was enchanted, we stayed and tried again next day, but the result was precisely the same. Then we vowed that Dhowtea of the Bheels should be written down with the blackest of spots in our mental map. We were utterly ruined, of course, with the Bheels. Having seen these multitudes of ghostly sámbar tracks, we never again found any place vacant of game but to be told with a grin, "Oh, they are gone to Dhowtea, of course!"

We were utterly beaten, and the unburnt jungle having also proved too thick for our boundary operations, we determined to retreat to the plains. But we were unwilling to return by the awful road we had come; and, a possible way down the northern face of the hill being reported, we left Dhowtea behind us the next morning, marching along the top of the range for eight or ten miles to a place called Jámtí, the residence of another of these petty Bheel chieftains, and marked by a conspicuous banyan tree which is visible from every part of the surrounding country. Thence we descended the next day to the Táptí valley, intending to return to the hills when the jungle should be clearer. The truth was, we had happened to visit Dhowtea just when nearly all the sámbar had gone down the hills to feed on some jungle fruits that had ripened in the valleys; and the few that remained were not to be found among the long unburnt grass. I believe that the immense number of marks we saw were caused by the collection of large numbers of deer there during the rutting season (late autumn).

The path we went down by wound along the top of a long spur of naked basalt. On either side were deep and almost coal-black rifts in the rock, the summits clothed scantily with thin yellow grass, and here and there a Sálei tree stunted and twisted like a corkscrew. At one point the rock assumed the form of a sheer cliff, many hundred feet in height, of the columnar structure seen occasionally in this volcanic formation, where the rock seems composed of a vast conglomeration of pentagonal pillars standing together and broken off at different lengths. This singularly favourable situation for nest-building had been occupied by an immense colony of vultures, the whole face of the rock for miles being whitened by their droppings, while numbers of the birds were perched on the cliff or sailing over the ravine. Among them were a good many of the common brown carrion vulture;[1] but the majority were the foul white scavengers[2] to be seen on every dunghill in the villages of the plains. I had often wondered where these birds bred, for although there are myriads in all inhabited tracts of Central India only a few nests are to be seen here and there in the tops of trees. Here was the puzzle solved, in the grim and retired solitude of the Valley of the Vultures. But a single hill—a few minutes' flight—separated them here from the thickly peopled plain where they find their repulsive food; and yet that ravine is probably as seldom looked on by the eye of man as if it were a guano island in the Pacific Ocean.

A few weeks after our unsuccessful trip to the Hattí hills, I heard from T. that the grass was mostly burnt, and sámbar were plentiful on the northern slope of the hills. He had also come across a preserve of bison, out of which he had bagged a bull. Early in April, therefore,

[1] *Gyps Bengalensis.* [2] *Neophum Perenopterus.*

I rode out to his camp at Chóndí—one of the deserted village sites in the valley below Gharrí. A lovelier spot for a hunting camp in the hot weather could not be found. Close by a clear and beautiful pool of water stood an enormous banyan tree, so old that many of the suckers thrown out by the branches of the parent tree had themselves become mighty stems, with branches which again had given birth to trunks of considerable girth, while the stem of the original tree had utterly decayed away. Beneath its copious shade were sheltered from the sun several tents, and numerous servants, lascars, and Bheels, besides our horses, dogs, etc. The grass on the lower hills had mostly been burnt since we were last here, and the Mhowa flowers had been falling for some time. Sámbar nightly visited some fine clumps of that tree in the bottom of the valley, a little higher up than the camp.

The next morning we sent out about half-a-dozen pairs of Bheels to look out on the hill-tops long before daybreak; and soon after ourselves started up the valley to a point where we intended to separate and take different beats. A colony of monkeys in the trees overhanging the river were "swearing" lustily about half a mile to our left, and presently we found the remains of a sámbar that had been killed during the night under the Mhowa trees by a tiger. The brute himself was doubtless making off up the valley when seen by the monkeys. Many sámbar had been feeding on the Mhowa, and fresh tracks led off in almost all directions. Just where we were about to separate a long spur ran down from the hills on the right to the valley up which we were proceeding; and as we approached it we saw in the dim gray light a long line of deer file over the top, each pausing for a second on the sky line before passing over to the far side. Watching them for a few seconds, we saw that they were followed by a large stag at a good distance in the rear. In fact, he had just commenced to climb the spur when we saw him; and at the same time he must have seen us pausing on the path, for his leisurely walk then became a run—the low crouching run, almost like a tiger's, with antlers thrown back, often adopted by a stag who wants to escape quickly and without being seen. We only saw the ridge of his back and the tips of his horns as he stole up the other side of the spur after the hinds. It is of no use for two men to follow one lot of sámbar; so, as it lay in my beat, I took after these deer, while T. held on up the valley. When I got to the top—a stiff climb of five or six hundred feet—the eastern heavens were suffused with that beautiful greenish yellow flush which immediately precedes sunrise in an Indian sky. It was light enough (it never is very dark at any time of night at this season of the year) to distinguish a couple of the Bheels perched on a higher peak of the same range; and on seeing me top the rise one of them stole softly down to me, and said that the herd, followed by the stag, had proceeded leisurely down the thickly wooded declivity on the opposite side. After a consultation, it was determined that I should keep along the top of the ridge, while two of the Bheels were to follow the track of the herd, and if they saw them come up and let me know. I went along slowly from one commanding point to another, keeping a little ahead of the Bheels, who tracked the herd along the slope, not very far below the top. In the course of one of these moves I started the herd from some long grass near the top. There were fifteen or twenty of them, but no good stags, so far as I could see as they bustled away along the hill-side in a confused mob, the round light-coloured patches on their rumps looking like so many targets as they switched their tails in the air. It was very tempting, but I wanted the fine horns of the stag and let them go. I was rewarded soon after by the appearance of the stag, walking slowly along in the same line, and showing by his dignified gait that he had no suspicion of danger. He was passing about a hundred yards below me when I pulled on his shoulder with the little single "Express" rifle, and he fell to the shot without a sound. The Bheels came running up at once, and as I had not gone down to the stag proceeded to cut his throat in the orthodox Mahomedan fashion, though I am certain he was stone dead long before they arrived. He was one of the finest harts I ever saw—in beautiful condition, with much of the cold-weather mane remaining, and of a peculiar and rare rich chestnut colour. His horns were very stout and handsome, though about four inches shorter than those of the Borí stag. The colour of the sámbar of these open light jungles is generally decidedly lighter than that of those which inhabit the more shady forests further east. Sometimes a very black stag will be found, however, even here; and the colour of all varies a good deal at different times of the year.

The next day we again went out long before daybreak. I was beckoned up a very steep hill by the Bheels on the top; and when I got there some time after the sun was up, and a good deal fatigued by the climb, I found it was only to tell me that they had seen two stags go up the *opposite* hill slope, between which and our hill there lay a valley as deep as that from which I had come up. They had never been at this scouting work before, or they had well deserved a thrashing for their pains. There was nothing for it but to descend to the valley again, which was almost severer work than coming up. The slipperiness of these trap hills when every particle of grass on them has been burnt into fine charcoal is dreadful. I never found the deer that had been seen, and soon got involved in a troublesome series of cross ravines, so that by about nine o'clock I was pretty hot and wearied in the April sun. I had almost given up hunting, and had turned for home, when something caught my eye in the bottom of a slight hollow in the hill. It looked exactly like one of the bunches of twigs that grow out of old teak stumps on these hills, with one or two dried leaves attached to them; and yet I fancied I had seen it move. I looked at it intently for at least a minute, trying to make out if it was a bunch of teak twigs or a sámbar's head and horns. It never moved the whole of this time; and, as the Bheels who were with me said it was only a stump, I turned to pass on. The glint of my rifle barrel must then have caught in the sun, for a noble stag started up from his lair, and without pausing for a second wheeled round and clattered away. My hasty shot missed him clean, and he then plunged into a ravine that lay at the back of the hollow he had been in.

I followed across, thinking I might find blood, but there was no sign, and I turned for home, swearing to expend a bullet in future on every teak stump that bore the most distant resemblance to a deer's head. The resemblance is so very close between the two objects that I cannot but think that the instinct of the animal leads him to dispose of his head so as to resemble the bunch of teak. Even the motion of the large ears of the sámbar, which they restrain only when actually in the presence of dangers, answers exactly to the stirring of a dried teak leaf in a light breeze. Indeed no one can hunt in these scantily covered hills without wondering at the extreme difficulty of making out such large animals as sámbar, bison, and bears on the open hill-side. The bison and bear precisely resemble the large black trap boulders that thickly strew every hill; and thus the glaring contrast of their black hides with the bright yellow grass frequently attracts no attention whatever.

On my way back I knocked over a four-horned antelope with very perfect horns, a long distance across a valley, with the "Express." These little creatures are very common in the hills we were hunting in, living solitary or in small groups in all parts of the range. The female is hornless, while the buck has four distinct sheathed horns. The posterior pair are four or five inches long, and set upon high pedicles covered with hair. The anterior pair are generally mere knobs, and never exceed in length an inch and three-fourths. In some specimens they are even absent altogether. The animal is found throughout India, and appears to be generally without the anterior horns in the south. Here, in Central India, some have them and some have not. I never could see any other difference between them; but it is not altogether certain that there are not two distinct species. The preponderance of females appears to be very great, quite as great as in the case of the ordinary Indian antelope, though from their not congregating in large herds, it is not so much observed. To kill a buck at all is rare, and to kill one with four well-developed horns is much rarer still. They seem to be very retiring little creatures, never coming to the crops, and moving very little out of the limited area where they find food and water. There is scarcely a water-hole in all these regions which is not frequented by one or more, and they are nearly certain to be found during the day lying in the nearest patch of grass. They make little forms like those of the sámbar, and allow themselves almost to be trodden on before they start. They run for a short distance at an incredible velocity, with their necks low, and making themselves as small as possible, till they suddenly stop, but always with such art that a tree stump, or mound, or thick bush shall screen them from the observer; then another short dash, and another halt, and so on till out of sight. They are nearly sure to be found in the same place next day, however. When seen walking about undisturbed in the jungle their pace is most curious, raising their feet absurdly high as if stepping over large stones, and putting them down with a fastidious delicacy and softness as if they were walking on eggs—a simultaneous "bobbing" action of the head and neck giving them altogether very much the gait of "that generous bird the hen." They live on the green shoots of bushes, young grass, and fallen jungle fruits; and their venison is coarse and tasteless.

The same afternoon two of the Bheels, who had been out scouting in a very solitary part of the hills to the east of the valley, came in and reported a large herd of bison as always to be found where they had been. Nothing is more difficult than to get really reliable news about the haunts of animals, until you can get the few jungle people who do know thoroughly enlisted in your interests. If you ask any one else, or even them when they don't care to tell you, ten to one they will charge their faces with a stare of utter vacuity, and ask you "if it is not a jungle," implying that, if you allow so much, of course you must know where to find beasts. The little block of hills we were going to visit is quite shut in from all the ordinary lines of travelling in these parts. There is no road into it by which carts can be taken; cattle are never sent to graze there by the neighbouring villagers; and thus no one ever goes into it, excepting a single family of Bheels, who are the hereditary Turvees[1] of an ancient village, said to have existed in the palmy days of Mahomedan rule in one of its valleys, and now represented by half-a-dozen Mhowa trees, the fruit of which these Bheels still go annually to gather. Two of the family happened to be among our scouts, and knew every inch of the country. The one who brought us the news rejoiced in the name of Jhingra, or "The Shrimp;" and really, by some fortuitous accident, his long attenuated arms and legs, and curiously shrivelled features, with a few long feeler-like bristles in the place of a beard, gave him a very strong resemblance to that innocent crustacean. The name of the other, who had been left perched in a tree to watch the beeves, cannot be handed down to fame, having been lost in the secondary appellation of "The Skunk." I must say the olfactory powers of the bison lost greatly in my estimation when I found that they had remained quietly grazing for half a day within a mile or so of this most odorous of Turvees! The Shrimp was very anxious that we should proceed there and then to attack the bison, urging how uncomfortable the Skunk would be if left clinging to the upper branches of a tree all night, and patting his shrivelled stomach to show how delighted they both would be to be at close quarters with a bison steak. We pitied the Skunk, and pointed out to the Shrimp a quarter of sámbar venison hanging up from which he might satisfy his own cravings; but we had no idea of starting off after bison six miles away in *that* country at three o'clock in the afternoon.

It wanted a good deal of arrangement, in fact, to hunt that country; and we never found out the proper way to do it till just as we were leaving it. As it was, we sent round a tent and the needful supplies by a very circuitous road, down our valley to the plain, along the foot of the hills for a good many miles, and then up another valley that was said to run into the heart of the bison country. The people had directions to go as far up the valley as

[1] The Turvee is the chief of a Bheel clan or settlement; and all heads of Bheel villages in this part of the country are so called by courtesy.

they could find water, and pitch there. We were to go straight across next day, and, after hunting up the bison, come down the head of the further valley to the camp; and dearly we paid for giving such indefinite instructions before we were done.

Next morning we started under the guidance of the Shrimp, and mounted on two redoubtable Deccanee ponies, who we had found could go in these hills wherever we could, and saved us a good lot of hard work in the sun. The way lay up a long burnt valley, in which tracks of sámbar, and the pug of a large tiger who had been following them during the night, were plainly visible. It was too late, however, to see any game out in such open country; and we wound up the rugged pathway leading to the top of the hill without having come across a single animal.

We now came on to a tolerably level plateau, and rode on for some miles, keeping a sharp look-out for animals. The plateau was beginning to shelve down towards a ravine filled with clumps of bamboo, beyond which rose another flat-topped ridge, when my eye rested on a spot of denser shadow in the thin sálei jungle that topped the further ridge. Pulling up to use the binocular, I discovered the whole herd of bison grazing quietly in the cover. We were a couple of miles away at least, and silently withdrew into a hollow that would lead us down into the ravine. T. and I now advanced with the Shrimp, leaving our ponies and the other Bheels to follow us on hearing a shot. We had a long, hot stalk, and on reaching the plateau found that the herd had disappeared. The place was evidently a regular resort of the wild cattle, the long grass being twisted about into wisps by their feet, and all the bushes broken and grazed away. We stalked over the plateau with cocked rifles, the Shrimp swarming trees to look out ahead; but no beeves did we see, except a cow and her little calf making off over a distant rising ground at a slow trot, the sunlight glancing every now and again on their beautifully bronzed hides. There were so many tracks that to follow the herd was hopeless; the Skunk was nowhere to be seen; and so we coasted round the edge of the plateau, peering down among the bamboo clumps in the hope of discovering the herd. After going about half round I suddenly almost ran up against a cow in some long grass; and immediately T., who was a little to my right called out that the whole herd was standing down below among the bamboos. My cow had bolted off in a great fright, and I ran up to T. in time to see ten or twelve bison scrambling up the opposite side of the ravine—a long shot from where we were. A bull brought up the rear, and there was another covered by the clump of cows; so we opened fire on the former, and the third shot broke his leg. He had the other shots too, and after limping on a bit, staggered and fell over down the hill. Being much fatigued by the heat of a very sultry April day, we waited there till the people came up with our leathern water-sack to have a drink, and then went over to the bull, who was still alive but unable to rise. The Skunk, who had luckily been exactly in the line of the herd's retreat, now came running up, and, standing afar off by special request, told us whither they had gone.

There was a mighty black bull among them, whose horns we determined to have, if possible; so, sending the ponies, and with them, alas! the water, under the guidance of the Skunk, to wait us at a point in the valley beyond for which we thought the herd was making, we started off on their tracks. In going along the edge of a spur T. saw three or four of the bison standing under the ridge of the hill, and we went round to stalk them. It was a long way and the heat was really fearful, so that we were not perhaps so cautious in our approach as we should have been, and the result was that before we got up we heard the alarmed snort of the sentry, and the crash of the herd through the jungle. We now walked along a ridge between two deep valleys—on the right hand that in which the camp should be, and on the left another leading down to where we had started from in the morning. We saw the startled herd far below us in the latter, crossing over at a swinging trot, and afterwards mounting the range beyond. The Shrimp said they were doubtless making for "Dhow-tea"! Further on, the Shrimp pointed to a motionless coal-black form standing against the sky-line, which the telescope showed to be a mighty bull. He stood for a few minutes till the cows came up and passed across him and then stalked solemnly after them. He, too, was no doubt going to Dhowtea! We were walking on disgusted when my eye caught another jet-black figure among the trees ahead of us, and we crouched into nothing as another bull walked slowly into an open space about half a mile ahead. After gazing round in every direction he slowly began to descend to the same valley. He, too, appeared like the rest of them, to have started for Dhowtea. But he was not there yet, and we determined at least to give him a run for it; so, waiting till he was concealed by the fall of the ground, we doubled down a rocky watercourse, to cut him off, if possible, from the valley. We succeeded; for he evidently got our wind, and sheered off from the pass down to the river, walking slowly and magnificently along the edge of a precipitous fall, apparently looking for another way down. There was none such, however; and we followed him along in short running stalks, gaining on him every time he got hidden for a minute by inequalities of the ground. The hill we were on gradually narrowed to the saddleback form so common in this range, and not far ahead seemed to terminate in an abrupt descent to the valley. There seemed to be no doubt we had him in a trap if we would only have patience; for he must either take that header to reach the valley, or charge back along the ridge over our mangled corpses! He became very cautious as he neared the end, zigzagging across the narrow ridge, and using all his senses to detect the pursuer he evidently suspected. We were slowly roasting on the bare, shadeless sheet of basalt that topped the ridge, lying as we had to do prone on it to escape his sight. I would have given a rupee per drop for the contents of our water-sack just then. At last, after what seemed an age, the tall black form of the bull slowly sank over the end of the hill. He was going down, then, after all, and there was nothing for it but a rush. A rush we accordingly made; but suddenly pulled up, much taken aback, as we saw the bull again emerge and stand in full sight of us, though much covered about the body by scrubby sálei stems, on the extreme point of the ridge. It was really a most ticklish situation. Had he charged, and our shots failed to stop him, T. might have escaped with a few broken bones by rolling down on his side of the hill; but on mine there was a sheer descent of a hundred feet, and the ridge itself offered not the slightest shelter. But we each had a double-barrelled, breech-loading, twelve-bore rifle — a battery against which few animals can stand. I saw T. sighting him, and heard the bull emit a low tremulous moan that sounded like mischief. His vitals were protected from me by the sálei stems, so I kept my double shot in reserve in case of accidents. The ball thudded against something, as it turned out, probably a sálei tree; and the bull at once disappeared over the edge. We now ran to the spot, and saw him below thundering down the steep hill-side at a tremendous pace. Utterly winded by running, and half dead with heat and thirst, the remaining three shots had no effect; and then we sat down, perfectly exhausted, to watch the bull as he gained the valley and crossed the stream-bed, halting for a few seconds under a shady tree to look back ere he set himself to mount the further slope, which he did in the line taken by the other bison. He, too, was fairly off for Dhowtea—and, as it seemed and we hoped, seeing that we could not have him, without a wound.

Life was now a blank. The Shrimp had lingered far behind, and there was no one to show us the way, while the Skunk was goodness knows where with the ponies and water. So we slowly and sadly descended the hill to our own valley, and walked on in the probable direction of camp, chewing grass in our speechless mouths. About a mile further on we were joined by the villainous Shrimp, who had taken a line of his own for home when he saw us bent on pushing the big bull to extremities. There was no water in all this valley, he said, excepting one pool miles ahead where our camp should be. After getting the direction, we started him off to find the ponies and water and bring them to meet us. It was now midday, and the sun was blazing hot—a quivering haze that made the eyes twinkle playing along the surface of the earth. After plodding along for some miles more, we came to a pathway by which we thought the ponies must pass; and there we sat down completely exhausted in the scanty shade of a wild fig-tree. A Mhowa grew close by, and some of its luscious flowers tempted us to try if they would assuage our raging thirst. Bah! never was anything more horrible than the clammy taste and fetid odour of that sickening product. Our mouths were now glued up as well as parched, and when at last the people came we could only make signs for the water, and replied not at all to the Skunk when he assured us that a big bear had been besieging him and the ponies on the road for ever so long not very far from where we were. After a draught that no one could appreciate unless he has hunted the "bounding bison" through an April day in the trap hills of Nimár, we jumped on the welcome ponies and galloped up the valley to our tent. Revived by breakfast and cold claret cup, we spent the rest of the day in skinning and preserving the head of the bison we had shot. A fine solemn look have the features of a dead bull. The horns alone are nothing of a trophy compared to the complete head, which should if possible be saved entire.

Next morning our Bheels were out early, and we ourselves made for the hill of Alí-Bál-Kót, or the "High Exalted Fort," which being translated means the ruinous little mud keep of one of these pensioned Bheel chiefs. They are all "Rájás" of course, and maintain standing armies of one or two ragamuffins apiece. We always had the "king" of the territory we were in in our camp, and it was really disappointing to find how little His Majesty differed from any other of these debauched-looking, opium-eating, and utterly ignorant and brutal Mahomedan Bheels. Our shikárí and scouts—Shrimp, Skunk, and Co.—were ordinary unconverted Bheels, and far superior in every respect to the converts, who, however, looked down upon them as an unregenerate lot.

We had not proceeded far towards the foot of the hills when a Bheel on a hill-top waving a cloth caught our sight; and on going up we saw about five or six stag sámbar slowly wending their way along the far side of a valley towards the interior of the hills. Our yesterday's shooting had no doubt cleared this part of the hills of all the bison, so we made after these deer, watching them over the rising grounds and then running close in behind them. At last we saw them apparently halted for the day in a shady place. Two of them appeared to have first-rate antlers, and we stalked round a long way to get in on them from above, and without giving them our wind. We blundered it, however, coming down at the wrong point, and the herd broke a long way to our left hand. T. fired into their backs as they struggled up the opposite slope in a confused gang, but without apparent effect; and the last of them was disappearing over the brow when I took a long shot at him with my single "Express." It was two hundred and fifty yards at the least, but I had often before killed as far with this rifle, and down he dropped. Crossing over, we found the stag lying dead; but, though it was one of the two we had marked, his antlers were very inferior. Nothing is more deceptive than the apparent size of sámbars' horns while stalking; as they have all the same number of points, the guide to size and quality afforded by the branches of the red deer is here wanting. On examination we found this to be still another instance of the curious occurrences before mentioned; for it was T.'s ball after all that had killed him, while mine had missed!

After this we made a long round through the hills looking for bison, but without success; and were descending towards the camp by a long narrow spur of bare basalt, when we saw the Skunk near the top of an isolated eminence rising out of the valley violently signalling to us; and soon after we were scanning the proportions of a fine bull bison lying down on the further side under the shade of a small tree. It was a very easy stalk, and we crept in to about seventy yards in the grass. T. fired both barrels at him as he lay, which is always a mistake, the vital regions being then greatly shielded by the enormous development of the shoulder and dorsal ridge. He sprang up and plunged away across our front, swerving round towards us in a fashion that made the Bheels take to their heels. On receiving my shots, however, he turned again; and, executing a most extraordinary series of plunges, with his head between his fore-legs and hind-quarters and tail in the air, disappeared down a small ravine. We were soon up, and followed along the side. I

SÁMBAR HORNS. (*Scale, one tenth.*)

was rather ahead, and found him lying very sick in the bottom of the hollow. When he perceived me he staggered up and shook his horns in a threatening manner; but it was all up with the poor brute, and a shot in the neck rolled him over finally on his back. I think if our yester-day's bull had been as viciously inclined as this fellow, we might have had more of it than we bargained for on that narrow ledge.

We had to return next day to the station, and bid adieu to these singular hills. The hot season was fairly on, when no one can long endure the exertion of hunting on foot the sámbar and bison in hilly country. My readers will probably think I have described to them but poor sport compared to what they have often read of before. It is so easy to throw in half-a-dozen bull bison in a day's sport by a stroke of a pen, that the temptation to meet the wishes of the reader is difficult to resist. I have, however, stuck to the exact facts of a by no means heavy bag, on purpose to give a more accurate idea of what such shooting really means—namely, very hard work and much exposure for an average of certainly not more than one head of game a day, and often much less. One of the hardest workers and best shots I ever knew, who had only time for a few weeks' bison and sámbar shooting in the year, and then went at it tooth and nail, told me he was always proud if he could keep his average up to one a day for the time he was out; and I am certain that very few ever do so much. By taking every chance at cow bison and doe sámbar, of course the bag could be largely increased; and I heard of two men who one year murdered in this way twenty-eight bison in a week. This is not sport, of course, nor are the performers sportsmen. The bison is already, it would seem, diminishing in numbers; certainly his range is becoming greatly contracted. He is one of the most harmless animals in the whole world to the industry of man, and, fairly hunted, affords perhaps the best sport in India; it would be a pity, then, if his numbers should be unduly diminished by unsportsmanlike conduct.

CHAPTER VII

THE TIGER

While wandering about during the months of April and May, in the teak forests of the Bétúl district, I devoted a day now and then to the sport of tiger-shooting; and it was the laudable custom of the forest officers to spare, if possible every year, a few weeks during the height of the hot season, for the purpose of making an impression on the numerous tigers which at that time rendered working in the forests and carrying timber so dreaded by the natives, and consequently costly to Government.

Although there is much in the sport of tiger-hunting that renders it inferior as a mere exercise, or as an effort of skill, to some other pursuits of these regions (for many a man has killed his forty or fifty tigers who has never succeeded in bagging, by fair stalking, a single bull bison or a stag sámbar), yet there is a stirring of the blood in attacking an animal before whom every other beast of the forest quails, and an unarmed man is helpless as the mouse under the paw of the cat—a creature at the same time matchless in beauty of form and colour, and in terrible power of offensive armature—which draws men to its continued pursuit after that of every other animal has ceased to afford sufficient excitement to undergo the toil of hunting in a tropical country.

It will have been gathered from previous descriptions that the hot season, the height of which is in April and May, is the most favourable time for hunting the tiger. Then the water supply of the country is at its lowest ebb; and the tiger, being very impatient of thirst, seeks the lowest valleys, where, too, much of the game he preys on has congregated, and where the village cattle are regularly watered. In Central India tigers vary a good deal in their habits and range; and they may be roughly classed into those which habitually prey on wild animals, those which live chiefly on domestic cattle, and a few that confine their diet to the human species. Not, of course, that any tiger adheres invariably to the same sort of prey. But there are a large number that appear to prefer each of the former methods of existence, and a few that select the latter.

The regular game-killing tiger is retired in his habits, living chiefly among the hills, retreating readily from man, and is altogether a very innocuous animal, if not even positively beneficial in keeping down the herds of deer and nílgái that prey upon the crops. His hot-weather haunt is usually some rocky ravine among the hills, where pools of water remain, and shelving rocks or overhanging trees afford him shelter from the sun. He is a light-made beast (called by shikárís a *lodhia bágh*), very active and enduring, and, from this as well as his shyness, generally difficult to bring to bag.

The cattle-lifter, again, is usually an older and heavier animal (called *oontia bágh*, from his faintly striped coat resembling the colour of a camel), very fleshy, and indisposed to severe exertion. In the cool season he follows the herds of cattle wherever they go to graze; and then, no doubt, in the long damp grass brings many a head of game also to bag. In the hot weather, however, the openness of the forest and the numerous fallen leaves preclude a lazy monster of this sort from getting at game; and he then locates himself in some strong cover, close to water, and in the neighbourhood of where the cattle are taken to drink and graze about on the greener herbage then found by the sides of streams, and, watching his opportunity, kills a bullock as he requires it, and drags it into his cover. Of course, a good many head of game are also killed by such a tiger when they come to drink, but so long as he can easily procure cattle, he does not trouble himself to hunt for them.

Native shikárís recognise more or less two kinds of tigers, with the names I have given above. It may be matter for speculation which is cause, and which is effect. Is it that as tigers grow old and heavy they take to the easier life of cattle-lifting? Or has the difference of their pursuits, continued for generations, actually resulted in separate breeds, each more adapted for its hereditary method of existence? I, myself, believe the former to be the truth, and that there really is only one variety of tiger in all peninsular India. It is only to extreme specimens that the above distinctive names are applied; and the great majority are of an intermediate character, and not distinguished by any particular name. The larger and older the animal, the more yellow his coat becomes, and the fainter and further apart are the stripes. Small tigers are sometimes so crowded with the black stripes as almost to approach the appearance of a *melanoid* variety. A few specimens of white tigers with fulvous stripes have also been mentioned, though I have never heard of one in Central India. The tiger, like all animals that I am acquainted with, is subject to slight variations of appearance and conformation amongst individuals; and local circumstances, and perhaps "natural selection," may tend to give the race something of peculiarity in different localities. But none of these has as yet, I believe, reached the point of even permanent variation.

It is useless to devote much time to hunting the hill tigers that prey on game alone. They are so scattered over extensive tracts of jungle, and are so active and wary, that it is only by accident that they are ever brought to bag.

Favourably situated covers are almost certain to hold one or more cattle-eating tigers during the hot weather; and however many are killed, others will shortly occupy their place. A favourite resort for these tigers is in the dense thickets formed of jáman, karondá, and tamarisk—evergreen bushes whose shade is thickest in the hot weather, and which grow in islands and on the banks of partially dried-up stream-beds. A thick and extensive cover of this sort, particularly if the neighbouring river banks are furnished, as is often the case, with a thick scrubby jungle of thorny bushes, through which ravines lead up to the open country where cattle graze, is a certain find in the hot season. Sometimes considerable gatherings of tigers take place in such favourable places. I have twice known five, and once seven, tigers to be driven out of one cover at the same time; and I think the season of love-making has something to do with these meetings. More usually it is a solitary male tiger, or a tiger and tigress, or a tigress with her grown-up cubs, that are found in one place. The tigress cannot breed more than once in three years, I believe; for the cubs almost invariably stay with her till they are over two years old, and nearly full-grown. The greatest number of cubs I have ever found with a tigress was three. These were small, however, and I never saw more than two grown-up along with the female.

A single tiger will kill an ox about every five days, if not disturbed, eating, if very hungry, both hind-quarters the first night. He will not go further than he can help after this meal, but will return again next night to the carcase, which in the meantime he often stores away under a bank, or covers with leaves, etc. This time he will finish all but the head; next night he will clean the bones; and then for a couple of days he will not take the trouble to hunt for a meal, though he will strike down another quarry if it comes near him. Should he have been fired at, however, when thus returning to his kill, he will frequently abandon such measures of economy, and kill a fresh bullock whenever he is hungry. A tigress and grown cubs are also far more destructive, finishing a bullock in a night, and, like the daughters of the horseleech, always crying for more. The young tigers seem to rejoice in the exercise of their growing strength, springing up against trees and scratching the bark as high as they can reach by way of gymnastics, and, if they get among a herd of cattle, striking down as many as they can get hold of. The tiger very seldom kills his prey by the "sledge-hammer stroke" of his fore-paw, so often talked about, the usual way being to seize with the teeth by the nape of the neck, and at the same time use the paws to hold the victim and give a purchase for the wrench that dislocates the neck.

Tigers that prey on cattle are generally perfectly well known to the cowherds and others who resort to their neighbourhood. They seldom molest men, and are often driven away from their prey, after killing it, by the unarmed herds. Frequently they are known by particular names; and they really seem in many cases to live among the villagers and their herds much like a semi-domesticated animal, though, from a mutual consent to avoid direct interviews as much as possible, they are chiefly known by their tracks in the river beds and by their depredations on the cattle. They do not, of course, confine their attacks to the cattle of a single village, usually having a whole circle of them where they are on visiting terms, and among which they distribute their favours with great impartiality. The damage they do on the whole is very great, sixty or seventy head of cattle, worth from £5 to £10 apiece, being destroyed by one such animal in the course of a year. Generally there is at least one native in every circle of villages whose profession is that of "shikárí," or hunter, and who is always on the outlook to shoot the village tiger. When he hears of a bullock having been killed he proceeds to the spot, and, erecting a platform of leafy boughs in the nearest tree, watches by night for the return of the tiger, who, though he may kill and lap the blood during the day, never feeds before sunset. Generally he does not get a shot, the tiger being extremely suspicious when approaching his "kill," and the shikárís being usually such bunglers at their work as to disturb him by the noise of their preparations. Often he misses when he does shoot, the jungle-king being somewhat trying to the nerves; and if he kills one tiger in the course of the year he considers himself lucky. His weapon is a long matchlock, which he loads with six "fingers" of powder and two bullets. These fly a little apart, and if they hit are usually the death of the tiger. His method of shooting is sometimes imitated by lazy European sportsmen.

Another way of hunting ordinary tigers is to beat them out of their midday retreat with a strong gang of beaters, supplied with drums, fireworks, etc., the guns themselves being posted at likely spots ahead. This plan is often successful, when the operations are directed by some one who knows the ground. Frequently, however, the tiger is not found at all, and moreover he very commonly manages to escape at the sides, or break back through the beat, without coming up to the guns at all. It has also the disadvantage of exposing the beaters to much danger; and there are few who shoot in this fashion who have not had more than one beater killed before them. To stalk in on a tiger in his retreat on foot is generally impracticable, as a man commands so little of a view in thick cover that he rarely sees the tiger in time for a shot. In some places, however, where tigers lie in rocky places inaccessible to elephants, this is the only way to do; and a very certain one it then is, there being generally little cover and plenty of commanding elevations whence to see and shoot. The best way of hunting the tiger is undoubtedly that usually adopted in Central India—namely to bring in the aid of the trained elephant, and follow and shoot him in his midday retreat. Any one who thinks he has only got to mount himself on the back of an elephant, and go to a jungle where he has heard of tigers, to make sure of killing one, will find himself very much mistaken on trying. A number of sportsmen with a large line of elephants may kill tigers if they simply beat through likely covers for a long enough time—and many tigers are thus killed—or by driving the jungle with beaters, without the possession of any skill in woodcraft whatever. But no sort of hunting requires more careful arrangements, greater knowledge of the habits of the animal, perseverance, and good shooting, than the pursuit of the tiger by a single sportsman with a single elephant.

At the outset of one's experience in forest life it is impossible to avoid the belief that the tiger of story is about to show himself at every step one takes in thick jungle; and it is not till every effort to meet with him has been used in vain that one realises how very little danger from tigers attends a mere rambler in the jungles. During ten years of pretty constant roaming about on foot in the most tigerish localities of the Central Provinces, I have only once come across a tiger when I was not out shooting, and only twice more when I was not actually searching for tigers to shoot. In truth, excepting in the very haunts of a known man-eater, there is no danger whatever in traversing any part of the jungles of this, or I believe any other part of India.

Some people affect to despise the practice of using elephants in following tigers, and talk a great deal about shooting them on foot. As regards danger to the sportsman, nine-tenths of the tigers *said* to be shot on foot are really killed from trees or rocks, where the sportsman is quite secure. The only danger then is to the unfortunate beaters, if used; and when this is not the case the sport generally resolves itself into an undignified sneaking about the outskirts of the covers, in the hope of getting an occasional pot-shot from a secure position. In this method of hunting many more tigers are wounded than are finally secured, the only danger lying in following up a wounded animal, which is usually avoided; and thus an innocuous animal is often converted into a scourge of the country-side. A very few sportsmen do, for a short period of their lives, make a practice of hunting and shooting tigers really on foot; but they are seldom very successful, and sooner or later get killed, or have such narrow escapes as to cure them of such silly folly for the remainder of their days. A man on foot has no chance whatever in thick jungle with a tiger that is bent on killing him. He cannot see a yard before him, and is himself conspicuous to every sense of the brute, who can completely hide in a place that looks scarcely enough to conceal a rat, and can move at will through the thickest cover without the slightest sound or stir. At the same time the sportsman who as a rule uses an elephant in thick cover will find quite enough opportunities, in special cases, of testing his nerve on foot, particularly if he marks down and tracks his own game instead of employing shikárís to do so. Even on the elephant all is not perfect safety, instances being not rare of elephants being completely pulled down by tigers, while accidents from the running away of the elephant in tree jungle are still more common. Much of the excitement of the sport depends on the sportsman's method of attacking the tiger. Some men box a tiger up in a corner and push in at all hazards, getting repeatedly charged, while others keep at a distance, circling round and offering doors of escape to the tiger, and never get a charge at all. As a rule, when on an elephant in fair ground, the object should be to get the tiger to charge instead of letting him sneak away, as the hunt is then ended in a short and exciting encounter, while if let away it may be hours before he is found again, if he ever is at all.

The first difficulty is to get reliable information of the presence of tigers in a particular neighbourhood. A great many reasons, besides the simple one to which it is usually attributed, namely, that "they are cursed niggers," combine to make the natives in most places very unwilling to give information about tigers. Firstly, it is likely to bring down a large encampment of "Sahibs" on their village, which they, very justly in most cases, dislike. The military officer who scorns to learn the rural language, and his train of overbearing, swindling servants, who fully carry out the principle that from him who hath not what little he hath shall be taken away, and that without a price, too, stink in the nostrils of the poor inhabitants of the tracts where tigers are found. The tiger himself is, in fact, far more endurable than those who encamp over against them to make war upon him, and demand from them grain and other supplies which they have not, and carts, etc., to carry the camp, which they want to use for other urgent purposes. Then they fear that they will be made to beat for the tiger—both those who are willing and those who are not—with a considerable chance of getting killed, and very little of being paid for their services. There are few well-known resorts of tigers where some story of the sort has not been handed down among the people. The first essential towards getting sport is to conciliate the willing co-operation of the people, and make it plain to them that your arrangements for supplies are such as to throw no unbearable burden on a poor country, and that your method of hunting is not one to lead to the constant risk of life. Such, however, is the want of sympathy often engendered in the naturally generous Englishman by the fact of his becoming a member of the ruling caste in India, that sportsmen will sometimes be heard on their return from an unsuccessful expedition in which they had harried a quiet population who did not want their tigers killed at all on their terms, cursing and swearing at them, and perhaps even expressing little regret that a few of them had been sacrificed to their bungling ardour. On the other hand, a properly organised expedition, where the sportsman provides his own supplies and his means of hunting the tigers, is certain to meet with every co-operation from the people. They will even crowd in to help in driving the jungles, when they know they are to work for a good sportsman and shot who will not unnecessarily risk their lives.

With luck and first-rate arrangements a few tigers may be got in the cold weather. A good many persons will remember a hunt in the month of January, 1861, when we secured a royal tiger for the Governor-General of India, on his first visit to the centre of his dominions, within a mile or two of the cantonment of Jubbulpúr. I mounted sentry over that beast for nearly a week, girding him in a little hill with a belt of fires, and feeding him with nightly kine, till half a hundred elephants, carrying the cream of a vice-regal camp, swept him out into the plain, where he fell riddled by a storm of bullets from several hundred virgin rifles. He had the honour of being painted by a Landseer, by the blaze of torchlight, under the shadow of the British standard; and my howdah bore witness for many a day, in a bullet-hole through both sides of it, to the accuracy of aim of some gallant member of the staff!

At this season tigers sometimes venture very close to large towns, and even to the European stations. Several tigers have been shot within the walls of the town and station of Mandlá, and in the "Páu" gardens round about; and at Seoní I formed one of a party who drove a large tiger out of a tobacco field, within a stone's-throw of a considerable village, and shot him in the main street thereof. There was nothing but fields of short green wheat for many miles round about this place; and the only reason we could discover for so singular an appearance of a tiger among the habitations of man was that he had received a slight wound a few days before.

But it is not until the greater part of the grass has been

burnt in the jungles, and a hot sun has contracted the supply of water to the neighbourhood of the great rivers, that regular tiger-hunting can be commenced with a fair prospect of success. At this season, having discovered a tract where tigers are reported, a good central place should be selected for a camp, in the deep shade of some mango grove near a village, or under the still more grateful canopy of some spreading banyan tree. The graciousness of nature in furnishing such plentiful shade at this arid season cannot but be admired. It is just at the time when all nature begins to quiver in the fierce sun and burning blasts of April that the banyan and peepúl figs and the ever-present mango begin to throw out a fresh crop of leaves, those of the first tree being then moreover charged with a thick milky juice that forms an impenetrable non-conductor to the sun's rays.

Riding up to his camp, pitched in the cool shadowy depths of some grove like this, the sportsman will probably find assembled the village headman, with a small train of cultivators and cowherds, waiting to receive him with some simple offering—a pot of milk, or a bunch of plantains from his garden. If he is welcome, tales will not be wanting of the neighbouring tigers—how Ram Singh's cow was taken out of the herd a few days before; or Bhyron, the village watch, going on an errand, went down for a drink to the river, and there came on a tigress with her cubs bathing by its brink. That youth himself will chime in, and graphically describe how he took to a tree and was kept there all night—the same being probably a euphemism for a night passed with some boon companions at a neighbouring grog-shop. The usual haunts of the tiger will be described; and the size of his footprints and width of his head be drawn to a greatly exaggerated scale. The shikárí of the neighbourhood will be present, or can be sent for—a long gaunt figure, clad in a ragged shirt of Mhowa green, with a dingy turban twisted round his shaggy locks, and furnished with the usual long small-bored matchlock, with its bulky powder-flask of bison horn, and smaller supply of fine priming powder kept carefully in a horn of the gazelle. Rupees, or a prospect of them, will be wanted to loosen his tongue, and then his statements will likely be studiously vague. His hearty services must be secured, however, for he alone knows intimately the ways and haunts of the tiger, and he alone will have the pluck to accompany you or your shikárí to mark him down. If you are known to be a good paymaster he will willingly serve you, otherwise you must promise him a handsome *douceur* in case of success, to induce him to spoil his own chance of claiming the Government reward. This reward was, till financial difficulties reduced it to half, fifty rupees (£5); and, as all sportsmen were entitled to claim it, it used to go far to cover the cost of the hunt. I used always to divide it equally between the village shikárí, if he worked well, and my own shikárí and elephant driver. Now, however, the sportsman will find himself a good deal out of pocket by every tiger he kills.

More precise information must be sought for by the sportsman himself. The village shikárí knows nothing of our system of hunting by attacking the tiger in his mid-day lair. His personal experience of him has probably been confined to nocturnal interviews from the tops of trees; but he will be certain to know his habits and usual resorts, and also whereabouts he is at the time being. It is necessary, therefore, for some one to go out with him who knows our style of work and what particulars to note for guidance when the actual hunt commences; for it is absolutely necessary to have some preliminary knowledge of the ground, and habits of the particular tiger, to ensure success. In my earlier sporting days I always went out to make the preliminary exploration for tigers myself; and this is the only way to learn the business thoroughly, so as to be able afterwards to devolve the labour on your shikárís. A sportsman who is not thoroughly master of this business will never have a reliable shikárí; and the best men are those who have been trained up in it along with their masters.

The morning is the best time for this work. It is then cool, and every footprint of the previous night is sharp and clear. All the wild animals, from whose movements much is to be learnt, are then on the move. The movements of the tiger even may often be traced up to eight or nine o'clock by the voices of monkeys and peafowl, the chatter of crows and small birds, and the bark of sámbar and spotted deer. The whole nocturnal life of the beasts of the forest is then displayed in the clearest manner to the hunter whose eye has been trained to read the book of nature; and I know nothing more interesting than a ramble in the cool gray of a summer morning along the stream-beds of a tract in which live a great variety of wild animals. The river beds usually contain large stretches of sand and gravel, with here and there a pool of water, the margin of which will be covered with tracks of deer, wild hogs, bears, etc., and here and there the mighty footprints of the jungle king himself. All must come here to drink in the cool night succeeding a burning day; and in the neighbourhood of the water occur most of the tragical interviews between the herbivora and their carnivorous foes. Everywhere the cruel tyranny of the tiger has imprinted itself on the faithful page. His track to the water is straight and leisurely, while that of the nílgái or spotted deer is halting and suspicious, and apt to end in a wild scurry to right and left where it crosses the tiger's. Here and there bleaching skulls and bones show that the whole herd have not always made good their escape. The ambush of dried leaves by the pass down the bank marks, perhaps, an unsuccessful stratagem; and not seldom the trampled soil and patches of blood and hair, show where a stubborn boar has successfully resisted the attack of a tiger. Bruin alone is tolerably safe from the assault of the tiger; but he, too, gets out of his way like the rest, and drinks at a different pool.

The sportsman will not be long under the guidance of the village shikárí before he comes on tracks of tigers. Where one or more have been living some time in the neighbourhood, footprints of many dates will be found in the sandy bed of almost every nálá. The history and habits of the tigers will generally ooze out of the local hunter at the sight of these marks. When the fresh tracks of the previous night are found his impassive features will be lighted into interest, and, as he follows the trail with the end of his gun, his speech will be low and hurried from suppressed excitement. There is little chance, however, of coming on the brute himself at that early hour. He is probably lying somewhere on an elevated place commanding the approaches to his favourite lair, sunning himself in the soft morning light, and watching against the approach of danger, until the growing heat about ten o'clock shall have extinguished all signs of movement in the neighbourhood, when he will creep down into some shady nook by the water, and, after a roll in the wet sand, proceed to sleep off the effects of his midnight gorge. Sometimes, however, if the sportsman be out early enough, he will find, from the cries of animals, that the tiger is moving not far ahead of him, and he may then by cutting him off even obtain a shot.

On one occasion I followed a tiger in the early morning for several miles up the bed of a stream, entirely by the demonstrations of the large Hanúmán monkey,[1] of which there were numbers on the banks feeding on wild fruits. As the tiger passed below them the monkeys fled to the nearest trees, and, climbing to the highest branches, shook them violently and poured forth a torrent of abuse[2] that could be heard a mile away. Each group of them continued to swear at him till he passed out of sight, and they saw their friends further on take up the chorus in the tops of their trees, when they calmly came down again and began to stuff their cheeks full of berries as if nothing had happened. The river took a long sweep a little further on, and by cutting across the neck I managed to arrive very much out of breath in front of the tiger, and crouched behind the thick trunk of a *Kawá* tree till he should come up. He came on in a long slouching walk, with his tail tucked down, and looking exactly like the guilty midnight murderer he is. His misdeeds evidently sat heavily on his conscience, for as he went he looked fearfully behind him, and up at the monkeys in a beseeching sort of way

[1] *Presbytis entellus.*

[2] The voice of the monkeys on such occasions is quite different from their ordinary cry. It is a hoarse barking roar something like that of the tiger.

as if asking them not to betray where he was going. He was travelling under the opposite bank to where I was, in the deep shadow of the overhanging trees; but, when nearly opposite me, he came out into the middle, in the faint yellow light of the just risen sun, and then he looked such a picture of fearful beauty—with his velvety step and undulating movements, the firm muscles working through his loose glossy skin, and the cruel yellow eyes blinking in the sun over a row of ivory teeth, as he licked his lips and whiskers after his night's feed. He passed within about twenty yards of me, making for a small ravine that here joined the river from the hills. I let him get to the mouth of this before I fired; and on receiving the shot, he bounded forward into its cover—a very different picture from the placid creature I had just been looking at, and with a roar that silenced the chattering of every monkey on the trees. I knew he was hit to death, but waited till the shikárís came up before proceeding to see; and we then went round a good way to where a high bank overlooked the ravine in which he had disappeared. Here we cautiously peeped over, and, seeing nothing, came further down towards the river, and within fifty yards of where I had fired at him I saw a solitary crow sitting in a tree, and cawing down at an indistinct yellow object extended below. It seemed like the tiger, and sitting down I fired another shot at it; but it never stirred to the thud of the ball, while the crow, after flying up a few feet, perched again and cawed away more lustily than before. We now went down, and found the tiger lying stone dead, shot very near the heart.

I think it is the pranks of juvenile tigers, rather than the serious enmity of old ones, that cause such a terror of them to exist among the monkey community. The natives say that the tigress teaches her cubs to stalk and hunt by practising on monkeys and peafowl. The gorgeous plumage of the latter, scattered about in a thousand radiant fragments, often marks the spot where a peacock has thus fallen victim to these ready learners, but the remains of a monkey are seldom or never seen. Indeed, these sagacious simians rarely venture to come down to the ground when young tigers are about, though this sign is not always to be relied on as denoting the absence of tigers. I thought so for a long time, till one day in the Bétúl country, after hunting long in the heat of a May day for a couple of tigers whose marks were plentiful all about, we came up to a small pool of water at the head of a ravine, and saw the last chance of finding them vanish, as I thought, when a troop of monkeys were found quietly sitting on the rocks and drinking at the water. I was carelessly descending to look for prints, with my rifle reversed over my shoulder, and another step or two would have brought me to the bottom of the ravine, when the monkeys scurried with a shriek up the bank, and the head and shoulders of a large tiger appeared from behind a boulder, and stared at me across the short interval. I was meditating whether to fire or retreat, when almost from below my feet the other tiger bounded out with a terrific roar, and they both made off down the ravine. I was too much astonished to obtain a steady shot, and I was by that time too well acquainted with tiger shooting to risk an uncertain one, so they escaped for the time. I quickly regained my elephant, which was standing above, and followed them up. It was exceedingly hot, and we had not gone more than a couple of hundred yards when I saw one of the tigers crouched under a bush on the bank of the ravine. I got a steady shot from the howdah, and fired a three-ounce shell at his broad forehead at about thirty yards. No result. It was most curious, and I paused to look; but never a motion of the tiger acknowledged the shot. I then went round a quarter of a circle, but still the tiger remained motionless, looking intently in the same direction. I marched up, rifle on full-cock, growing more and more amazed—but the tiger never moved. Could he be dead? I went round to his rear and approached close up from that direction. He never stirred. Then I made the elephant kick him, and he fell over. He was stone dead—converted, without the movement of a hair, into a statue of himself by the bursting of the large shell in his brain. It had struck him full in the centre of the forehead. We then went on with the track of the other. It led down into the Móran river, on the steep bank of which there was a thick cover of jáman bushes in which the tiger was sure to stop. I had just before come through it, and found the place as full of tracks as a rabbit-warren. Having a spare pad elephant out that day, I sent her round to keep down the bottom of the bank and mark, while I pushed my own elephant—Futteh Ráni ("Queen of Victory")—through the cover. About the centre I came on the tiger, crouched like the other, with his massive head rested on his forepaws, the drawn-up hind-quarters and slightly switching tail showing that he meant mischief. At the first shot, which struck him on the point of the shoulder, he bounded out at me; but the left barrel caught him in the back before he had come many yards and broke it, when he rolled right down to the bottom of the bank, and fell, roaring horribly, right between the fore-legs of the pad elephant. She was a new purchase for forest work, called Motí Málá or "Pearl Necklace" (such are the fantastic names given to elephants by their Mahomedan keepers), and quite untried; but she stood admirably this rather abrupt introduction to her game, merely retreating a few steps and shaking her head at the contortions of the tiger. There is no more striking incident in tiger-shooting than to witness the fearful and impotent rage of a tiger with a broken back. He cannot reach beyond a short circle, but within that limit stones, trees, and the very earth are seized and worried with fearful savageness, and the wretched brute will horribly mangle even his own limbs. It is too ghastly to look on long; and, though the agony is that of a monster who has caused so much himself, a merciful bullet in the head should quickly end the horrid scene.

These were regular cattle-eating tigers, and perhaps had not been molesting the monkeys. On another occasion, however, I was much struck with the caution of the monkeys under very trying circumstances. I had tracked a man-eating tigress into a deep ravine near the village of Pálí in the Seoní district. She was not quite a confirmed man-eater, but had killed nine or ten persons in the preceding few months. She had a cub of about six months old with her, and it was when this cub was very young and unable to move about that want of other game had driven her to kill her first human prey. I knew when I entered the ravine that this was her regular haunt; for, though every bush outside had been stripped of its berries by a colony of monkeys, I saw them perched on the rocks above the ravine wistfully looking down on the bushes at the bottom, which had strewed the ground with their ripened fruit. They accompanied me along the ravine on the top of the rocks, as if perfectly knowing the value of their assistance in getting the tigress—and better markers I never had. I should probably have passed out at the top without seeing her, as she was lying close under a shelving bank, but for the profane language of an ancient gray-bearded Hanúmán, who posted himself right above her, and swore away until he fairly turned her out of her comfortable berth. The excitement of the monkeys soon told me she was on the move; and presently I saw her round face looking at me from behind a tree with a forked trunk, through the cleft of which I caught sight of about a square foot of her striped hide. It seemed about the right place, so covering it carefully I put in a shell at about forty yards, and she collapsed there and then, forming a beautiful spread-eagle in the bottom of the nálá. The youngster now started out, roaring as if he were the biggest tiger in the country; and, though I fired a couple of snap shots at him as he galloped through some thick bushes, I could not stop him. It is important to extinguish a brute, however young, who has once tasted human flesh; and I followed him up till it grew nearly dark, when I returned to the ravine to take home the tigress, and there I found my monkey friends tucking into the berries in all directions, and hopping about close to the body of the dead tigress. The cub was met, much exhausted with its run, by a gang of wood-cutters, and killed with their axes.

The barking of deer, and the alarmed cry of peafowl, also frequently indicate the movements of a tiger. The sámbar, the spotted deer, the barking deer, and the little four-horned antelope, all "bark" violently at a tiger suddenly appearing in the daytime. Once having marched nearly a thousand miles exploring in the forests almost without firing a shot, I halted to hunt a very large cattle-eating tiger near Chándvél in the Nimár district. This animal was believed by the cowherds to have killed more than a thousand head of cattle; and one of the best grazing grounds in all that country had been quite abandoned by them in consequence. His haunts lay in a network of ravines that lead down to the Narbadá river—now included in the Ponásá Reserved Forest, which I was then exploring. The herds of cattle having been withdrawn from the grassy glades on the banks of the Narbadá where he usually preyed on them, he had lately been coming out into the open country, and had been heard for several nights roaming round about the village of Chándvél on the edge of the forest. I found his tracks within a hundred yards of the buffalo pens of the village the morning I arrived; and a few nights before he had broken into a Banjárá encampment a little way off, and killed and dragged away a heifer, which he ate within hearing distance of the encampment, charging through the darkness and driving back the Banjárás and their dogs when they tried to interrupt him. I picketed a juicy young buffalo for him the night I arrived, about half a mile from the village where his tracks showed he regularly passed at night. Next morning it was found to have been killed and dragged away about a hundred yards to a small dry watercourse; and, after having been cleaned as scientifically as any butcher could have done it, eaten up all but the head, skin, feet, and one fore-quarter. If his footprints had not already shown him to be an unusually large tiger, this feat of gormandising would have sufficiently done so. We started about ten o'clock on his trail. It was the 12th of April, and a hotter day I never remember. Long before midday the little band of cowherds and shikárís who accompanied me had most of their wardrobes bound round their heads to keep off the sun; and I looked for a tussle with such a heavy old tiger, long accustomed to drive off the people he met, if we found him well-gorged on such a grilling day as this. We took the track down fully five miles till it entered a long narrow ravine with pools of water at the bottom, and shaded over with a thick cover of trees and bushes. We could not go into so narrow a place to beat him out with an elephant; and after much deliberation we decided to leave a pad elephant at the head of the ravine, and post the people we had with us on the trees round about to mark, while I went down to the other end and quietly stalked along the top bank on the chance of finding him asleep below. There never was such a beautiful retreat for a tiger, I think. In many places I could not see through the dense shade at the bottom, and several times had to fling down stones to assure myself whether some indistinct flickering object were the tiger or not. I was proceeding quietly along, probing the ravine in this fashion, when the pad elephant we had left at the further end gave one of those tremendous screams that an untrained elephant sometimes emits when suddenly put in pain. She had stumbled over a stone when swinging about in their impatient fashion. There was little chance of finding the tiger undisturbed after this, and I had only to stand and watch for a chance of his coming down the ravine or being seen by the scouts on the trees. The first intimation I had of his presence was from a couple of peafowl that scuttled out of a little ravine on the opposite side; and then I saw the tiger picking his way stealthily up the face of a precipitous bank, where I could hardly think a goat would have found footing. He was about a hundred and fifty yards from my rifle; and the first bullet only knocked some earth from the bank below him. When I fired the other he was just topping the bank, and clung for a second as if he would have come over backwards, but by an effort recovered himself and disappeared over the top. Running to a higher piece of ground I saw him trotting sullenly across the burnt plain, and looming as large to the eye as a bull buffalo. He certainly looked a very mighty beast; but he was a craven at heart, or he would never have left such a stronghold to face the fearful waterless, burnt-up country he did. I lost no time in getting round the head of the ravine and giving chase on the elephant. His tracks in the ashes of the burnt grass were clear enough, and we followed him for about two miles, sighting him on ahead every now and then, till he disappeared in a little ravine, and we lost the track in its bare rocky bottom. I was going along the bank, with the other elephant in the bottom of the ravine, when I heard the bark of a sámbar to my left on some high ground, and, urging Futteh Ráni at her best pace in that direction, shortly came on the tiger slouching across the open plain—evidently suffering from a wound, with his tongue hanging out, and wearing altogether a most woebegone look. He made an effort when he saw me, and galloped a hundred yards or so into a patch of bamboo jungle. I knew from the local shikárí that he was making for a water-hole about half a mile ahead, and cut across with the elephant to intercept him. I had the pace of him now, and got clean between him and his water. I never saw such an air of disgust worn by any animal as that tiger had when he came down the hill and saw the elephant standing right in front of him. He said as plainly as possible, "Come what will, I don't mean to run another yard; and it won't be the better for anybody that tries to make me." So he lay down behind a large anjan tree, showing nothing but one eye and an ear round the side of it. I marched up within fifty yards, and now saw the switching end of a tail added to the eye and ear. I could not fire at him thus, and therefore sidled round till I saw his shoulder. He saw the opening thus left, and eyed it wistfully, as if he would rather escape that way, if he could, than fight it out. But I planted a ball in his shoulder before he had time to make up his mind; on which he rose with a languid roar, and lumbered slowly down the hill at the elephant. So slowly! He actually hadn't steam left in him to get up a proper charge when he tried. A right and left stopped him at once and another ball in the ear settled him; and then Futteh went up and kicked him, and it was all over. He was a very large tiger, measuring ten feet one inch in length as he lay, and was a perfect mountain of fat—the fat of a thousand kine, as the cowherds lugubriously remarked when they came up. He had a perfect skin, clear red and white, with the fine double stripes and W mark on the head, and long whiskers, which add so greatly to the beauty of a tiger trophy. The whole of the pads of his feet were blistered off on the hot rocks he had been traversing, and his tongue was swollen and blue. We were nearly dead ourselves, and went down to the water he had been making for, while a messenger went to the village for more men—the dozen lusty cattle-herds and my own men together being totally unable to put him on the pad elephant to carry home. An ordinary tiger will weigh about four hundred and fifty or five hundred pounds, but this beef-fed monster must have touched seven hundred pounds at least; and a tiger, from his length and suppleness, is a very awkward object to lift off the ground.

I have said that ten feet one inch is the length of an unusually large tiger. The average length from nose to tip of tail is only nine feet six inches for a full-grown male, and for a tigress about eight feet four inches. The experience of all sportsmen I have met with, whose accuracy I can rely on, is the same; and it will certainly be found, when much greater measurements than this are recorded, that they have either been taken from stretched skins or else in a very careless fashion. The skin of a ten-feet tiger will easily stretch to thirteen or fourteen feet, if required; and if natives are allowed to use the tape they are certain to throw in a foot or two "to please master." Master also, no doubt, sometimes pleases himself in a similar manner. A well-known sportsman and writer whose recorded measurements have done more to extend the size of the tiger than anything else, informed me himself that all his measurements were taken from flat skins. But the British public demands twelve-feet tigers, just as it refuses to accept an Indian landscape without palm-trees. So a *suppressio veri* went forth; and not only that, but his picture of a dead tiger being carried into camp was improved by a few feet being added to the length of the beast, while, to make room for it, the most of the bearers were wiped out, leaving about four men only to carry a tiger at least fifteen feet long!

Sporting stories are apt to breed each other, incident leading on to incident, so that I find I have already killed some five or six tigers while yet only on the threshold of my subject—discoursing of the preliminary exploration of the tiger's haunts. I have little more to say on that matter, however, the sum of it all being that every information regarding the tiger's country, the route he usually takes from one haunt to another, the points where he may be most easily intercepted or come upon unawares, good points for scouts, etc., must be obtained. Places must also be fixed on for tying out baits for him at night. He must be induced, if possible, to kill a buffalo or an ox so tied out; and it must be in such a position that he can be easily tracked from there to one of his usual haunts.

It may seem cruel thus to bait for a tiger with a live animal, but there is no doubt that the death of a tiger saves much more suffering than is caused to the single animal sacrificed to effect it. A natural kill will not do so well for many reasons. It will probably not be discovered in time to hunt the next day, and the day after it would be useless. Further, it would seldom be conveniently situated with respect to some haunt of the tiger favourable for finding him in, and the whole day might be lost in trying to find him in wrong places. In fine, experience shows that no bag can ever be made worth speaking of without tying out baits. I usually purchased at the commencement of the season a dozen or fifteen half-grown buffaloes, these being the cheapest as well as the most readily killed by tigers. A thin old brute of an ox, or a tough full-grown buffalo, a well-fed tiger will scorn to touch, and often in the morning his footprints will be found all round such a bait, which he has come and smelt, and (metaphorically) poked in the ribs, and left untouched. But a tender juicy young buff of about three and a half feet high would tempt the most *blasé* of tigers to a meal. The cowherds being good Hindús, will not sell cattle avowedly to be tied up for tigers; nor will your Hindú shikárís tie them up with their own hands, though few will object to superintend the operation. The flimsiest disguise is, however, sufficient to quiet the consciences of the cattle men, who will sell a herd of young buffaloes in open market to your Mahomedan shikárí dressed up as a trader in kine, though they may have known him for a bloody-minded baiter for tigers all their lives. I remember being very hard up for a bait once in the Nimár district, having come to a place where tigers were very destructive when I had none of my own. All I could say would not induce the Gaolís (cow-keepers) of the place to sell me a single head during the day-time, the owner of the village being a Baghél Rájpút, a clan which claims descent from a royal tiger, and protects the species whenever they can. I was standing outside my tent in the evening, when the village cattle were being driven in, having given up all idea of halting for the tigers another day, when a fine tall young Gaolí stepped up with a salaam and said, "Sahib, I have lost a very fine young buffalo in the jungle, and it will very probably be snapped up by the tigers; but if you would send some one along that road perhaps he might find it, and we will be pleased if your Highness will keep it, as you are going away from this to-morrow." He grinned a broad grin as he finished, and I spotted his game; so sending along the "Lálla" about a quarter of a mile we found a very sufficient young wall-eyed buffalo tied by a piece of straw rope to a little tree! We had barely time to get the little brute put out in a proper place before nightfall; but he was duly taken, and we shot a fine tigress, and wounded and lost a tiger, the next day!

The morning after the baits have been tied out a shikárí should go to see the result, untying and bringing in those that have not been taken, and following up the tracks from any that have, so far as to ascertain fully whereabouts the tiger is likely to be found later in the day. I have mentioned above the "Lállá," and that brings me to the subject of *shikárís*. A really first-class tiger shikárí is extremely rare. The combination of qualities required to make him is seldom found in a native. I shall best explain what he should be by describing the Lállá. And first as to his name. "Lállá" means in upper India a clerk of the Kàyat caste, to which our friend belonged; so that though utterly ignorant of all letters save those imprinted on a sandy ravine-bed by a tiger's paw, he was nicknamed the Lállá by the people, and thereupon his real name disappeared for ever; and, when he was afterwards killed by a tiger, no one had any idea what it was. He was a little, wee man, so insignificant and so dried and shrivelled up that, as he used to say, "No tiger would ever think of eating *me*." His early days had been passed in catching and training falcons for the nobles of upper India, and in shooting birds for sale in the market. He had come down to Central India to make a bag of blue rollers and kingfishers, whose feathers are so much valued in the countries to the east for fancy work, when he was caught, nobody knows how, by a gentleman with a taste for bird-stuffing, from whom he passed into the possession of a sportsman who put him on tigers, and eventually he came to me with a little experience of the business. His early training had made him exceedingly keen of eyesight, and in reading the signs of the forest; while in his many wanderings he had accumulated a store of legends of demons and devilry, and a wild jumble of Hindú mythology, that never failed, when retailed over a fire at night to a circle of gaping cowherds and village shikárís, to unlock every secret of the neighbourhood in the matter of tigers. Such an oily cozener of reticent Gónds never existed. Then, miserable as he looked, he could walk about all day and every day for a week in a broiling sun, hunting up tracks, with nothing but the thinnest of muslin skull-caps on his hard nut of a head, and would fearlessly penetrate into the very lair of a tiger perfectly unarmed. He had a particular beaming look which he always wore on his ugly face when he had actually seen or, as he said, "salaamed to" a tiger comfortably disposed of for the day; and in late years, when I had to leave all the arrangements to him, I hardly recollect ever going out when he reported the find a likely one without at least seeing the game. He could shoot a little, say a pot-shot at a bird on a branch at twenty paces, and kept guns, etc., in beautiful order. But he soon came to utterly despise and contemn everything except tiger-hunting, of which he had, I believe, really an absorbing passion. Even bison-hunting he looked down on as sport not fit for a gentleman to pursue. For ten months in the year he moped about looking utterly wretched, and taking no interest in anything but the elephants and rifles; and woke up again only on the first of April—opposite which date

"Tiger-shooting commences" will be entered in the Indian almanack of the future, when the royal animal shall be preserved in the Reserved Forests of Central India to furnish sport for the nobility of the land!

Poor old Lállá! He fell a victim in the end to contempt of tigers, bred of undue familiarity. I was very ill with fever, and meditating a trip home, and had sent out the Lállá with a double gun to shoot some birds for their feathers with a view to salmon flies. He came upon the tracks of a tiger, and, contrary to all orders, tied out a calf at night as a bait, and sat over it in a tree with the gun. The tigress came and received his bullet in the thigh, going off wounded into a very thick cover in the bed of a river. The plucky but foolish Lállá followed her in there the next morning by the blood; but soon found that tracking up a wounded tiger with a gun is a very different thing from following about uninjured tigers without intent to disturb them. Before he had gone a dozen paces the tigress was upon him, his unfired gun dashed from his hands and buried for half its length in the sand, his turban cuffed from his head to the top of a high tree by a stroke of her paw that narrowly missed his head, and himself down below the furious beast, and being slowly chewed from shoulder to ankle. He was brought in a dozen miles to Khandwá, where I was, by some men who had gone in for him when the tigress left him. The fire of delirium was then in his eye, and he raved of the tiger's form passing before him, red and bloody. But he recognised me when I came to him, and conjured me to go out forthwith and bring in her body next day if I wished to see him live. I knew that the natives have a superstition to this effect; and, though I was then in a high fever, I sent off my elephant at midnight to a village near the spot, following myself on horseback at daybreak. Much rain had fallen, and all old tracks were obliterated. The jungle was also very green and thick, and I spent the whole day till the afternoon, hunting, as I afterwards found, in a wrong direction. At last I came on a fresh trail, with one hind-foot dragging in the sand, and then I knew I was near the savage brute. We ran it up to a dense jáman cover in the river-bed, and

I had barely time to get the people on foot safely up trees when the tigress came at me in the most determined manner. She looked just like a huge cat that had been hunted by dogs—her fur all bedraggled and standing on end, eyes glaring with fury, and emitting the hoarse coughing roar of a charging tiger that no one, to the very close of his tiger-shooting, hears without a certain quickening of the blood. The first two shots hit fair, but did not stop her; and she was not more than a few yards from the elephant's trunk when the third ball caught her clean in the mouth, knocking out one of her canine teeth and passing down the throat into the chest. She could do no more, but lay roaring and worrying her own paws till I put an end to her with another shot in the head. She was a lean, greyhound-made brute, scarcely bigger than a panther. The Lállá was avenged. but the poor fellow was beyond any help that the sight of his enemy might have afforded him; and notwithstanding every care—for he was the favourite of everybody who knew him—he sank under the exhausting drain of so many fearful wounds.

Very different from the old Lállá is the usual pattern of tiger shikárí. He will probably be a tall swaggering Mahomedan, brushing out his whiskers to the likeness of a tiger's, and, to add ferocity of expression, dyeing them when young a steely blue and when old a rusty red; clad in elaborate jungle-coloured raiment, and hung with belts and pouches of sámbar leather supporting a perfect armoury of cut-throat weapons which he has not the faintest idea of using; bragging sky high of his own and his master's doughty exploits; insufferable to the people, and lazy as a pampered lap-dog; with just enough knowledge of his work, gained in his early days by carrying the water-bottle of some real sportsman, to concoct a plausible but utterly fictitious story at every place he comes to; and convicted at every turn of lying, stealing, and every deadly sin;—yet possibly the admiration of a gullible master, on whom a portion of the glory of his whiskers and tall talk is reflected, as he struts about his house in cantonments in full war-paint, snapping the locks of his brand-new sixty-guinea rifles.

How the tiger marked down in the morning is to be hunted and killed at midday, when all life in the forest is still beneath the scorching heat of the sun, and the brute himself is least on his guard and most unwilling to move, will have been seen from previous descriptions. To read the hunting of one tiger is like that of every other; but a different set of incidents marks each day's sport in the memory of the hunter, who pictures vividly the death of each long after incidents of his sport with every sort other of game have faded away. The main features are the careful preliminary arrangements, the settling the direction of approach so as to cut off all roads of escape to inaccessible fastnesses, the posting of scouts to notify the possible retreat of the tiger, and the cautious, silent approach, the excitement gathering as the innermost recess of the cover, where the brute is expected to lie, is approached by the wonderfully intelligent and half-human elephant.

A strange affection springs up between the hunter and his well-tried ally in the chase of the tiger; and a creature seeming to those who see him only in the menagerie, or labouring under a load of baggage, but a lumbering mass of flesh, becomes to him almost a second self, yielding to his service the perfection of physical and mental qualities of which a brute is capable, and displaying an intelligent interest in his sport of which no brute could be thought to be possessed. No one who has not witnessed it would believe the astonishing caution with which a well-trained elephant approaches a tiger, removing with noiseless adroitness every obstacle of fallen timber, etc., and passing his huge bulk over rustling leaves, or rolling stones, or quaking bog, with an absolute and marvellous silence; handing up stones, when ordered, for his master to fling into the cover; smelling out a cold scent as a spaniel roads a pheasant; and at last, perhaps, pointing dead with sensitive trunk at the hidden monster, or showing with short nervous raps of that organ on the ground that he is somewhere near, though not actually discovered to the senses of the elephant. Then the unswerving steadiness when he sees the enemy he naturally dreads, and would flee from panic-stricken in his native haunts, perhaps charging headlong at his head, trusting all to the skill of his rider, and thoughtless of using his own tremendous strength in the encounter—for a good elephant never attempts to combat the tiger himself. To do so would generally be fatal to the sport, and perhaps to the sportsman too; for no one could stick to an elephant engaged in a personal struggle with a tiger, far less use his gun under such circumstances. The elephant's business is to stand like a rock in every event, even when the tiger is fastened on his head—as many a good one will do and has done.

It is not one elephant in a thousand that is so thoroughly good in tiger-shooting as this; and such as are command very high prices in the market. From £200 to £400 is now the value of a thoroughly first-rate shooting elephant, though much sport may be had with one purchased for a much smaller sum. The supply of elephants has much fallen off in late years, since the Government ceased to capture them in the forests of the north of India. I visited the great annual fair on one occasion at Sónpúr, on the Ganges, to purchase elephants for our forest work in Central India. It occurs on the occasion of a great congregation of Hindú pilgrims to worship at a noted shrine of Sívá, and bathe in the Ganges at the full moon of the month of Kártik (September—October). Several hundred thousands of Hindús from every part of India are then collected on the banks of the holy river; and such a gathering together of people is of course seized by traders in every sort of ware, from wild yáks' tails of Tibet to croquet implements in lac varnish, and dealers in every sort of animal, from white mice to elephants. The European gentlemen of Bengal have also here constructed an excellent race-course, with grand stand complete; and some of the best races in India are run during the fair. The year I was there something like twelve thousand horses were brought by dealers for sale—ranging from the tiny woolly-haired pied pony of Nepál, which makes the best child's pony in the world, to Australian thoroughbreds and "made-up" casters from the Indian cavalry.

About five hundred elephants offered a considerable

choice in my particular department. It is difficult to buy horses at a fair; but the difficulty is ten times greater in the case of elephants. Every one connected with the keeping of elephants (and camels) is by nature and training from his youth upwards a consummate rascal; and the animal himself is subject to numerous and often obscure vices and unsoundnesses. I have given in an appendix some hints regarding these, as well as on the management of elephants, which would scarcely interest the general reader. Elephants differ as widely in their "points" as do horses; and it is very difficult for an uneducated eye to distinguish these, particularly in the fattened-up condition the animals generally carry at the fair. Furthermore, and fortunately enough for us, a native's idea of good points in an elephant (as in a horse) differs *in toto* from ours. He looks not at all to shape, or good action, or likelihood of standing hard work; but first of all to the presence or absence of certain accidental marks—such as the number of toe-nails on the foot, which may be five or six but not four; the tail, which must be perfect and with a full tuft; and the colour of the palate, which must be red without spot of black. Some of the best elephants I have known failed in each and all of these points. Then a female or tuskless male is of small value to a native, who wants big white tusks. A rough high action, and a trunk and forehead of very light colour, are greatly in request by the native buyer, who looks entirely to show, and covers up every part of the animal except the face with an enormous parti-coloured cloth. We, on the other hand, dislike the high rough action, and never by any chance purchase a tusker, who is nearly certain to be ill-tempered. We look for a small well-bred-looking head and trunk, and a clear confident eye devoid of piggish expression, fast easy paces, straight back and croup, wide loins, and generally well-developed bone and muscle—a great test of which is the girth of the forearm, which should measure about three feet eight inches in an elephant nine feet high. A very tall elephant is seldom a good working one, and generally has slow rough paces; so that in a male nine feet, or a female eight feet four inches at the shoulder, should not be exceeded. A smaller animal than eight feet two inches will be undersized for tiger-shooting purposes. A female makes the best hunting elephant when she is really staunch with game, as her paces and temper are generally better, and she is not subject to the danger of becoming "must" and uncontrollable, as male elephants do periodically after a certain age. But females are more uncertain as to courage than males; and it is a risk to buy the former untried for shooting purposes. Most "muknas" (tuskless males) can, I believe, be relied on to become staunch with tigers when properly trained and entered; and, for my own part, if buying an entirely untried elephant, I would always select a "mukna." They are generally more vigorous and better developed than tuskers, though not usually so tall. A not improbable explanation of this was given me by a wild inhabitant of the forests to the east of the sources of the Narbadá, where wild elephants then existed in large numbers. He said he had noticed that the young tuskers, after their sharp little tusks began to prick the mother in the process of sucking, were driven off by her and allowed to shift for themselves, while females and muknas continued to be nourished by her until she got another young one.

After some trouble I bought the ten elephants I wanted —eight of them muknas and two females. Their average price was £150, the dearest being £200, and the cheapest £100. The highest price I heard of being obtained at the fair was £800 for a noble tusker, bought for a Rájá in the Punjáb. So far as I know, none of them had ever seen a tiger; but they all became excellent shikárís, except one large mukna in whom I found I had been stuck with a regular man-killing brute. He was quite quiet at the fair, having been probably kept drugged with opium; but on the march down to Central India he broke out and killed a man, and afterwards became quite uncontrollable. He fetched his full price, however, for a native notable; for he was a very handsome animal, and a wealthy native is rather proud of having an elephant that no one can go near, chained up at his gateway for an ornament.

All elephants intended to be used in hunting tigers

must be very carefully trained and entered to their game. A good *mahout*, or driver, is very difficult to obtain. They differ as much in their command over elephants as do riders of horses; and a plucky driver will generally make a staunch elephant, and *vice versâ*. The elephant should first be accustomed to the firing of guns from his back, and to seeing deer and other harmless animals shot before him in company with a staunch companion. He must not be forced in at a tiger, or at a hog or bear, which he detests even more, until he has acquired some confidence, though in some few cases he will stand to any animal from the very first. When they have seen a few tigers neatly disposed of, most elephants acquire confidence in their human allies, and become sufficiently steady in the field; but their ultimate qualities will depend much on natural temperament. The more naturally courageous an elephant is, the better chance there is of his remaining staunch after having been actually mauled by a tiger, an accident to be avoided, of course, as long as possible. It will occur sometimes, however, in the best hands; and then a naturally timid animal, who has only been made staunch by a long course of immunity from injury, will probably be spoilt for life, while a really plucky elephant is often rendered bolder than before by such an occurrence.

Some elephants which are in other respects perfect shikáŕis will retain some ineradicable peculiarity which may almost unfit them for use in hunting. For some time I had a female who would stand anything in the way of animals (I once had her charged close up by a whole family of bears—a terrible trial for any elephant), but who bolted invariably in the utmost panic from the loud shout of a human voice. On one such occasion she carried a cargo of native clerks into the middle of a deep river, and left them to swim for their lives. On another, I thought I should die of laughing, though her prank nearly ended in the death of an unhappy Gónd. He had been taken out with her by the attendant whose business it is to cut branches of trees for fodder, and was left on her back to pack the load, while the other went up the tree to cut down branches. In the meantime a loud shout in the neighbourhood sent her off at full speed for camp, and, a deep weedy tank lying in the way, she marched right into it, and began to surge up and down in the water, her unwilling rider piteously screaming at every plunge. He was half drowned and nearly finished with fright before we could release him by sending in two other elephants with their drivers, who drove her with their spears into a corner and secured her.

The keeping of an elephant is very costly, coming in Central India to about £80 or £90 a year. The Government has, however, great numbers of elephants, many of them trained shikárís; and there is seldom much difficulty in obtaining the use of one for a few weeks. They may also be frequently borrowed from wealthy natives; but in that case will seldom be found to possess the hard condition necessary for severe work in the hot season. In the later years of our forest work we always had several Government elephants allowed for the carriage of baggage and riding purposes, and, as I always kept one of my own besides, I could generally muster enough to drive effectively any tiger ground in Central India. But I rarely took out more than one elephant besides my own when shooting alone, finding that quiet hunting was far more successful than the bustle of many elephants and the rabble of men that usually accompany a tiger hunt.

In the end of April and May of 1862, I bagged six tigers and one panther in the Bétúl jungles, wounding two more tigers which escaped. I was unable regularly to devote myself to tiger-shooting, having much forest work to do, and my shooting was also much interfered with by accidental circumstances. A sprained tendon laid me up for fifteen days of the best weather (the hottest), and there was so much cholera about that many of the best places had to remain unvisited. Another party were also shooting in the same district; and, though they arrived after me in the field, contrary to the well-understood rule in such circumstances, proceeded ahead and disturbed the whole country by indiscriminate firing at deer and peafowl. It is scarcely necessary to say that when after tigers nothing else should be fired at. The Lállá came out strong under these unfavourable circumstances, working ahead and securing by his plausible tongue a monopoly of information in which he was well seconded by the conduct of our rivals in harassing the people in the matter of provisions, and thrashing them all round if a tiger was not found for them when they arrived. On one occasion I reached their ground just as their last camel was moving off to a new camp. They had stayed here a week trying in vain to extort help in finding a couple of tigers whose tracks they had seen. The tigers were all the time within half a mile of their tents, and before ten o'clock that day I had them both padded. During a whole month I believe they only succeeded in getting one tiger, and that by potting it from a tree at night.

I spent nearly a week of this time in the destruction of a famous man-eater, which had completely closed several roads, and was estimated to have devoured over a hundred human beings. One of these roads was the main outlet from the Bétúl teak forests towards the railway then under construction in the Narbadá valley; and the work of the sleeper-contractors was completely at a standstill owing to the ravages of this brute. He occupied regularly a large triangle of country between the rivers Móran and Ganjál; occasionally making a tour of destruction much further to the east and west; and striking terror into a breadth of not less than thirty to forty miles. It was therefore supposed that the devastation was caused by more than one animal; and we thought we had disposed of one of these early in April, when we killed a very cunning old tiger of evil repute after several days' severe hunting. But I am now certain that the brute I destroyed subsequently was the real malefactor even there, as killing again commenced after we had left, and all loss to human life did not cease till the day I finally disposed of him.

He had not been heard of for a week or two when I came into his country, and pitched my camp in a splendid mango grove near the large village of Lokartaláe, on the Móran river. Here I was again laid up through over-using my sprained tendon; but a better place in which to pass the long hot days of forced inactivity could not have been found. The bare brown country outside was entirely shut out by the long drooping branches of the huge mango trees, interlaced overhead in a grateful canopy, and loaded with the half-ripe fruit pendent on their long tendril-like stalks; while beneath them short glimpses were seen of the bright clear waters of the Móran stealing over their pebbly bed. The green mangoes, cooked in a variety of ways, furnished a grateful and cooling addition to the table; and the whole grove was alive with a vast variety of bird and insect life, in the observation of which many an hour that would otherwise have flown slowly by was passed. A colony of the lively chirping little gray-striped squirrel lived in every tree, and from morning to night permeated the whole grove with their incessant gambols. My dogs would have died of *ennui*, I believe, but for the unremitting sport they had in stalking and chasing these unattainable creatures, whose fashion of letting them get within two inches of them while they calmly sat up and ate a fallen mango, and then whisking up and sitting just half a foot out of reach, jerking their long tails and rapping out a long chirp of defiance, seemed highly to provoke them. Clouds of little green ring-necked paroquets flew from tree to tree, clambering over and under and in every direction through the branches to get at the green mangoes. A great variety of bright-coloured bulbuls, several species of woodpecker, and the golden oriole or mango-bird, flashed about in the higher foliage, while an incessant hum told of the unseen presence of multitudes of the insect world.

I was much amused by the result of my tent being pitched between two trees inhabited respectively by colonies of the common black and red ants, so plentiful in all wooded parts of the province. Each side sent detachments down the ropes of the tent attached to their trees, and numerous were the skirmishes and reprisals I watched between them. At last, on coming in from a short stroll one morning, I found the top of my tent had been the scene of a pitched battle between the entire forces of each party, multitudes on each side having been killed and wounded. Their telegrams to head-quarters in the tops of the trees must have much resembled those of the French and Prussians, for both sides seemed to claim the victory, and each was busily engaged in carrying off the fallen of the *other* side, perhaps with a view to provender in case of a siege! There were far more of the black ones, however, killed than of the red. The latter are most unflinching and venomous little devils, and prefer to leave their heads and shoulders sticking where they have bitten rather than loose their hold. I shall never forget disturbing a nest of these red ants in an overhanging tree when hot on the fresh footprints of a tiger. In an instant the elephant, howdah, and myself were covered with a multitude of the creatures rearing themselves on end and watching for a tender place in which to plunge their nippers. No philosophy—not even in the hot pursuit of a tiger—could stand this; and everything was forgotten in a wild rush to the nearest water, where half an hour was lost in clearing ourselves and the half-maddened elephant of the tormentors, and in picking out the fangs they had left behind.

A few days of a lazy existence in this microcosm of a grove passed not unpleasantly after a spell of hard work in the pitiless hot blasts outside; but when the Lállá brought in news of families of tigers waiting to be hunted in the surrounding river-beds I began to chafe; and when I heard from a neighbouring police post that the man-eater had again appeared, and had killed a man and a boy on the high road about ten miles from my camp, I could stand it no longer. I had been douching my leg with cold water, but now resorted to stronger measures, giving it a coating of James's horse-blister, which caused of course severe pain for a few days, but at the end of them resulted, to my great delight, in a complete and permanent cure. In the meantime, while I was still raw and sore, I was regaled with stories of the man-eater—of his fearful size and appearance, with belly pendent to the ground, and white moon on the top of his forehead; his pork-butcher-like method of detaining a party of travellers while he rolled himself in the sand, and at last came up and inspected them all round, selecting the fattest; his power of transforming himself into an innocent-looking woodcutter, and calling or whistling through the woods till an unsuspecting victim approached; how the spirits of all his victims rode with him on his head, warning him of every danger, and guiding him to the fatal ambush where a traveller would shortly pass. All the best shikárís of the country-side were collected in my camp; and the landholders and many of the people besieged my tent morning and evening. The infant of a woman who had been carried away while drawing water at a well was brought and held up before me; and every offer of assistance in destroying the monster was made. No useful help was, however, to be expected from a terror-stricken population like this. They lived in barricaded houses; and only stirred out when necessity compelled in large bodies, covered by armed men, and beating drums and shouting as they passed along the roads. Many villages had been utterly deserted; and the country was evidently being slowly depopulated by this single animal. So far as I could learn, he had been killing alone for about a year—another tiger who had formerly assisted him in his fell occupation having been shot the previous hot weather. Bétúl has always been unusually favoured with man-eaters, the cause apparently being the great number of cattle that come for a limited season to graze in that country, and a scarcity of other prey at the time when they are absent, combined with the unusually convenient cover for tigers existing alongside most of the roads. The man-eaters of the Central Provinces rarely confine themselves *solely* to human food, though some have almost done so to my own knowledge. Various circumstances may lead a tiger to prey on man; anything, in fact, that incapacitates him from killing other game more difficult to procure. A tiger who has got very fat and heavy, or very old, or who has been disabled by a wound, or a tigress who has had to bring up young cubs where other game is scarce—all these take naturally to man, who is the easiest animal of all to kill, as soon as failure with other prey brings on the pangs of hunger; and once a tiger has found out how easy it is to overcome the lord of creation, and how good he is to eat, he is apt to stick to him, and, if a tigress, to bring up her progeny in the same line of business. The greater prevalence of man-eaters in one district than in another I consider to be that I have mentioned. Great grazing districts, where the cattle come only for a limited season, are always the worst. Where the cattle remain all the year round, as in Nimár, the tigers rarely take to man-eating.

As soon as I could ride in the howdah, and long before I could do more than hobble on foot, I marched to a place called Chárkhérá, where the last kill had been reported. My usually straggling following was now compressed into a close body, preceded and followed by the baggage-elephants, and protected by a guard of police with muskets, peons with my spare guns, and a whole *posse* of match-locked shikárís. Two deserted villages were passed on the road, and heaps of stones at intervals showed where a traveller had been struck down. A better hunting-ground for a man-eater certainly could not be. Thick scrubby teak jungle closed in the road on both sides; and alongside of it for a great part of the way wound a narrow deep water-course, overshadowed by thick jáman bushes, and with here and there a small pool of water still left. I hunted along this nálá the whole way, and found many old tracks of a very large male tiger,[1] which the shikárís declared to be the man-eater. There were none more recent, however, than several days. Chárkhérá was also deserted on account of the tiger, and there was no shade to speak of; but it was the most central place within reach of the usual haunts of the brute, so I encamped here, and sent the baggage-elephants back to fetch provisions. In the evening I was startled by a messenger from a place called Lé, on the Móran river, nearly in the direction I had come from, who said that one of a party of pilgrims who had been travelling unsuspectingly by a jungle road had been carried off by the tiger close to that place. Early next morning I started off with two elephants, and arrived at the spot about eight o'clock. The man had been struck down where a small ravine leading down to the Móran crosses a lonely pathway a few miles east of Lé. The shoulders-stick with

[1] A little practice suffices to distinguish the tracks of tigers of different ages and sexes. The old male has a much *squarer* track, so to speak, than the female, which leaves a more oval footprint.

its pendent baskets, in which the holy water from his place of pilgrimage had been carried by the hapless man, was lying on the ground in a dried-up pool of blood; and shreds of his clothes adhered to the bushes where he had been dragged down into the bed of the nálá. We tracked the man-eater and his prey into a very thick grass cover, alive with spotted deer, where he had broken up and devoured the greater part of the body. Some bones and shreds of flesh, and the skull, hands, and feet, were all that remained. This tiger never returned to his victim a second time, so it was useless to found any scheme for killing him on that expectation. We took up his tracks from the body, and carried them patiently down through very dense jungle to the banks of the Móran; the trackers working in fear and trembling under the trunk of my elephant, and covered by my rifle at full cock. At the river the tracks went out to a long spit of sand that projected into the water, where the tiger had drunk, and then returned to a great mass of piled-up rocks at the bottom of a precipitous bank, full of caverns and recesses. This we searched with stones and some fireworks I had in the howdah; but put out nothing but a scraggy hyæna, which was of course allowed to escape. We searched about all day here in vain, and it was not till nearly sunset that I turned and made for camp.

It was almost dusk, when we were a few miles from home, passing along the road we had marched by the former day, and the same by which we had come out in the morning, when one of the men who was walking behind the elephant started and called a halt. He had seen the footprint of a tiger. The elephant's tread had partly obliterated it; but further on, where we had not gone, it was plain enough—the great square pug of the man-eater we had been looking for all day! He was on before us, and must have passed since we came out in the morning, for his track had *covered* that of the elephants as they came. It was too late to hope to find him that evening; and we could only proceed slowly along on the track, which held to the pathway, keeping a bright look-out. The Lállá indeed proposed that he should go a little ahead as a bait for the tiger, while I covered him from the elephant with a rifle! But he wound up by expressing a doubt whether his skinny corporation would be a sufficient attraction, and suggested that a plump young policeman, who had taken advantage of our protection to make his official visit to the scene of the last kill, should be substituted, whereat there was a general but not very hearty grin. The subject was too sore a one in that neighbourhood just then. About a mile from the camp the track turned off into the deep nálá that bordered the road. It was now almost dark, so we went on to the camp, and fortified it by posting the three elephants on different sides, and lighting roaring fires between. Once in the night an elephant started out of its deep sleep and trumpeted shrilly, but in the morning we could find no tracks of the tiger having come near us. I went out early next morning to beat up the nálá; for a man-eater is not like common tigers, and must be sought for morning, noon, and night. But I found no tracks, save in the one place where we had crossed the nálá the evening before, and gone off into thick jungle.

On my return to camp, just as I was sitting down to breakfast, some Banjárás from a place called Dékná—about a mile and a half from camp—came running in to say that one of their companions had been taken out of the middle of their drove of bullocks by the tiger, just as they were starting from their night's encampment. The elephant had not been unharnessed, and, securing some food and a bottle of claret, I was not two minutes in getting under way again. The edge of a low savanna, covered with long grass and intersected by a nálá, was the scene of this last assassination; and a broad trail of crushed-down grass showed where the body had been dragged down towards the nálá. No tracking was required; it was horribly plain. The trail did not lead quite into the nálá, which had steep sides, but turned and went alongside of it into some very long grass reaching nearly up to the howdah. Here Sarjú Parshád (a large Government mukna I was then riding) kicked violently at the ground and trumpeted, and immediately the long grass began to wave ahead. We pushed on at full speed, stepping as we went over the ghastly half-eaten body of the Banjárá. But the cover was dreadfully thick; and though I caught a glimpse of a yellow object as it jumped down into the nálá, it was not in time to fire. It was some little time before we could get the elephant down the bank and follow the broad plain footprints of the monster, now evidently going at a swinging trot. He kept on in the nálá for about a mile, and then took to the grass again; but it was not so long here, and we could still make out the trail from the howdah. Presently, however, it led into rough, stony ground, and the tracking became more difficult. He was evidently full of go, and would carry us far; so I sent back for some more trackers, and with orders to send a small tent across to a hamlet on the banks of the Ganjál, towards which he seemed to be making. All that day we followed the trail through an exceedingly difficult country, patiently working out print by print, but without being gratified by a sight of his brindled hide. Several of the local shikárís were admirable trackers; and we carried the line down within about a mile of the river, where a dense thorny cover began, through which no one could follow a tiger.

We slept that night at the little village, and early next morning made a long cast ahead, proceeding at once to the river, where we soon hit upon the track leading straight down its sandy bed. There were some strong covers reported in the river-bed some miles ahead, near the large village of Bhádúgaon, so I sent back to order the tent over there. The track was crossed in this river by several others, but was easily distinguishable from all by its superior size. It had also a peculiar drag of the toe of one hind-foot, which the people knew and attributed to a wound he had received some months before from a shikárí's matchlock. There was thus no doubt we were behind the man-eater, and I determined to follow him while I could hold out and we could keep the track. It led right into a very dense cover of jámin and tamarisk, in the bed and on the banks of the river, a few miles above Bhádúgaon. Having been hard pushed the previous day, we hoped he might lie up here; and, indeed, there was no other place he could well go to for water and shade. So we circled round the outside of the cover, and, finding no track leading out, considered him fairly ringed. We then went over to the village for breakfast, intending to return in the heat of the day.

There I was told by one of the mahouts a story, which I afterwards heard confirmed from the lips of one of the principal actors, regarding a notable encounter with tigers in the very cover where we had ringed the man-eater. It was in 1853 that the two brothers N. and Colonel G. beat the cover for a family of tigers said to be in it. One of the brothers was posted in a tree, while G. and the other N. beat through on an elephant. The man on the tree first shot two of the tigers right and left, and then Colonel G. saw a very large one lying in the shade of a dense bush, and fired at it, on which it charged and mounted on the elephant's head. It was a small female elephant, and was terribly punished about the trunk and eyes in this encounter, though the mahout (a bold fellow named Rámzán, who was afterwards in my own service) battered the tiger's head with his iron driving-hook so as to leave deep marks in the bones of his skull. At length he was shaken off, and retreated; but when the sportsmen urged in the elephant again, and the tiger charged as before, she turned round, and the tiger, catching her by the hind-leg, fairly pulled her over on her side. My informant, who was in the howdah, said that for a time his arm was pinned between it and the tiger's body, who was making efforts to pull his shikárí out of the back seat. They were all, of course, spilt on the ground with their guns; and Colonel G., getting hold of one, made the tiger retreat with a shot in the chest. The elephant had fled from the scene of action, and the two sportsmen then went in at the beast on foot. It charged again, and when close to them was finally dropped by a lucky shot in the head. But the sport did not end here; for they found two more tigers in the same cover immediately afterwards, and killed one of them—or four altogether in the day. The worrying she had received, however, was the death of the elephant, which was buried at Bhádúgaon—one of the few instances on record of an elephant being actually killed by a tiger.

About eleven o'clock we again faced the scorching hot wind, and made silently for the cover where lay the man-eater. I surrounded it with scouts on trees; and posted a pad-elephant at the only point where he could easily get up the high bank and make off; and then pushed old Sarjú slowly and carefully through the cover. Peafowl rose in numbers from every bush as we advanced; and a few hares and other small animals bolted out at the edges —such thick green covers being the midday resort of all the life of the neighbourhood in the hot weather. About the centre the jungle was extremely thick, and the bottom was cut up into a number of parallel water-channels among the strong roots and overhanging branches of the tamarisk. Here the elephant paused and began to kick the earth, and utter the low tremulous sound by which some elephants denote the close presence of a tiger. We peered all about with nervous beatings of the heart; and at last the mahout, who was lower down on the elephant's neck, said he saw him lying beneath a thick jáman bush. We had some stones in the howdah, and I made the Lállá, who was behind me in the back seat, pitch one into the bush. Instantly the tiger started up with a short roar and galloped off through the bushes. I gave him right and left at once, which told loudly; but he went till he saw the pad-elephant blocking the road he meant to escape by, and then he turned and charged back at me with horrible roars. It was very difficult to see him among the crashing bushes, and he was within twenty yards when I fired again. This dropped him into one of the channels; but he picked himself up, and came on again as savagely though more slowly than before. I was now in the act of covering him with the large shell rifle, when suddenly the elephant spun round, and I found myself looking the opposite way, while a worrying sound behind me and the frantic movements of the elephant told me I had a fellow-passenger on board I might well have dispensed with. All I could do in the way of holding on barely sufficed to prevent myself and guns from being pitched out; and it was some time before Sarjú, finding he could not kick him off, paused to think what he would do next. I seized that placid interval to lean over behind and put the muzzle of the rifle to the head of the tiger, blowing it into fifty pieces with the large shell. He dropped like a sack of potatoes; and then I saw the dastardly mahout urging the elephant to run out of the cover. An application of my gun-stock to his head, however, reversed the engine; and Sarjú, coming round with the utmost willingness, trumpeted a shrill note of defiance, and rushing upon his prostrate foe commenced a war-dance on his body, that made it little less difficult to stick to him than when the tiger was being kicked off. It consisted, I believe, of kicking up the carcase with a hind-leg, catching it in the hollow of the fore, and so tossing it backwards and forwards among his feet, winding up by placing his huge fore-foot on the body and crossing the other over it, so as to press it into the sand with his whole weight. I found afterwards that the elephant-boy, whose business it is to stand behind the howdah, and, if necessary, keep the elephant straight in a charge by applying a thick stick over his rump, had had a narrow escape in this adventure, having dropped off in his fright almost into the jaws of the tiger. The tiger made straight for the elephant, however, as is almost invariably the case, and the boy picked himself up and fled to the protection of the other elephant.

Sarjú was not a perfect shikárí elephant; but his fault was rather too much courage than the reverse, and it was only his miserable opium-eating villain of a mahout that made him turn at the critical moment. He was much cut about the quarters; but I took him out close to the tents two days after and killed two more tigers without his flinching in the least. The tiger we had thus killed was undoubtedly the man-eater. He was exactly ten feet long, in the prime of life, with the dull yellow coat of the adult male—not in the least mangy or toothless like the man-eater of story. He had no moon on his head, nor did his belly nearly touch the ground. I afterwards found that these characteristics are attributed to all man-eaters by the credulous people.

Before dismissing Sarjú from these pages, I would

like to record an anecdote of his sagacity which I think beats everything I have heard of the elephant's intellect. He was a consummate thief, and had grown so cunning that he would unfasten any chains or ropes he was tethered with, which he often would do of a dark night if not watched, and proceed to roam about seeking what he might devour. His favourite object on such occasions was sugar-cane, and if he got into a field of this would trample down and damage the greater part of it. Many a long bill have I paid for such depredations. He would never allow himself to be caught again after such an escapade while his keepers pursued him with sticks and threats, but surrendered at once as soon as they resorted to persuasion, and promised not to beat him. One night the people of the camp were sitting up late over a small fire, and saw Sarjú unloose his foot-chain and stalk off through the camp. Presently he appeared sniffing about the place where a grain-merchant had brought out his sacks during the day to supply the wants of the camp. A sack of rice, nearly empty, lay under the head of a sleeping lad, and Sarjú paused and seemed to ponder long how he might annex its contents. At last he was seen to gradually withdraw the bag with his trunk, while he replaced it with the sloping edge of his big fore-foot in supporting the head of the boy. Having gobbled up the rice with much despatch, he then rolled up the bag, and returning it under the boy's head, stalked away! I was told this story next morning by several respectable natives who saw the whole affair, and who had no object in telling a lie about it. For my own part, knowing what Mr. Sarjú was capable of, I believe it.

Before quitting the subject of tigers I may notice the obstacle presented by the number of these animals to the advance of population and tillage. Between five and six hundred human beings, and an uncalculated number of cattle, are killed by wild beasts in the Central Provinces alone every year. This enormous loss of life and property has been the subject of much discussion, and many schemes for their destruction have been proposed—most of them unpractical, and some even absurd. For some years heavy rewards were given for every tiger and other dangerous animal killed, special rewards being placed on the heads of man-eaters; and I am convinced that many more were killed during that time than previously, though statistics of former years when there was no reward are not available for comparison. The number destroyed increased every year under this stimulus. Rewards for the killing of 2414 tigers, panthers, bears, and wolves were claimed in 1867 (the last year for which statistics are available), against 1863 in 1865. Tigers are certainly not now so numerous by a great deal in many parts with which I am personally acquainted as they were even six or eight years ago. The reward has now again been much decreased; and the experience of a few years will show whether the tigers again get the upper hand. It is practically only the cattle-killing and man-eating tigers that are productive of injury, those which principally subsist on game being probably more useful than noxious. Poison has sometimes been successful in destroying a man-eater —a famous tigress, that long ravaged the western part of Chindwárá district, having been killed with strychnine just a day before I arrived after a forced march of a hundred miles to hunt her. More commonly, however, poison is of no avail with these cunning brutes; and, as a rule, man-eaters can only be killed by the European sportsman with the help of an elephant, the native shikárís rarely attempting to molest them. Elephants have been made more available than formerly, some of the jungle districts having a Government one attached to them, besides many possessed by various public departments; and man-eaters of a bad type now rarely survive long. It is a great point to extinguish those brutes at the outset of their career, for, if not killed when he commences to prey on human beings, a tiger becomes so cunning that it is afterwards a most difficult thing to circumvent him.

On the 27th of May I shot my last tiger for that season in the famous cover of Dapárá, being seized the next day with the preliminary symptoms of what turned out to be a severe attack of jungle fever, brought on by constant exposure to the hot sun by day and the malarious air of these close valleys by night; cholera, too, was raging all around us, and so I determined to return to the cool heights of Puchmurree, which I did by the Borí route, in four longish marches. I was sick of the constant severe heat of the burnt-up plains below, and parched with the coming fever as well, and I think I never enjoyed anything so much as when I bared my head to the cool breeze that swept over the Puchmurree plateau, as I topped its edge after climbing up the stiff ascent of the Rorí Ghát. The thermometer in my tent below had been ranging from 98 degrees to 110 degrees during the heat of the day, and had once reached 120 degrees, when I went out and lay like a tiger under some jáman bushes by the waterside. In the verandah of the lodge on Puchmurree, which was now nearly finished, it stood at 86 degrees, while the nights, which below had not for weeks been free from hot winds, were cool and delicious up here. Soon after coming up I was fairly prostrated with fever, and remained delirious for about a couple of days, emerging at last, thanks to a very attentive native doctor we had, much shaken and weak, but free from the fever. Nearly all my servants and the camp followers who had been through the hot weather with me also got fever on coming up to Puchmurree, and the place presented much the appearance of an extensive hospital for some weeks.

The first rain of the monsoon fell on the 12th of June, a smart shower, that, as if by magic, covered the plateau with the greenest of tints. The wild flowers, too, again burst forth on all sides, under the influence of the gentle showers that now almost daily visited the hill. It was inexpressibly delightful to be up here, in a perfectly English climate, with cool gray skies, and greenery all about, after the terrible grilling we had suffered for two long months down below. My Korkú friends seemed glad to see me back again, and I tried to go out after the bison with them, but I found myself far too weak to negotiate the formidable slopes of Dhúpgarh. The early part of the rainy season which was now approaching is the very best time of all for hunting the bison, tracks being easily followed, while the sky is generally overcast with clouds, and the weather cool in these high regions. Towards the end of the month the clouds began to bank up into deep purple masses behind the higher peaks, and at night lightning played incessantly round the horizon. By great exertions we got the house roofed just in time to hang a bison's frontlet over the door, and christen it "Bison Lodge," before the full force of the monsoon broke upon the plateau on the last day of June. I must not now tell of the many pleasant days and jovial nights passed between those four walls in after years, when the fire blazing in the arched grate I had builded with my own hands, and the *jorum* of whisky toddy imported from my native hills, deluded us into the belief that we were far away from the exile, if still a pleasant exile, of the highlands of Central India. Such a terrific storm I never saw as on the night of the breaking of the monsoon, crash after crash seeming to burst within the rooms, while a blaze of green lightning incessantly lit up the whole features of the hill. It lasted about the whole night, and nearly four inches of rain fell along with it, but on its clearing up in the morning, such is the beautiful drainage of this plateau that in less than an hour a horse could have galloped over it comfortably in any direction. Rain-clouds continued to shroud the higher peaks, and roll round the edges of the plateau, the whole time I remained on the hill, but we never had another heavy storm, and, what is very unusual at such altitudes, the clouds never invaded the centre of the plateau at all. I had repeated returns of the fever, and neither could my people shake it off. Conveniences to help recovery were also wanting, and I left the plateau on the 20th of July to march to Jubbulpúr. It was a melancholy procession down the hill, that march of my gaunt and fever-stricken followers, crowded on the backs of the elephants that carried them in several trips to the carts that awaited them below.

Another officer relieved me at Puchmurree, and remained nearly till the end of the rainy season; meteorological observations being kept up, in order to compare with others which were being taken at the same time by a party resident on the rival plateau of Motúr. The result was that a mean temperature of about 73 degrees, and a rainfall of rather more than 60 inches, were registered for both places during the four months from June to September, which shows a range of heat about 8 degrees or 10 degrees lower than on the plains, and nearly double the rainfall. Unfortunately, however, the comparative difficulty of access to Puchmurree was allowed to tell against its infinitely superior beauty and suitability in other respects; and swampy, jungly, hideous Motúr, which lies

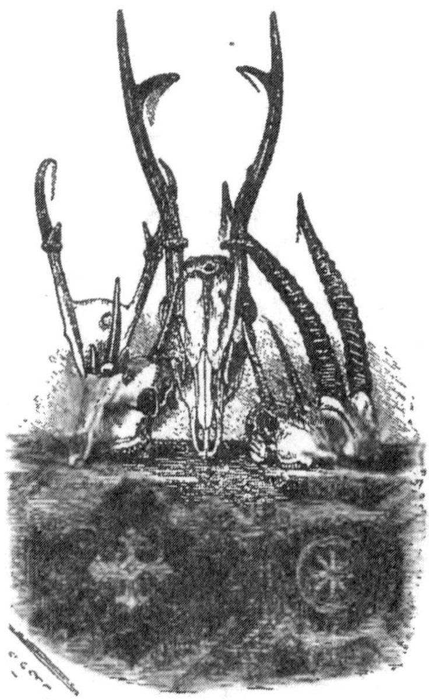

HORNS OF HOG-DEER, BARKING-DEER, MALE AND FEMALE CHIKÁRA, AND FOUR-HORNED ANTELOPE. (*Scale, one-tenth.*)

on the trap formation, and very much resembles the country along the Táptí river described in the last chapter, was preferred to this beautiful plateau for trial as a sanitarium for European troops during the ensuing season. It was an utter failure, the climate being bad, and there being nothing to interest the men in such a place.

Since then the Forest Department has regularly occupied the lodge on the hill, and laid out extensive gardens round about. Attempts to cultivate the quinine-yielding cinchona made on a small scale have failed, owing probably to want of the needful attention and knowledge, rather than to unsuitability of the place and climate. The potato, and all sorts of European vegetables and flowers, have been found to thrive admirably at Puchmurree. Another house has been built, and many European and native officials have enjoyed excellent health during visits to the place for some years.

I shall not say much of my long ride of a hundred miles to Jubbulpúr in the soaking rain, through the stiff black mud and unbridged streams of the Narbadá valley. It was very miserable, with the chills of ague in one's bones. With the exception of a few days, when I had the excellent society of my friend Captain Pearson, I had not seen a white face during these six months of jungle wanderings; and though by no means tired of the wild, independent life of a forester, or of the company of the hill people and the kindly little band of dependants I had gathered about me, the society of a pleasant station like the Jubbulpúr of those days was an agreeable change.

CHAPTER VIII

THE HIGHER NARBADÁ

JUBBULPÚR is now rather an important place, being the point of junction of the two lines of railway which between them connect the political with the commercial capital of India, Calcutta with Bombay, and over which pass all the passengers, and much of the goods, in transit between England and upper India. At the time of which I write it was a small civil and military station, of which few who had not been there knew anything, except that it was situated somewhere in the wilds of Central India. I remember when we first got our orders to march there from upper India no one could give us a route to it. It was trooped from Madras at that time, and so of course the Bengal authorities could not be expected to know anything about it. We found it the pleasantest of Indian stations; situated in a green hollow among low rocky granite hills always covered with verdure; with tidy hard roads and plenty of greensward about them; with commodious bungalows embowered in magnificent clumps of bamboo; remarkable for the delicacy and abundance of its fruits and other garden products, including the pineapple, which will not grow anywhere else in Central India; and withal, from its land-locked condition forbidding exports, a most absurdly cheap sort of place to live in. All this is now changed. The steam-horse has torn his way through the parks, and levelled the bamboo clumps that were the glory of the place. Hideous embankments, and monstrous hotels, and other truly British buildings, stare one in the face at every turn. Crowds of rail-borne "picturesquers" assail the Marble Rocks and other sights about the place. Everything has run up to the famine prices induced by the rapid "progress" of the last ten years. And progress it is, in every proper sense of the word. The Narbadá valley is now a part of the great bustling world outside, instead of being a mere isolated oasis in a desert of jungle, thinking and caring only about its own petty wants and concerns. The agriculturist, the merchant, and all who "paddle their own canoe" on the great ocean of life, are all the better for it. Their gains have grown in more than proportion to their outgoings. Only such wretches as sail in "foreign bottoms" have to regret the change; their fixed incomes have not grown with the growth of their expenses. The poor clerk, who could barely in the old times keep body and soul together on his pittance of ten rupees a month, gets no more now that his expenses are doubled. Government schools have flooded his market with competitors, who prevent his wages from rising by their importunity for office; and the Government, not having yet discovered the way to raise its own income, when appealed to for more, buttons up its pockets, and points to the crowds ready and willing to serve for less. The poor clerk has his remedy; he can pick and steal enough to make up the deficiency; and he does so. But the subaltern of infantry, or the young civilian, being incommoded with the troublesome commodity called honour, have no such resource; and so they have nothing for it but to knock off their Arab, and other little luxuries, and fag away through an ill-concealed period of indigence to higher grades and better pay.

All this civilisation has of course greatly deteriorated the place as a residence for him whose pleasures lie with the jungle and its wild inhabitants. In the old times, Jubbulpúr was almost the perfection of a sportsman's head-quarters. It lay nearly at the head of the last of the great basins of the Narbadá valley, which have been reclaimed by population and agriculture. These basins are a characteristic of the valley, and within the limits of our province are four in number; great circular plains surrounded by steep hills, filled with deep alluvial soil, through which the river moves slowly in long silent reaches, with here and there a gentle stream. Between them lie shorter sections of rugged ground, where the hills on either side converge, and through which the river tumbles in a less placid course, short pools being connected by long broken rapids. A little way above Jubbulpúr, the last of these basins is terminated by the again converging hills, and from this point up to the little civil station of Mandlá the river flows through a narrow valley, very scantily cultivated here and there, and generally covered along the riverside by bamboos, and on the hills by a low jungle composed of the commoner sort of trees. Many little tributary streams joined the river in this part of its course. These ran up into the partially cultivated uplands on either side of the valley; and in the cold season, when they contained water and green vegetation, afforded cover to great numbers of wild animals of all sorts. When the hot season advanced their waters gradually dried up, and then the game all moved down into the Narbadá valley, congregating at that time, when the great mutiny had for some years prevented their molestation, in very great numbers.

I have marched up this valley, on my way to explore the Sál forests in the eastern part of the province. But want of time then prevented my lingering to shoot. The year before joining the Forest Department, however, I had made an excursion up this valley during the hot season; and while cantoned at Jubbulpúr, made many excursions through the hilly regions surrounding the valley. Several sorts of game which have not yet been much mentioned were then met with in great abundance; and before taking my readers towards the Sál forests I will devote a little space to these excursions.

I was then a good deal of a "griffin," and was obliged to rely much on the assistance of native shikárís in finding game. The chief of these about Jubbulpúr was an arch-villain who haunted the purlieus of the cantonment messes, and hawked about his news of panthers, bears, deer, etc., to the highest bidder. I don't think I ever heard his name. He was always called "Bamanjee," or the "Brahman," for such was his caste. He knew intimately every inch of the jungle for twenty miles around, and had sons and nephews in close relations with the tigers and other wild animals in all directions. He was thoroughly acquainted with all the different sorts of game and their habits, and really could, when he chose, furnish first-rate sport to his clients. But he was by nature a rogue of the first water, generally taking his information all round the station for offers; and taking out the highest bidder to a hunt which almost invariably ended, through some perverse accident, in the escape without scathe of the object of pursuit, which he would very likely bring in the next day himself to claim the Government reward. He had "stumbled on it," of course, quite by accident, and in self-defence, etc., he was compelled to shoot it!

His great quarry was the panther, of which he was known to have killed an almost incredible number in the course of his long life. He lived in a little village about four miles out of the station, just under one of the steep isolated granite hills that rise at intervals from the plain; and he once showed me a notched stick, on which fifty-two cuts recorded the number of panthers he had killed on this hill alone. The number of these animals in the districts round about Jubbulpúr is very great. The low rocky hills referred to, full of hollows and caverns, and overgrown with dense scrubby cover, afford them favourite retreats; while the numbers of antelope and hog deer, goats, sheep, pariah dogs, and pigs, supply them with abundant food. A large male panther will kill not very heavy cattle; but as a rule they confine themselves to the smaller animals mentioned. They seldom reside very far from villages, prowling round them at night in search of prey, and retreating to their fastnesses before daybreak. Unlike the tiger, they care little for the neighbourhood of water even in the hot weather, drinking only at night, and generally at a distance from their midday retreat.

There has been much confusion among sportsmen and writers as to the several species of Cat called "Panther," "Leopard," and "Hunting Leopard." Jerdon, in his *Mammals of India*, has at last correctly distinguished them under the above names, recognising two varieties marked with rosettes (the fulvous ground of the skin showing through the black), instead of plain black spots, which are peculiar to the Hunting Leopard (*F. Jubata*). He calls both *F. Pardua*, considering them only as varieties, not distinct species. In English he calls the larger the panther and the smaller the leopard, and it will be well if sportsmen will avoid future confusion by adopting this appropriate nomenclature. The points of difference between the two varieties of *F. Pardus* he states to be the larger size of the panther, which reaches in fine specimens seven feet eleven inches in length from nose to tip of tail, the leopard not exceeding five feet six inches; the lighter colour, and taller and more slender figure of the panther, and the rounder, more bulldog-like head of the leopard.

In my early sporting days I fell into the mistake of most sportsmen in supposing that the panther might be hunted on foot with less caution than the tiger. On two or three occasions I nearly paid dearly for the error; and I now believe that the panther is really by far a more dangerous animal to attack than the tiger. He is, in the first place, far more courageous. For though he will generally sneak away unobserved as long as he can, if once brought to close quarters he will rarely fail to charge with the utmost ferocity, fighting to the very last. He is also much more active than the tiger, making immense springs clear off the ground, which the tiger seldom does. He can conceal himself in the most wonderful way, his spotted hide blending with the ground, and his lithe loose form being compressible into an inconceivably small space. Further, he is so much less in depth and stoutness than the tiger, and moves so much quicker, that he is far more difficult to hit in a vital place. He can climb trees, which the tiger cannot do except for a short distance up a thick sloping trunk. A few years ago a panther thus took a sportsman out of a high perch on a tree in the Chindwárá district. And lastly, his powers of offence are scarcely inferior to those of the tiger himself; and are amply sufficient to be the death of any man he gets hold of. When stationed at Damoh, near

Jubbulpúr, with a detachment of my regiment, I shot seven panthers and leopards in less than a month, within a few miles of the station, chiefly by driving them out with beaters; all of them charged who had the power to do so; but the little cherub who watches over "griffins" got us out of it without damage either to myself or the beaters. One of the smaller species, really not more than five feet long, I believe, charged me three several times up a bank to the very muzzle of my rifle (of which I luckily had a couple), falling back each time to the shot, but not dreaming of trying to escape, and dying at last at my feet with her teeth closed on the root of a small tree. This animal had about six inches of the quill of a porcupine broken off in her chest. Another jumped on my horse, when passing through some long grass, before she was fired at at all; and after being kicked off charged my groom and gun-carrier, who barely escaped by fleeing for their lives, leaving my only gun in the possession of the leopard. I had to ride to cantonments for another rifle, and to get together some beaters. When we returned, I took up my post on a rock which overlooked the patch of grass; and the beaters had scarcely commenced their noise before the leopard went at them like an arrow. An accident would certainly have happened this time had my shots failed to stop this devil incarnate before she reached them. She had cubs in the grass, which accounted for her fury; but a tigress would have abandoned them to their fate in a similar case. The last I killed was a man-eater, which took up his post among the high crops surrounding a village, and killed and dragged in women and children who ventured out of the village. He was a panther of the largest size, and had been wounded by a shikárí from a tree, the ball passing through his external ear and one of his paws, and rendering him incapable of killing game. I was a week hunting him, as he was very careful not to show himself when pursued; and at last I shot him in a cowhouse into which he had ventured, and killed several head of cattle, before the people had courage to shut the door.

When a panther takes to man-eating, he is a far more

terrible scourge than a tiger. In 1858 a man-killing panther devastated the northern part of the Seoní district, killing (incredible as it may seem) nearly a hundred persons before he was shot by a shikárí. He never ate the bodies, but merely lapped the blood from the throat; and his plan was either to steal into a house at night, and strangle some sleeper on his bed, stifling all outcry with his deadly grip, or to climb into the high platforms from which watchers guard their fields from deer, and drag out his victim from there. He was not to be baulked of his prey; and when driven off from one end of a village, would hurry round to the opposite side and secure another in the confusion. A few moments completed his deadly work, and such was the devilish cunning he joined to this extraordinary boldness that all attempts to find and shoot him were for many months unsuccessful. European sportsmen who went out, after hunting him in vain all day, would find his tracks close to the door of their tent in the morning. When, a few years later, I passed through the scene of his chief depredations (Dhúmá), a curious myth had grown round the history of this panther. A man and his wife were travelling back to their home from a pilgrimage to Benares, when they met on the road a panther. The woman was terrified; but the man said, "Fear not, I possess a charm by which I can transform myself into any shape. I will now become a panther, and remove this obstacle from the road, and on my return you must place this powder in my mouth, when I will recover my proper shape." He then swallowed his own portion of the magic powder, and assuming the likeness of the panther, persuaded him to leave the path. Returning to the woman, he opened his mouth to receive the transposing charm; but she, terrified by his dreadful appearance and open jaws, dropped it in the mire, and it was lost. Then, in despair, he killed the author of his misfortune, and ever after revenged himself on the race whose form he could never resume.

The Seoní panther is not a solitary case, several other man-eating panthers having done scarcely less amount of mischief in other parts of the province. Their indifference to water makes it extremely difficult to bring them to book; and, indeed, panthers are far more generally met with by accident than secured by regular hunting. When beating with elephants they are very rarely found, considering their numbers; but they must be frequently passed at a short distance, unobserved, in this kind of hunting. I was hunting for a tigress and cubs near Khápá, on the Lawá river, in Bétúl; their tracks of a few days old led into a deep fissure in the rocky banks of the river, above which I went, leaving the elephant below, and threw in stones from the edge. Some way up I saw a large panther steal out at the head, and sneak across the plain. He was out of shot, and I followed on his tracks, which were clear enough for a few hundred yards, till, at the crossing of a small rocky nálá, they disappeared. I could not make it out, and was returning to the elephant, when I saw the driver making signals. He had followed me up above, and had seen the panther sneak back, along the little ńálá, which led into the top of the ravine, and re-enter the latter. I then went and placed myself so as to command the top of the ravine, and sent people below to fling in stones, and presently the panther broke again at the same place, this time galloping away openly across the plain. I missed with both barrels of my rifle, but turned him over with a lucky shot from a smooth-bore, at more than two hundred yards. I then went up to him on the elephant, and he made feeble attempts to rise and come at me, but he was too far gone to succeed. The panther will charge an elephant with the greatest ferocity. Near Sambalpúr, a party of us were beating a bamboo cover for pigs, with a view to the sticking thereof, my elephant accompanying the beaters, when a shout from the latter announced that they had stumbled on a panther. They took to trees, and I got on the elephant to turn him out, while the others exchanged their hog-spears for rifles, and surrounded the place on trees. She got up before me, bounding away over the low bamboos, and I struck her on the rump with a light breech-loading gun as she disappeared. Several shots from the trees failed to stop her, and she took refuge in a very dense thorny cover on the banks of a little stream. Twice up and down I passed without seeing the brute, but firing once into a log of wood in mistake for her, and was going along the top of the cover for the third time when the elephant pointed down the bank with her extended trunk. We threw some stones in, but nothing moved; and at last a peon came up with a huge stone on his head, which he heaved down the bank. Next moment a yellow streak shot from the bushes, and, levelling the adventurous peon, like a flash of lightning came straight at my elephant's head, when, just at the last spring, I broke her back with a breech-loader, and she fell over under the elephant's trunk, tearing at the earth and stones and her own body in her bloody rage. She had a cub in the cover, about the size of a cat, which I shot on the way back.

The method usually resorted to by old Bamanjee and other native shikárís for killing panthers and leopards was by tying out a kid, with a line attached to a fish-hook through its ear, a pull at which makes the poor little brute continue to squeak, after it has cried itself to silence about its mother. No sentiment of humanity interferes with the devices of the mild Hindú. A dog in a pit, with a basket-work cover over it, and similarly attached to a line, is equally effective. I have known panthers repeatedly to take animals they have killed up into trees to devour, and once found the body of a child, that had been killed by a panther in the Bétúl district, so disposed of in the fork of a tree. They are very often lost, I believe, by taking unobserved to trees. Beating them out of cover with a strong body of beaters and fireworks is, on the whole, the most successful way of hunting these cunning brutes; but it is accompanied by a good deal of risk to the beaters as well as to the sportsman, if he is over-venturesome; and it is apt, also, to end in disappointment in most instances. My own experience is that the majority of panthers one finds are come across more by luck than good management.

Old Bamanjee, with whom I had often been out on short trips with considerable success, induced me to take a month's leave, and accompany him up the Narbadá valley from Jubbulpúr to shoot. The game promised consisted of tigers, bears, sámbar, and spotted deer; and I found that all these were really attainable in no small numbers. The sámbar and bears lived on the hill ranges on either side of the river; while the spotted deer, as usual, kept to the banks of the river, where a network of ravines, covered with clumps of bamboo, afforded them the plentiful shade and abundance of water they delight in. In attendance on them was the tiger, who revelled in the abundance of game then congregated about the river. The herds of cattle and buffaloes that were grazing in the valley were seldom touched, excepting in one place, where I found a family of tigers wholly subsisting upon them; but nearly every day we stumbled on the remains of spotted deer, sámbar, and nílgái, which had fallen victims to the destroyer. The destroyer himself, however, kept, with a good deal of success, out of our way. I was too green a hand to hunt him then with the silent perseverance which alone ensures success, and could rarely resist a promising shot at other game on the distant chance of finding a tiger. Nor do I think that Mr. Bamanjee much desired to have very many interviews with his jungle majesty. Spotted deer were in immense numbers, and the bucks were everywhere bellowing along the banks, and in the bamboo-covered ravines that radiate from the river. It was very easy to shoot the poor brutes at that time, the best plan being to embark in a canoe dug out of a single log, and paddle slowly down the reaches a little way from the bank, between daybreak and ten or eleven o'clock. The air of repose worn by the whole scene at that time is scarcely broken by the movement of animal life. The lazy plunge of a crocodile, the eddying rise of a great fish, the hover of a gem-like kingfisher, the easy flight of the dark, square-winged buzzard, all add to, rather than diminish, the sense of quietness in the scene. Immense numbers of peafowl live on the banks. This is the season of their loves, and almost every bare knoll may be seen covered with a flock of them, the hens sitting demurely in the centre, while the cocks ruffle out their magnificent plumage, and spread their gorgeous trains, and waltz round and round them in a most absurd fashion. The boatmen are fond of trying to catch them when absorbed in this dance of love; and, though I have never seen one actually secured, I have seen an active fellow get so near as to pluck some feathers from the tail of the collapsed and retreating swain. No riotous sounds offend the ear in this peaceful valley. The Koël, bird of the morning, raises now and then his staccato note from some overhanging tree, or the giant Sárus crane floats his tremulous cry along the calm surface of the lake-like river.

But hark! From a clump of tangled bamboos, overhanging the mouth of a little burn that joins the river, rings the loud bellow of a spotted buck. The boatman sticks his long pole down to the bottom, and anchors the dug-out, while the sportsman, with cocked rifle, watches in the bow. Presently a rustle and a motion in the fringe of bright-green jáman bushes that edge the river, and the head and shoulders of a noble buck emerge, one fore-foot advanced hesitatingly to the strip of yellow sand beside the water. Another instant and he stands, a statue of grace and beauty, on the open beach. Now he has seen the boat, and his careless mien is changed for an attitude of intense regard. Motionless, head thrown up, and antlers sweeping his flanks, he might be photographed for the second or two he stands at gaze. In an instant more he will wheel round and plunge into the thicket, unless stopped by the deadly bullet. The true sportsman will often spare the beautiful creature, even when thus at the point of his rifle, when a week or two of the easy sport has satiated his ardour, and filled his camp with meat and trophies of graceful antlers. It was impossible in those days to walk half a mile along the river bank without seeing deer, and I have known an indifferent shot kill six bucks here in a morning.

There was some excitement in the chance of stumbling on a tiger in the cool thickets of green cover by the river, or, like the sportsman, stalking the spotted deer. I was following a wounded buck once, when I thus almost trod upon a tiger doing the very same thing. It was in the dusk of the evening, when I saw him about twenty paces ahead of me, roading up the bloody trail like a retriever on a winged pheasant. He was passing over a low ridge between two ravines, and I was below him—a situation awkward for a foot-encounter with any dangerous animal. I therefore waited till he disappeared on the other side, and then running softly up, peered down from behind a clump of bamboos. Presently I saw the wounded buck and two does start out of some cover beyond the further ravine, and then a motion of the tiger, who had been standing a little below them, as he quickly crouched out of their sight, revealed him to me. I sat down, and took a steady shot at his shoulder at about seventy yards. He rolled back into the nálá, above which I was standing, and, after a good deal of growling and struggling among the leaves, all was still. It would have been folly to go down to him in such uncertain light, so I returned to the boat, going back next morning with an elephant to see the result. It was just as well I had not ventured down in the dark the night before; for, after lying some time where he fell, and leaving a great pool of blood on the ground, he had afterwards recovered himself, and gone slowly and painfully off towards the river. We followed up the track, and about three hundred yards further down found him, by the chattering of birds, lying stiff and stark under a bush. He had never reached the water he sought.

About twenty-five miles above Jubbulpúr is a curious place called "The Monkeys' Leap." A small tributary of the Narbadá, called the Bághórá (or "Tiger River"), here comes down from the southern hills, and, after approaching the Narbadá within about a hundred yards, sheers off again, and runs some miles before it finally joins it. Deep water fills both the channels opposite the narrow neck, and the strip of cover between the rivers is a favourite resort for all sorts of game in the hot season. I was invited by a neighbouring Thákúr, a Rájpút, to join a drive for game he was arranging at this place, in which he hoped to secure a famous tiger that had long defied every effort to kill him. Long will "Whitehead," of the Gairá Bairá, be remembered on the banks of the Narbadá. He furnished sport to a whole generation of the sportsmen of Jubbulpúr, and, so far as I know, never was killed. He disappeared in the course of time. Several hundred beaters were assembled to beat the leg-of-mutton shaped tract, of which the narrow "Monkeys' Leap" between the two rivers formed the shank. A large old stump of a banyan tree stood right in the centre of the neck, hollowed like a cup at the top by the weather, and filled a few inches deep with drift sand. A better post for the gunner could not be, and here the Thákúr and I took our places. It was a long drive, and it was not for an hour or more that the game began to appear, and groups of spotted deer gradually collected on all the knolls within sight on the inward side. They grew and grew in numbers, gazing back at the beaters and forward at the tree, where they had often run the gauntlet before. They were very unwilling to come on, but the drive was strong and not to be eluded. I watched for the tiger till many of the deer had gone past; at first a straggling doe with her fawn, then small groups, and finally a great hustling mass of dappled hides and tossing antlers. There was no tiger evidently in the beat. The Thákúr's long matchlock had already been the death of a buck, and he was painfully reloading its long tube from his primitive charging implements. I had a couple of rifles, single and double, and it was the work of as many seconds only to fire the three barrels, killing two and wounding another. There were no breech-loaders in those days; but I had time to reload the double while the stream of deer poured past, and secure two more bucks before the beaters came up. The wounded buck was afterwards recovered. There cannot have been less than a thousand spotted deer in this beat; and I never before or since saw such a sight. With a breech-loader twenty or thirty bucks could easily have been killed. One of the bucks I killed had the largest horns I have ever seen, measuring each thirty-eight inches round the curve.

I had another beat for "Whitehead" afterwards, near

the same place. The beaters came on him in a patch of long grass jungle, from which he obstinately refused to move. He had been once wounded in a drive, and never would face the guns again. At last we set fire to the jungle, while I awaited him on a tree at one end. The raging flames must have passed completely over him, and it was not till they had nearly reached my post, and the heat was exploding the dried fruits of a *leael* tree[1] next to me, with reports like pistol shots, that I retreated from my post. I had barely reached the ground when I heard a shout from the beaters, who were all in the trees round about the cover, and the tiger broke out among them. Then ensued a drawing-up of black legs, and a perfect Babel of abuse of his remotest ancestors was poured on him from the trees as he halted below, and looked up at them with a longing gaze. I hurried round, but was just in time to see him pause for a moment on the top of a ridge, his grand form appearing dilated to an unnatural size, from the bracing of the muscles, lashing tail, and bristling coat, bathed in the red glow of the setting sun and the blazing jungle. The next instant, before my rifle could be got to bear on him, he plunged down the farther side and disappeared.

I had one piece of really wonderful luck in this trip, which compensated for a good deal of heavy fagging in vain after the monarch of the jungle. I will quote the account as written at the time, which betrays an enthusiasm I should scarcely be able to call up in such a description nowadays, and which gives the details of a method of hunting tigers which in later years I abandoned as involving too great a risk of human life, namely, driving with beaters. In such a country as the upper Narbadá valley, however, the more legitimate method of stalking with the elephant could scarcely be followed, owing to the extent and density of the cover and the abundance of water.

Three tigers, namely, a tigress and her two nearly full-grown cubs, had long been the plague of some villages on the banks of the river. Their depredations extended

[1] *Ægle marmalos.*

over about five miles of country, where they found beef so plentiful and easily got that they seldom wandered above that distance from their usual haunts, which lay in a mesh of most difficult ravines bordering the Narbadá, and running up towards the hills. The covert here was of the densest description, though thinner, of course, at this time of the year than at any other. On my arrival in the neighbourhood, I was immediately solicited to go and rid it of these pests, and every assistance promised. So I pitched my camp at the village nearest to their haunts, and began to lay plans for their destruction. There was no need to tie animals out as baits for the tigers, as is sometimes done, for here they killed a cow or two every other day, although, food being so plentiful, they seldom remained long near the carcases. The third evening after I came, two cows were killed about a mile from camp. I would not allow them to be touched, trusting that, having eaten well during the night, the tigers would lie up in some place close at hand, to which we might track them next morning, and beat them out in the heat of the day.

When any tracking has to be done, it is of great importance to be at the spot very early in the morning, as the breezes, which generally rise shortly after daybreak, are apt to destroy the fine edges of the impressions left, and by nine o'clock it is often impossible to tell whether the marks are old or new. We accordingly started for the "murrees" before daylight, and had no difficulty in finding the place, which was deeply marked by the feet of both tigers and cows, and a broad trail led off in the direction the tigers had dragged the carcases. Following this up, it led us shortly into a ravine, where we found the remains of both cows deposited in different narrow clefts, where the tigers had retired to dine at their leisure. Of one the head alone was left, and the head and fore-quarters of the other. The carcases had evidently been most scientifically cleaned out by these professional butchers before setting to work, the dung and other refuse being carefully piled up at a little distance, so as not to come between the wind and their nobility during the repast. Vultures, kites, and crows had already commenced to demolish the remainder

—a sure sign that our game had left the immediate neighbourhood.

Taking up the tracks, we followed them for about half a mile along the ravine towards the river. The prints of the old lady and her daughters were nearly the same in size, and scarcely distinguishable. The Gónds who were tracking declared that they could tell that the cubs were both females. This, I confess, I was somewhat incredulous of, although I had frequently had occasion to admire their extraordinary skill in tracking; and I thought they were merely trusting to the well-known preponderance of female over male cubs,[1] to get a little *kudos* in the event of their prediction turning out true. This was subsequently the case, but I have since learned that the footmarks are really distinguishable. On inquiry, I found that while the foot of the male leaves an impression nearly round, that of the tigress is almost oval. On seeing them both together the difference is at once perceived. This is likewise true of the male and female panther. With a single exception, the footprints of all these great cats can be distinguished with certainty after a little practice, which is no small assistance to the hunter at times. The exception is, that a large male panther and a young male tiger leave marks absolutely identical, and not to be distinguished by the best native trackers.

After following the easily read trail in the sandy bottom of the ravine for some half-mile or so, the ravine branched off into two; the main branch leading straight down to the river; and the other a narrow, rock-bound gully, striking off almost at right angles to the left. The sturdy little Gónd who was then leading seemed to grow somewhat anxious as we approached the junction, and his swarthy countenance lighted up with a smile pleasant to see, when he found that all three tigers had entered the gorge to the left.

[1] Natives account for this by saying that the old male tiger kills all the male cubs he comes across when they are young; and they describe so similarly, in different parts of the country, the manœuvres of mamma to protect her young "hopefuls" against their unnatural papa, that I have little doubt of the truth of the story.

"We have them!" he exclaimed; "they are in the dewur, and as good as killed."

Dewur is the local name for a place where two or three nálás meet, and form a hollow in which water remains throughout the hot weather; if sufficiently shady and cool, it is a favourite haunt of the tiger; and it really seemed very likely that the tigers, having gorged themselves at night, had proceeded to lie up in the dewur, as surmised by the Gónd. To make all sure, we described a circle round the place, carefully examining all the nálás that led from it, and finding no marks to indicate their exit, returned to camp, pretty confident of having "ringed" the family, and that we would find them asleep about twelve o'clock. A scorching hot wind was blowing fiercely across the plain when I left my tent after breakfast, and mounted the howdah. It was fearfully hot, and the flickering haze that plays over the bare ground at this season, like an exhalation of gas from its surface, playing the strangest pranks with houses, trees, and figures, was exceedingly painful to the eyes. Never mind! all the more chance of finding the tigers at home, and we were soon under way for the dewur. About a hundred and fifty beaters had collected, for, the whole wealth of these people lying in their herds, they were naturally anxious for the destruction of the family of pests.

On arriving at the scene of operations, they were told off into four parties, each placed under charge of one of the more respectable inhabitants; and, after strict injunctions about taking to trees, etc., were despatched to their several posts. There were only two places where the tigers were likely to break, of which one led to the river, and the other, a dry watercourse, towards the neighbouring hills. Some peculiarities in the ground induced me to select the latter for my own post, while I entrusted the former to the old shikárí with his matchlock. I got an excellent position in a thick covert of jáman bushes, while at the same time effectually commanding the pass.

Half an hour elapsed, as agreed on, and then burst forth from the beaters the most terrific Babel of barbarous noises ever heard out of Pandemonium. I had engaged a "band," that had come from some distance to assist at the marriage of a wealthy merchant in the village, and we were, consequently, powerful in instrumental music. Fancy drums, great and small, "ear-piercing fifes," "rumtoolahs" of formidable dimensions (a hideous copper wind instrument, indescribable in simple English, but which I fancy must be identical with the "cholera horn" of southern India), mingled with a tempest of watchmen's rattles (each of fifty landrail power), and abundantly supplemented by vocal abuse of the tigers' ancestors to the tenth generation, delivered in the loudest key of native Billingsgate, and you have a faint idea of the row!

As they approached, it of course got more and more exciting, and soon the various inhabitants of the dewur began to make their appearance. First came a peacock and two hens, pattering over the fallen leaves. Sharper in eyesight than any other denizen of the forest, they soon observed me, and, rising in a panic, sailed off with their beautifully steady flight towards the river, the gorgeous plumage of the cock flashing in the sun—six feet of living gold and purple!

Another rustle, and a herd of spotted deer came trotting over a little eminence ahead, led by a well-antlered buck, with two more good ones bringing up the rear. Entirely taken up by the noise of the beaters, they never observed me, and, passing within fifteen paces of my elephant, disappeared in the jungle. I could have shot any one, or perhaps two, of the bucks, but seeing what was more interesting at the time, held my hand. This was a troop of baboons—hoary-bearded old fellows, and matrons with their young ones in their arms—who were perched on the trees ahead, and had already commenced their angry warnings that *the tigers were there.*

Then came the glorious moment of excitement—ample reward for days of bootless toil. The tigress came sneaking along amongst the bushes that fringed the nálá, and, halting about sixty paces off, turned round her head for a moment towards the beaters. Steady now! the bottom of the neck is exposed, and the sight of the big rifle bears full upon the proper spot. Bang! and with a gurgling roar, over she rolls into the nálá. Is it she? or the devil, or what? Certainly she fell; but, from the very spot she stood on, bounds forth the image of herself, with blood pouring in torrents from a gaping wound in the neck! More still; a third leaps the nálá just in front of my elephant, and the jungle seems alive with tigers. I had instantly exchanged the single for the double rifle, and as this one passed me at full speed, I rolled her over with a broken back and a bullet through the shoulder. Meantime the wounded one had disappeared behind me, and I proceeded to inspect the field, and count the killed and wounded. The last shot was a cub; so was the one that had rolled into the nálá to the first shot; and it was the old tigress that had escaped behind me. This was all a mystery, till I found that the first one was shot through the heart, the ball entering through the ribs, whereas, the first tiger I had fired at was standing almost facing me when I pulled; and then it was explained. One ball, the crashing two-ounce one, had passed through the tigress, and killed cub No. 1 on the other side.

My little elephant, a female called Káli, quite untried, which I had borrowed from the Jubbulpúr commissariat, had behaved nobly. Curling her trunk out of harm's way, and placing her sturdy fore-legs firmly before her, she stood like a rock in the midst of all the noise (for the trio roared like very bulls of Bashan). I had therefore perfect confidence in proceeding to follow up the wounded tigress. We soon found blood in plenty leading along the nálá towards the hills. I had taken the precaution of placing scouts on all the principal trees, some of whom had seen her cross an open space and enter the nálá where it debouched from a cleft in the hill-side; she was going quite strong, they said, although bleeding freely from the neck. On inquiry I found that the gorge in the hill was a mere *cul-de-sac*, having no exit at the other side, except on to an elevated plateau, as bare as my hand, which a wounded tiger would never dare to face. There was no doubt, therefore, that she had stopped in this gully and would fight, so I proceeded to make arrangements for the attack. The first thing done was to send men up the hill, by a circuitous route, to post themselves on trees all round the top of the ravine, as outlooks. This done, I advanced along the nálá till I found the blood again, which I followed up slowly, keeping a bright look-out ahead. The ravine was densely covered on both banks by clumps of bamboo jungle, and I had just reached the first of these when up jumped the tigress with a roar, and galloped off as fresh as ever towards the head of the ravine; I had two snap shots at her, which made her speak still louder, but otherwise had no effect. The people above now shouted out that she had again laid down higher up the nálá among some bamboos half-way up the banks. It would not do to approach her in this position from below, as a charge would probably have resulted in a general roll to the bottom of the ravine; so, with considerable labour, we climbed up to the table-land, and went round till we were right above her. Here, however, the bank was too steep to admit of a descent; so, getting a supply of stones into the howdah, I commenced bombarding the bamboo clumps, and at the third shot the tigress charged out. On she came within twenty paces, when her heart failed her; she turned sharp off to the left, and I got two pretty fair shots at her, which told loudly, but still she went on as strong as ever. This time she crossed quite over to the opposite side of the ravine, and ascended the bank, as if with the intention of bolting across the open ground. The scouts kept shouting out to me to come round, which I did, and found them in a terrible panic, for the tigress, seeing them on the trees, kept walking about and eyeing them in a cat-and-mouse sort of manner, growling fearfully and lashing her tail about. The first of them I came to told me she was then lying down at the foot of a tree further on, watching two Gónds in the branches. I soon reached the place: the wretched Góńds were too much frightened to speak, but pointed to the ground below the tree, and sat jabbering like monkeys as I approached. I now made out the tail of the tigress impatiently switching up and down; she herself being crouched in the long grass, I could not see her body. On perceiving the elephant she jumped up, and, making a short run forwards, crouched again. We steadily advanced, and, finding she could not put us to flight, she took to it herself, and suddenly bounded again towards the ravine. I had another shot as she was disappearing over the bank. This time it was the large rifle, and she caught it unmistakably; for, on coming to the place where she had vanished, we could hear her down below, growling and struggling on the ground. The descent here was more gradual, though the bamboo cover was dreadfully thick. The elephant was sliding down on her haunches, stones and earth rolling down before her. The growling grew deeper as we descended, and the noise of struggling ceased, as if the tigress had collected herself for a last charge. The bamboo stems kept whipping me in the face as I stood in the howdah with my double smooth-bore ready for the *coup de grâce*. My face was soon covered with blood, and my shooting-jacket torn to ribands. A raging thirst parched my throat, for I had now been some five hours in the sun; and my hat having been swept off on first entering the bamboos, its rays had been for some time beating full on my unprotected skull. I felt my head begin to swim, and the bamboo stems to dance before me in an indistinct maze. Had it lasted much longer, I feel certain I must have had a sunstroke; but the last act was playing out. Crash went the elephant into a dense clump of bamboos; a jagged stem seized me by the neck; and as I raised my hand to disengage it, the roar of the tigress burst forth in my very face; a striped form rose in the centre of the clump, in the act of bounding on the elephant's head. Leaning over the railing of the howdah, I levelled the gun, double-shotted in both barrels, at her chest; and the next moment was shouting out: "For God's sake, bring that claret and water, will you, and come down, half-a-dozen of you, and take up this carcase!"

So I bagged the whole family, to the no small delight of the cattle-keepers of the place.

A large panther was making himself very troublesome at that time in the neighbourhood of the Jubbulpúr and Mandlá road. He had killed several children in different villages, and promised, unless suppressed, to become a regular man-eater. I encamped for some days in the neighbourhood of his haunts, and the very first night the villain had the impudence to kill and drag away a good-sized baggage pony out of my camp. The night being warm, I was sleeping outside, for the sake of coolness, and was awakened by the riving, gurgling noise close to my bed. It was too dark to see; so I pulled out the revolver, that in those uncertain times always lay under my pillow, and fired off a couple of shots to scare the intruder. Getting a light, I was relieved to find it was only the pony, instead of a human being, as I had half feared, and we proceeded to investigate the condition of the deceased.

The brute had seized him by the neck, which was dislocated; the jugular was also divided, and he had evidently been drinking the blood when my shots, or perhaps the light, scared him off. The night was too dark for any attempt to kill the panther, who, moreover, had probably been scared completely away from the neighbourhood of the camp. It was, however, very probable that he would return next evening in quest of the pony before it was too dark to shoot, and I was persuaded by the old shikárí to sit up on a "machan" and watch for him. A small nálá ran from the river nearly up to the camp, as is always the case when a misadventure like this occurs. This I had overlooked when selecting a site for my tent. We dragged the carcase, without touching it ourselves, to the head of this nálá, where there was a convenient tree. The shikárí—an old hand at this sort of work—strewed the ground for some paces round the pony with fresh white wheat-chaff, which he said would not prevent the panther coming to feed, while it certainly rendered the chance of hitting in the dark much greater; and about sunset he and I took our places on the machan. There was small chance of the panther making his appearance so early in the evening, so I commenced a whispered conversation with the old man about machan-shooting in general, which he evidently considered the finest sport in the world, as well as the safest. He was full of stories of curious events that had occurred to himself and others; and told me many as we sat through the long hours together, of which I only remembered one next morning sufficiently well to note it down in my journal. Somehow we got on the subject of man-eating tigers, and I happened to ask him if he had ever watched for a man-eater over the body of a man he had killed.

"Yes," said he, "but I didn't much fancy it, as it stinks abominably, and, besides, I don't care to have more to do with ghosts than I can help, after what happened to Pádám Singh, Thákúr of Ponhrí."

With much pressing, I got him to tell me this wonderful tale, which was much as follows :—"The village of Ponhrí, about thirty coss from here, was haunted a few years ago by a perfect *shitan* of a man-eating tiger. He was very old and very cunning. There were two ghâts that led from the village to the open country, and on the hill between these he used to live. Whenever he saw any persons leave the village, he would rush across to the ghát they selected, and waylay them there; springing out with a roar, and carrying off one of the party like a flash of lightning. Often did the people of the village see him thus stalking some wretched traveller, and sometimes were in time to warn him to take to a tree; but still oftener the monster was too cunning for them, and approached his victim in the stealthy manner only a man-eater can. He sometimes left his post for a few days, and was then sure to be heard of at some one of the surrounding villages at his old tricks. The road by Ponhrí was soon completely blocked up, and no one would pass that way, although it was the high-road to several large villages. The tiger soon became straitened for food, as, having become confirmed in his taste for human flesh, he could now eat no other; so he took to frequenting the outskirts of the village, and two or three times stalked the Aheers, who were driving home their cattle, up to the very doors. The buffaloes, however, which you know do not in the least fear a tiger when in a body, always discovered him and drove him off before he could do any mischief. Thus repeatedly baffled, the man-eater conceived the bold idea of lying in wait for one of the cowherds in his own house. This he did, somehow managing to smuggle himself in unobserved; and when the wretched man, after securing his charge in their shed, returned blithely home to his dinner, just as he reached the door forth sprang the terrible scourge of the village, and, racing off to the hills with the Aheer in his horrid jaws, disappeared in an instant!

"It was about the hour of sunset, and most of the villagers returned from their work were collected by the image of Máhádeo, under the village pepul tree, discussing the events of the day. Amongst them was a Gónd Thákur, named Pádám Singh, who had killed his tiger, and was consequently considered the village authority on sporting matters. He was a man of determination, as his after-conduct will show, and at once proposed that they should proceed in a body and rescue the remains of their fellow-villager from the maw of the spoiler. Arming themselves as best they could, and taking all the drums and other noisy instruments in the village, they sallied forth and approached the spot where the man-eater had retired to devour the Aheer. Bold and undaunted as the tiger is when himself the aggressor, the most terrible man-eater wants the courage to stand the approach of a body of men like this; so he retreated (as, indeed, the villagers very well knew he would). They found the corpse half eaten, the upper half remaining untouched. Pádám Singh, the possessor of the only matchlock in the place, proposed that the remains should be left untouched, that he might sit up in a tree, and, awaiting the return of the tiger, rid the village for ever of the pest. To this the dead man's relations yielded an unwilling assent, and Pádám Singh was left to the ghastly company of the corpse, perched high on a neighbouring tree. Ere long the man-eater returned, and the Thákúr watched his approach with immense satisfaction from his lofty position. The tiger approached within eighty yards or so—thirty too far for a sure aim with the rude matchlock. Then he paused, and to his horror the Thákúr saw the mutilated corpse slowly raise its right arm, and point with a warning gesture at himself! On the signal, the man-eater instantly disappeared in the jungle. Transfixed with horror, the Thákúr remained glued to the tree. Shortly the tiger again returned, and again was the same mute warning given by the dead man, the tiger disappearing as before. A bright idea now struck the Thákúr, who had somewhat recovered his senses, and cutting two sharp stakes with his knife, he slipped down the tree and pegged both hands of the corpse firmly to the ground. Scarcely had he regained his perch when the man-eater again appeared; and, concluding from the absence of the signal that the danger no longer existed, proceeded quietly to resume his horrid feast. He had buried his jaws in the neck of the corpse, when the matchlock of the avenger flashed forth its contents. Struck full on the shoulder by the two bullets with which Pádám Singh had loaded his weapon, the dreaded man-eater rolled over dead on the body of his last victim."

It is singular how widely spread is this superstition regarding the malice against their fellows entertained by the spirits of persons killed by wild beasts. According to Sir J. Lubbock, many other savage races, besides those of India, have entertained it; and it will be seen further on that it forms the ground of a singular ceremony among the wild Bygás of the Mandlá district.

The panther of course never came to the carcase of the pony. I never saw an animal do so yet; but I have, I confess, only tried it a few times. Some sportsmen have been very successful in this machan-shooting by night; but it would be poor fun even if one killed a tiger every night.

Sámbar were extremely numerous at that time on the hills on both sides of the valley, but particularly on the north side. Shots at them could be procured by driving almost any of the hills with beaters, and I killed a number of them both this way and by stalking. Although it was near the end of the month of April, when, according to theory, both sámbar and spotted deer should have cast their horns, yet, out of the immense number of both species that I saw on this trip, only one sámbar, and two or three spotted bucks, were without horns. Some of the most interesting sport I have had in this valley has been in coursing the sámbar with dogs. During this trip I fell in with a gang of Gónd woodcutters, who possessed a number of fine large red-coloured dogs, with the aid of which they were able to run down and spear many deer and wild pigs.

This red breed of pariahs is certainly the indigenous one of these parts, whether or not, as I suspect, descended from the wild species which frequent these jungles. The large parti-coloured animals, seen about Hindú villages in the open valley, were probably imported along with their masters. The wild dogs live in packs of fifteen or twenty, and prey exclusively on game, running down all sorts of deer like a pack of hounds. Where a pack has been hunting for any time, most of the game naturally disappears. This applies to the tiger even, which they are said to attack wherever they meet him. Tigers would naturally follow the herds of deer on which they prey, if they were moved by the wild dogs; but there is such a consensus of native opinion as to the wild pack actually hunting, and even sometimes killing tigers, that it is difficult altogether to discredit it. I do not believe that any number of the dogs could overcome a tiger in fair fight; but I think it quite possible that they might stick to him, and wear him out by keeping him from his natural food. Many stories are related of tigers climbing into trees (which of course is quite against their nature) to escape from them; and I once saw the bones of a tiger lying on a ledge of rock, where more than one person assured me that they had seen him lying surrounded by a large pack of the wild dogs.

The wild dog of this part of India[1] is about the size of a small setter, and the colour of the old "mustard" breed of terriers. In shape, however, he is more vulpine than any European breed of dogs, with a long, sharp face, erect but not very long or pointed ears, and slouching tail never raised higher than the line of the back. In these respects he very much resembles the red pariahs above mentioned, the most noticeable distinction being that the latter raise their tails at times a good deal higher, with something of a curl. Very often, however, and particularly when moving fast, the pariahs carry their tails just like the wild dog; and so close is sometimes the resemblance between them, that I remember on one occasion, near Mandlá, I allowed what afterwards proved to be really a wild dog to escape from before my rifle, as he trotted across the road before me,

[1] *Cuon rutilans.*

thinking him to be one of those red pariahs strayed from some village. There is of course the considerable distinction, that the wild dog cannot bark, while the tame one can. But how readily the voice of the latter reverts to the howl of the wild animal must have been remarked by every one who has passed by a village when they came forth to salute him.

But to return to our muttons. I arranged with the owners of some of these red dogs to have a morning's sámbar hunting with them, assisted by two capital hounds of my own. Scouts were out before daybreak, and marked down a herd of about twenty sámbar on a spur which jutted out into the plain from the main range of hills. This spur was covered with Mhowa trees, the deciduous flowers of which have a strong attraction for all sorts of deer, as well as bears and Góuds. The former come long distances at night to eat the flowers that drop in great profusion as soon as ripe, Bruin, if too late for the feast, having no objection to scramble up and get some for himself. The plan was to send a strong body of beaters round to the neck of the spur, while we were to post ourselves with the dogs where it ended in the plain. I call it plain, but it was so only comparatively speaking. Broken and treacherous "cotton-soil" it was, intersected by numerous nálás, and about as bad ground to ride over as could well be wished.

We were wending our way down a somewhat precipitous pathway that led from the village to the scene of operations, when the Gónd to whom I was talking dropped behind on some pretence or other, and shortly afterwards we passed one of the primitive altars they erect near almost every pathway. This consists of a platform of hard mud, on which are constructed, of the same material, small models of the necessary implements of their simple life, such as a cooking-place, flat plate, etc. Near the platform is a stake planted in the ground, from which project two wooden arms, drilled with holes; through these a peeled wand is passed, the top of which is decorated with a streamer of red cloth. Close by is a cairn of stones, to which every passer-by adds another. These altars are generally erected to the names of some one of their race who bore a saintly reputation during life, and offerings placed on them are supposed to propitiate his spirit. On this occasion the Gónd who had dropped behind, and who was the leader and concocter of the present hunt, stopped before the altar; and, after a prostration, extracted from the folds of his waistcloth, and placed on the plate constructed for such purposes, a peeled onion! Each of the band then added a stone to the heap, muttering at the same time something I could not make out, and passed on. This was for luck.

We soon reached our station, and taking up a properly concealed position, awaited the approach of the game. The beaters had a long way to go round, and we had waited about an hour when their voices began to be heard, as they advanced in a long line that stretched completely across the spur. They were still about a quarter of a mile off, when I made out that something unexpected had occurred, by their shouts suddenly ceasing, and then breaking out into a terrific and concentrated yell! By my glass I saw that some of them had taken to trees, and that all were looking down the hill-side to the left of the line. Advancing my Dollond in that direction, I made out some black objects trundling down the hill, and a few moments afterwards, as they emerged on the plain, I saw that they were a bear and two cubs; they were making for another spur of the hill that ran parallel to the one we were beating, at a distance of about half a mile. Between them ran the dry bed of a nálá, formed of a natural pavement of huge flagstones, and strewn with boulders that had been rolled down from the hills above. Jumping on my pony, I started up this nálá at a rattling pace, scrambling and sliding in a most wonderful manner over the stones, till I again caught sight of the bears going leisurely about two hundred yards ahead. I had gained about fifty more on them before they saw me, and was just going to pull up and fire, when they set off at a shambling gallop, which, owing to the badness of the ground, soon left me far in the rear. Coming to a better place, I rapidly gained on them again, but the hill was too near, and I was full one hundred and fifty paces behind when they commenced the ascent. Pulling up, I administered my two barrels with as much steadiness as my panting steed would admit of; the second shot told somewhere, as testified by the growls it elicited from the old "she," but it was too far for such a snap shot, and their movements seemed to be only accelerated. Throwing my bridle over a branch, I was reloaded in a few seconds, and scrambling up in Bruin's tracks, I heard them above me on the hill-side rustling among the dried leaves, but could not get another shot; nor did I find any blood. This was very unlucky, for if I had had a suspicion of there being bears on the hill, I would never have taken up the position I did, as a bear would break back through an army of beaters rather than take to an open plain, where he has no stronghold to make for. The bear is very sweet upon the Mhowa, and these had evidently come down to feed on it; for, had they been regular residents, the villagers must have been aware of it from seeing their tracks and excavations.

The beaters, who had suspended operations to witness the result of the bear chase, now resumed their beating, while I rode slowly along the bed of the nálá, in case there might be any more of the family left. We had reached within about two hundred yards of where the dogs were concealed, when I observed a dun hide glance between two bushes, and shortly afterwards the whole herd of sámbar filed slowly down the face of the hill. Indecision still swayed them, and, fearing lest they might yet break back, I fired off my rifle; at the same time a round stone from the beaters rolled down the hill among them, and down they galloped straight for the hounds. The Gónds, in their eagerness, slipped their dogs too soon, and about half the herd broke back through the beaters after all; the rest took across the plain in the direction of the spur the bears had reached. Shouting to my man to let loose the greyhounds, as the deer were in full view, I started off at the best pace I could muster over such ground. Had it not been for my own dogs, the sámbar would probably have reached the hills and been safe; but, as it was, they shot ahead of the Góndi pack, and the sámbar, finding they could not make the hills, turned off towards the river. By cutting off an angle here I gained a good deal on the chase, and could see that my hounds, dog and bitch, were well up. The dog is a heavy, powerful, Rampúr hound, while the bitch, more lightly made, has considerably the speed of him. As I came up, she made a gallant rush at the hindmost stag, and, springing at his hocks, deer and dog rolled over together. She wanted power, however; and, before the dog was up to help her, the stag was up and pegging away as fast as ever. Two or three of the Góndi dogs now joined in at a respectful distance, but going as if they meant something. Shortly afterwards I came up to a deep nálá, and missing the pass by which the deer and dogs had crossed, lost a deal of distance in trying to find it out. Everywhere else the bank was about twenty feet deep, and nearly perpendicular. At last I found the place, and crossing over, had the satisfaction of finding that I was utterly alone, dogs and deer having disappeared.

I knew the direction of the river, and rode for that, but soon got into the labyrinth of nálás that fringe its bed, and had the greatest difficulty in forcing my nag through amongst the bamboos. The nálás themselves were a perfect puzzle; in and out and round about, they twisted like the alleys in Fair Rosamond's bower; and I several times found myself in the place I had just left. At last I got into the bed of one of the principal of them, that led straight down to the Narbadá; and, by dint of occasionally putting my head under my pony's neck and forcing him through the bamboos, and here and there leaping a fallen tree, I soon emerged on the shingly banks of the river, and, pulling up to listen, I thought I heard a faint yelp far, far up the stream.

A broad belt of sand and shingle intervened between the jungle and the shrunken river, along which I galloped for about a mile, the baying of the dogs becoming more and more distinct as I rode. A few minutes after, I reached the scene of conflict—a shady nook of the river, arched in by the massive boughs of trees, interspersed with the feathering stems of the bamboo. A giant forest-tree lay felled by the brink of the pool, worm-eaten and water-logged, as if it had lain there for centuries, and beyond this stood the stag at bay, chest deep in the water. Four of the Góndi dogs and my greyhound bitch were baying him from the log; and just as I arrived a black little Gónd, spear in hand, emerged from the forest and jumped on to the tree. Two or three prods he made at him with his weapon failed to reach him; and he was just about to leap into the water when the greyhound, encouraged by our arrival, made a fierce leap at the stag, falling short by about a yard of her intended mark. Instantly the deer bounded forward, and with his fore-feet struck the hound under water; but in so doing he forgot his fence, and exposed his flank within striking distance of his human foe. The spear was buried twice in his side, and the dark water was streaked with crimson as the blood poured from the wounds. The poor brute now tries to struggle to the shore, but in vain; the dogs are upon him in a body, and their united weight bears him down; a few more spear-thrusts, and the gallant stag is bubbling out his life under water.

The distance run must have been about four miles, but I had ridden probably double that distance. The dogs were a good deal done up, as the heat was by this time tremendous; but a swim in the river, and half an hour in the cool shade made them all right again. These Góndi dogs must have wonderful noses to follow deer by scent over the burning ground at full speed, as they are said to do. They had not much trouble on this occasion, as the greyhound bitch had never lost sight of the stag to the finish, and cut out the work for the others.

At other times I have had excellent sport with the fine breed of dogs possessed by the Banjárá carriers referred to in a former chapter. If the wild dog were available to breed from, a still better hound for sámbar-hunting might probably be obtained. With more regular organisation, better dogs, and more sportsmen, sámbar-hunting in this country might give admirable sport. The best breed, if the wild dog is, as is probable, unavailable, would be the cross between the Scotch deerhound and the Banjárá dog, the former being the mother. Pups of a Bankárá bitch almost invariably grow up with "vernacular" habits, and a hatred of Europeans. A real specimen of the Banjárá should however be selected, and this is not easy, the breed having got much mixed with the common village pariah dog. The true Banjárá is a fine, upstanding hound, of about twenty-eight inches high, generally black mottled with gray or blue, with a rough but silky coat, a high-bred, hound-like head, and well feathered on ears, legs, and tail. He shows a good deal of resemblance to the Persian greyhound, but is stouter built, and with a squarer muzzle. Probably this wandering race of gipsies may have brought the originals with them from western Asia, the subsequent modification of them being due to a cross with some of the indigenous breeds. The Banjárá breed possesses indomitable pluck, can go about as fast as a foxhound, and will run all day. His nose is superior to that of any other domestic breed in a hot climate; but he wants better speed for coursing deer, and attachment to Europeans.

The common black sloth-bear of the plains of India [1] is very plentiful in the hills on either side of the Narbadá, between Jubbulpúr and Mandlá. Indeed, there are few parts of these highlands where a bear may not at any time be met with. They are generally very harmless until attacked, living on roots, honey, and insects, chiefly white ants, which they dig out of their earthen hillocks. The natives call them *ádam-zád*, or "sons of men," and, considering them half human, will not as a rule molest them. Really, their absurd antics almost justify the idea. Sometimes, however, a bear will attack very savagely without provocation—generally, when they are come upon suddenly and their road of escape is cut off. As a rule, in frequented parts, they do not come out of their midday retreats, in caves and dense thickets, until nightfall; but, in remoter tracts they may be met with in the middle of the day. I was once charged by four bears all at once, which I had come upon near the high-road between Jubbulpúr and Damoh, feeding under a Mhowa tree. I had two guns, and hit three of them; but had to bolt from the fourth, who chased me about a hundred yards, and then dived into a ravine. Returning to the scene of action, I found one sitting at the foot of a tree, bewailing his fate in most melancholy whines, and finished him with a ball in the ear. The other two had gone down the slope of a hill, and I started off to head them. The ground was rocky and very slippery, and I had not gone far when I fell, my rifle sliding away down the hill, to the considerable damage of its stock and barrels. I picked myself up, however, and

[1] *Ursus labiatus.*

by dint of hard running, arrived above and parallel to the bears, and commenced a running fight with them, in which my chances would have been a good deal better had I had a breech- instead of a muzzle-loader. As it was, I had to keep one barrel unfired in case of a charge, and peg away at long intervals with the other. At last, one of them came round up the hill at me, rising on his hind-legs, pulling down branches, and dancing and spluttering in so ludicrous a manner, that I could scarcely shoot for laughter. When I did, he got both barrels through the chest, and subsided. I never got the other, as it had sufficient headway to escape into some hollow rocks near the river-side. A wounded bear will often charge with great determination. He comes on like a great cannon-ball; and the popular idea, that he will rise on his hind-legs in time to give a shot at the "horse-shoe" mark on his chest, to penetrate which is fatal, is, as a rule, a mistake. But a shot, when he is ten or fifteen yards off, will nearly always turn, if it does not kill him. The most successful way of getting bears is to get up very early, and go up to some commanding position, that overlooks the pathways taken by the animals on their return from the low ground, where they go nightly to feed. They can then either be intercepted, or marked into some cover, and afterwards beaten out. It is a sport of which a little is great fun; but one soon tires of it, the animals being generally so easily killed, and furnishing neither trophy (an Indian bearskin being a poor affair) nor food. Most sportsmen ere long come to agree with the natives, and let the *ádam-zád* alone, except when they turn up by accident.

It was in these jungles that I first saw the great rock python of India, which is the subject of so many wonderful tales. I was following the track of a wounded deer, and, the day being very hot, had mounted my horse, a chestnut Arab, from which I could shoot, carrying a rifle. The horse almost trod upon him, lying on a narrow pathway, and started back with a snort, as the great snake slowly twisted himself off the road, and down the slope of the hill, along which it wound. A loud rustling, and here and there the wave of a fold in the grass, told me that something was moving down the bank, and I forced the horse after it, very unwillingly on his part, till with a loud hiss, and a swish of his folds, the serpent gathered himself into a great coil, just under the horse's nose. A very unpleasant sound, like the boiling of a big kettle, came from the gathering pyramid of coils, and I lost no time in leaning over and firing both barrels of the rifle into the mass, at the same time drawing the horse back to the pathway, as I did not know the customer I had to deal with. The snake made off down the hill, and my horse refused to follow, so that, before I could dismount and get down on foot, all trace of him was lost. I was taken by surprise, or should perhaps have made a better business of it. My impression was that the creature was about twenty-five feet long, of a leaden colour, and about as thick as a large man's thigh. I have seen one killed in the same jungles, which measured sixteen feet in length. They are of a very sluggish disposition, and do not molest man. The stories of their swallowing spotted deer whole, antlers and all, I believe to be utter myths.

HORNS OF SPOTTED DEER. (*Scale, one-tenth.*)

CHAPTER IX

THE SÁL FORESTS

ABOVE Mandlá, the valley of the Narbadá opens out into a wide upland country, the main river, between this and Jubbulpúr, joined by few and unimportant tributaries, here radiating like the fingers of a hand, and draining the rainfall of an extensive triangular plateau, known as the Mandlá district. These converging valleys rise in elevation towards the south, where they terminate in a transverse range of hills, which sends down spurs between them, subdividing the drainage. The valleys themselves also successively rise in general elevation, by a step-like formation from west to east. Furthest to the west, that of the Banjar river possesses a general height of about 2000 feet; next is that drained by the Hálon and the Phén at about 2300; still further to the east the basin of the Khormér has risen to about 2800 feet; and furthest east of all is the plateau of Amarkantak, the chief source of the Narbadá, which attains a general altitude of about 3300 feet, with smaller flat-topped elevations reaching to 4000 feet above the sea. The hilly range which runs along the southern border of the district is called the Mýkat, and overlooks, in a steep descent to the southward, a flat low-lying country called Chattísgárh, or "the land of thirty-six forts."

The elevated cradle of the infant Narbadá, thus described, contains within its outer circle of hills an area of not less than 7000 square miles; much of it, of course, of a broken and unculturable character, but comprising also in the valleys much of what may properly be called virgin soil of the finest quality. The Mýkat range, and the radiating spurs which separate the plateau, are mostly clothed with forests of the sál tree, which, here as elsewhere, almost monopolises the parts where it grows. The sáj alone grows in any quantity along with it. Some of the hills are covered with the ordinary species of forest trees of other parts; the species of vegetation appearing, as I have said before, to depend much on the geological formation.

The valleys themselves are generally open and free from all underwood, dotted here and there by belts and

SÁL FORESTS IN THE HÁLON VALLEY.

islands of the noble sál tree, and altogether possessing much of the character ascribed to the American prairies. In their lowest parts the soil is deep, black, and rich, covered with a growth of strong tall grasses. As the valleys merge into the hilly ranges, the soils become lighter and redder, from the lateritic topping that here overlies the basaltic and granitic bases of the hills; the grasses are less rank and coarse; and in many places springs of clear cold water bubble up, clothing the country with belts of perpetual verdure, and conferring on it an aspect of freshness very remarkable in a country of such comparatively small elevation in the centre of India. Everything combines to deprive this region of the sterile and inhospitable appearance worn by even most upland tracts during the hot season. The sál tree is almost the only evergreen forest tree in India. Throughout the summer its glossy dark-green foliage reflects the light in a thousand vivid tints; and just when all other vegetation is at its worst, a few weeks before the gates of heaven are opened in the annual monsoon, the sál selects its opportunity of bursting into a fresh garment of the brightest and softest green. The traveller who has lingered till that late period in these wilds is charmed by the approach of a second spring, and it requires no slight effort to believe himself still in a tropical country. The atmosphere has been kept humid by the moisture from the broad sheets of water retained by the upland streams, which descends nightly in dews on the open valleys. The old grasses of the prairie have been burnt in the annual conflagrations, and a covering of young verdure has taken their place. Now and then the familiar note of the cuckoo[1] (identical with the European bird), and the voices of many birds, including the deep musical coo of the grand imperial pigeon, heighten the delusion. But for the bamboo thickets on the higher hills, whose light feathery foliage beautifully supplements the heavier masses of the sál that cling to their skirts, the scene would present nothing peculiar to the landscape of a tropical country.

The climate of these uplands is very temperate for this part of India, showing a mean of about 77 degrees of the thermometer during the hot season. The variation between the temperature of day and night is, however, considerable, ranging from about 50 degrees to 100 degrees as extremes during the hot season under canvas. It would of course be much more equable in a house, and the range is also far less on the higher plateaux than in the lower valleys. In the cold season (which corresponds to our

[1] *Cuculus canorus.*

winter) it generally descends at night to freezing-point in the open air, rising in a tent no higher than 65 degrees or 70 degrees in the middle of the day.

The country can scarcely be said to be populated at all, except within a short distance of Mandlá itself, where the rich soil has been cultivated by an outlying colony of Hindús from the Lower Narbadá valley. Mandlá was at one time the seat of one of the Gónd-Rájpút ruling dynasties, and the remains of their forts and other buildings still crown in crumbling decay the top of many a forest-covered mound.

The Gónds are here a very poor and subdued race, long since weaned from their wild notions of freedom, with its attendant hardships and seclusion; but still unreached by the influence of the general advancement which has in some measure redeemed them in most parts from their state of practical serfdom to the superior races. They usually plough with cattle, instead of depending on the axe, and are nearly all hopelessly in debt to the money-lenders, who speculate in the produce they raise. There is no local market, and the difficulty of exporting grain over the seventy or eighty miles of atrocious road to the open country is such that the prices obtained for their produce are contemptible. They congregate in filthy little villages, overrun by poultry and pigs, and innocent of all attempt at conservancy.

Far superior to them in every respect are the still utterly unreclaimed forest Bygás, another aboriginal race, whose habitat is in the hills of the Mýkat range and its spurs, which intersect these valleys. The same tribe extends over a vast range of forest-covered country to the west of Mandlá, where we shall subsequently meet them again under the name of Bhúmiás. A few have somewhat modified their original habits, and live, along with the Gónds, in villages lower down the valleys. These have been slightly tainted with Hindúism, shave their elfin locks, and call themselves by a name denoting caste. But the real Bygá of the hill ranges is still almost in a state of nature. They are very black, with an upright, slim, though exceedingly wiry frame, and showing less of the negretto type of feature than any other of these wild races. Destitute of all clothing but a small strip of cloth, or at most, when in full dress, with the addition of a coarse cotton sheet worn cross-wise over the chest, with long, tangled, coal-black hair, and furnished with bow and arrow and a keen little axe hitched over the shoulder, the Bygá is the very model of a hill aborigine. He scorns all tillage but the dhya clearing on the mountain-side, pitching his neat habitation of bamboo wicker-work, like an eagle's eyrie, on some hill-top or ledge of rock, far above the valleys penetrated by pathways; and ekes out the fruits of the earth by an unwearying pursuit of game. Full of courage, and accustomed to depend on each other, they hesitate not to attack every animal of the forest, including the tiger himself. They possess a most deadly poison wherewith they tip their little arrows of reed; and the most ponderous beast seldom goes more than a mile, after being pierced with one of these, without falling. The poison is not an indigenous one, but is brought and sold to them by the traders who penetrate these wilds to traffic in forest produce. I believe it to be an extract of the root of *Aconitum ferox*, which is used for a similar purpose by some of the tribes of the eastern Himáláyá. The flesh is discoloured and spoilt for some distance round the wound. This is cut out, and the rest of the carcase is held to be wholesome food. Their bows are made entirely of the bamboo, "string" and all; they are very neat, and possess wonderful power for their size. A good shot among them will strike the crown of a hat at fifty yards. Their arrows are of two sorts, those for ordinary use being tipped with a plain iron head, and feathered from the wing of the peafowl, while those intended for poisoning and deadly work have a loose head, round which the poison is wrapped, and which remains in the wound. These poisoned arrows are altogether remarkably similar to those used by the Bushmen of South Africa. Their axes are also of two sorts—one, like the ordinary axes of the Góbnds, for cutting wood, and the other, a much more formidable implement, called a *tongiá*, with a long semicircular blade like an ancient battle-axe in miniature. All the iron for these weapons, and for their agricultural instruments, is forged from the native ore of the hills, by a class called Aguriás, who seem to be a section of the Gónds. A Bygá has been known to attack and destroy a tiger with no other weapon than his axe. This little weapon is also used as a projectile, and the Bygá will thus knock over hares, peafowl, etc., with astonishing skill.

Though thus secluded in the wilderness, the Mandlá Bygá is by no means extremely shy, and will placidly go on cutting his dhya while a train of strangers is passing him, when a wild Gónd or Korkú would have abandoned all and fled to the forest. They are truthful and honest almost to a fault, being terribly cheated in consequence in their dealings with the traders; and they possess the patriarchal form of self-government still so perfectly, that nearly all their disputes are settled by the elders without appeal, though these of course, under our alien system, possess no legal authority. Serious crime among them is almost unheard of. The strangest thing about them is that, though otherwise certainly the wildest of all these races, they have no aboriginal language of their own, speaking a rude dialect of which almost every word can be traced to the Hindí. They can also communicate with the Gónds in their language, though they do not use it among themselves. A similar case is that of the Bheels, in the western continuation of these hills, who, though also extremely wild, have no peculiar language of their own, and never have had, so far as history informs us. There are many points of resemblance between the Bygás and the Bheels, and there seems to be no evidence to connect either with the Kolarian or the Dravidian families of aborigines. Further inquiry may show them to be remnants of a race anterior in point of time to both, and from which the Hindí may have borrowed its numerous non-Sanscrit vocables. We know that, at an early period in Hindú history, Bheels held the country up to the river Jamná, which they do not now approach within many hundred miles.

There is every reason to believe that these Bygás are, if not autochthonous, at least the predecessors of the Gónds in this part of the hills. They consider themselves, and are allowed to be, superior to the Góṇds, who may not eat with them, and who take their priests of the mysteries, or medicine-men, from among them. Theirs it is to hold converse with the world of spirits, who are everywhere present to aboriginal superstition; theirs it is to cast omens, to compel the rain, to charm away the tiger or disease. The Bygá medicine-man fully looks his character. He is tall, thin, and cadaverous: abstraction and mystery residing in his hollow eyes. When wanted, he has to be sent for to some distant haunt of gnomes and spirits, and comes with charms and simples slung in the hollow of a bottle-gourd. A great necklace, fashioned with much carving from the kernels of forest fruits, marks his holy calling.

The Bygá charmer's most dangerous duty is that of laying the spirit of a man who has been killed by a tiger. Man-eaters have always been numerous in Mandlá, the presence during a part of every year of large herds of cattle fostering the breed, while their withdrawal at other times to regions where the tigers cannot follow causes temporary scarcity of food, too easily relieved in the abundant tall grass cover by recourse to the killing of man; the desultory habits of the wild people, and the numbers of travellers who take this short route between the Narbadá valley and the plains of Chattísgárh, furnishing them with abundant and easy victims. The Bygá has to proceed to the spot where the death occurred—which is probably still frequented by the tiger—with various articles, such as fowls and rice, which are offered to the manes. A pantomime of the tragedy is then enacted by the Bygá, who assumes the attitude of a tiger, springs on his prey, and devours a mouthful of the blood-stained earth. Eight days are allowed to pass; and should the Bygá not, in the interval, be himself carried off by the tiger, the spirit is held to be effectually laid, and the people again resort to the jungle. The theory rests on the superstition, prevalent throughout these hills, that the ghost of the victim, unless charmed to rest, rides on the head of the tiger, and incites him to further deeds of blood, rendering him also secure from harm by his preternatural watchfulness. To remove pestilence or sickness, they have a pleasant notion that it must be transferred to some one else; and so they sweep their villages, after the usual sacrifices, and cast the filth on the highway or into the bounds of some other village.

The real Bygá medicine-man possesses the gift of throwing himself into a trance, during which the afflatus of the Deity is supposed to be vouchsafed to him, communicating the secrets of the future. I never saw the performance myself, but persons who have affirm that it is too severe in its physical symptoms to be mere acting; and there is sufficient evidence from other quarters to prove that some persons can educate themselves into the power of passing into such fits at will, to lead us to credit the Bygá at least with nothing worse than self-deception in the matter. In religion the Bygás have admitted a few of the Hindú deities of the destructive type; but their chief reverence is paid to the spirits of the waste, and to Mother Earth, who is their tribal god. One of their tribal names is Bhúmiá, meaning "people of the soil," and it is curious that among every aboriginal tribe of these hills, including the Bheels, the priests or medicine-men are called by the same name. The rite of charming the souls of deceased persons into some material object, before described, and which seems peculiar to these hills, is practised also by these Bygás.

A male Bygá is easily distinguished from a Gónd; but their women are scarcely in any respect different—perhaps a little blacker, but dressing in a similar manner, wearing the same ornaments (including a chignon of goat's hair), and, like them, also tattooed as to the legs. Though the Bygás are, like the Bheels, less given to congregate together in large villages than some other tribes, often indeed living in entirely detached dwellings, there are a good many villages of a considerable number of houses. These are arranged with much neatness in the form of a square, and the whole place is kept very clean.

The Bygá is the most terrible enemy to the forests we have anywhere in these hills. Thousands of square miles of sál forest have been clean destroyed by them in the progress of their dhya cultivation, the ground being afterwards occupied by a dense scrub of low sál bushes springing from the stumps. In addition to this, the largest trees have everywhere been girdled by them to allow the gum resin of the sál (the dammer of commerce) to exude.

The dammer resin, called here *dhók*, is extensively used as a pitch in dockyards, and for coating commercial packages. It is extracted by cutting a ring of bark out of the tree three or four feet from the ground, when the gum exudes in large bubbles. Several half-circles are, however, equally effective, and do not destroy the life of the tree, like the former method. The ringing of sál trees has now been entirely prohibited within our territories; but I do not think that any more economical method has as yet been substituted, the vast area of sál in native states being sufficient to supply the present wants of the trade. The dammer is collected, and, together with lac dye, is exchanged for salt, beads, and arrow-poison, brought by peripatetic traders with pack-bullocks, who annually visit their wilds for the purpose. This may be said to be the only commercial transaction of the Bygá in the whole year. He rarely visits the low-country markets, like the other tribes, and has scarcely a knowledge of coined money.

Fortunately the sál tree, unlike the teak, is possessed of a most inextinguishable reproductive power, the seeds being shed by every mature tree in millions, and ready to germinate at once in a favourable position. The seedlings shoot rapidly above the danger of jungle-fires, and grow straight and tall before branching out. The timber of the sál, if inferior to the teak for some purposes, such as carpentry and transverse beams, is superior for others, such as wheel-work and uprights, its straight, firm grain giving it immense power of resistance to crushing. It is almost the only timber tree of upper India, where teak is unknown. The unlimited water-power of these rivers will supply the means of converting it on the spot; and the Narbadá will form a highway for floating it to the open valley. Sál will not swim by itself, until seasoned for several years; but the hills produce an unlimited quantity of the finest bamboos, a bundle of which tied round a log will support it, and which are themselves of the highest economic value. At present these forests have scarcely been drawn on for the supply of timber, being distant from the Narbadá some thirty or forty miles, without a road capable of conveying heavy timber. I have already remarked on the appearance of the sál tree. Singly it is a little formal in outline, though possessing a fine aspect from its horizontal branching, bright evergreen leaves like broad lanceheads, and straight, tapering stem covered with gray and deeply fissured bark. Its great charm, however, resides in the fresh, cool aspect of the masses and belts in which it chiefly grows.

Besides the dammer resin of the sál, several other kinds of minor forest produce are collected here, as in other tracts, for sale to the traders of the plains. Some of these have already been mentioned. Another is the stick-lac of commerce, which is deposited by an insect on the smaller twigs of several species of trees, among which *Butea frondosa*, *Schleichera trijuga*, and *Zizyphus jujuba* are the principal. The twigs are broken off, and sold as they stand, looking like pieces of very dark red coral. About twenty pounds will be procured annually from a tree, so long as any of the insects are left on it to breed. But just as often as not the improvident wild man will cut down the whole tree to save himself the trouble of climbing. The inborn destructiveness of these jungle people to trees is certainly very extraordinary; even where it is clearly against their own interest, they cannot apparently refrain from doing wanton injury. A Gónd or Bygá passing along a pathway will almost certainly, and apparently unconsciously, drop his axe from the shoulder on any young sapling that may be growing by its side, and almost everywhere young trees so situated will be found cut half through in this manner. The stick-lac is manufactured into dye in considerable quantities at a factory in Jubbulpúr, whose agents penetrate the remotest corners of these jungles in search of the raw material.

The cocoons of the wild *tusser* silk-moth are also collected in great numbers for sale to the caste of silk-spinners who live by this business in the villages of the plains. Experience has shown that these moths will not breed a second generation of healthy silk-producing insects in captivity, and a fresh supply is therefore procured annually from their native hills. They live chiefly on the leaves of the sáj tree, whose foliage, being deciduous, would not afford safety to the insect in its chrysalis stage, if the cocoon were attached, as other species are, to the leaf alone. The instinct of the little creature teaches it therefore to anchor its cocoon by a strong silken rope to the leaf-stalk, where it sways about in safety after every leaf has dropped from the tree. The cocoons brought from the jungles by the breeders are attached to pollarded sáj trees, grown near their villages, till the moths have hatched and paired, when the females are captured and made to lay their eggs in close vessels, where they are incubated by heat. The worms reared from the eggs are again placed on the sáj trees, where they form their cocoons, which are then spun into the rough silk known as "tusser." The business is a very precarious one, much depending for success on favourable weather. Superstition of course seizes this uncertainty for her own, and the purchased blessings of the Bygá priest must accompany the cocoons from their native hills, if the breeder of the plains is to expect success.

Besides such scanty exportation of the minor produce of these wilds as I have described, almost their only economic use has hitherto been the splendid grazing they afford for countless herds of cattle, annually brought to them from great distances in the open country on both sides during the hot season. Fine grass and abundance of shade and water make this one of the finest grazing countries in all India, and the amount of wealth which thus actually seems to depend on its continuance as a waste is very great.

At first sight some hesitation might be felt at the prospect of these great grazing-grounds being reclaimed for cultivation, when it is considered how all-essential to the life of a country like India is the breeding of large stocks of oxen. Here the draught ox takes the place of the farm-horse and the steam-engine of England. Cattle are bred, not as an article of food, but as affording perhaps the only description of power by which the operations of agriculture could be performed at all. Horses could not take their place in converting the hard, burnt-up soils, under the blazing sun of the season, when ploughing and sowing the autumn crop goes on, nor, so far as we know the resources of the land, could steam power, even if otherwise suitable, find sufficient fuel at anything like a moderate cost. Thus it may not have been without a teaching of far-seeing policy that the Hindú has been prohibited by his religion from converting the race of horned cattle to the purposes of food. It may be true that the rigid prohibition against touching the carcases of such animals, or in any way trafficking in their death, may have excluded the Hindú cattle-owner from much legitimate profit in the way of leather, horn, tallow, glue, etc.; but it is impossible to draw fine shades of distinction in religious sanctions, and, if, as is probable, the slaughter of cattle useful for the plough could not otherwise be prevented, then the sanctification of the animal from all such uses was probably a measure of the highest policy. Even looked on as an article of food, it is probable that the sacredness of the cow has been productive of more gain than loss, milk and butter being much more wholesome articles of diet than beef in a hot climate. Certainly, any measure which would be likely to endanger the existing supply of plough-cattle would be highly objectionable. But I think that no apprehension of the sort need be entertained from the probable reclamation of such tracts as the Mandlá savannahs. Sufficient forest land must always remain in the higher regions to furnish the green bite at the end of the hot season, which is all that is necessary to tide the herds over the most trying part of the year, and, for the rest, the people will soon learn to do as other countries have done, and as other parts of India even have done, namely, devote a part of the cultivated area to the raising of green pasture, by irrigation, for the cattle. This fine natural pasture is no doubt a great advantage; but it is not at all indispensable even in India.

The resources of the country in iron and other mineral wealth have never been fully examined, though it is evident on the surface that they are abundant. Gold is washed out of the sands of more than one of the streams, in small quantities, however, which barely repay the labour, and it is probable that its lodes are buried in the quartz of the primitive rocks deep below the flow of volcanic material that has overlaid them.

In the matter of climate, like all uncleared regions in this latitude at so low an elevation, the tract is subject to malarious fever during the months of October to January. But experience shows that this influence lasts only so long as the country continues uncleared. It is probable that the Lower Narbadá valley was equally unhealthy at one time, yet it is now as healthy as any part of the country. Several stations in these provinces have been set down in the middle of jungles with as evil a reputation as this, and along with the clearance of the jungle the fever was found to disappear. The Wynaäd, Ássám, and Cachar are also standing instances of the successful occupation of malarious countries by the help of European enterprise. The malaria excepted, the climate is highly favourable to colonisation, considering the situation of the tract. No region out of the great mountain ranges could probably be pointed to as possessing such advantages of coolness and freshness as are here conferred by the elevated situation, abundance of moisture, and its attendant evergreen verdure.

As for the obstacles supposed to be presented by the rank vegetation and noxious animals, they are chiefly imaginary. Immense plains lie ready for the plough, if merely the coarse natural grasses were cleared away, there being no brushwood or heavy timber to speak of. The luxuriance of these grasses is only evidence of the fatness of the land that lies below; and a torch applied in the month of May will, over large tracts, remove all obstacle to the immediate application of the plough. The wild animals, here as elsewhere, would retire before the axe and plough of the settler. Such as are noxious to human life are not really more so here than in many other much more open parts of the country. In the districts of Doní and Bétúl there is certainly a larger number of tigers in the same area than in Mandlá, and there they have not been found to constitute any serious obstacle to the steady advancement of population and tillage.

I am not one of those who believe that Europeans can ever labour profitably with their own hands in the "plains" of India; and even at this elevation I believe that the power of the sun, although much alleviated by the coolness of the breezes, the low temperature of the nights, and the freshness of the vegetation, would still be prohibitive of severe manual labour by natives of a temperate region. But I think that we have here a tract eminently fitted to yield results from the application of European energy, intelligence, and capital to the supervision and direction of native labour.

The great difficulty would be to obtain the labour to supervise. I doubt if the regular Hindú cultivators of the plains outside could be induced to move into these wilds by any temptation, so long as they can obtain a pittance where they are. The aborigines are too timid and unstable to furnish reliable workmen. I would rather look to the teeming millions of the coast districts to furnish the needful supply of labourers, if these inland wastes are to be reclaimed within any reasonable period of time. It really seems to be matter for astonishment that these littoral races have for many years shown themselves to be ready to cross the seas to the West Indies, the Mauritius, and other distant countries, and have actually been transported thither in great numbers, while all the time vast areas of the finest land are pining for labour in the interior of their own country. There cannot be a doubt which they would most willingly go to, in order to escape from their densely crowded condition at home, were the inducements offered to them the same. What has tempted them to other countries has been the superior wages which their industries could afford to offer; and in India, wherever, as in Ássám, Cachar, and the Wynaäd, such articles of European demand as coffee, tea, etc., have attracted European enterprise, and where similar wages have been held out, an abundant supply of labour has been furnished by these fountains of population. What appears to be necessary, then, to effect the rapid reclamation of these wilds, is the introduction of some special industry which will attract the European energy and capital which alone can ever effect the movement of Indian labour in large bodies from one part of the country to another. That there are such industries capable of introduction there cannot be a doubt.

At present cattle-breeding would seem to be the most promising opening, both because it wants the fewest hands, and because the absence of roads is of less consequence in such a business.

Before leaving the subject of these waste lands, I should refer to the only attempt ever made to form a settlement in them under European supervision, and which ended in lamentable failure. Some thirty years ago four German missionaries attempted to form a colony among the aboriginal tribes, on the Moravian system, in one of these upland valleys. They selected a spot just under the Amarkantak plateau, near a small village called Karinjeá, in the middle of a fine plain of rich soil, a few miles south of the Narbadá. The place had an elevation of about 2700 feet, and was well situated in every respect but one. In a country abounding with shade and water, they pitched on a bare mound without an evergreen tree, and more than two miles distant from the nearest running water. They went out in the hot weather, and failed to prepare sufficient shelter before the arrival of the rainy season. Thus they remained exposed to constant damp and cold winds, and dependent for their water on a small stagnant pool polluted by the drainage of decaying vegetation. The result was death from cholera, or some other malignant bowel-complaint, of three out of the four, and the retreat of the only survivor. However worthy of praise, such an enterprise cannot be looked on as a fair experiment. But it cast a gloom over the prospect of further attempts of the same sort, and has never again been repeated. The example of the missions to the Kóls of Bengal and the Karens of Burma, where the combination of profitable industrial enterprise with theological teaching has been found to be singularly effective in the propagation of the Gospel among aboriginal races, may point to the desirability of some such system being attempted among the unsophisticated savages of these wilds by those who are now preaching in vain to the semi-Hindú tribes further west.

Some time ago a French gentleman took up a considerable tract of the finest land in one of these valleys. But it soon appeared that he had no intention of real colonisation, and had, in fact, been merely speculating on the value of the forest produce of the land. This and other symptoms of land-jobbing have, I believe, induced some reconsideration of the rules for the sale of the fee simple of waste lands. One thing may be relied on, however—that whatever title a settler may here obtain from the Government will be an absolute one, every existing or possible private interest having been fully determined before the available wastes were declared by law to be state property.

In such a well-watered, shady, and grassy region as this upper Narbadá valley, it is inevitable that wild animals should abound. The hilly ranges which separate the valleys contain the bison, the sámbar, and the black bear, like similar tracts in other parts of the province. These are animals peculiar to no part of India, and the same may be said of the spotted deer, which affects the densely wooded banks of the larger streams. But, as I have said, we are here within the limits of the great sál belt, and come upon some animals which I have noticed as coinciding in range therewith.

Chief in interest among these is the beautiful twelve-tined deer (*Rucervus Duvaucellii*), called by some the Bárá-singhá, a name which simply means "twelve-tined," and which is applied also to the Káshmír stag (*C. Cashmiriensis*). In size it is intermediate between the sámbar and the spotted deer, and almost the same as the red deer of Scotland. In colour it is a reddish brown during the cold season, passing through a bright rufous chestnut in spring to a rich golden red in summer. The antlers are very handsome, and differently shaped from those of any other deer in the world. They have but one basal tine over the forehead, no median tines at all, and all the other branches arranged at the summit of the beam.

Here they show a tendency to approach the Rusine type, to which belong the sámbar and the axis, the beam being first divided into a terminal fork, each branch of which afterwards splits into several points. Usually the outward or anterior branch bears three such points, and the inward or posterior two, making, with the brow-antler, six points on each horn. Very old stags sometimes have more; but, as in the *Rusinæ*, when there are more than three the extra ones are abnormal monstrosities, and the antlers are usually unsymmetrical and stunted in size. The horns are grayish in colour, and of a smoother surface than those of the sámbar. They are not nearly so massive, nor so long, but have a very handsome outward sweep, which renders them, I think, more effective as a trophy for the deerstalker. They are very difficult to procure fully developed and perfect. They are cast more regularly, I think, than those of the *Rusinæ;* and as the stags seem to be very combative, some of the points are usually broken off after they lose the velvet at the close of the rainy season, when their haunts first become accessible to the sportsman. In form the *Rucervus* is one of the most beautiful of the family—lightly and gracefully made, and with a stately carriage; and altogether, with his splendid golden colour and finely shaped antlers, this stag is not surpassed, I think, in appearance, by any member of the deer tribe.

This animal has been called in north-eastern India the "swamp deer," but here he is not observed to be particularly partial to swampy ground. They graze in the mornings and evenings, chiefly along the smaller streams, and by springs, where the grass is green, in the open valleys, and rest during the day about the skirts of the sál forest. A favourite midday resort is in the shade of the clumps of sál dotted about the open plain, at some distance from the heavy forest. They are not nearly so nocturnal in habits as the sámbar, being often found out grazing late in the forenoon, and again early in the afternoon; and I do not think they wander about all night like the sámbar. Their midday rest is usually of a few hours only, but during that time they conceal themselves in the grass much after the manner of the sámbar. I have never heard of their visiting cultivated tracts, like the latter; nor can I learn that their apparent adherence to the sál forest is due to their employing any part of that tree as food.

In the middle of the day the red deer (so they are called by natives, and often by Europeans) may be shot by beating the grass with elephants in the manner before described. During the height of the cold weather many parts of this tract can hardly be traversed except on an elephant; and in such places shooting would otherwise be impossible, owing to the height and thickness of the grass jungle. In the course of a day's beating of this sort in the Mandlá district a very great variety of game may easily be met with. On one occasion, when spending Christmas with two friends in the lovely Matiárí valley, a day's march east of the station of Mandlá, we secured, I think, a specimen of nearly every kind of game to be found in the country, excepting the bison and the panther. On the 26th we marched from a place called Bartólá to Gobrí, both on the Matiárí—a clear sparkling stream that here runs through a valley, filled with long grass cover, and bounded on either side by chains of low hills, flat on the tops, and clothed with low tree jungle and bamboos on their sides. We took separate lines, F. going by the pathway, D. along the tops of the hills on one side, while I beat along the river below on an elephant. I had not gone far before I put up a large herd of sámbar in long grass, and, firing right and left, dropped one small stag, and heavily wounded a very large fellow with splendid antlers and as black as a buffalo. I got off, and tracked the wounded animal for about three miles by his blood through the long, dewy grass, till I was as thoroughly wetted through as if I had been wading in a tank, when, as the deer had reached heavy bamboo cover, and seemed to be still strong, I gave it up, and again made for the river. On the way I came on a herd of red deer, grazing about in an opening in the low jungle, where a fine spring kept the grass beautifully green. They saw me before I was within shot, however, and retreated into grass cover.

Waiting a little, I got on the elephant, and proceeded to beat the long grass; and, after going about a quarter of a mile, started the herd, which must have contained fully thirty individuals. They dived into a deepish hollow, filled with low brushwood, in front of me, and I waited on the edge for their appearance on the far side. Presently they clattered up in single file, stags and does intermixed, the last of all being a very large dark red stag, with beautiful antlers that seemed almost to overpower him as he slowly trotted up the rise. I had the sight of the double rifle then full on his broad back, and was just touching the trigger when the man behind me seized and detained my arm in a vice-like grasp. The moment was lost, and I turned viciously on the culprit, who, however, pointed silently to an object in a tree close to our heads. It was a huge colony of bees—the terrible *Bonhrá*, whose swarms had, a march or two before, routed our whole following, leaving a good-sized baggage pony dead upon the ground. Lucky it was I had not fired, and I thought little of the lost stag in the hurry to get out of so dangerous a vicinity. About half a mile farther on, near the river, a spotted doe leaped out of a patch of grass, and scoured across the plain. It was too tempting, she looked so round and fat; and a snap shot rolled her over, shot through the loins. We were now not far from camp, and I was beating through some longish grass, when a full, round countenance was seen peering over the top of it at the advancing elephant. I did not make it out for a while, and presently it disappeared, the motion of the grass showing the progress of a large body towards the river. A little further on it stopped, and the round face again glared at me over the grass. Surely it must be a tiger? A glimpse of a striped red hide settled the question, and I moved a little down to cut her off from the river bed. All was motionless for a few minutes, and then again the slowly waving grass showed the stealthy progress towards the deep gully in which ran the river. A shallow ravine was a little ahead, down which she could steal unobserved, except in one place, where a little jungle pathway crossed it, and I took up a place commanding this at about sixty yards, waiting with cocked rifle and beating heart. Now she is close to the opening, the grass rustling gently above her. Now she sneaks rapidly across, crawling low, but halts for a moment to look again before entering the further cover. Fatal pause! A ball speeds through her shoulder, and, turning with a roar, she gallops back again up the hollow. I thought she meant a charge, and hastily reloaded the discharged barrel of my breech-loader, as I had only one gun out, being on a pad. But she left the nálá, when nearly opposite me, on the wrong side. I think she must have forgotten, for she evidently looked out for her assailant, jumping high above the grass at every bound—a really beautiful sight, with her very bright-coloured skin, hair erect, and tail streaming behind her. About the third bound I caught her with another bullet, and she fell, crumpled up in mid-air, for all the world just like a partridge struck full by a charge of shot. She was lying stone-dead when I came up, and no wonder, for the ball had entered near her tail, traversed the whole length of her body, and was resting under the skin of her forehead. The rifle was a twelve-bore breech-loader, on my own spherical ball principle, the penetration of which may be judged of by this performance. The first shot was a little high on the shoulder, but would soon have killed her, and fully accounted for her confusion of ideas. She had evidently been lying on the watch for spotted deer coming to drink. A large herd of them broke out of the grass while our interview was in progress. Coming to camp, I found that F. had shot a black buck antelope on the road; while D. returned with a young *bárá-singhá* stag and a spotted deer. In the evening F. went out, and killed a large bear, which came down to the river to drink beside him. Next day we were almost equally fortunate, though no tiger was met with; and we spent a Christmas of considerable joviality in that remote wilderness, the dinner consisting, as far as I recollect, of a (peacock) turkey and sámbar tongue, supported by roast haunch of red-deer venison, as *pièces de résistance*, with cheetul cutlets and fillet of nilgái veal as *entrées*, followed up by boiled quails and roasted teal, and concluded by the orthodox plum-pudding and mince-pies out of Crosse and Blackwell's tins. Sundry glasses of whisky toddy, imbibed round a rattling bonfire lit in front of the tents, were fully justified by the really severe cold after sunset. Stalking the *bárá-singhá*, however, affords the finest sport; and from the less exclusively nocturnal habits of the animal, as well as the open character of the country, resembles deer-stalking in Scotland more than any other of our field sports.

When hurrying through this country in January, *en route* to the eastern forests, I halted for two days in the upper valley of the Hálon to stalk the red deer, which I had never before seen. The grass was very thick and long, and, being still green, was entirely unburnt. At a place called Motínálá, where a deep branching watercourse crosses the pathway several times, I was walking ahead of my followers, when I came on the remains of a poor wanderer, who had evidently not long before been killed by a tiger. He was a religious mendicant; and his long iron tongs, begging-bowl hollowed from a skull, and cocoa-nut hooka were scattered about in the bottom of the nálá, where he had been resting on his weary march, together with tresses of his long matted hair and a shred or two of cloth. The bones were all broken to pieces, and many of them were missing altogether. A Banjárá drover had been taken off near the same spot about a week before, so that it was not without some misgivings that I wandered off the road through the long grass to look for red deer towards the skirts of the hills. To hunt for the tiger in such an ocean of grass-cover would have been hopeless. I skirted the hills to the right of the road from here to the camping-ground at Manglí, very soon getting drenched to the skin passing through the high grass dripping with the morning dew. Towards the hills the grass was shorter, and the plain much cut up by deep fissures in the black, heavy soil. I saw several small herds of deer wending their way towards the clumps of sál forest on the skirt of the hills before I found any in a position that would admit of stalking. At last I marked a small parcel of hinds, with two fair-looking stags, disappear over a low rising ground, slowly feeding their way towards the forest; and making a long détour to gain the shelter of a deep crack, which led into the valley they had entered, I stalked almost into the middle of them before I was aware. My first intimation of the fact was the sharp bark of a hind, who had observed the top of my head over the bank, and the next moment a rush of feet informed me that the herd was off. Stepping on to the bank, I made a clean miss of the first running shot; but, taking more time with the second barrel, I saw the hindmost stag reel and almost fall over to the shot. He made off, however, along with the herd; but presently left them, and took a line of his own towards the long grass-cover in the middle of the plain. I soon hit on his track where he had entered the grass, and found a little blood; but as the grass was a long way over my head, I sent back for the elephant with which to beat him out. Following the blood-marks on the yellow stems for about a mile, we started him out of a patch of grass near the river, and I shot him through the back as he ran away.

The next day, being encamped at Toplá, in the centre of a wide valley among the sál forest, I went out in the afternoon towards the Hálon river. Here the country was open and prairie-like, short grass plains, dotted with clumps of sál, intervening between the heavier masses of forest. The river was very bright and clear, running over a pebbly bed. I took out two young half-bred hounds, between the Rámpúr breed and the Scotch deerhound, in the hope of getting them a run at a wounded red deer, as they were as yet guiltless of blood. Their mother, and the bull mastiff "Tinker," of wolf renown, accompanied to help them in the kill. A couple of lithe, black, and nearly naked, Bygás, with their war-axes, guided the party. We wandered a good many miles in the early afternoon without coming on game, but I, at least, was gratified by the delightful park-like scenery. About four o'clock, by the advice of the Bygás, we sat down on a little eminence crowned by a clump of sál trees, to watch for deer coming out to drink or feed. Very soon a good-sized herd suddenly appeared in the middle of a long, flat stretch of grass-land beyond the river; and after stretching themselves, and enjoying a game at romps, commenced feeding pretty quickly down towards the bank of the river. We at once retreated over the bank of our knoll; and, getting into a hollow protected by a fringe of bushes, crept up to the banks and again reconnoitred. They were quite unsuspicious, the wind being highly favourable; and they seemed likely to come and drink in our very faces. When within a few hundred yards, however, they halted a long time behind a little rising ground. I was in agony lest the dogs should make us known, as they were dreadfully excited by the restraint of the stalks, and seemed to know perfectly well that there was something to hunt at hand. Presently a single hind topped the rise, and for full five minutes stood sniffing round in all directions, her great ears cocked in aid of her sense of smell. At last she seemed to be satisfied, and moved slowly forwards, now pausing to crop a mouthful of grass, and then again starting and looking about as if she had heard or smelt something. A stag now walked up past her, and without the least precaution came boldly on to the water, which he entered about a hundred yards above our post. The rest of the herd were still mostly hidden by the rise. Creeping through the bushes I prepared to fire at the stag, and gave orders for the hounds to be slipped at once after I should fire. I was barely in time to secure a shot, before the stag, alarmed by a yelp from one of the dogs, turned to flee up the bank. As it was I dropped him on the pebbly bank, shot through the shoulder; and, turning the rifle on the hind who was pausing startled at the shot, the other bullet passed through her thigh, injuring the hip joint. She fell on her hind-quarters for a few moments, but presently recovered, and made off after the herd across the flat. The four dogs had sprung from the slips, and splashed through the shallow stream before she had well got on her legs; and they very nearly had her before she got fairly into her pace. Then, however, she distanced them at once for a few hundred yards, when the old bitch "Bell," who was extremely fast, began to draw steadily up to her. The pups were a hundred yards behind, giving tongue like foxhounds, and old Tinker laboured along scarcely half-way from where they had started. Bell was very near the hind, when I saw her disappear bodily into a hole. But the deer was now failing fast; and, seeing no chance of making the forest, turned round and came back towards the river. The pups and Tinker now made up considerably by cutting off the corner, and very soon the brindled one, "Sheroo," who was rather the faster, was racing alongside of her, making uncertain snatches at the shoulder. The yellow dog soon joined him, and together they managed to throw over the deer just as she reached the bank of the river. They all three rolled down the bank together; and before the deer could recover herself Tinker was up and pinned her by the throat. The bitch was not far behind, and among them they nearly tore the poor animal limb from limb. Fearing a row between Tinker and the young dogs I ran up as fast as possible; but a Bygá with his axe was before me, and attempted to get the quarry from the dogs. He didn't know Tinker, however, who loosed his hold on the deer's throat only to fly at the Bygá. The latter defended himself as well as he could with his axe-handle, very thoughtfully for such a savage, not attempting to use the head; but he had several pretty severe bites in the arms and legs before I could arrive to his rescue. As a rule Tinker was as quiet as a lamb with men; but when roused by blood he was a perfect devil; and as his size and weight were immense I was often rather afraid of him myself. Poor fellow, his formidable aspect and a few outbursts of this sort were the death of him, being poisoned by a dog boy a few months afterwards. Bell broke her neck by chasing an antelope down a blind well, a few marches after the hunt I have related; the best of the two pups was carried off by a leopard or hyæna; and altogether I was so disgusted with the bad luck I had always had in keeping large dogs in India that I gave it up altogether; and I cannot say that I found very much loss accrue to my sport in consequence. I believe they lose more wounded animals, by driving them out of reach, than they recover.

On the way back I shot another hind, who stood too

long to gaze at the unwonted intruders, and saw the tracks of a wild elephant sinking deep into the soft, black soil. I was told afterwards that this elephant was one which had broken loose from captivity about ten years previously, and had since inhabited the dense covers about the head of the Hálon river. He afterwards annoyed the forest officers not a little by systematically demolishing all the masonry boundary pillars erected by them round the reserved forest. Really wild elephants do not come so far west as this; the country to the east of Amarkantak (the source of the Narbadá), or at the most the Samní valley, a little nearer than that place, being their most westerly range in this part of India. Formerly, however, the whole of this country, and far to the west of it, was the home of the wild elephant. The etymology of many names, such as the "elephant enclosure," the "elephant pool," etc., would suffice to indicate this; but, besides, we have it distinctly recorded, in that valuable work, *The Institutes of Akber*, that in the sixteenth century elephants were found and captured in the Narbadá valley as far west as the Bíjágarh and Hándiá Sirkárs,[1] which lie partly to the west of the meridian of the present military stations of Mhow and Ásírgarh. This is probably the most westerly range of the wild elephant that has been recorded; and their subsequent disappearance over so large a tract of country speaks volumes for the advancement which has taken place in that period.

The night I was at Toplá, two tigers roared loudly round about the camp. We were pitched in a little glade in the sea of grass, and the effect in the clear, cold night was very fine. The night voice of the tiger has a very impressive sound, conveying, though not nearly so *loud* as the bray of a jackass, the idea of immense power, as it rolls and trembles along the earth. Four months later, when I was encamped near Mátín, in the forests of the far east, I listened one night to the most remarkable serenade of tigers I ever heard. A peculiar, long wail, like the drawn-out mew of a huge cat, first rose from a river course a few hundred yards below my tent. Presently

[1] Gladwin's *Azeen Akbery*, vol. ii. p. 249.

from a mile or so higher up the river came a deep, tremendous roar, which had scarcely died away ere it was answered from behind the camp by another, pitched in a yet deeper tone, startling us from its suddenness and proximity. All three were repeated at short intervals, as the three tigers approached each other along the bottoms of the deep, dry watercourses, between and above which the camp had been pitched. As they drew together the noises ceased for about a quarter of an hour; and I was dozing off to sleep again, when suddenly arose the most fearful din near to where the tigress had first sounded the love-note to her rival lovers, a din like the caterwauling of midnight cats magnified a hundredfold. Intervals of silence, broken by outbursts of this infernal shrieking and moaning, disturbed our rest for the next hour, dying away gradually as the tigers retired along the bed of the river. In the morning I found all the incidents of a three-volume novel in feline life imprinted on the sand; and marks of blood showed how genuine the combat part of the performance had been. For the assurance of the timid, I may as well say that I have never had my camp actually invaded by a tiger, though constantly pitched, with a slender following, and without any sort of precaution, in the middle of their haunts. It strikes a stranger to jungle ways a little oddly, perhaps, to see a man in the warm summer nights calmly take his bed out a hundred yards from the tents, lie down under the canopy of heaven, listen, pipe in mouth, for half an hour to the noises of wild animals, and then placidly fall asleep. He soon learns to do the same himself.

About the end of the rains, in September and October, the red deer collect in large herds on the tops of the plateaux; and I have been told of assemblages of several hundred head at that season. They are then beginning to rut, and are very easy to get at, the Gónds and Bygás killing great numbers with their axes, aided by their strong tall dogs. The best heads are to be got from these people; and that figured opposite, which is a very typical one, was killed either thus or by a tiger. I myself never got a complete head with more than ten points, though I have secured some heavier than the twelve-pointed one figured below. Its length is $33\frac{1}{2}$ inches round the curve of each antler, and extreme spread 36 inches. There are few larger in the forests.

In the rains the wild buffalo wanders in herds all over these Mandlá highlands. They mostly disappear, however,

HORNS OF BÁRÁ-SINGHÁ DEER. (*Scale, one-tenth.*)

when the tame cattle are brought up to graze in the open season, a few only lingering in the most secluded valleys; and they must then be sought in the less accessible jungles to the south and west. Thither I must carry the reader to introduce him to the animal, as I never was in the Mandlá district at the time when the buffaloes are found there.

CHAPTER X

AN EXPLORATION IN THE FAR EAST

THE Highlands of Central India may perhaps properly be said to terminate where the steep southern face of the Mýkal range, trending away to the north-east, culminates in the high bluff promontory of Amarkantak. Standing here on this prominent point, the very focus and navel of India, the eye ranges over a panorama perhaps inferior in extent to no outlook in the whole peninsula. The rain that clothes this little plateau of a few square miles with the greenest of verdure, having the peculiarity of seldom ceasing for more than a few days at any part of the year, forms the first beginnings of three great rivers, whose waters flow in opposite directions to the seas on either side of India. The infant Narbadá bubbles forth at the feet of the observer, enclosed by religious care in a wall of masonry, and surrounded by Hindú temples, and thence meanders on for some miles through a narrow glade, carpeted with beautiful grass, and fringed by forests of sál; at first a tiny burn, but growing rapidly by union with others, till, some three miles from the fountain, it leaps over the edge of the plateau in a clear shoot of about thirty feet. Seven hundred and fifty miles further on it rolls, a mighty river, into the waters of the Arabian Gulf. In the local Sivite Mythology the Narbadá is the maiden Mýkal-Kanyá, daughter of the Mýkal Mountain, from whose brow she springs. Resistless in her divine might, at her first birth she overflowed the earth in a destructive flood, till, in answer to the prayers and sacrifices of men, the Great God sent the Vindhyá Mountain and his seven stalwart sons [1] to restrain her, when she shrank into her present channel,

[1] Thence the name Sát-purá, applied to these highlands, *Sat pura* meaning literally the "Seven Sons."

leaving behind her the Ganges and other rivers, as pools are left by the receding tide. Hence the sanctity of the Narbadá is superior to that of all other rivers, though the gods gave the preference for the first five thousand years of the Kálí-Yug to the Ganges. Twenty-eight years only of this period now remain unexpired, when the local Brahmans fully expect the Narbadá to surpass as a place of pilgrimage all other rivers of India. As it is, the parent spring at Amarkantak, and many places along its course, are places of great sanctity to pilgrims from all parts of India; and the help of the railway, which is by no means scorned by the devout Hindú (who likes to "boil his peas"), bids fair to realise in some degree the prophecy of the Puránás. A little to the north of the source of the Narbadá rises the Johillá, a stream which shortly joins the Sone, also born in these hills, and flows north into the Ganges; while, still only a few steps from these, another little stream, the Arpá, bubbles forth, and shortly tumbles over the sheer cliff to the south, and mingles with the great Mahánadí, which drains the plains of Chattis′garh into the Bay of Bengal. From this height of 4000 feet the eye embraces a view of three-fourths of a circle, uninterrupted by anything but the blue haze of distance which limits the vision. Far below to the south, lying like a chessboard, is the open cultivated plain of Chattis′garh, stretching out to the uttermost range of vision. To the east and north, 2000 feet below, appears a flat sea of greenery, broken here and there by an isolated peak that appears to reach the level of the observer. In the faint distance beyond rises another wall of rock, visible only on a clear day as a faint violet-coloured shade across the sky. The green plain is a vast forest of sál, unbroken by tillage, and scarcely inhabited by man, and the rocky rampart beyond is the buttress of another table-land called Sirgújá, the land of the Kól aborigines, and beyond the limits of our province. My mission for the succeeding six months was to explore this vast region of sál forest, lying to the north and east of Amarkantak, and stretching far beyond and to the south of the plain of Chattis′garh, in the semi-independent country called the Garhját States.

Over all this country roams the wild buffalo, and in the forests north and east of Amarkantak were then found large herds of wild elephants, which descended at the ripening of the crops of Chattis'garh to the skirts of the forest, doing immense damage, and forming a serious obstacle to the cultivation of the country. To penetrate to their haunts, ascertain their numbers, and propose means for their destruction, was another object of our expedition.

In the end of January I descended the Rajádhár pass from the Mandlá district, and marched across the Chattis'-garh plain, where antelope, ducks, snipe, etc., afforded perpetual occupation for the gun, to the station of Rái'púr, where I met the Chief Commissioner's camp and my future companion in this expedition—Captain B., of Her Majesty's —— Regiment. Thence we proceeded to the eastern and southern forests, marching rapidly to get from one portion of these forests to another, where days and weeks would be passed in tramping about the hills and making notes, the great part of which would possess no interest for the general reader. We never allowed ourselves to linger for sport; but the herds of buffaloes are in some parts of this country so numerous that it would have been almost impossible to avoid encountering them.

The extreme western range of the wild buffalo[1] in Central India is almost exactly marked by the 80th meridian of longitude, or in physical features by the Wyn-Gangá tributary of the Godávarí river, and below their junction almost by the latter river itself. I say *almost*, because in a trip down the Godávarí river which I made during the rains, I saw the tracks of a herd of buffaloes on the western side of that river, at the "third barrier"[2] south of the station of Chándá, that is, a short distance to the west of the 80th meridian. The natives, however, told

[1] *Bubalus arni.*

[2] These "barriers" are points in the course of this river where its otherwise still, lake-like character is broken by spaces in which the river assumes more the character of a mountain stream. They interrupt what would otherwise be an unbroken stretch of waterway into the heart of the country, and are now being dealt with by a staff of skilful engineers. Probably a herd of buffaloes would find it easier to cross at one of these barriers than elsewhere.

me there that they only cross the river in the rainy season, and that they do not penetrate very far to the west, so that so slight an exception may fairly be held to prove the general rule. So far, then, from the common adage of the sportsman being true that the wild buffalo does not extend *south* of the Narbadá, the truth is that the animal is unknown to the *north* of it, in the longitude of that river. It has been stated that the feral buffaloes of these parts are only the descendants of tame ones run wild, an idea that will not hold water for a second. They have all the habits of fully wild animals, are extremely numerous in the parts they inhabit, and exactly correspond in size and every particular with the aboriginally wild buffaloes of eastern Bengal. Two varieties are recognised in India, differing chiefly in the length and shape of the horns. They have been called by Hodgson, *B. Macroceros*, and *B. Speiroceros*, the horns of the former being long, straight, and more slender, and of the latter, shorter, thicker, and more curved. All the Central Indian species that I have seen pertain to the latter race, the average length of the horns of a mature bull being three-and-a-half to four feet. No animal has changed so little in domestication as the buffalo. In appearance the wild animal is extremely like the tame one, but fully a third larger, and showing fine, plump, sleek condition, instead of the slouching, scraggy appearance of the domestic " buff," and possessing the free action and air of a denizen of the wilds. I have never heard an authentic case of their interbreeding with the domestic race, though individuals of the latter sometimes join the wild herds, and become difficult to reclaim. In height I have never seen a wild buffalo exceed sixteen hands; but though thus less in stature than the bison, the buffalo stands on much shorter legs, and is altogether a heavier built animal, so that in bulk and weight he must a good deal exceed the wild bull of the hills. They never interfere with each other, the bison adhering to hilly tracts, while the buffalo is essentially a lover of plains and level plateaux, where the extensive swamps he delights in can be found. The very different structure of their hoofs would suffice of itself to indicate this, those of the buffalo being broad and platter-like, to support him on soft ground; while those of the bison, who has to pick his way among rocks, are wonderfully small for his size, as neat and game-like and little larger than those of the sámbar deer. The buffalo is also much less intolerant of man and his works than the bison, invading the rice cultivation, and often defying all attempts to drive him from the neighbourhood of villages. They are altogether very defiant of man, and, unlike the bison, will generally permit a close approach without any concealment, where they have not been much molested, trusting apparently to their formidable aspect to secure the retreat of the invader, which is usually successful. If the attack be followed up, however, they almost always make off at last, and are then not so easily got at again. The favourite resorts of the buffalo are on the skirts of the lower sál forests, where they run out into the open plain, and between them and the rice cultivation of these regions, in the great open, swampy plains, where long rank grass affords the sort of cover they like.

Our first introduction to the wild buffalo in this trip was near the high-road between Rái'púr and Sambalpúr, when B., who had the shot (in stalking a herd together we always arranged by turns who should have the first shot), killed a cow. We followed the herd a long way, and wounded another, but could not bag. For a long time after this we were employed in the forests, and though we saw a few, never had time to hunt them, until, near the Mahánadí river, we came out on a cultivated plain, of which a large bull and four cows had completely taken possession, devastating the rice, and charging indiscriminately at all who approached. A Baboo from the nearest police station had come out a little while before to rid the place of the invader, but contented himself with firing away all his ammunition at half a mile's distance from the top of a house, and the bull remained monarch of all he surveyed. We had scarcely entered on the plains when the owner of the ruined rice-fields pointed out his enemy, looming out against the horizon as large as an elephant, and we at once made preparations for the attack. The place was as level and open as a billiard-table, so we had to rely on our rifles alone. We were both heavily armed with two-ounce rifles, however, and several smaller guns in reserve, so we marched straight on the foe, with our very miscellaneous pack of dogs under orders to be let go at the first shot. The bull and his harem came boldly down to meet us, and as we approached commenced his usual demonstrations to put us to flight—pawing the earth with his feet, tossing his mighty horns, and making short runs in our direction. But we steadily advanced, and when within about eighty yards separated a little, so that one should get a flank shot, the full front of the buffalo being practically proof against lead. It was my turn for first shot, and when about sixty yards intervened I knelt down and brought the heavy rifle to bear on the point of his shoulder. Crash went two ounces of lead, propelled by eight drachms of powder, against his tough hide, and he fell upon his knees. Bang went several more of our shots, and he stumbled off dead lame and very much crestfallen. Following him up with the dogs, who were now baying round him, we overhauled him in an open field, and repeated the dose again and again till he fell heavily against the embankment of a rice-field, and then, stepping up, I put a three-ounce shell behind his shoulder, and with a quiver of the limbs he gave it up. He was a fine animal, in the prime of life, and we were amazed at the bulk and strength exhibited by his massive form. The horns were each three feet ten inches long, which is nearly the extreme length they ever attain here.[1] He had sixteen bullets in him before he died, several of large calibre, and at close quarters. We were, however, shooting with bullets of plain lead, and I found that my first two-ounce ball, propelled by eight drachms of powder, had flattened out on his shoulder, pulverising the bones, however, and completely laming him. After this we shot with hardened projectiles.

Next day we embarked in a long canoe, hollowed from the stem of a mighty sál tree, on the bosom of the Mahánadí and sailed down to Sambalpúr in two days and a night. It was mighty exciting work, the stream passing at intervals

[1] Fossil horns of much larger size have been found in the Narbadá gravels, along with bones of the hippopotamus, etc.

over long rapids, where the water, broken into many channels, rushed between narrow banks overhung with bushes, the boatmen steering the canoe with long poles in the most dexterous manner, now warding her bows from a rock on which the stream broke in a sheet of foam, then prostrating themselves at the bottom of the boat to avoid the sweep of the branches, while the canoe shot through some narrow passage, and presently emerging, after a final shave against a sunken rock, into a deep and silent pool, where the splash of huge fish, and the eye-knobs and serrated backs of crocodiles sailing about, showed that we had entered one of the long, silent reaches that break at intervals the torrent of these mountain rivers. My companion had got a severe attack of fever, which marred what would otherwise have been a sufficiently jolly trip. After resting awhile at this most secluded of stations (they get their supplies from Calcutta, several hundreds of miles away, on men's heads, and a convoy had just been trampled up by wild elephants before we arrived), we started again for the Garhját States, where the next month was spent in unremitting toil among their rugged hills. Here we were among the Khónd aborigines, famous for the Meriá sacrifices of human beings to the dread goddess Kálí. How they can have been confounded with our Central Indian Gónds I cannot imagine. They are much blacker and more negro-like in their physique, and speak a wholly different language, a few words only of which approximate, like Góndí, to the Támil of the south. Their country is wholly beyond the limits of the Central Highlands; and it would be out of place to enter here into a detailed description of the tribe, even did the few weeks I passed among them justify such an undertaking. We returned from this trip with most of our following severely ill of fever, contracted in these close jungles, where water is so scarce and bad at this time of year (April) that we rose, like river gods, from our daily bath hung with the green slime of the fetid pools from which our supplies were drawn. As we marched northward again we entered the valley of the Jónk river, a tributary of the Mahánadí, and here we fell in again with great herds of buffaloes, and halted for a day or two to recruit our followers and shoot. Our camp was pitched below a great spreading tree at the deserted site of the village of Jildá. Eaten up by the buffaloes, the people had moved off to a less open space. Around us was a sea of long grass, bounded by low hills and sál forests on the far horizon. Here our poor fever-stricken people paraded themselves in rows to let the sun into their shivering bones, and three times a day got a dose of quinine all round, a course of treatment (preceded by a smart dose of jalap) which soon frees a native from this hot-weather fever.

When marching in the morning, about a couple of miles from camp we saw a herd of fifty or sixty buffaloes standing up to their knees in a swamp among long grass. It was B.'s turn for the shot, and we spent several hours trying to get near enough to shoot. The buffaloes were very wild, having been much fired at a few weeks before by a sportsman with long-range small-bore rifles. As we approached on one side they waded through the swamp and went out on the other, reversing the process when we changed the direction of approach. At last I got on my horse, and took a light breech-loading gun, to try and get round and drive them across to B. They now got alarmed, and made off towards the head of the swamp; and on our following them on either bank, left it altogether, and started at their best pace across a rising ground. The ground seemed very favourable for riding for that country, so I could not resist the temptation to breathe my little nag at them, and was soon galloping full speed in their rear. My animal was an Arab pony, about thirteen three in height, but game as a bantam, and wonderfully sure-footed over bad ground. To my surprise and delight, I found myself ahead of them in less than half a mile; and, shooting past, looked out for a worthy quarry among the labouring mass. I fixed on a bull with long horns, whose shining tips danced in the sunlight conspicuous above them all, and was just ranging alongside to fire when a tremendous bound of my little nag nearly unseated me, and we just escaped the long pointed horns of a lean brute of a cow that shot past my quarter, and then pulled up beyond me, shaking her head and looking very wicked indeed. I sheered off, and let her proceed to rejoin the herd, giving her a broadside of two barrels as she passed, which was followed by another end-on charge for several hundred yards. Eventually she went off again towards the retreating herd; but, though the ground had now become very bad, cut up in all directions by deep rifts in the black soil and pitted by the old footmarks of the buffaloes, I was not going to decline the challenge of this fighting cow. So after reloading my breech-loader, which was a very light snipe gun pressed into ball service, and wholly unfit for this sort of work, I cantered after her, and, when within distance, made a rush past, intending to fire into her at close quarters. But she was too quick for me, and we almost met, my gun going off, I believe harmlessly, in her face. I had another narrow shave as she again charged me, the little horse stumbling heavily several times in the frightful ground. Again she sheered off, and once again I rode up, though not so close as before, and gave her both barrels, holding the gun out like a pistol. She felt these, and, though shaking her head in a threatening manner, did not charge again. She now held on slowly behind the herd; and as I felt I could not kill her with this weapon, I waited behind, hoping she would lie down and the heavy rifles come up. Presently she slackened her pace to a walk, and I watched her from behind a bush. Peering cautiously all round, she went on a little further, and then, after standing about five minutes watching, lay down in the long grass. I marked the spot carefully, as I thought, by a bush, and then rode back full split for a heavy rifle. About a mile behind I met B. with the rifles and dogs, and we proceeded together to finish off the cow. My large rifle had got bulged on one barrel some time before, being unable to bear the proper charges for buffalo-shooting, so I had only one barrel to depend on. We walked up through the grass close to the the spot I had marked, but she was not there. I soon lost the bearings, there being fifty bushes just like the one I had marked her by, and we wandered about, a little apart, looking for her. I had stood up on an ant-hill to get a better look, when just below me up started her savage-looking head and long horns, and she plunged towards me

[To face page 332.

A VICIOUS COW

in the grass. A ball from the heavy rifle in the neck turned her, and she passed between B. and me, preventing both of us from further firing. The dogs now tackled her, "Tinker" in particular (whose deeds of valour in the wolf line have already been recorded) striving to seize her by the nose as she tore along. A couple of hundred yards further on she stopped in another patch of grass, the dogs baying round her, and Tinker, exhausted by the great heat, lying down in the shade of a bush, but flying at her the moment she tried to move. We marched up, at a short interval from each other, and, arriving first on her blind side, I saw her glance at B., shake off the dogs, and creeping forward in a stealthy manner like a tiger, watch for him, with horns laid back, behind the screen of grass and bushes that intervened. Before he arrived, however, I took a steady shot at her neck with the little double fourteen-gauge rifle, dropping her stone dead. We found she had an old bullet wound in the flank, which was full of maggots, accounting for her extremely poor condition and unusual savageness. The small-bore rifle of our predecessor in these hunting-grounds was probably the cause. Her horns were of full cow length, the pair measuring eight feet four inches round the curve and across the skull.

The herd was now clean gone, of course, in the meantime, and we turned towards camp. On the way B. shot a cow, and I wounded a bull, and lost him in the long grass. While smoking our pipes after breakfast, one of the men who had remained to look after the wounded bull came in to say that he had been found lying down in an open plain about a mile away, looking very savage. We sallied forth immediately to encounter him, and found him lying close to a little ridge that had been the embankment of a rice field when the country was cultivated, and was now overgrown with tall grass. He had taken up a position which commanded all approaches, and, as there was no cover, there was nothing for it but to march up on foot. When within about sixty yards I took a shot with a small rifle, on the accuracy of which I could rely, at his broad forehead reclining on the bank. But the angle was wrong, and the ball glanced off without injury to the bull, who sprang on his feet and retreated to the middle of the field. The dogs were now loosed, and bayed round him till he began to chase them all round the field; but as soon as our heads appeared over the fringe of grass, he left them and charged down at ourselves. There was no sort of shelter, and every one had to look out for himself. I stood till he was within about half-a-dozen paces, and then jumped out of his course in the grass, not a moment too soon, my rifle being whirled out of my hands and its ramrod broken. Recovering it, I fired the undischarged barrel into the back of his shoulder, and at the same time the report of B.'s rifle in front of him rang in my ears. Next moment I saw B. fall spinning to one side, while the bull came down on his knees, Tinker, who had dashed past along with him, clinging nobly to his nose. Neither spare gun, gun-bearer, nor the dog-boy was in sight, as I dashed about, looking for the wherewithal to finish the struggling bull. At last I saw them, shrunk into nothing, in a shallow hollow in the black soil, and, seizing a couple of the guns, was hurrying up to the scene of action, when I met B., safe and sound, though rather pale, and at the same time heard the report of a rifle, and saw the bull fall over dead. My Mahomedan shikárí, a man accustomed to shoot, had fortunately ensconced himself, with my spare rifle, close to where the bull stopped after knocking B. over; and, putting the muzzle to his head, had pulled the triggers of both barrels at once! Tinker was covered with mire and blood from the bull, but otherwise uninjured, while the nose of the buffalo showed how determined had been his grip. B. had been caught fortunately with the *outside* edge of his horns, and but slightly, in the arms and ribs, and was not hurt beyond loss of wind and the shock of his fall.

The next day B. had fever, and was so shaken as to require a rest, and I went out alone in another direction. I came on a herd of about forty, grazing in an open plain some two miles south of the camp, and proceeded to stalk them. I had an elephant with me, and sent him round a long circuit to attract their attention while I crept in. Getting within about a hundred yards, I saw that the buffaloes had a bull nílgái along with them, which maintained a sharp outlook all round, while the buffaloes gazed stupidly at the elephant. I was crouched in grass about three feet high, and could not get any nearer for this singular sentinel. So I remained still, and presently the elephant disappeared in some low jungle, and the herd began again to graze. They fed down towards me, and when about seventy yards off I fired at the leader, who was standing end on to me, and was raked fore and aft by the heavy hard ball, falling prone, toes upwards, on the ground. Instead of retreating, the herd now gathered about their comrade, and trotted round, snuffing the blood, and looking about for their concealed enemy. The wreathing smoke of my rifle betrayed our position, and it was not without some alarm that I saw them draw up in a semicircle of pawing hoofs and snorting nostrils, surmounted by forty pairs of monstrous horns. My gun-bearer, Peer Khán, and I thought discretion the better part of valour under such circumstances, and espying, some way to our right, the pollarded trunk of a sáj tree, we retreated, snake fashion, through the grass, and clambered up it. Getting to the top, I sat on its smooth summit, while Peer Khán roosted crow-like on a branch, the only one, a foot or two lower down. I now opened fire on the herd, the first shot from the large rifle almost knocking me off my perch with the heavy recoil; I believe Peer Khán, who had reloaded it, had put in a double charge of powder. I then fired two rounds from the fourteen-bore, the herd pausing irresolute, and finally breaking into a panic-stricken flight. The balls had knocked the dried mud in clouds from their hides, and one remained standing on the ground, while another lagged, very lame, behind the retreating herd. I went up and finished the first, and then tracked up the other a long way till it went with the herd into a heavy swamp, when I returned to camp. I did not see, in the confusion, what became of the nílgái; but he was not with the herd when it retreated.

Our experience of the wild buffalo was thus different from that of some, who have reported it to be a timid, inoffensive animal. As is the case with most wild beasts, it all depends, I believe, on whether you press them hard or not; and probably many might be slaughtered at long ranges without even eliciting a charge. If followed up on foot, I believe the buffalo to be a much more dangerous opponent than the bison, being less timid, and also found in country where there is usually no protection to be derived from trees or rocks. In Bengal they are scarcely ever shot in any way but from elephants; and then have been known to prostrate an elephant in their charge. The prime sport with the buffaloes is on horseback; but it is rare that ground is found fit to ride them on with any degree of safety, and I never heard of its having been accomplished excepting on the occasion above related. I am sure, though, that with a horse clever over rough ground, and a light, breech-loading carbine, capital runs at buffaloes might often be secured by watching them into favourable ground. To kill them with the spear would, I conceive, be utterly out of the question. We cut open one bull down the chest with an axe, to see what stopped our balls so strangely in front shots, and found that a bullet fired into the chest has to pass through more than two feet of hide, bone, and gristle before reaching the cavity of the lungs. Nor is the brain more accessible, the animal holding its head either elevated till the nose is level with the eyes, or, if charging, down between its fore-legs, and quite protected from a shot. A plain leaden bullet of an ounce weight, with three drachms of powder, will go clean through the skull if hit perpendicularly, which, however, it is nearly impossible to do. The best places to fire, both at bison and buffalo, are through the point of the shoulder, if the rifle be powerful enough, or, if not, then behind and a little above the elbow. The centre of the neck is also very deadly, if the aim be true; natives almost always fire there with their matchlocks. The skull and horns of a bull buffalo are so large and heavy as to form a considerable encumbrance as a trophy to the sportsman marching fast with a light camp. Its value is completely spoilt, however, by sawing off the horns and throwing away the skull, as is often done. The better way is to boil away the flesh, and wait a few days till the horn-sheaths loosen on the bony cores, when they can be taken off, and the cores sawn down, leaving only a few inches to give the set of the horns. In doing this, the wonderful provision for giving requisite strength to the structure, without undue weight, by constructing the bony cores like hollow cells, crossed by stays in every direction, will not fail to be perceived.

We marched on down the valley of the Jónk through tracts of sál, mostly devastated by dhya cultivation, to the Mahánadí, and then along it and its tributary, the Arpá, to the little civil station of Bíláspúr, where we arrived on the 28th of April, and began to make arrangements for an expedition to the elephant haunts in the great sál forest to the north of that station. It was reported to be scarcely inhabited except by a few utterly savage Bhúmiás; and it was certain that no supplies of any sort would be procurable. Our first business was, therefore, to hire a large herd of Banjárá bullocks, with their drivers, and load them up with grain; and such was then the land-locked condition of this fertile country that we purchased as much wheat, gram, and rice as we required at the rate of about 100 lb. for a shilling!

On the 3rd of May we rode out to Ratanpúr, the ancient capital of a Rájpút dynasty which ruled over the greater part of this eastern country from the earliest times till the invasion of the Maráthás in the eighteenth century. This ancient place is an example of the decay which has overtaken many of the old Hindú cities since the extinction of the native dynasties, and the decay of orthodox Hindú religious sentiment. Standing on a little central hill, on whose summit the white painted dome of a temple forms a landmark to the surrounding country, the eye looks over great vistas of enormous banyan and mango groves, embosomed in which sleep the waters of a hundred and fifty tanks, and shrouded in whose recesses, with here and there a ribbed spire visible above, lie the crumbling ruins of a vast number of temples, palaces, and forts. A day's ramble scarcely discovers a tithe of the archæological treasures which here await the inspection of the curious. Much of the city has already fallen to pieces. Great untenanted masonry buildings attest the former wealth and state of its inhabitants, while mean little mud shanties and thatched hovels clustering against their walls witness to the poverty of the diminished number of its modern residents. As the temples of the old faith have suffered decay, so, too, has the religion itself; and orthodox Hindúism has over all this country been extensively displaced by a deism, planted less then fifty years ago among the Chamár inhabitants of Chattis'garh by a prophet of their own race. It is, like the Búddhism of old, an uprising of the down-trodden low castes against the tyranny of Brahmanism, its leading principles being abjuration of priestdom and caste, and substitution for the Brahmanistic pantheon of the worship of one God, whom they call *Sal Nám*, or the "True One."

Lying in a low hollow between surrounding eminences, the foul water-tanks, fetid with the slime of centuries, breed among the people of Ratanpúr every sort of loathsome disease; and everywhere the hideous leper, and sufferer from elephantiasis, are seen stalking gloomily about in the shadows of these decaying groves. I was myself destined to share in the pestilence that is rapidly depopulating the place. Coming in heated from our ride, and the tents not having arrived, I was foolish enough to throw myself down on a string beadstead I found under a tree and go to sleep, and in the evening found myself overtaken by a sensation which I did not recognise. It was fever, but not that of malaria I had become accustomed to. Next morning I marched, though very ill, ten miles to the next halting-place; and the day after, being much worse, was carried on six miles further. After tossing about all night I suddenly felt relieved from the burning fever, and became aware of a fine crop of small-pox pustules on my feet. This promised to be the end of my exploration; but, as I had been duly vaccinated, I hoped the attack might be a light one, and determined not to return to the station while a hope remained of accomplishing my desire to see the elephant-country. It was very hot where we now were; but about seven miles further on rose a high conical hill, crowned by an old fortress, called Laäfágarh, which seemed to possess an elevation of at least 3000 feet; and as, on inquiring about it, I found there was shade and water on the top, I determined to get myself carried up there to a cooler temperature, and fight through it with the help of the worthy though not very skilful native apothecary attached to our camp, while B. went off to do as much of the exploration as possible in the meantime. Next morning I was carried up to a small village half-way up the hill, and which the aneroid showed to be about 2450 feet above the sea. Here I was met by the Thákúr of Laäfá, the landowner of a considerable hilly tract round about Laäfágarh, who, with the utmost civility, led the way to a commodious hut he had prepared for my accommodation, of leafy boughs from the forest, under the shade of a large banyan tree, while my tent was being made comfortable in the old fort on the top of the hill. A gang of wild Bhúmiás from the Thákúr's hill villages had been collected to carry up my things; and throughout the day I was "interviewed" by little knots of them, who would steal to the door of the hut, squat down on their hams, with their axes hitched over their arms and their funny little leaf pipes stuck behind their ears, and remain perfectly contented as long as we let them, drinking in the strange appearance and surroundings of the sahibs. Without his formidable battle-axe (tongiá) and his leaf pipe (chongee) you will rarely see the Bhúmiá of these eastern regions. The pipe is twisted in a few seconds out of the leaf of the palás tree,[1] a peculiar twist making the bowl and its narrow neck in the most perfect manner. It looks simple, but I never could acquire the knack of it, and my pipes always came to pieces before they were well lit. The Bhúmiás smoke them once or twice, and then make another. They spoke capital Hindí, and were not at all shy in conversation, though wilder in appearance even than those of their race who live in the Mandlá district. Here the tribe is known only by the name of Bhúmiá, the term Bygá, which is their commoner tribal name in Mandlá, being restricted to their priests and medicine-men in these more eastern regions. It was queer to see what trifles sufficed to bring a grin of delight on their black and unhandsome but good-humoured countenances. Their broadest

[1] *Butea frondosa*, after which the whole district of Biláspúr is named.

grins were elicited by my three lemon-and-white spaniels, when they sat up in line to beg—"Wah Kookur! Koo-oo-Koo-rá!" exclaimed among them, testifying their delight; and when the visitors who had been initiated to this awful mystery were excluded from the hut to let me have a sleep, I saw them, through the leafy wall, form a deputation from the whole population of the place, to solicit my dog-boy to give one more exhibition, by the aid of a bone, of the wonderful performing "kookurs." For days afterwards fresh parties of these simple savages used to come up to my tent on the hill, and sit down over against me in the hope of seeing the wonderful spectacle, the news of which was carried, I believe, to the uttermost ends of this wilderness. When our elephants arrived from below with my tent and things (there was a pathway as far as the village), all the Bhúmiás saluted them by placing a hand on their broad footprints and then touching their foreheads. The wild elephants were truly, as they said, the rájás and demons of their country at that time, wandering whither they listed, and devastating their fields of hill-rice at will. So, as usual with the offensive powers of nature among these tribes, they were ranked and propitiated as an expression of the Deity. The next morning I was carried up to the top of the hill, where my tent had been pitched under a shady tree by the banks of a small tank, which in olden days had been excavated for a supply of water to the fort. The way up was a steep zigzag of 730 feet. Near the top a clear scarp of light gray rock rises out of the sloping forest-covered hill-side, sweeping right round the hill, an inaccessible barrier excepting at the point we ascended, where a pathway has been formed by excavation and piling up huge blocks of rocks. The entrance itself lay through a massive double gateway of great blocks, laid without mortar; and a low wall, of similar cyclopean structure, had surmounted the top of the precipice. Much of this had now fallen into ruins, which could be seen lying in great heaps in the jungle below; but in some places, particularly at the bastions, it was still almost complete. The top was a tolerably level plateau, broken by a few knolls, and was at that time covered by long yellow grass, and dotted with trees. Among the latter I found some specimens of the ebony tree,[1] which had evidently been cultivated, their plum-like luscious fruit being much larger and more fleshy than the wild species, and with very small stones. The only building on the top is a small temple dedicated to the consort of Sívá. The extreme elevation of the hill, on a rising ground above my tent, was shown by the aneroid barometer to be 3410 feet, which is almost identical with that of the source of the Narbadá at Amarkantak.

I stayed up here till the 15th of May, rapidly recovering from my attack, for which I took no medicine but seidlitz powders. The only physic I ever took from our worthy medico was what he called a "carminative," valuable in fits of ague—brandy and soda, to wit. But he had a great effect, with his purges, and emetics, and seven-leagued medical talk, on the native following. The Thákúr was exceedingly kind, visiting me constantly, and sitting for hours talking about the affairs of his jungly domain. He was a fine, tall, middle-aged man, claiming to be a pure Rájpút, and a descendant of the ancient dynasty of Ratanpúr, whose stronghold for many years was the fort of Laäfágarh. He brought me numerous delicacies produced by his wilds, among which two were particularly acceptable, namely, a fine pure arrowroot (*Tikúr*), made from the roots of the wild *Curcuma angustifolia*, and a beautiful small grain called *Sikér*, which is nothing but the produce of old plants of the grain called *Kútkí* (*panicum*), generally cultivated by those hill-tribes in their dhya clearings. After a clearing has been abandoned, the plants of kútkí rapidly degenerate, and in their third and fourth year the grain has become this sikér. It is much smaller than the fully cultivated grain, but also much sweeter, and with a nutty flavour about it, which is particularly delicious. Very little of it is gathered, the labour being great for a small result; but it is so much appreciated as to be generally kept for the *Purshád*, or sacrificial food of the gods. It made the best porridge I ever tasted. The Thákúr had been a mighty hunter in the days of his youth,

[1] *Diospyros melanoxylon.*

and was full of yarns of his sport. I remember few of them, and was too listless at that time to note them down. He showed me a scar received from a man-eating tiger, which he and another had done to death with their bows and arrows. He told me much about the wild elephants, which wandered all over his own and the neighbouring chieftaincies, their head-quarters being in Mátín and Uprorá, about twenty-five miles to the north. He only knew of one of these animals having ever been killed by a native. He was a very old male, with a broken tusk, and was shot in the trunk with a "bisár," or poisoned arrow, from a tree by the Bhúmiá, whose rice-field he was devastating below. He wandered long in the neighbouring jungle, growing thin and weak, and at last sank down helpless in a water-pool, where he had gone to bathe his miserable body. Then a neighbouring Thákúr came and fired all day into him from his matchlock, *two bushels* of bullets being taken from his carcase after he expired.

He had another story of a "loathly worm" that haunts the forests of the Uprorá country—slimy and horrid like a great caterpillar, a cubit and a half in thickness, and dull gray in colour, with a scarlet head, to look upon which was death. Many had seen it, but none had lived to tell the tale. On pressing him as to the source of the accurate portrait of the monster he had drawn for me, since all who had seen it had died, he was at no loss for a reply. The Thákúr of Uprorá was travelling, with an attendant behind him, when at the crossing of a stream the latter called out, "What is that great slimy caterpillar-like monster with a scarlet head, etc.?" on which his master warned him not to look at it, and did not do so himself. He was too late, however, for the servant was dead in a few moments.

Evening after evening I sat on the highest point of the hill listening to the incessant music of the "myriad crickets" that seemed to permeate every nook and cranny of the hill and its covering of trees, and gazing over the vast forest prospect spread below. To the south the open plain of Chattis'garh from which we had come, to the north the great green wilderness of the elephant country, dotted here and there with isolated hills. A long valley led up into this region from the foot of Laäfágarh, in which a few specks of village clearings could be seen. Everywhere else was utter waste. Far to the west a pink promontory glowed hazily in the setting sun. That was Amarkantak, the source of the Narbadá, to which I took the reader at the opening of this chapter.

Many wild animals had their haunts in the wooded sloping skirts of the hill. The harsh, grating roar of the panther was heard nearly every night; sámbar deer were sometimes seen picking their way up the hill from the plains in the early morning; and once I saw a black bear hurrying up the rocks to his cavern long after the sun had risen. Gangs of Hánumán monkeys stalked about the ruined ramparts and the precipice they crowned. On the top were many hares, peafowl, and painted partridges; and my dogs had endless chases after the yellow wild cat,[1] and the tree cat,[2] which were both more numerous on this hill than anywhere else I have seen them. Once when strolling round the camp in the dusk, looking for a shot at the green pigeons, which every night came to feed on the wild fruits, I saw a pair of gleaming eyes looking down on me from the dark shadow of an overhanging banyan tree; and a charge of No. 4 brought down among the dogs a fine red lynx,[3] which they soon dispatched in his wounded condition. It takes hard fighting for the best of dogs to kill an unwounded lynx, as my pack knew to their cost.

I pined sadly over my imprisonment on the top of this hill. The climate was milder by many degrees than it had been below, with no hot wind, even at this height of the summer season; and it was in particular delightfully cool at night. But there were only a few weeks remaining of the dry season; and we had to march nearly two hundred miles after leaving the elephant country to get into Jubbulpúr; so as soon as I could move at all, I descended the hill, and marched on an elephant for Mátín. At a place called Sirkí, fifteen miles from Laäfá, a tiger had just been

[1] *F. chaus.* [2] *Paradoxus musanga.*

[3] *F. Caraçal.*

killed with a poisoned arrow. His companion was reported to be still in the jungle, and I foolishly went out to hunt him in the heat of the day, ending in my being brought fainting back to camp. When I reached Mátín, I was again very ill. It was far hotter than in Laäfágarh, lying as it does in a low valley surrounded by hills. B. did not rejoin me for the next eight days, and I had a very dreary time of it indeed. There was abundance of game about, and several cow elephants drank daily at a pool not a mile from camp. Shooting females, or anything but old males, had been prohibited by the Government, as there was an intention of establishing a *khedda* here to capture them alive. But there was an old "rogue" about who had killed several persons not long before, and I sent some Bhúmiás out to search for him. The second night after my arrival I was sleeping outside for coolness, when I was rudely awakened, and sat up to listen to the crashing and trumpeting of a herd of elephants on the slope of the hill above the village. All night long, till within a few hours of daybreak, they kept on breaking the bamboos and crying shrilly at intervals. Our tame elephants were very uneasy the whole time; and I took the precaution of securing them by additional ropes, and stationing people with spears beside them to suppress any attempt at an *émeute*. In the evening I went out to the place, and found the hill-side completely levelled, bamboos torn down, crushed between their teeth, and many of their young shoots eaten away, and many trees of the Boswellia and other scantily rooted species overthrown and stripped of the tender bark of their top branches. The limit of their powers in overthrowing trees appeared, however, to be confined to those of not more than about eight inches in diameter, and my experience with trained tame elephants leads to a similar conclusion. Even these are not torn up by the roots, but merely borne down by the application of their full weight, by means of the forehead and one foot, or, as the natives here assured me, of the stern. The tales of some African travellers of elephants employing large trees as projectiles (one declares he saw two trees of eighteen inches diameter torn up and hurled ten or twelve yards) must be utter myths. A broad track through the jungle, like a high-road, led off in the direction taken by the herd; and, where they had crossed the dry sandy bed of the Mátín river, their tracks of every size, ranging from that of the tusker of a foot and a half diameter to the youngster's the size of a teacup, showed that the herd must have numbered some fifty or sixty individuals. I was of course quite unable to follow them in my present condition.

In the afternoon, when I was asleep, some of the Bhúmiás came in with news of a solitary tusker being within half a mile of the camp. Ill as I was I could not stand this, so getting on my pony, in sleeping drawers and slippers just as I was, I went out at least to see him. He was standing in the sandy bed of the Mátín river, where he had dug out a great hole down to the moisture below the surface, and plastered himself all over with wet sand to keep off the flies. He was a very large tusker, resembling the Nepál breed in shape. The only striking difference I noticed between him and domesticated elephants was the much greater fleshiness of his neck and forequarters, a circumstance also to be remarked in the wild buffalo bull, as compared with the tame species. He stood leaning on his tusks against the bank, gently swaying his tail about, and seemingly half asleep. There was no way of getting nearer him than about a hundred and fifty yards—much too far to shoot at an elephant; and I sat long watching him in the hope that he would move, but he didn't. Then I went and found the road he had taken down the steep bank of the river, and posted myself behind it, sending a Bhúmiá round a long way to give him his wind. It was interesting to see the elephant when he caught the first whiff of the savage. He still stood leaning on his tusks, but his tail ceased to sway, and the point of his trunk was curled round below his ear in the direction of the scent, while his ears stood cocked to catch the faintest sound. Long he stood thus, perfectly motionless. The Bhúmiá soon got more directly to windward, though still unseen by the elephant, and got up a tree. Those wild creatures had a wholesome dread of this jungle deity of theirs, it seemed. Then the elephant gently walked out of his hole, and never a look did he take towards the foe; slowly and heavily making for another pass up the bank a couple of hundred yards from where I was. I stole along through the grass as near this point as I could without coming into his view, and again sat down by an elephant path up which I hoped he would come. And I was not mistaken, for after a breathless pause of a minute or so, his great solemn forehead and gleaming tusks appeared, waving to and fro as he moved, and within eighty or ninety paces of my post. I felt sure of him with my big rifle if he came along the path, and determined not to fire till he was quite close. About forty yards only now intervened between us, and I was lifting the rifle to my eye, when a short cough behind caused me to look round, and there, oh horror! was a tall figure, clad in a yellow coat and bright red turban, standing on an ant-hill and striving to get up a tree! Instantly I turned again to the elephant; but all I saw was his vast round stern in full retreat through the trees. It was a little provoking, and I did not bless very much the owner of that yellow garment as I sped along frantically after the vanishing tusker. I remembered no more than this, till I found myself being supported on my pony back to camp. They said I had fallen senseless in the grass after running about a hundred yards. The culprit was a relative of the Thákúr of Mátín, who had stolen out after me, and, coming up unperceived in the grass, had lain still enough till the formidable aspect of the man-killer had overcome his opium-shaken nerves. He looked so utterly wretched and ashamed of himself that I could not tell him all that I thought of him. There was also rather a panic abroad just at the time, as not long before a young son of the Thákúr of Uprorá had been taken out after some elephants which had come down near the plains, by some sportsmen from Bíláspúr; and a large tusker charging down on them, after having been followed and shot at for half a day, was trampled up before he could get clear. It was a terrible disappointment, and neither B. nor I ever had another chance at an elephant which we might shoot. I made a number of little excursions from Mátín to the principal elephant haunts of the neighbourhood. All about there were great quantities of game of other sorts, spotted deer along the nálás, and red deer in nearly every glade of the sál forests. Bears were numerous, and I saw a few prowling about in the early morning, but, being unable to work on foot, never got a shot. I picked up four or five deer, of sorts, shooting from the elephant; and, having to follow up the tracks of several which were wounded, had an opportunity of admiring the wonderful tracking powers of these wild Bhúmiás. An ordinary track that I could barely see, they ran breast-high, and scarcely looking at the ground, and it was not till all sign disappeared to other eyes that real interest in the work began to be displayed. No natives of these highlands can compare with a Bhúmiá in real knowledge of woodcraft. A short distance north-east of Mátín is a small hill called Málíndeh. Many bones of elephants lay strewn about below the steep precipice at one end of this hill; and it seemed that, the year before we were there, a singular accident had led to the destruction on this spot of almost the whole of a small herd. The Thákúr and villagers were going up the narrow path, by which alone it is accessible, to pay their annual devotions to the god of the hill. The procession was accompanied by the noise of drums and much shouting in honour of the deity; and they were wholly unaware that they were driving before them a herd of five elephants which had been ahead of them on the path. Arrived at the summit, and the noise still pursuing them, the elephants became panic-stricken, and four of them tried to descend on the opposite side. Here a slope of loose shingle led down from the top, ending in a sheer cliff. Once embarked on this there was no retreat for their ponderous weight, and the poor brutes were hurried over the perpendicular fall. The fifth—the big tusker whom I had so recently encountered, it was said—charged back through the procession, scattering them like chaff, and made his escape down the path.

On the 26th, B. rejoined me, having covered a great extent of country by dint of hard marching, and explored the eastern portion of the sál forest and elephant country which belongs to the Thákúr of Uprorá. He had seen little game, and had never stayed to shoot. From Mátín we proceeded again together, due north, to examine the country between this and Amarkantak; and till the end of the month we travelled on through an unbroken forest of the sál tree. This wild is very scantily peopled by a few utterly primitive Bhúmiás, a sight of whom could only be secured by sending on an embassy of some of their own tribesmen, whom we took with us from Mátín. On one occasion I had wandered off the elephant track that served for a road in these parts, into the thick sál forest, without a guide, trusting to regain it after a short détour. But the country is here so level, and the prospect so circumscribed by the never-ending array of great gray stems of the sál, that I soon found I had entirely lost my way, while the midday sun, hanging like a globe of glowing silver right overhead, threw only vertical shadows, which afforded no guide to the points of the compass. I was riding on an elephant, and we wandered on for some hours through glade after glade and clump after clump of the sál trees, each exactly like the one before it, till at last we emerged into a little open space, where a few tall naked stems of sál trees killed by ringing stood up from among a thick copse of bushes sprung from the roots of the cleared forest. In the middle was a small Bhúmiá hamlet of a few huts of bamboo basket-work, surrounded by a fence of the same material. We marched up to the little wicket-gate of this enclosure, and the barking of a dog brought out the two or three inhabitants. To stare wildly like startled deer at the amazing sight of an elephant ridden by a white man, fly over the fence with a shriek, and plunge into the thick copse-wood of the little clearing, was the work of a moment. But I could not do without a guide to regain the road, and pushed in the elephant after them. It was just for all the world like beating hog-deer out of thick bush-cover, the naked black savages lying close in the thickets till the elephant put her foot almost on the top of them, when they bolted out and ran crouching across to another patch. I thought we would never catch one, until the man behind me slipped down the elephant's tail and ran round, intercepting a lad in the act of leaving the last of the underwood for the open forest. When laid hold of he struggled a little, but soon resigned himself, trembling in every limb, to his fate. It was many minutes before we could get him to speak at all, a blank shake of the head meeting every question before he could have heard it. At last, after much reassuring and comforting, with presents of tobacco and the almighty rupee, and the withdrawal of the elephant to a distance, he found a tongue, and that in good broad Hindú, but only to declare that he knew nothing of the road; and, indeed, as we were making for nothing more definite than a water-hole in the forest rejoicing in the name of *Boogloogee*, I dare say the poor youth spoke the truth. We insisted on his trying, however, and at last he started, taking the way back to the huts, and peering about among the bushes as if he had lost something. Presently he put his hand to his mouth and gave a succession of piercing yells, the last of which was answered from the copse-wood, and in a while a very old wrinkled little man crept out, holding his hands across his shrivelled stomach to deprecate the wrath of the riders on the elephantine gods of the forest. More tobacco and another bright rupee, and the sight of the youth safe and sound after his awful adventure, brought a grin over the highly simian countenance of this ancient; and the pair of them, first diving into a hut for their pipes and axes, stalked away before us through the trees. Soon they got quite chatty, gabbling and grinning to themselves about the elephant and its riders, on whom, however, they kept a sharp look-out over their shoulders. Once or twice I made the elephant take short runs close up behind them to try their nerves; and the alacrity with which they skipped behind the nearest trees, and chuckled and grinned from their secure positions, was worth seeing. They took us straight across country to Boogloogee without a mistake; and when we got there, and set them down among their tribesmen to fill themselves with venison, and wheat-flour from our store, they were perfectly happy.

The Bhúmiás of these parts are much wilder than those of the Mandlá district, cultivating not at all, and subsisting solely by their bows and arrows, and the roots and fruits of the jungle, and collecting the dammer resin of the sál tree to barter for the few necessaries of life not produced by their wilds with the traders who reside at the head-quarters of their Thákúrs. They have scarcely an idea of the use of coined money, the rare rupees that reach them being pierced and worn as ornaments by the women. They are said to have, besides their little hamlets in the forest, a retreat in some still more secluded wild, known only to the family it belongs to, in which all their worldly substance beyond a few days' supply is kept, and to which they are ready to fly at a moment's notice. The sál forest has thus escaped much of the devastation it has suffered where the tribe is more numerous, and where they cut it down for dhya cultivation. Many of the trees are annually ringed for the extraction of dammer; but the forest is too extensive to be much injured by the operations of this handful of savages; and as it is the oldest trees that are selected, which, if not cut down, soon become useless from heart-shake and dry-rot (a peculiarity of the sál), probably little harm is done by them in so remote and inaccessible a region. The general elevation of the country we traversed is about 1700 feet above the sea. It is very level, and with a light porous soil formed by the detritus of the primitive rocks which here mostly lie near the surface. The water-courses are broad, shallow, and sandy, showing that large floods do not occur. Thus in the summer there is little or no water on the surface, but a little below it the soil is everywhere full of moisture; and the brilliant greenery of the sál forest thus plentifully supplied with sap, melting in the distant vistas with startling rapidity into wonderful blues, is unspeakably delicious at that torrid season of the year. Wild animals are very scarce, owing to the absence of water, though in the rainy season elephants, buffaloes, bison, and innumerable red deer are reported to frequent the forest. In this march the dainty footmarks of a few four-horned antelopes at the water-holes, the voice of the cuckoo in the early morning, and rare glimpses of some hornbill or woodpecker glancing among the foliage of the sál, was all the sign we saw of the presence of animal life.

It is very difficult to ascertain distances in these extensive level forests, where there are no eminences from which the country can be examined; and we had some tremendous marches in consequence of relying on statements of distance made in "coss" by the Bhúmiás. Considering that their coss is derived from so indefinite a basis as the distance at which a yell from a hill-top can be heard, it is little surprising if the coss itself should be uncertain. This is their table of long measure :—

2 yells = 1 *daab* (or "bittock"),
2 "bittocks" = *coss*,
12 coss = 1 day's march;

which seems to be about thirty miles.

In the jungles of Kéndá and Péndrá, which form the most easterly section of this forest, and lie right under the range of the Mýkal hills, great numbers of wild buffaloes were reported to us; but we had not time at this season to stop to look after them. Doubtless it is chiefly to these regions that they retire from the Mandlá uplands when the latter are invaded by the grazing of domestic cattle.

So far as we could learn, an area of about 1200 square miles was occupied by herds of wild elephants, whose number we estimated, from all accounts, to range from two hundred to three hundred. They undoubtedly did very serious damage to the crops in the neighbourhood; and for many years the annual tribute of the Thákúrs whose possessions they disturbed had been remitted on this account. The people were totally unable to defend themselves from such powerful foes, and most of the villages I met with on the borders of the jungle are furnished with platforms in high trees, to which the people were accustomed to retreat on the occurrence of an invasion. Shooting at wild elephants only increases the damage they occasion, by breaking up the herds and spreading their ravages over a larger area; and, besides, to shoot an elephant is like hanging a man, the worst use that can be made of him. After a good deal of reporting and correspondence, the Government of India was induced to send down one of its regularly organised elephant-catching establishments to these wilds, which attacked the herds during the years 1865 to 1867. The system pursued in this country was somewhat peculiar, and has been thus described by an eye-witness : [1]

"Several modes of capture were tried here, but the most successful was a simple stockade erected hurriedly in one of the runs near the spot where the elephants were tracked. To make this process successful, a very large establishment is required, for all necessary arrangements to be of any use must be made at once. A rough ring-fence of bamboos is thrown round a large area, traversing in circumference some two or three miles, within which the elephants have lots of moving room. This enclosure must contain water and fodder, or the elephants are certain to break through. At every few paces there are two coolies who relieve one another, and by striking the fence with a stick, keep up a continual clatter. Then at every hundred yards or so, there is a matchlock-man supplied with blank ammunition. Near this fence the jungle is cleared, so that at any point the elephants make for, they are at once visible and when they are seen approaching, a rush of men occurs to the threatened locality with an immense shouting and firing of matchlocks. This has the effect of driving the herd back, and as it is at night that these efforts are chiefly necessary, they entail much watchfulness and labour. In fact, at night the whole circle is, as it were, a blaze, for each party has lighted a grand pile of wood. These fires surround the elephants in a ring of light, which they believe themselves powerless to break through, especially as they are assailed with all the din of battle if they approach too near, so that it is a sheer case of desperation, or gross carelessness, or a weak establishment, if they succeed in getting out. From a neighbouring camp the scene is exciting enough, for the hill-side resounds with shouting, and the discharge of blank ammunition seems incessant, partly from necessity and partly from the inherent affection an Asiatic has for noise. All this time the stockade is progressing, made of immense piles of wood, capable of standing any charge, and enclosing a few hundred square yards of ground. The

[1] Report on the Settlement of tke Biláspúr district of the Central Provinces, by J. W. Chisholm, Esq.

elephant runs are clearly marked-out tracks, to which they usually keep. The stockade is on one of them, with an open gate at one extremity, from which an immense arm of piled logs stretches on either side, so that the rush may be, once the arms are entered, into the single opening that has been left. The first day after the stockade is finished the driving commences. If fortune smiles, once the herd is started by shouting and firing in their rear, they make a rush for the stockade run and are enclosed without further trouble; if not, they require to be driven several times—a service often of difficulty and danger. When enclosed, the decoy elephants with trained men are employed for noosing and tying them."

An enormous area of the tract we travelled over, in the neighbourhood of the Hásdú river and its tributaries, was found to be full of coal measures, which have since been professionally examined, and reported to furnish mineral of a highly valuable character. But the extreme remoteness of these regions from any of the great centres of commerce or transport puts out of the question any immediate utilisation either of the coal or the rich store of timber which are now ascertained to exist. The same reason renders all idea of colonising these wilds, except by the slow process of extending population, a matter which it would not be useful to discuss. Far superior lands in every respect, whether of natural quality or situation, exist in great areas in the Mandlá highlands, which must come to be taken up before a plough can furrow the remote regions to the east of Amarkantak.

On the 1st of June we climbed the steep ascent leading up to Amarkantak from the east, and rested there for two days. I was still very ill and weak, and obliged to travel on an elephant; and though it was very tempting to linger on this elevated region, where, at this season of excessive heat below, the temperature in a small tent all day was delightful, while at night it was cold enough to enjoy a couple of blankets, the season was getting very late, and banks of clouds collecting on the horizon threatened heavy rain, which might block the way to Jubbulpúr. So we determined to march straight to that station by the direct road to the north of the Narbadá. That frightful march still lives in my dreams. For the first ten days we kept to the elevated country south of the river, which we then crossed. The country to the north is an utterly bare sheet of black basalt, without a field or a tree, or, I believe, hardly a blade of grass. Sharp glancing flakes of white quartz alone relieved the inky black of the horrible rocks. The sun was at its very hottest, and heavy thunderous clouds now gathered round the sky, oppressing the air with a sultry stillness far worse than the fiercest hot blast of the earliest summer. Day after day we toiled along in the fierce heat, pitching in a burning plain, without a particle of shade; and I really thought that before we reached Jubbulpúr on the 16th of July, I should have had to sit down decently and give up the ghost. I had marched close on a thousand miles in changes of camp alone since I left the station in the preceding January. How much more should be added for our explorations it would not be easy to say.

The monsoon burst a day or two after; and in the comfort of the beautiful little station, and its pleasant society, I soon got over my troubles. I was very much broken in health, however, by constant exposure to the malaria of the jungles, at all seasons of the year. I had never lost the remains of the fever I had contracted the previous year; and, I may add, never did so till I had a trip to England.

I have no intention of attempting a treatise on Indian forestry, for which, indeed, there are as yet few available materials; but a few remarks on the present aspect of the question may not be out of place before concluding my work.

The Government of India has been fully awakened to the necessity of watching over the important part of their trust which resides in the forest regions. Even now it is doubtful whether the clearances already effected have not seriously deteriorated the rainfall of the country, as they certainly have much impaired the supply of useful timber; and the example of many countries, ancient and modern,[1] is a warning against rash interference with the life-giving forests of hilly regions where rivers are born. The scientific forester must now take the place of the explorer; and the Government have taken the proper course in seeing that all newly appointed forest officers shall in future go through a course of instruction in the advanced schools of forestry in Germany and France. The danger is lest a too purely professional view of forest questions be allowed to exclude considerations bearing powerfully on the general economy of the masses of the people, and particularly of the hill-tribes; and lest cut-and-dried theories, based on the example of moist temperate regions, be applied without sufficient caution to the very different conditions of tropical forests. For example, one of the practices of continental forestry, the working of forests in blocks by rotation, though probably quite inapplicable to a hot country, where stripping the soil of all the trees at once converts it into an arid desert, is still aimed at in our Indian forests, and is the cause of much, and I believe wasteful, expenditure of money. Many important matters can even now be dealt with only in a tentative manner; and the wisdom of the administrator must always be joined to the technical skill of the forester to secure the best results.

My narrative is now done, having carried the reader over every portion of these Central Highlands, and even taken a step with him below their eastern termination. In the course of our rambles he has made the acquaintance of every wild animal he is likely to meet with in the forests; and it only remains for me to offer a few hints to the traveller or sportsman who may contemplate an excursion in these regions. Few men would probably come to India merely to shoot over this central wilderness. But as a field for general travel, and even as a sporting ground, India is rapidly coming into favour among the wandering section of Englishmen. I need not dilate on the general interest of the country. It may be hoped that most Englishmen will benefit as much from a tour through this greatest of

[1] A pamphlet, admirable for learning and research, on this subject, by Dr. Dalzeil, Conservator of Forests in Bombay, exhausts the subject.

our dependencies, as India herself will assuredly benefit from having the bull's-eye of outside observation turned on to her obscurity. I will here speak only of the glorious field that the country offers to the sportsman—incomparably the finest in the world. As a field for sportsmen, Africa may be thought to be better, but it is not so if India be looked at as a whole. Perhaps more animals in number or in size may be slaughtered in Central Africa; but that does not surely imply superior *sport*. In reading accounts of African shooting, I have often wondered how men could continue to wade through the sickening details of daily massacre of half-tame animals offering themselves to the rifle on its vast open plains. In India fewer animals will perhaps be bagged; all will have to be worked for, and some perhaps fought for. The sport will be far superior, and the sportsman will return from India with a collection of trophies which Africa cannot match. Africa and India both have their elephants. We cannot offer a hippopotamus; but we have a rhinoceros superior in a sporting point of view to his African relative. We have a wild buffalo as savage and with far superior horns to the Cape species; and we have *four* other species of wild bovines besides, to which there is nothing comparable in Africa. In felines, besides a lion, a panther, and a hunting-leopard, almost identical with those of Africa, we have the tiger, and one, if not two, other species of leopard. Our black antelope is unsurpassed by any of the many antelopes of Africa; and besides him we have fourteen species of antelopes and wild goats and sheep in our hills and plains, affording the finest stalking in the world, to compare with the other antelopes of Africa. Africa has no deer properly speaking at all, except the Barbary stag, which is out of the regular beat of sportsmen. India, on the other hand, has nine species of antlered deer. We have three bears; Africa has none at all. There is no country in the world that can show such a list of large game as we can in India. And for minor sport, what can compare with our endless array of pheasants, partridges, and wildfowl?

All this, too, is now so easy of access. The traveller may step ashore, in Bombay, with nothing more than a

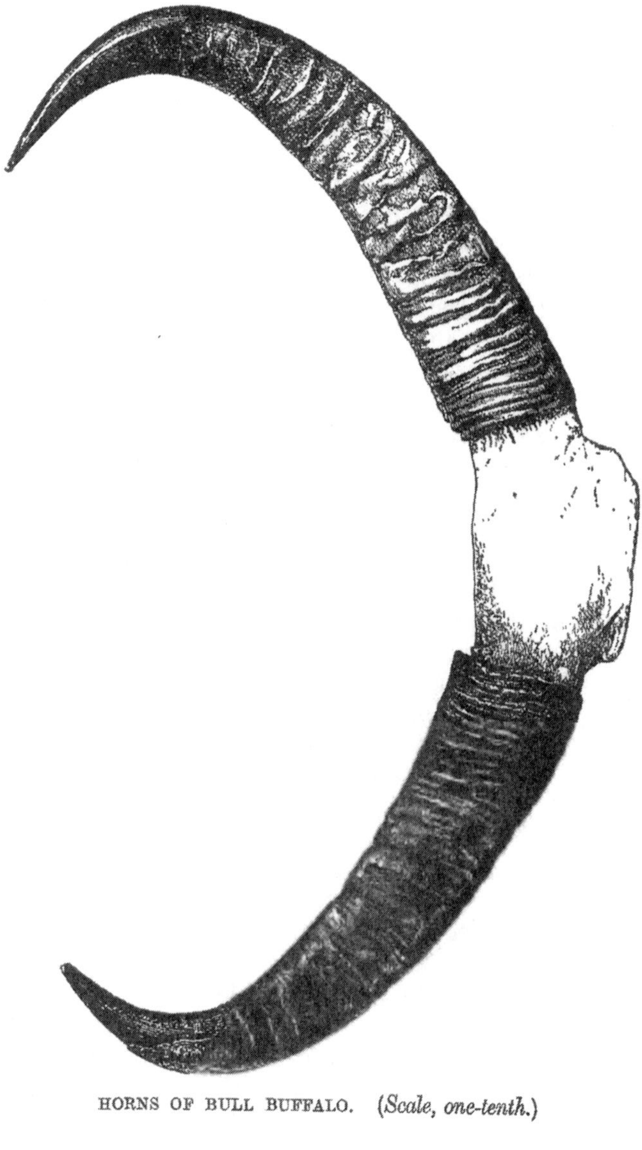

HORNS OF BULL BUFFALO. (*Scale, one-tenth.*)

carpet-bag if he pleases, and at once fit himself out for a year's tour through the country. If he joins a regular camp in the "plains," he will find the most perfect system of open-air life that has anywhere been devised. Though an Indian camp may not, as, according to Mark Twain, did that of the Yankee pilgrims in Palestine, contain "a thousand boot-jacks," he will find pretty nearly everything that civilised man can want, ready to move about with him at the rate of from twelve to twenty miles a day. By the help of railways, he may see almost the whole country south of the Himalayas, and shoot specimens of all its game, during the pleasant cold months from October to March; and by the time that April ushers in the hot blasts of summer, he may find himself, if he pleases, stalking the ibex among the snows of Káshmír.

For mere sport England need not be left earlier than December; but should the traveller, as is probable, have other objects in view, he should take an extra month or two to see the lions of the civilised parts at their best, which he may combine with some small game shooting and pig-sticking if he likes, in November and December. Should these central regions be selected by the sportsman, the shooting camp should be organised, if possible, beforehand, at some station on the Great Indian Peninsular Railway, the exact spot depending much on whether the sportsman has any friends on the spot who would assist him. The help of the local civil authorities is of course of the greatest value; and I may say that it is always freely rendered to gentlemen projecting a tour through their charges. Some previous acquaintance with the language, and the general requirements on such a trip on the part of at least one of the party, is almost essential to ensure success. In the absence of inducements to take another line of country, I would recommend the traveller to leave the railway at the large city of Burhánpúr, in the district of Nimár, and commence his hunting in the country round the head-waters of the Móná tributary of the Táptí river. Bison, sámbar, and bears are as numerous and easy to get at there as in any part of the country I know. Painted partridges, jungle fowl, and other small game, would also diversify the sport, and supply the pot. Thence he should cross over to the Bétúl district, north of the Táptí, where tigers are plentiful, and devote the month of March to their pursuit. Spotted deer, antelope, nílgái, and other game, are also abundant in this tract, and the end of March might see the sportsman stalking the bison on the Puchmurree hills. If he means to devote the hot weather also to these regions, the district of Mandlá and the sources of the Narbadá should be selected, where plenty of tigers will be found, and the sámbar, red deer, and wild buffalo, will add to the variety of the sport.

The cost of such an expedition need not be very great. Most of the outfit required would be re-sold at the conclusion at no very great loss. One hill-tent, ten feet square, and a small "pál," would be sufficient for two sportsmen; and would cost at the Jubbulpúr School of Industry (whence they should be ordered beforehand and sent to the railway station) about £30. A strong rough pony is the best animal to ride, unless hunting on horseback is contemplated, when a good Arab should be bought in the Bombay stables. The former are not always to be picked up on the spot, but can generally be bought in Bombay at a cost of about £20. A good Arab, fit to hunt under eleven stone, will cost £80 or £100. Arrangements should be made to get the loan of or purchase a staunch shooting-elephant and howdah; for, though much good sport can be got without one, a far heavier bag will be realised with the help of an elephant. They are difficult to obtain, however, at any time; and a really good one will not be bought for less than £200 to £300. Decent shikárís can generally be obtained on the spot, though they will not of course come up to men who have been brought up by the sportsman himself to the work. The current expenses, after the outfit has been bought, will come to about £30 per mensem for each sportsman. Of course a man accustomed to rough it could get on, and obtain the best of sport at a much less expense than this, which is laid down for a party wishing to enjoy all the comforts of the Indian style of travelling in camp. Such an adventurous sportsman need only get for himself a small pál tent and a few necessary implements of travel, and hire a camel to carry them, buy a rough pony for £5 of £10, hire a couple of servants, and plunge with his rifle into the wilderness. If capable of speaking the Hindí language, and conciliatory towards the wild men, he would soon have about him a knot of real jungle hunters who would take him up to every sort of game; while his monthly expenses would not exceed £10 or £15. Saddlery, hunting implements of all sorts (excepting boar spears, which are made better in India), ammunition, and clothes, should be brought from England.

In the matter of guns and rifles, improvements are still so rapidly progressing that the *dicta* of one year are very likely to be upset before the next. Regarding breech-loading it is sufficient to say that by the universal consent of sportsmen, the use of the muzzle-loader is now confined to exceedingly remote countries where the cartridge cases cannot be carried. No part of India answers to this description, and a muzzle-loader is now rarely seen there. The "Express" system consists in the use of a short conical bullet, hollowed at the point like a shell—but without any bursting charge, and propelled by a very great charge of powder in proportion to its weight. The first result of this is that the bullet, striking with extreme velocity, has its hollow point opened out by the shock into the shape of a mushroom, or even, when the hollow is very deep and the speed great, broken altogether into fragments, which take different courses through the animal and inflict a terrific wound. This complete breaking up of the bullet has as yet been effected only with very small gauges, not larger than the half-inch (·500) diameter; but projectiles of even this size have been found to be amply sufficient to kill effectually all animals of the deer class, and hardly any other description of rifle is now used for that purpose.

Their only serious disadvantage is the smallness of the hole they make on entering, while they rarely pass through an animal of any considerable size, rendering the work of tracking, should the animal leave the spot, a matter of some difficulty. I have found that generally a deer struck by the Express bullet, even in the lungs, will run from fifty to a hundred yards before falling. It is then generally stone dead, having bled internally. But very often there will not be the slightest mark of blood on the track. The very first two shots I ever fired with an Express were remarkable illustrations of this. The first was at a lovely spotted buck, who suddenly stood before me like an apparition, drinking at the margin of the mirror-like lake of Lachórá, as I rounded the point of one of its bays on my way back, tired and muddy, from an evening's snipe-shooting. It was over two hundred yards across the arm of the lake from where I was. I had taken out a single Express, by Henry, to raise the flocks of wild fowl that sat in safety in the centre of the lake, and this my gun-boy now thrust unloaded into my hand. The buck had turned, and was picking his way leisurely up the bank, before I had the cartridge in; and his graceful form and long tapering antlers stood out clear against the sky-line as I fired point-blank at his shoulder. With a startled toss of the head, and a desperate bound over the top of the bank, he was off into the thick cover that here surround the lake. We tracked his footprints in the gravelly soil for near a hundred yards, when, light failing us altogether, we had to give it up. Next morning I returned, and a solitary crow cawing on a branch, pointed out the buck lying dead and stiff within a few paces of where we had left the trail. The next chance I had with this rifle was equally unexpected. Walking along near midday in the Punásá forest, by a little-travelled pathway, the ridge of a great black back appeared through the trees, slowly passing behind a little eminence. It was a splendid stag sámbar, who had, very unusually, ventured down to that silent valley in the midday heat to drink at a little stream. He seemed to be dazed by the sunlight as he came out on the pathway, and failed to notice a *cortége* of three or four horses with their riders, an elephant, and ten or a dozen men on foot. I fired at about a hundred and seventy yards, and heard the little bullet strike against his brawny shoulder. But he galloped away up a little glade, leaving no blood, and I felt inclined to throw down the little rifle in disgust. Less than a hundred yards from the pathway, however, the great stag lay perfectly dead, shot through the middle of the shoulder. I afterwards acquired complete confidence in this weapon, and killed a far larger percentage of the animals I fired at than I had ever accomplished with any other. On one occasion I shot three out of a herd of five Chikárá antelopes running across me, the nearest being over a hundred yards. This little creature offers an extremely small mark to fire at, and these were fairly struck in the shoulder. I could not have done such work as this with any other rifle of my acquaintance.

These small bores, however, have not been found so effective for destroying the larger animals, such as tigers, buffaloes, bison, etc., the small fragments into which the bullets are broken up not possessing sufficient penetrative power to reach the vitals. It is a great object, too, with these large and dangerous animals to break the large bones, so as to cripple them at once and prevent accidents; and this the small Express, with its very hollow bullet, is quite unable to effect. The bone-breaking and penetrative power of these bullets can, however, be much increased by diminishing, or altogether omitting, the hollow in the point. A good many elephants have been killed by the dead shot, with the smaller gauge, using solid hardened projectiles; and the larger rifle, with a short hollow, has been effectively used against tigers and bears. Much of the shock to the system, caused by the spreading of the hollow bullet, is of course lost if a solid ball be employed.

The next advantage of the Express system, where it is suitable as regards killing power, is the very flat trajectory at sporting ranges obtained by the use of a light ball and heavy charge of powder. Two sizes of the small Express are now made: the smaller, ·450 of an inch, having a charge of nearly four drachms, and the larger, ·500, shooting five drachms of powder. The first gives a perfectly point-blank range of a hundred and sixty yards, with an extreme effective range of two hundred and fifty; the latter a point blank of rather more than two hundred, and an extreme of four hundred. They both shoot with extreme accuracy at these ranges. The smaller weighs seven and a half pounds, and the larger eight and a quarter as a minimum; though the addition of half a pound to the weight of each gives more steadiness and regular shooting.

The very great improvement thus effected in the shooting of any one who uses an Express rifle, goes a long way towards compensating for any loss of smashing power in comparison with the old wide-bored rifles. I unhesitatingly therefore recommend the adoption of the ·450 or ·500 Express for *all ordinary* purposes. If its greater weight be not objected to, the larger is certainly preferable in every other respect; but very good work can be done with the smaller bore, and the saving of weight is a great advantage for work in the hills.

For dangerous game, such as tigers, there is nothing better yet available for sportsmen than the large rifle firing the spherical ball, or the explosive shell. This should be at least twelve-gauge, and eleven pounds in weight. The application of breech-loading to these rifles renders it possible also to use a spherical or short conical ball with the same rifle, either of which gives flatter trajectory than the shell, and which are preferred to it by some sportsmen. If the shooting is to be from an elephant I think the spherical twelve-bore is amply sufficient. This ball, or the short conical, hardened with one-twelfth part of mercury or tin, with four and a half or five drachms of powder, will also form an excellent charge for buffalo or bison shooting.

All rifles should, by preference, be double-barrelled. To use a single rifle is to sacrifice many chances, while it possesses no advantage whatever over a well-made double.

The rifles should be fitted in small, handy, solid leather cases, unencumbered by much apparatus, or by space for cartridges. The latter should be soldered up in tin cases, to hold two hundred and fifty each, and should be carried unloaded until about to take the field.

I have added in Appendices some information which may be useful to travellers in the region I have thus attempted to describe.

APPENDICES

SELECTION AND TREATMENT OF ELEPHANTS

THERE are few subjects on which so little is generally known as that of the diseases and unsoundnesses, and the general management of tame elephants. Although there are many elephants under the charge of officers of different public departments in India, as well as a good number which belong to private persons, it always seems to be assumed that to attain to any acquaintance with the nature of the animal and its veterinary treatment is a hopeless task. The consequence is that their mahouts, or native keepers, than whom a more ignorant or careless class does not exist, are commonly allowed to do with them what they choose very often to their serious detriment, and sometimes complete disablement. They profess to possess many secret specifics, most of which are useless, and only intended to extract money from their masters on the pretence of purchasing drugs; and many of them founded on the grossest superstition. For instance, it is common among them to give the elephant a piece of tiger's liver to make him courageous! And, in order to make him see well at night, to thrust down his throat the great yellow eyes of the brown horned owl torn fresh from the living bird!

Having had much to do with elephants, both in my private possession and in the forest establishment, I am induced to put on record what I know of their management, not with the idea of furnishing a complete guide to their treatment, but in the hope that it may go some way towards obviating some of the mismanagement they are now so generally subjected to, and also be of assistance to persons engaged in purchasing elephants. In a rough country like the forest tracts of Central India, elephants, when properly looked after, are the most useful of animals, whether for riding purposes or for carrying baggage and other heavy work. When neglected, however, they are subject to numerous small ailments, which have led some persons to reject them for such services.

On looking over an elephant, the most inexperienced eye would at once detect the presence of the disease called by natives *Zérbád*. There are two varieties of it, called *Asl* and *Súkhá*. The former is a dropsical affection, in which the neck, chest, and stomach fill up to an enormous size. It occurs most frequently in newly caught animals, and is probably attributable to a sudden change of food. I once had an elephant attacked with it immediately after changing from wheat to rice, on entering a district where the former was not procurable. Generally, an elephant that has been two or three years in captivity is considered pretty safe from it. *Súkhá Zérbád* is usually developed out of the other, but sometimes comes on at once. It is a sort of general atrophy, or falling away; and is characterised by a shrivelled, cracky skin, much emaciation, and weakness. It is apt to become complicated with troublesome sores in various parts of the body. In purchasing an elephant it is not likely that the actual presence of Zérbád would be overlooked; but without care it is easy to buy an animal so recently caught as to be still likely to develop it. Such an animal should be got for much less money than one longer domesticated. The state of training the animal has reached will generally indicate the period of his capture. If thoroughly obedient to its driver, lying down patiently to let you examine its feet, etc., it will probably have been sufficiently long in hand to be pretty safe.

This brings me to unsound feet—the most common failing in an elephant. It is of two kinds, called by natives *Kándi* and *Sájhan*. The former is a sort of canker, that begins on the sole and gradually eats deep into the structure of the foot, until at length it breaks out above the toe-nails. In its earlier stages it is easily concealed by plugging the holes; and many of the elephants brought to the great fairs, like that of Sónpúr, are in fact affected with Kándí, though to outward appearance perfectly sound. It can generally be discovered by making the elephant lie down, and administering a series of sharp raps with a stick all over the soles of the feet, when, if Kándí be present, the animal will be sure to show it by shrinking.

Sájhan is what would be called "cracked heels" in a horse. Its deep cracks, discharging matter, situated about the junction of the horny sole with the skin, can hardly be passed over in a bad case, though a slight one may escape observation. It is a serious unsoundness, being generally constitutional, and often rendering useless during every rainy season elephants that are subject to it.

The eyes of the elephant are extremely delicate, and appear to possess in an unusual degree a sympathetic connection with the digestive organs. Nearly every indisposition of the animal is accompanied by a clouding or suffusion of the eyes. Few elephants that have been long caught, especially if in the hands of natives, have perfect eyes. Heating food, or undue exposure to bright sun, is often followed by the appearance of a film over one or both eyes, which, if not attended to, and its cause remains in operation, increases till the cornea becomes quite opaque, and the animal loses its sight. The leaves of the peepúl fig-tree, which form excellent fodder in the cold season, are almost sure to produce this affection if given for any considerable time in the hot season. I would not reject an elephant, otherwise suitable, merely because it had a slight film over the eye; for it is easily removed when attended to in time. But its presence would of course lessen the value the animal would otherwise bear.

Another very tender point in the elephant is the back. A highly arched back is very liable to get galled; and such sores, when fairly established, are exceedingly obstinate. Such a back will almost always show traces of old sores about the ridge, and frequently they are only healed over on the surface, leaving deep sinuses below ready to break out on the slightest pressure. Such a back should be avoided and a flat back, showing as nearly as possible a straight line from the withers to the croup, should be selected. Besides its immunity from galling, such a back always carries a load, or the howdah, well and steadily.

The above are almost all the external points to which the attention of the purchaser requires to be directed. Old strains will sometimes affect the paces, but this can be seen at once. I have alluded, in the text, to the points of build and carriage that should be looked to in choosing an elephant. There is no critical test of the animal's age. The ears are always a good deal split and frayed at the edges in an old animal; but so they sometimes are also in young ones. The general appearance will, however, indicate the age sufficiently well for practical purposes. The full size and development is attained at from thirty-five to forty years; and from that age till about sixty, the elephant is in the prime of life. It is desirable to buy an elephant of full age if required for shooting, young animals being nearly always timid and unenduring. A very old, or "aged," elephant will be easily recognised by the loose, wrinkly state of the skin, deep hollows above the eyes, and very deeply cracked ears. I do not think that the number of concentric rings in the ivory of the tusk is a reliable criterion, though the natives talk a good deal about it.

At the great Sónpúr fair, mentioned in the text, which is the principal market for elephants, the elephants offered for sale are usually the property either of landowners from the districts of Bengal, or of Mahomedan dealers who move about between the places where they are captured and the chief markets and native courts. The former are much the safest to purchase, having generally been purchased young by the landowner, and brought up among his own people at his farm, with plentiful food and good treatment. It is quite a part of their business this buying of youngsters, which they prefer for their own riding, keeping them till of full size, and selling them at a good round profit. The dealer's strings, on the other hand, are too often made up of the halt and the blind. There is no end to their tricks. A dangerous man-killer is reduced to temporary harmlessness by a daily pill of opium and hemp. Kándí sores are plugged, and Sájhan cracks "paid" with tow. Sore backs are surface-healed; and the animals are so bedizened with paint, and so fattened up with artificial feeding, that it is hard to tell what any one of them would look like if "stripped to the bones." Then the space is so confined, and the crowd so great, that very little "trotting out" is possible; so that altogether buying elephants at such fairs is anything but plain sailing.

The usual food of elephants in Upper and Central India consists of cakes of wheaten flour, baked without leaven, to a weight of about 2 lb. each, and given with a slight spreading of clarified butter. In the South and East, where wheat is scarce, plain uncooked rice is given instead. The daily ration of a full-sized animal of, say 8½ feet high, is 24 lb. of flour, or 32 lb. of rice. When one of these sorts of food is substituted for the other, it should be done gradually; and when rice is first given a part of it should be boiled for some weeks. The above rations are for an animal in hard work. In the Government Commissariat Department, where great numbers of elephants are kept almost in idleness for a great part of the year, lower rations are given. But the treatment of these elephants is by no means a model for imitation. In a state of nature the animal takes an immense deal of exercise. Here they get no work to speak of between the close of one marching season (March) and the beginning of the next (November). They pass quite out of condition during this time; and many are lost from complaints generated by these sudden alternations of work and idleness. In the text I have urged the employment of these elephants during this season in the organised destruction of wild beasts. Of course the amount of the ration will vary somewhat with the size of the animal, and elephants, like horses, have their idiosyncrasies in the matter of feeding. A sharp look-out requires to be kept over the mahouts at feeding-time, otherwise great part of the allowance will probably go to Moula Bux, wife, small family, and the several fathers, brothers, and cousins, who usually aim at getting "half a seer of flour" apiece out of their great milch cow—master's elephant. About half a pound of clarified butter, and the same amount of salt should be allowed daily with the food; and spice-balls should be administered about once a week. Besides these rations an elephant devours an enormous amount of fodder. The principal substances given him are the branches of various trees of the fig tribe, banyan, peepúl, and goolar. The leaves of the peepúl are eaten, but should be avoided in the hot season for reasons before mentioned. Of the others the inner bark of the larger branches, and the whole substance of smaller twigs alone are eaten. It is astonishing to observe the adroitness with which the elephant peels off the delicate inner bark in long strips, and rejects all the rest. This fastidiousness necessitates an immense supply of branches every day; and the elephant always goes out with his keeper to bring in as much as he can carry at a time. The bamboo is also eaten, but will not be accepted very long at a time. Other trees are also eaten in the jungle, but as they are seldom accessible to tame elephants, they need not be referred to. A long species of grass (*Typha elephantina*), which grows in many tanks and rivers during the rainy season, forms excellent fodder for elephants, who are very fond of it; and when they have been much pulled down by a season's hard work, they should, if possible, be sent to pick up again where this fodder is plentiful. In the absence of the above descriptions of fodder, the stalks of millet, called *Kurbee*, or even dry grass, may be given, but it will not satisfy them long without a mixture of green food. Sugar-cane is a great treat, and in moderate quantities is very good for them, particularly if in poor condition.

Elephants should be picketed on dry ground, standing in damp being a great cause of diseased feet. They do not require any protection from the weather but the shade of a tree, and a *Jhool* or *Numda* (cloth of string or felt) thrown over them on cold nights. They should be bathed as often as possible in tanks and rivers; and a small quantity of clarified butter should afterwards be rubbed over their foreheads, ears, chests, and such parts as are liable to crack, or suffer from the rubbing of the accoutrements or from the sun. They should be allowed to drink as much water as they like. They are often very nice about it, and reject it when muddy or stagnant. The pad should be of full size and well-stuffed with grass. The felt cloth that goes under the pad (Gadéla) should always be in proper repair, or a sore back is the certain consequence. Both these articles require to be renewed about once a year, if a whole season's work has been done. The smaller felted cloth on which the driver sits should be made large enough to project a little in front of the elephant's forehead, and protect him from a vertical sun. It is not the nature of the animal to remain out in the open in the heat of the day; and I am sure that he suffers from it if made to do so unprotected. If not allowed a tree to stand under in the heat of the day, an elephant always heaps all the leafy branches he can get on his head and back.

After much marching on stony ground, the feet are apt to get tender from undue wearing away of the horny soles. This is to be remedied by the process called "Chóbing," which consists in the application to the feet of a boiling hot mixture of a good many ingredients, generally resembling coal tar. Its principal component is the gum resin of the sál tree; but every mahout professes to have a mixture of his own, which he keeps a profound secret, and which it is as well to let him use, so long as the desired result ensues, and it does not cost more than about five shillings. There is no doubt that the process is beneficial, the most footsore elephant getting round under it in about a week. It requires to be done about twice a year, if the animal is regularly worked on hard ground.

In dropsical Zérbád the food must be reduced to a minimum, about 4 lbs. of wheat or 6 lbs. of rice; and if the latter be the diet it should be given boiled. No green fodder should be allowed, only dry grass or Kurbee. A purgative should also be given; and the following recipe, which I got from a very experienced elephant doctor, is as good as any:—

Croton seed	1 ounce
Calomel	$1\frac{1}{2}$ drachms
Aloes	6 drachms

made into a ball with rice flour and "goor" (crude sugar). Most elephants take physic without any trouble. In a bad case the swellings will have to be tapped. Many mahouts know how to perform this operation. The skin should be pierced about the middle of the abdomen where the greatest quantity of liquid is usually collected, and a fleam of 1¼ inch blade will be required. The fluid which comes out is said to be infectious to other elephants if they are allowed to stand near it. The root of the *Mudar* plant (*Calotropis gigantea*) is often given by the mahouts in this disease in doses of one drachm twice a day, apparently with good effect. This is also their great remedy in the more advanced stage of the disease called Súkha Zérbád. It should be accompanied, however, by abundance of food, including green fodder and sugar-cane, plenty of bathing, and regular exercise.

For *Kándi* in the foot, the horny sole must be pared down till the sinuses can be got at, and well washed out with warm water. The holes should then be filled with an ingredient composed of :—

Tar	1 part
Leaves of the Ním tree (*Melia Azidirachta*) . .	1 part
Gum of the Sálei tree (*Boswellia thurifera*) . .	2 parts

A piece of stout leather should then be fastened over the open parts with small tacks driven into the adjoining horny sole, or tied on if there is no place for the tacks.

Sájhan, or cracked heels, cannot be remedied unless the feet are kept dry. This alone will suffice to cure moderate cases. The following lotion was recommended me by the experienced friend above alluded to; but I never had occasion to use it myself. Take ½ lb. of dry tobacco and boil it down in a quart of water till it becomes a pint. Then mix with it 2 lb. of quicklime, with 4 ounces of bluestone, and apply at intervals to the cracks.

For dimness in the cornea of the eye caused by heating food, change the diet, particularly avoiding peepúl leaves. Give the elephant grass if in season. In the earlier stage of the disease this treatment, and bathing the eye with a weak solution of nitrate of silver (5 grains to the ounce of water), will usually effect a cure. If a film has been formed it may generally be removed by blowing a pinch of very finely powdered glass into the eye once or twice a day.

Sore backs are the most troublesome of all elephant affections to cure effectually. They must not on any account be allowed to heal up superficially; and should sinuses or a sac have formed, they must be cut open and kept open until they heal up from the bottom. A downward orifice should, if possible, be secured to permit the escape of the matter. Cutting open a sore back is generally a terrible business, as the elephant, not realising the utility of the operation, fights against it with all his might. He must be well secured and held down, and a sharp razor is the best weapon to use. The wounds should then be thoroughly washed out with a solution of alum; and then filled with a stuffing composed of two parts of Ním leaves and one part common salt, well pounded together. If they should slough or throw up proud flesh, they must be touched with bluestone at intervals. This cleaning and dressing will have to be repeated at least twice a day; and the practitioner will have his hands full while it lasts in keeping the lazy elephant attendants up to their work. They will always, if allowed, let a sore back heal up superficially only to break out again on the first pressure. They rather like their elephant to have a sore back, as it saves them the trouble of loading it and going out to cut fodder. I have known them cause a sore back on purpose by inserting a stone below the pad; and I knew one case in which an elephant was destroyed by these ruffians, by the continued application of quicklime to a sore near the spine.

Elephants are very liable to intestinal worms. They generally cure themselves, when they get very troublesome, by swallowing from ten to twenty pounds of earth. They always select a red-coloured earth for the purpose. In about twelve hours after, purging commences and all the worms come away. When this occurs the hard food should be stopped for a week, fodder only being given; and a ball of spices should be given every day. Some elephants will not eat earth when they require it; and they are considered a very bad lot in consequence. I do not know how to treat them for worms. Should an elephant get wounded by a tiger, or otherwise, the places should be well cleaned and kept moistened with cold water. If they get foul apply Holloway's ointment. The mahouts have a cruel practice in such cases of heating balls of elephant's dung in the fire and splitting them open, applying them hot and hot to the wounds. I believe it to be as useless as it is barbarous. Fomentations and rest are required in the rare event of a strain.

The above are the commonest cases that will call for treatment by the elephant owner. They seldom prove fatal (excepting Zérbád), but are very troublesome when not properly attended to. Besides these elephants are subject to several obscure internal diseases, which fortunately are of very rare occurrence, but when they do occur usually prove fatal from the difficulty of diagnosing or treating them. Among them are fever and inflammation of the internal organs. Bleeding can, I believe, be effected from some small arteries behind the ears; but I have never seen it done. It would probably offer the only chance of a cure in such cases.

Occasional injuries and complaints will give an opportunity for the display of ingenuity in the application of remedies. One of the most singular operations of dentistry I ever heard of was the removal of a large excrescence on the back tooth of an elephant, which had grown into the poor brute's cheek, and almost prevented his feeding. One of the best mahouts I ever knew volunteered to remove it. He got a good thick log of wood, and made a hole through it large enough for his arm to pass. Outside he covered it all over with nails, leaving about a quarter of an inch of each sticking out of the wood. The elephant was made to lie down and fastened with hobbles, while the log thus prepared was placed in his mouth like a bit, and bound with ropes across his neck. Twenty or thirty persons now sat upon his head and trunk (if these be kept down an elephant cannot rise from his side), and the operator introduced his arm through the hole and began to saw off the protuberance. He took several hours to effect it, the elephant after a while lying perfectly still, with the expression of a martyr in his upturned eye. The piece sawn off was as large as one's fist; and the animal got perfectly well very soon afterwards.

LIST OF USEFUL TIMBER TREES, AND OTHER VEGETABLE PRODUCTS, OBSERVED IN THE FORESTS OF THE CENTRAL PROVINCES

Botanical Name.	English Name.	Vernacular Names in different parts.	Remarks.
Acacia arabica	Gum arabic tree	Hind. *Babool*; in the eastern parts, *Bassim.*	Yields a light red wood, very tough and durable, much used for wheels and agricultural implements; also a clear, fine gum sold for the gum arabic of commerce; pods eaten by goats and wild animals; bark and pods for tanning.
Acacia catechu	Catechu tree	Hind. *Kheir*	A red timber, not much used; the astringent substance called Catechu or *Terra Japonica* is extracted from the wood, bark, and roots, by boiling; it is a fast red dye, and is also useful in tanning.
Acacia leucophlæa	—	Hind. *Renja*; in the east, *Gohera.*	A hard yellow wood of small size; used for pegs, posts, etc.; pods eaten by goats.
Acacia paniculata	—	Hind. *Doobein*	A light wood, not much used except for fuel.
Acacia procera	—	Hind. *Gurbari*; in the east, *Gurkur.*	Hard wood, used for agricultural tools. Not common.
Acacia speciosa	—	Hind. *Siris* or *Sirsa*	A light, easily worked timber, used for planks. Yields a gum sold with that of *A. arabica* as gum arabic. A remarkably fast-growing tree.

Botanical Name.	English Name.	Vernacular Names in different parts.	Remarks.
Ægle Marmelos	Bael tree	Hind. *Bel*	Not very common. The pulp of the fruit a very useful remedy in bowel complaints.
Andropogon Martini	Rusa grass	Hind. *Rusa*	A fragrant oil is distilled from the grass, considered valuable as an external application for rheumatism. Very plentiful in the eastern parts, particularly the Nimár district.
Andropogon muricatum	—	Hind. *Kuskus*	Extract used medicinally as a stimulant; roots made into "tatties" for cooling houses.
Bambusa arundinacea	Bamboo	Hind. *Bans;* large variety, *Kuttung;* by Korkoos, *Mad.*	Grows everywhere, and universally useful for a vast variety of purposes; seeds and dies once in about thirty years; seed is eaten, resembling grains of rice; particles of pure silica, *Bans lochun*, are found in the joints and are eaten medicinally.
Bassia latifolia	Mahwah tree	Hind. *Mhowá* or *Mhow*	A cinnamon coloured wood, tolerably durable; seldom used as timber, however, the flowers being much eaten by man and animals, and also distilled into the common ardent spirits of the country; seeds yield a concrete oil, valuable in commerce. Very common everywhere in low grounds.
Bauhinia racemosa	—	Hind. *Kan Raj*	Small tree; bark used for matches of matchlock guns, and making small ropes.
Bauhinia scandens } Bauhinia Vahlii }	Giant creeper	Hind. *Mahwal*	Bark made into ropes; seeds roasted and eaten by wild tribes.

Bignonia chelonoides	—	Hind. *Pader*	Red wood, used for implements; flowers used in temples.
Bombax malabaricum	Red cotton tree	Hind. *Semul*	A large tree, with a light strong timber, excellent for common boxes, etc.; seeds embedded in a white fibre, used for padding, etc., instead of cotton.
Boswellia thurifera	Olibanum tree	Hind. *Sálei*	A very common tree in all parts. Wood useless as timber; grows well from stakes planted during the monsoon; yields plentifully the fragrant gum resin called *labanu*, long supposed to be the *olibanum* used as incense by the ancients; is still used as incense in Hindú temples, but possesses no commercial value at present; probably capable of utilisation in the arts; leaves eaten by elephants.
Buchanania latifolia	—	Hind. *Achar*	Wood little used; seeds called *Chironji*, much eaten by natives, resembling almonds; oil is expressed from them.
Butea frondosa	Kino tree	Hind. *Palas* and *Dhak*; in east, *Pursha*.	Does not attain the dimensions of timber. The *Butea Kino* of commerce, useful for tanning and dyeing, is yielded by its juice; the large brilliant flowers are used in ornaments, and yield a fine yellow dye; ropes are made from the roots; the leaves are commonly employed instead of paper for covering bazaar packages, making temporary cups, pipes, etc.; the lac insect principally lives on this tree; wood makes excellent charcoal for gunpowder.

Botanical Name.	English Name.	Vernacular Names in different parts.	Remarks.
Careya arborea	—	Hind. *Pilu*	Bark used for ropes, and matches for guns.
Carissa carandas	Karounda	Hind. *Karunda*	A large evergreen bush, which makes the best possible hedge. Fruit slightly acid, makes an excellent preserve.
Chloroxylon Swietenia	Satinwood	Hind. *Girya* or *Bihra*	Found of good size in Seonie district. A highly ornamental wood, a little liable to split; makes beautiful furniture and picture frames.
Cochlospermum gossypium	—	Hind. *Gooloo*; in the west, *Koor*.	Wood only used for torches; yields the gum *Kuteela*, a substitute for Tragacanth; seeds embedded in a fibre similar to that of Bombax, and used for same purpose. A very common tree in most parts.
Conocarpus latifolius	—	Hind. *Dhowra* or *Dhow*	Hard, tough, yellow wood, chocolate colour in centre; much used for cart-axles, posts, beams, etc.; yields a very fine, pure gum arabic, superior to any other; is seldom, however, exported without adulteration. Very plentiful in some parts.
Conocarpus myrtifolius	—	Hind. *Kardahi*	Reddish white wood, similar in properties to *C. latifolius*. Not very common.
Cordia angustifolia	—	Hind. *Gondi*	Not very common, but yields the best wood of all for making gunstocks.
Cordia Macleodii	—	Hind. *Deughan*	A beautiful figured gray wood, excellent for furniture, found only in Central Districts (Jubbulpúr, Seonie).

Croton tiglium	—	Hind. *Jumalgota*	Seeds yield the croton oil of commerce. Is found in most forests.
Curcuma angustifolia	Arrowroot	Hind. *Teekur*	Arrowroot is prepared from the root, of excellent quality.
Cynodon dactylon	Doob grass	Hind. *Doob* and *Huryali*	An excellent pasture grass; grows along the banks of streams.
Dalbergia latifolia	Blackwood	Hind. *Sheeshum;* in eastern parts, *Siris*.	Found of large size in central and eastern parts. Yields the "blackwood" of Bombay, here used for furniture, and making combs, etc.
Dalbergia Ujenensis	—	Hind. *Tinnus* or *Tinsa*	Yields a hard, close-grained, and durable wood much like the Bengal Sissoo (*D. Sissoo*).
Diospyros melanoxylon	Ebony tree	Hind. *Tendoo* or *Temroo*. Heartwood, *Abnoos*	The heart wood is East Indian ebony. In large trees it reaches one foot or more in diameter. The white wood is soft, but good for purposes of ordinary carpentry; the fruit is fleshy and sweet, and much eaten by natives. A cultivated variety, without stones, grows in a few places.
Diospyros montana	—	Hind. *Kanchan* and *Kadal*	Produces a beautifully variegated wood with black and white streaks; does not grow to very large size; a fine furniture wood.
Elæodendron paniculatum	—	Hind. *Jumrassee;* in eastern parts, *Kalamooka*.	Yields a light variegated wood, useful for ornamental purposes; bark a virulent poison.
Emblica officinalis	—	Hind. *Aola*	A mottled red and yellow wood, used for matchlock stocks, and common purposes; bark used for tanning; every part of the tree used in native medicine; fruit made into pickle or preserve.

Botanical Names.	English Name.	Vernacular Names in different parts.	Remarks.
Epicarpus orientalis	—	Hind. *Seora*	An excellent hedge shrub, with an edible fruit; used also in medicine; stem produces a fibre.
Eugenia Jambulana	—	Hind. *Jamun*	Wood used for lining wells, being very durable under water; fruit edible and astringent; bark gives a brown dye; grows as a bush in nearly all stream beds, and attains the size of a large tree on higher plateaux, as on Puchmurree.
Feronia elephantum	Elephant apple	Hind. *Kaweet*	A gray-coloured timber of small usefulness; fruit is edible and slightly astringent; produces a fine gum used in medicine and the arts. Not very common.
Ficus glomerata	—	Hind. *Gular*	Timber used in wells, etc., being durable under water; fruit eaten by wild tribes and birds.
Ficus indica	Banyan	Hind. *Burr* or *Burgut*	Fruit eaten.
Ficus religiosa	Peepúl	Hind. *Peepúl*	Timber sometimes used for cart-frames, but being a sacred tree, is rarely cut down. Lac insect sometimes frequents it.
Gmelina arborea	—	Hind. *Seewun*	Produces a light-coloured wood, well adapted for gunstocks, for which it is much used in the Nagpore arsenal; it requires to be stained the usual dark colour, however.
Grewia elastica	Lancewood	Hind. *Dhamin*	This produces an elastic wood almost equal to the lancewood of commerce for gig-

			shafts, bows, etc., for which it is much employed. Very large trees of it are found in the remoter forests, but where accessible it has been nearly exterminated.
Hardwickia binata	—	Hind. *Unjun*	A large handsome tree, plentiful in a few localities, chiefly in the Nimár, Hoshungabad, and Chanda districts; wood extremely hard and heavy, of a deep brown colour, in old trees almost black; mature timber makes everlasting bridge posts, etc., but is too heavy for beams; smaller trees used as rafters; bark used in tanning, and for ropes.
Inga xylocarpa	—	Hind. *Jamba*	Hard, tough wood, used for handles of tools, etc. Not common.
Lagerströmia lanceolata	—	Hind. *Leudya*; in the west, *Bundarya.*	An excellent timber for ordinary building purposes.
Mangifera indica	Mango	Hind. *Am* or *Amba*	A durable timber; scarcely used, however, the fruit being in great demand. Grows wild in ravines of higher hills.
Melia Azadirachta	Neem	Hind. *Neem*	Mature timber makes a fine furniture wood; leaves used in a fomentation for strains and bruises, for which they are very effective; oil is yielded by the seeds.
Nauclea Cadamba	—	Hind. *Kadam* or *Kuhuni*	A light red wood, very straight in the grain and easily worked; a good common building timber, and also for planks, boxes, etc.
Nauclea cordifolia	—	Hind. *Hurdoo*; in east, *Halun.*	A yellow wood, good for all common carpentry, also furniture, boxes, etc.; one

Botanical Names.	English Names.	Vernacular Names in different parts.	Remarks.
			of the best common woods we have, resembling in qualities yellow pine.
Nauclea parviflora	—	Hind. *Kaim*	A reddish yellow wood, with a fine even grain, inferior to above in strength, but excellent for common furniture.
Odina Wodier	—	Hind. *Gunjak*, also *Moyen;* and in east, *Burna.*	A coarse-grained wood, sometimes used in common house-building, and for firewood.
Phœnix farinifera (?)	Wild date	Hind. *Sendi*	A dwarf species of date-palm, grows wild on higher plateaux; pulp of seeds, and a substance found in the stalks eaten by wild tribes.
Pterocarpus marsupium	Kino tree	Hind. *Beeja Sal* or *Beea;* in the east, *Bijra.*	Yields a fine building timber, rather heavier than teak, but nearly as strong; when wet gives out a yellow stain; yields from the juice a gum resin, which is one of the Kinos of commerce.
Schleichera trijuga	—	Hind. *Kosum*	A hard heavy wood, used for sugar and oil mills; seeds yield an oil; lac insect commonly prefers this tree.
Schrebera Swietenioides	—	Hind. *Moka*	A grayish brown timber, used for common purposes, of no great value.
Shorea robusta	Sál	Hind. *Surye;* and in east, *Rinjal.*	The principal timber tree in the eastern parts, and an excellent building timber; yields the *Dammer* resin of commerce; seeds eaten by wild tribes.

Soymida febrifuga	Ironwood	Hind. *Rohun* or *Ruggut-Rora.*	A very hard, heavy, red wood, extremely durable; bark a valuable febrifuge, and is also employed in dyeing and tanning.
Strychnos nux-vomica	—	Hind. *Koochla*	Of small size; seeds and other parts used in medicine; seeds also to poison fish.
Strychnos potatorum	—	Hind. *Nermulli*	Nut used, like alum for clearing muddy water, and also in fish-poisoning.
Tamarindus indica	Tamarind	Hind. *Imli*	Wood used for oil mills, etc.; fruit eaten.
Tectona grandis	Teak	Hind. *Sagon* and *Sag*	Our best timber tree in western and central parts.
Terminalia Arjuna	—	Hind. *Kowa;* and in some parts, *Aujun.*	A very large tree, growing generally on river banks. Mature wood, dark brown and durable, but little used from difficulty of cutting and working.
Terminalia Belerica	—	Hind. *Bahera*	Grows to a great size, but timber is little valued; nuts are the *Myrobolan* of commerce, but are little exported here.
Terminalia Chebula	—	Hind. *Hurra*	A handsome tree, very common in many parts; the nut is the *Kadukai* of commerce, and is extensively used in indigenous manufactories for dyeing, tanning, etc.
Terminalia tomentosa (? coriacea)	Black Eyne	Hind. *Saj;* and in west, *Sadur;* in east, *Sijra.*	One of the best timbers of the second class; much used for building and all common purposes; bark used for tanning; Tusser silkworm lives on the leaves.
Zizyphus jujuba	—	Hind. *Ber*	Fruit tastes like a crab-apple, and is eaten by wild tribes and many animals; wood small, but extremely tough, and used for a few purposes; parts of the tree are used in medicine.

VOCABULARY OF A FEW USEFUL TERMS IN THE LOCAL HINDÍ, GÓND, AND KORKOO LANGUAGES

ENGLISH.	HINDÍ.	GÓND.	KORKOO.
Antelope	Hirn	Hirn (H)	Kutsar
„ four-horned	Chonsingha	Bun-Bher (H)	Bherki
Axe, common	Kulhari	Maro	Akae
„ battle	(Bygas) Tonngya	Pharchia	——
Bamboo	Bans	Bans (H)	Mad
Bear	Reech	Yedjal	Bana
Bison	Bun-Boda	Bun-Bhainsa (H)	Hela (H)
Blood	Looh	Nattur	Puchna
Buffalo (wild)	Arna-Bhainsa	——	——
Camp	Dehra	Bungla (H)	Purno
Deer, barking	Kakur	Bherki	Bherki
„ hog	Bher-Samur	Bher-Samur (H)	——
„ red	Bara Nerwaree or Sal-Samur	Gowna	——
„ sámbar	Samur	Mauk	Stag, Kakur; Hind, Samri
„ spotted	Cheetul; Buck, Jank	Kurs	Darkar
Dog	Kutta	Nae	Seeta
Elephant	Hathi	Yani	Hathi (H)
Fever	Bokhar or Tup	Yerki	Rua
Fire	Angar	Kis	Sengal
Food	Khana	Nena	Jojam
Forest	Jungal	Kaira	Tharee (H)
Fowl	Moorghee	Pitte	Seem
Fox	Lóm	Khekree	Kakree
Gazelle	Chikara	Hirni (H)	——
Guide	Agwa	Agwa (H)	Agwa (H)
Gum	Gónd	Dhok	Deek
Gunpowder	Barood	Burko	Daroo
Hare	Kargosh	Malol	Koarli
Hill	Dongur	Mata	Bulla
Horn	Singh	Kor	Singh (H)
Hyena	Turrus	Renhra	Dhopre

ENGLISH.	HINDÍ.	GÓND.	KORKOO.
Jackal	Geedur	Kolial	Kolea
Jungle fowl	Bun-Moorgh	Bun-Moorgh (H)	Komba
Leather	Chumra	Chumra (H)	Kutrae
Leopard	Borbacha	Gordag	Sonora
,, hunting	Cheeta	Chitra	——
Man	Admi	Maursal	Koro
Milk	Doodh	Pal	Deedum
Monkey (Hunoo-Man)	Lungoor	Lungoor (H)	Sara
Morning	Bunsare	Sukre	Pathar
Nilgai	Rojh (male); Gorayen (female)	Goorya	Rooi
Panther	Tendwa and Adhnaira	Burkal	Kairea
Partridge, painted	Kala Teetur	Kukkura	Chitree
Peafowl	Mór	Mal	Mara
Pigeon, wild	Kabutur	Parewal	Kubdoor (H)
Plains, the	Khulotee	Maidan (H)	Sehwan
Plateau	Mal	Dadur	Tor
Porcupine	Seyal	Hoigu	Jekra
Quail	Batair	Batte	Ore
Rain	Bursaät	Pirr	Salla
Ravine	Khudda	Kori	Lór
River	Nuddee (small, Nala)	Dhoda	Gada
Road	Rasta	Sarri	Kora
Rock	Dhata	Tongung	Gota
Rope	Rursee	Dor (H)	Dora (H)
Sál tree	Sal and Renga	Surye	Surye
Sand	Balu	Waroo	Beetil
Snake	Surp	Turás	Beeng
Spurfowl	Chota Bun-moorgh	Bunteetur (H)	Toteang
Stone	Puthur	Puthur (H)	Gota
Teak tree	Sagon	Sag	Seepna
Tiger	Bagh and Nahr	Poolie	Koola
Torch	Massal	Doote	Marsal (H)
Track	Pug and Punja	Koj (H)	Mang (H)
Tree	Per	Mara	Seeng
Valley, or low ground	Neechwas	Daäb	Borro
Village	Bustee	Naru	Gaon (H)
Wild boar	Dookur	Puddee	Bun-Sookree
,, dog	Son-Kutta	Nerka	Bun-Seeta
Wolf	Bherya	Landgal	Lendya (H)
Wound	Ghao	Chot (H)	Gaae (H)

Numerals.

ENGLISH.	HINDÍ.	GÓND.	KORKOO.
One	Ek	Oondi . . .	Meea
Two	Do	Rand . . .	Barya
Three	Tin	Moond . . .	Apya
Four	Char	Nalu . . .	Opoonya
Five	Panch	Saighan . . .	Moonya
Six	Cheh	Sarung . . .	Toorae
Seven	Sát	Yedung . . .	Aie
Eight	Ath	Yermud . .	Elar
Nine	Nau	Nau (H) . . .	Araie
Ten	Dus	Daha (H) . .	Goolya

DIRECTIONS AS TO THE PRESERVATION OF THE SKINS AND OTHER TROPHIES OF ANIMALS ON THE FIELD

Contributed by Edwin Ward, F.Z.S.

GENERAL.—It must always be borne in mind that the value of any object secured and preserved depends on the completeness with which all its natural features are saved, as well as the condition in which they are kept. This is true in degree, for whatever purpose the object is designed; but it is an absolute essential in regard to specimens for the illustration of natural history.

LARGE GAME.—Those met with in the Central India district will most generally be, the *Felidæ*, most important of which is the Tiger; many smaller *Carnivora;* of horned beasts, the gigantic gour—Bos Sylhetanus—commonly called the Indian bison; buffalo, sámbar, cheetal, and other deer. There is also the elephant, largest of all, and other pachyderms.

When the great game is secured, first turn the animal on its back, and stretching apart the fore and hind legs, proceed to remove the skin. In all cases where the skin is wanted entire, this is best done by making incision from one corner of the mouth through the medial line of belly to the extremity of tail. Next make lateral incisions in order to strip the limbs; for the fore-legs, from the edge of central incision through the armpit along the inner side of the limb, the line of incision inclining slightly to the outer portion, in order that the seam may be less perceptible when the perfect specimen is mounted. A like process through the groin is necessary for the hind-legs. The incisions thus made leave the skin in form of tongue-pieces over the breast. First apply the knife to these points and detach the skin round to the spine. In doing this it is necessary to clear the limbs, and great care must be taken to leave intact the natural features of the foot. The last metacarpal and metatarsal bones must be left in the skin, whether in the case of *Felidæ* or *Cervidæ.* Now turn over the carcase and draw back the whole skin over the head, exercising particular care in separating the ears and the eyes from the skull. Similar care must be taken as to the lips. For if the rim of the eyelids be severed by the scalpel the injury spreads in a remarkable manner, often so badly as to render the damage seriously conspicuous. As to the ears, they should be separated from the skull close to the bone, or the lower structure will present too large an aperture. The lips must be cut off close to the gums. Having thus taken off the skin it must be cleaned of all superfluous fat and flesh. The cartilage of the ear must be turned through. The lip must be treated thus: Pass the knife between the mucous lining and the outer skin all round the mouth so as to admit of the preservative penetrating this thick portion of the specimen completely. The eyelids and feet must each be treated in a similar manner for the same reason. Now peg the skin out with the fur downwards for drying, and anoint it thoroughly with arsenical soap if preferred; but at the same time use freely a sufficient quantity of powdered alum, especially on the lips, eyelids, ears, feet, and all other fleshy parts. In regard to the employment of arsenical soap as a preservative against insect ravages, it is not in my opinion always completely efficacious. I therefore recommend that spirits of turpentine should at the same time be freely poured over both sides of the skin. When the skin is sufficiently dried it can be folded and packed.

Although the process just described is a very good one, I should myself adopt the following, which would be much more simple, and is thoroughly successful: The skin having been removed from the carcase and cleaned, instead of being pegged out for drying, should be thickly covered over the flesh side with powdered alum, then folded in convenient form, and thus immersed in a barrel of brine, what we technically call "liquor"; add parts of alum and common salt in the proportion of six pounds of alum and two pounds of salt to a gallon. A number of skins may be placed in the same barrel, which is thus ready either for storing or transit. They are quite exempt from the ravages of insects; native dressing with lime and other deleterious material is avoided. They will keep safely for a long period, and the process is at once inexpensive and a saving of time. In the case of horned beasts where the head only is frequently preserved, I have no hesitation in recommending this system as the best. Of course in such case the skull and horns are cleaned and packed separately. In cutting off bison and stag's heads be sure to leave a long neck; they are too frequently cut close to the jaws, and this considerably mars the effect when mounted.

It is important for the proper preservation of the skulls of *Felidæ* that they should be protected from injury to or loss of the teeth. This is best done as follows: When the skull has been boiled and cleaned, it should be tied up in a calico bag and placed in a separate compartment of the packing-case designed for it. Stuffing should moreover be put into each compartment to prevent the skull from injury from being shaken.

SMALL MAMMALIA, ETC.—In the case of the small mammals the skull and bones of the legs are to be left in the skins. The animal being placed on its back, incision is made from the sternum (breast bone) to root of the tail. The skin is then separated from the carcase as far as can be conveniently reached, and the limbs are severed from the body at the shoulder and thigh. Each limb can then be drawn out—as a glove might be turned inside out—but the bone must not be separated at its junction with the toe, or the skin of the foot or leg in any way injured. The muscles can then be removed from the bone, and this can best be done by cutting the tendons near the toes, and carefully drawing the whole mass away at one operation. It must come in one piece, not piecemeal. The bone will now be clean. Clean the skin of the limb, and at the same time the remainder of the skin of all superfluous flesh and fatty matter. Dress the inside all over with arsenical soap, and apply freely powdered alum all over it, but particularly to the fleshy parts, as the eyes, nose, lips, feet, etc. Then replace the bones in the limbs, having previously, if possible, bound them with tow or similar material, so as to replace the muscle that has been removed. A portion of stuffing should be placed in the skin of the head and trunk, and the whole can be suspended to dry.

BIRDS.—First of all plug up with cotton wool the throat, nostrils, and all shot holes. Place the specimen on its back, the head towards you. Break the wing bones (*humeri*) near the body. Next separate the breast feathers carefully, and make an incision along the medial line from chest to vent; having done which, turn back the skin and raise the specimen to a perpendicular position, resting it on the vent. Now skin round the chest, cut through the neck, windpipe, and gullet, detach the wings from the body, and remove the skin all down the back to the thighs. Push the thigh through at the same time, carefully drawing off the skin, and having cut the tendons near the tarsus remove the muscle of the thigh in one piece, leaving the bone clean. This bone must be cut near the femur joint, leaving the head of the bone, which is useless, with the flesh attached to the thigh and body. Having treated both legs thus, skin round root of tail; but in cutting the vertebræ take care to leave the small bone which supports the tail. The next operation is to turn back the skin of the head with care so that the eyes and ears may not be injured. Cut away the back part of the skull with neck, tongue, and palate. Remove the brain and eyes, skin the wings and trim the tail, and the whole skin is in condition to be cleaned and prepared. Having taken away all fat and superfluous flesh, dress it with arsenical soap, bind tow in place of the muscles on the bones, and return them to their places. It is not desirable to use powdered alum to bird skins, as it tends to make them brittle. The specimen should be filled out to natural size, and a band of paper placed round it in order to keep the wings and other parts in proper position till dry. During the whole operation wood-dust or other dry powder should be freely employed to absorb blood and grease, so that the plumage may be kept clean.

THE END